The Battle for Control of the Brass
and Instruments Business in the French
Industrial Revolution

The Battle for Control of the Brass and Instruments Business in the French Industrial Revolution

José-Modesto Diago Ortega

OXFORD
UNIVERSITY PRESS

Great Clarendon Street, Oxford, OX2 6DP,
United Kingdom

Oxford University Press is a department of the University of Oxford.
It furthers the University's objective of excellence in research, scholarship,
and education by publishing worldwide. Oxford is a registered trade mark of
Oxford University Press in the UK and in certain other countries

© José-Modesto Diago Ortega 2024

The moral rights of the author have been asserted

All rights reserved. No part of this publication may be reproduced, stored in
a retrieval system, or transmitted, in any form or by any means, without the
prior permission in writing of Oxford University Press, or as expressly permitted
by law, by licence or under terms agreed with the appropriate reprographics
rights organization. Enquiries concerning reproduction outside the scope of the
above should be sent to the Rights Department, Oxford University Press, at the
address above

You must not circulate this work in any other form
and you must impose this same condition on any acquirer

Published in the United States of America by Oxford University Press
198 Madison Avenue, New York, NY 10016, United States of America

British Library Cataloguing in Publication Data

Data available

Library of Congress Control Number: 2024932676

ISBN 9780198895053

DOI: 10.1093/oso/9780198895053.001.0001

Printed and bound by
CPI Group (UK) Ltd, Croydon, CR0 4YY

Links to third party websites are provided by Oxford in good faith and
for information only. Oxford disclaims any responsibility for the materials
contained in any third party website referenced in this work.

With love, to María-Cristina.

Acknowledgements

More than twenty years have passed since I found the first *factum*—one of many which will be discussed throughout this book—in the library of the Musée des Instruments in Brussels. Pulling on that thread meant beginning to weave the story that is contained in this book, an exciting adventure that has also had complicated moments that I have coped with better, thanks to the support of my mother Loreto, my sisters Juncal and Fátima, my nephew Daniel who gives me great joy, and equally and very intensely María-Cristina García Márquez, with whom I share my life and our particular 'Bourgeois Revolutions'. I also remember the people who were there at the beginning of this journey and shared stages with me, and although they are no longer with me physically, they are part of my heart and thoughts: my father José-Andres Diago Pérez for those values of effort and work that he instilled in me, and Paco and Esperanza. I would also like to remember at this point the closest friends who have been constantly cheering me on, namely Andrés Selva Orellana, Juan-Manuel Arrazola, Eduardo Vázquez, Ángel Romero, Jaime Pardeza Solinís, Viçent Giménez Pons, César de León, and Massimo Puglisi.

A work as eclectic and multidisciplinary as this would not have been possible without the support and efficiency of the staff of several institutions, among which I would like to highlight the Bibliothèque Nationale de France—Louvois, Opéra, Richelieu, and Miterrand sites—(Pierre Vidal, especially), the Musée de la Musique (Elisabeth Wiss-Sicard, Fabienne Gaudin, Thierry Maniguet, and Thierry Ollivier), the INPI [Institut National de la Propriété Industrielle] (Steeve Gallizia, Amandine Gabriac, and Isabelle Bougrina), Archives de Paris, the Musée des Instruments de Musique de Bruxelles, and the Association Internationale Adolphe Sax.

Of course, I would also like to write down the names of other colleagues and friends who have directly or indirectly provided me with help, empathy, example, or encouragement, among whom I must mention Angelita Márquez and Nino Fandiño, Arnold Myers, Benedikt Brilmayer, Bruno and Colette Kampmann, Cristina Bordas Ibáñez and Luis Robledo, Cyrille Grenot, David Flor García, Encarnación Barranquero, Frank García, Gavin Holman, Jeremy Montagu, Jesús Núñez, José del Rincón, Julio Pérez Serrano, Leo van Oostrom, Léon Touret, Malou Haine, Manuel Titos, Miqui Troncoso,

Pablo Ordóñez, Patricio Sáiz, Patrick Péronnet, Pere-Andreu Jariod, Philip Herman, Ramón Calabuig, Thierry Bouzard, and William Waterhouse.

I am especially grateful to other people whose work has been an example to follow and who have inspired me over the years, namely Géry Dumoulin, Albert Rice, Ignace de Keyser, James Kopp, Jerry-L. Voorhees, and most especially Juan-Antonio Gómez Barrera. Thank you not only for your wise counsel, for sharing your wisdom with me and some impressions of parts of the draft of this book—also thanks to the anonymous reviewers—but also for your friendship and generosity. I must also highlight two people—the most important ones—from whom I have learned a great deal over the last few years and who have been fundamental: Joaquín Piñerio Blanca and Eva Moreda Rodríguez. Finally, I am deeply grateful to my Commissioning Editor and Project Editor (Adam Swallow and Phoebe Aldridge) for their faith in the project, trust, and exquisite advice.

Contents

List of Figures xi
List of Tables xiv

    Introduction 1

PART 1. DEFENCE

    1. Chimeras, Tall Tales, and 'Joke-Horns' in the First Instance: Presentation of the Bases of Prosecution and Defence 31

    2. 'Let Him Calm Down' and the Judgement of the *Lumières*: The Position of the Prosecutor and the Technical Report 50

    3. Judicial Setback or 'Nothing Patentable': Change of Regime and Procedural Course 61

    4. *Appel-incident* or Escalation to the Second Level of Jurisdiction: Challenge and Pressures on the Court of Appeal 76

    5. *Persistence* and Jump to *Cassation*: The Paradox of Winning an International Prize and Going Bankrupt 88

    6. The Egg of Columbus and a Great Victory: The Denouement of the Civil Prosecution 107

PART 2. CHARGE!

    7. Hasty Raids: A Fiasco and a Second Wave of Aggressive Seizures of Instruments, Ledgers, and Machinery 123

    8. Gautrot or 'the Most Relentless Fighting Spectacle between Makers': Double Resistance and Exhaustion 130

    9. Masterstroke: The Extension of Contested Patents 150

    10. With Malice Aforethought: Squeezing Out the Deadlines 160

    11. Besson, a Brass Heavyweight Maker: Brave Competition and an Interesting Production Model 170

12. Versus Eighteen . . . at the Same Time: Collective Confrontation 'against Adversaries So Powerfully Allied and So Persistent' — 177

13. Tentacles in Strasbourg: Competition from Outside Paris and in Other Ways — 187

14. Transfer and Escape to London: Accusations of Defamation, High Resistance, and the Introduction of *Madame* Besson — 194

15. Drouelle or the Valve Big Business: The Challenges of Maintaining a Monopoly — 203

16. Endgame and Epilogue: Pressing Charges against Ex-Associates and the Confirmation of the Brasswinds Consumer Society — 213

17. Conclusions — 227

Appendix I: French Patent Law of 1791 — 243
Appendix II: French Patent Law of 1844 — 251
Appendix III: Saxhorn Patent (1843) — 260
Appendix IV: Saxotromba Patent (1845) — 265
Appendix V: Saxophone Patent (1846) — 270

Bibliography — 273
Index — 292

List of Figures

0.1	Saxophone main components: (1) mouthpiece; (2) neck; (3) keys; (4) bell	18
0.2	Saxhorn/saxotromba main components: (1) mouthpiece; (2) bell; (3) valves; (4) valve slide; (5) ferrule	19
2.1	Evolution of the number of patents and certificates of addition—the values in the graph represent this sum—for all aerophones during the nineteenth century in France	51
2.2	Growth of brasswinds companies and their profitability	52
3.1	Earliest drawings of Sax's instruments for sale	66
3.2	Gautrot's 'chromatic clarions' from his 1850 sales catalogue	68
3.3	The most important tools, machines, and details of the workshop on the ground floor of Sax's factory (1848), consisting of a press (1), a screw clamp (2), mandrels (3), flywheel (4), strap (5), other wheels (6), guillotine (7), furnace (8), bellows (9), smoke expelling tube (10), ladders (11), and worker honing (12)	69
3.4	View of a part of the workshops of the Gautrot *aîné* factory in the Marais district, Paris (1855) and its most significant elements, for example, brass sheets (1), scissors (2), hammers (3), drill or perforator (4), anvil (5), clamps (6), mandrel (7), bells (8), kettles or drumshells (9), furnaces (10), and tree stumps (11)	71
3.5	The most important details of the ground floor of Gautrot's factory, namely steam engine and straps (1), forges (2), mandrels? bells? (3), bellows (4), coal storage area (5), assembly sections (6), clamps (7), and ladders (8)	73
3.6	The most significant details of the workshop on the first floor of Sax's factory (1848), namely a screw clamp (1), a hammer (2), a furnace (3), wheels (4), small tools (5), bells (6), and assembly lines (X)	74
4.1	Instrumental demonstration by Sax in the concert hall of his house	81
5.1	Photograph of Sax's stand at the 1851 London International Exhibition	92
5.2	Comparison of the number of British and French patents relating to brasswind instruments registered during the nineteenth century	95
5.3	Bell of a Sax six-piston trombone with distinctive inscription 'F^{teur} de la M^{son} Mil^{re} de l'Empereur'	105
6.1	Timeline of the defence phase	114

List of Figures

7.1	'Opening of the Universal Exhibition of 1855. Imperial procession', colour engraving (1855?), anonymous. Musée Carnavalet, Paris	127
7.2	Great Hall of the 1855 Exhibition with the stand of Sax	128
8.1	Interior view of the shop and/or warehouse of the Gautrot factory in the Marais district, Paris	131
8.2	Presumptive E♭ *néo-alto* (left), B♭ Bass *bombardon* (centre), and a monster ophicleide (right)	133
8.3	Guichard's original patent design for an *ophicléide [ophicleyde] à pistons* (1835) (left) and Gautrot's original instrument—E♭ ophicleide with pistons or bombardon, E.1450 (possibly third quarter of the nineteenth century) (right)	134
8.4	Gautrot-Marquet soprano sarrusophone (second half of the nineteenth century), E.1164 (left) and design of the Patent of the sarrusophone (1865) (right)	140
10.1	Factory of musical instruments by Couesnon (*c.*1900), formerly owned by Gautrot	161
10.2	Bird's eye of Gautrot's Factory in Château-Thierry	161
10.3	Sax's stand in The London International Exhibition on Industry and Art of 1862	165
10.4	Gautrot's stand in London 1862 Fair	166
11.1	Concert of a military band in a grove in Versailles	175
12.1	False correlation between the measured levels of the saxotromba patent	182
12.2	Comparison of the E♭ saxotromba with the rest of the instruments of the same pitch (*altos*), including *clavicors*, ophicleides, and a *néo-alto* of the rest of the manufacturers	183
14.1	Types of regulation instruments for ensembles mounted with the precise shapes of saxhorns, saxotrombas, cornets, trumpets, and trombones	199
14.2	Possible variables of the shape of the saxotromba from a patent of Besson	202
15.1	Performer with a chromatic bugle or deep brasswind with valves perpendicular to the bell, probably by Gautrot	209
16.1	Timeline of the attack phase	218
17.1	(Added) quantity of patents and certificates of addition of the main eight branches of instrumental manufacturing in nineteenth-century France	231
17.2	French amateur civilian fanfare (*c.*1895)—including minors—and the usual military look	240

III-1	Main designs of the saxhorn patent (figures 7, 6, 5, 8, and 9)	263
III-2	Main designs of the saxhorn patent (figures 4 and 3)	264
III-3	Main designs of the saxhorn patent (figures 11, 10, 2, 1, 13, and 12)	264
IV	General design of the saxotromba patent 1845	269
V	General design of the saxophone patent 1846	272

List of Tables

0.1 Common French judicial system in civil and criminal matters during the July Monarchy, the Second Republic, and the Second Empire, with an approximation to its present-day equivalent (2023) — 13

1.1 Price of the saxophone, brasswinds, and percussion instruments of the manufacture Sax et Cie for the infantry and cavalry regiments according to the new organization of 1845 — 46

3.1 Comparison of the instrumental palette for infantry bands according to the 1845 (pro-Sax) and 1848 (republican) regulations, as well as their (theoretical) nominal correspondence arranged in parallel — 63

3.2 Comparison of the instrumental palette for cavalry bands according to the 1845 (pro-Sax) and 1848 (republican) regulations, as well as their (theoretical) nominal correspondence arranged in parallel — 64

3.3 Comparison of the prices of instruments made by Sax and Gautrot (*c.*1848–50) — 67

6.1 Price of instruments for a 55-person infantry band according to the 1854 provision — 116

6.2 Price of instruments for a 37-person cavalry band according to the 1854 provision — 117

9.1 Instrumental palette of the military bands (*Décret impérial* of 26 March 1860) — 151

14.1 Production costs and profit of a low brass aerophone according to Sax — 196

14.2 Comparison of the retail prices of Sax's with those of three of his licensees (Millereau, Lecomte, and Gautrot) — 197

16.1 Standard prices of some brasswinds during the early part of the Third Republic (*c.*1870–98) from various catalogues, Army regulations, and Pierre's book — 224

Introduction

The liberal bourgeois revolutionary period opened up a new socio-economic and political dimension that spread throughout all aspects of human activity in Europe and, later, much of the world. Nineteenth-century leaders established an order—first nationally, then internationally—that would allow coexistence among individuals, but they also decreed new regulations within the economic and social spheres. The former parameters were presided over by capitalism, a system that intensified as the century progressed and caused not only the polarization of the middle classes and the proletariat but also other tensions and conflicts between traditional structures which were then disappearing and the new realities that were being dynamically implemented.

The main purpose of this book is precisely to narrate, develop, and analyse one of those scenarios of confrontation: the largest judicial battle in culture and industrial property in nineteenth-century Europe, the echoes of which still ring today. Obviously, what lay behind those contentious disputes was the pursuit of commercial profit, or more specifically, the consolidation of a dominant position that would yield the maximum possible economic return. Interestingly, the object of dispute was not related to opera—the musical genre that moved the most money and people at the time—nor was it related to the always revered and contentious high art; rather, the fight was motivated by some rather simple wind instruments made of brass. Likewise, this approach shows that something as (apparently) prosaic as music and the tools with which it was made were also at the mercy of speculative and economic interests, just like the sale of raw materials or essential manufactured goods.

The centre of our story is France, a state that culturally and politically acted as a sounding board for other European and American countries, including the United Kingdom and the United States of America, which were also the two main importers of wind instruments from the French in the middle decades of the nineteenth century.[1] Although the UK was industrially more developed, France was living a golden age of innovation and creativity at the

---

[1] *Statistique de l'industrie à Paris résultant de l'enquête faite par la Chambre de Commerce pour l'Année 1860* (Paris: Chambre de Commerce, 1864), 754.

time which overlapped with the productive plateau of its first Industrial Revolution. It was thanks to the development of transformation techniques in metallurgy and new possibilities and improvements in working with brass, that there was an explosion and proliferation of brass instruments.

However, almost all of these inventions and advances that emerged throughout of the nineteenth century had a common characteristic: they were protected by patents or property titles on a piece of technical information or knowledge.[2] The control of know-how and skills was not unique to this era. However, the way in which these tangible and intangible components or resources were managed and legislated, especially in a context where the middle class was the de facto economic authority and dominated—or greatly influenced—the governmental spectrum, is indeed unique. Therefore, these ideas and the zeal with which they were cultivated became tools and sources of power, transcending the particular interests of an individual to turn into issues that affect collectives with common interests, including those of the political sphere.

Thus, the major themes we will explore are economic—after all, it was all about doing business—but they are intertwined with other legal, political, and cultural issues.[3] Therefore, this book not only aims to develop the comprehensive framework in which the case study—the brass instrument industry in nineteenth-century France—is placed, but also to transcend and relativize it. More precisely, it is about knowing not only what those companies were like and how they functioned, or how much money they put in circulation; but rather, find out how they adapted to the evolution of capitalism and its rules. Precisely, and although it may seem obvious, the musical instrument companies were not oblivious to one of the key components of the system, namely credit, which was essential to materialize the patents. In other words, beyond any lofty artistic message they served with their

---

[2] See, among others, B. Zorina Kahn, 'History Matters', in Stephen H. Haber and Naomi R. Lamoreaux, eds, *The Battle over Patents: History and Politics of Innovation* (New York: Oxford University Press, 2021), 319–59, Mario Biagioli, 'Patent Specification and Political Representation: How Patents Became Rights', in Mario Biagioli, Peter Jaszi, and Martha Woodmansee, eds, *Making and Unmaking Intellectual Property: Creative Production in Legal and Cultural Perspective* (Chicago/London: University of Chicago Press, 2011), 25–40, Joshua S. Gans and Fiona Murray, 'Funding Scientific Knowledge: Selection, Disclosure and the Public-Private Portfolio', in Josh Lerner and Scott Stern, eds, *The Rate and Direction of Inventive Activity Revisited* (Chicago/London: University of Chicago Press, 2012), 51–103, Gabriel Galvez-Behar, *La République des inventeurs. Propriété et organisation de l'innovation en France (1791–1922)* (Rennes: Presses Universitaires de Rennes, 2008), 21–52, or Josh Lerner, '150 Years of Patent Protection' NBER [National Bureau of Economic Research] Working Paper no. 7478 ([January] 2000), article available on the Internet at <https://www.nber.org/system/files/working_papers/w7478/w7478.pdf> (accessed 5 November 2022).

[3] Patent litigation is per se complex because it is nourished by technical, legal, business, and economic components (sometimes changing), all overlapping and interacting with each other. For a discussion of the patent system, see Michael Risch, 'The Layered Patent System', *Iowa Law Review* 101: 4 (2016), 1535–82.

products, the survival of these firms was conditioned to attracting investors and a correlative yield of profits, which brought considerable pressure.

The book will explain and contextualize the legal framework regulating industrial property and invention patents at the time, and how the law was applied to subtle and controversial technological and artistic developments— e.g. the alleged new properties brought into the sound of musical instruments. The decisions of the judges serve to connect us to the political area, which interfered with the legal one when interests or pressures materialized. As will be discussed later, the same laws were interpreted differently in times of the July Monarchy and the Republic, and even more so in the Second French Empire; similarly, other strong agents such as the Army or the press also exerted considerable pressure. Moreover, we will also discuss how political power used economic power, and vice versa, for example, in uncovering the strategies of Louis-Philippe or Napoleon III to favour certain instrument making companies—without getting their hands too dirty, that is—and how they returned the favour, most obviously through the establishment of large, powerful, and spectacular brass bands who honoured them outdoors before their devoted subjects. It is unquestionable that culture made money circulate and generated investments, but it also articulated the social machinery and was a powerful tool for legitimizing political positions.

The legal dispute at the centre of the action lasted more than twenty years and was partially led by Adolphe Sax, the well-known inventor of the saxophone. More precisely, there was a phase we might call defence (1847–54) and a period of offensive (1854–67), which allows us to structure the book in two main parts. The first period concerned civil proceedings—it was debated whether to give validity and authority to some patents—and began in 1847, when a group of French businessmen who built wind instruments saw their business and sources of financing threatened because the Army forced them to use a series of musical instruments that were different from the usual ones and protected by patents that belonged to Sax himself. That first lawsuit lasted seven years, but it was reactivated a few months later—and here is where the second part commences—when the original defendant took the initiative and simultaneously pursued (this time criminally) several of his competitors, also inflicting numerous raids on them. The latter period is more complicated because it was assumed that crimes had been committed deliberately and admitted more serious penalties and fines. In addition, the number of people involved (sometimes organized collectively and in the form of a lobby), the acceptance of new evidence and last, but not least, an unprecedented (and spectacular) extension of the duration of the patents in dispute—validated in 1860 by a law by the French Parliament and Senate themselves—made the dispute more bellicose. It goes without saying that such consent increased the intensity of the conflict on the main plane, the economic one, since it presumably damaged the capitalist framework of the theoretical free competition.

Retrospective

Before the discussion can start, a brief historical retrospective of the French trade of musical instruments and particularly brasswinds is needed. Perhaps going back to the burgs and towns of the Middle Ages would be a bit of an exaggeration, but it is helpful to refer to the guilds and corporations of the time that had strict rules of access and permanence in certain trades or productive activities. At that time, the concept of monopoly was also in force: the competent authority granting a concession in order to benefit from a particular trade or industry. The feudal order and the powers of the kings and nobles made use of that possibility and introduced new ways of control that they codified as privileges. These prerogatives were unique exploitation rights limited in time and space, but in accordance with the will and interests of the person or institution granting them, typically being the monarch. This was not exclusive to France, as this practice became common throughout Europe, which affected different areas of economic activity, for example the dyeing of garments in England in the thirteenth century or the permits to create parts of an important building such as the Florence Cathedral during the fourteenth and fifteenth centuries. Most of these contracts were formalized with the famous *patent letters* (open or public letters) that bestowed onto their holders an advantage—outside the range of common law—over aspects of prestige, employment, or sole rights.

The construction of musical instruments during that time was dependent on other major sectors outside the arts which normally used the same materials or similar tools. Moreover, manufacturers of flutes—and likely of oboes or shawms as well—that doubled up as manufacturers of chair or tables legs still existed in the seventeenth century.[4] That is to say, there were carpenters or cabinetmakers that, in addition to making common furniture utensils (ladles, bowls…) or more decorative items (such as boards and chess pieces), ventured at times into making a bowed string instrument (type of violin).[5]

---

[4] David Jenkins, *Woodwind Instruments in France 1690–1750. Their Makers, Theoreticians and Music*, vol. 1 (Thesis, Edinburgh, University of Edinburgh, 1973), 3–4 and François Lesure, 'La facture instrumentale à Paris au seizième siècle', *The Galpin Society Journal* 7 (1954), 11–12.

[5] Florence Gétreau, 'Entre l'oral et l'écrit: pratique, transmission et théorie du métier de facteur d'instruments de musique', *Ethnologie Française* 26: 3 (1996), 504–6.

Furthermore, those who dedicated themselves to making horns and trumpets were bound by the statutes of the *forcetiers* (grinders or profilers) or the boilermakers. It was precisely within this last activity of making metal kitchen containers where Diderot and d'Alembert grouped the manufacturing of brasswinds in their *Encyclopédie* (1756), and this association lasted in some cases well into the nineteenth century.

The Renaissance saw a very significant increase in the creation of musical instruments, but the trade remained closed. Usually, a worker would start out as an apprentice in the workshop of a despotic owner and, after much hardship, only a (very) few would achieve their own independence. One of the first French edicts that exclusively concerned the manufacturers of musical tools (*Lettres de création du métier de faiseur d'instrumens* [sic] *de musique en maîtrise et de leurs privilèges et statuts*) was sanctioned by Henry IV in 1599. This arbitration granted the group financial advantages and institutional support, but also the legitimacy to self-manage and continue obstructing third party access into the profession. The situation was so generalized across the sector and across regions that even professional musicians were subjected to similar regulations and made to obey the head of that corporation, being that of the minstrels (*ménétriers*). This subject attended to the voice of 'King and Master of all Masters Players of Instruments and Masters of dance in the kingdom of France (*Roi et Maître de tous les Maîtres Joueurs d'Instruments et Maîtres à danser par tout le royaume de France*)' and had the right to name a representative (*lieutenant*) in each city to represent the central authority.[6]

The situation did not change significantly in the Baroque era and even worsened after the paternalistic legislative and propagandistic system through which the kingdom was governed, that is, Colbertism, a political and economic doctrine that granted the state authority total power over most of the nation's productive activities. This *dirigiste* system continued to sanction monopolies and privileges at will, which, of course, resulted in large profits to the royal house itself. With respect to the arts, it is worth mentioning a letter patent dated 28 June 1669 by which the minister of Louis XIV granted Pierre Perrin a monopoly 'to establish, throughout the Kingdom, Academies of Opera, or music performances in the French language (*pour establir* [sic], *par tout le Royaume, des Académies d'Opéra, ou représentations en musique en Langue française*)' which three years later—originally it was to last twelve—passed to Jean-Baptiste Lully. This composer, who was already directing the thriving *The Little Violins of the King* (*Les Petits Violons du Roy*)

---

[6] Paul Loubet de Sceaury, *Musiciens et facteurs d'instruments de musique sous l'Ancien Régime. Statuts corporatifs* (Paris: A. Pedone, 1949), 68–72 and 168–71.

since 1655, received the power to manage and produce opera in the kingdom of France with extraordinarily advantageous conditions.[7] In addition, this monarch was the first in France to pay attention and in a significant way to military music, a genre that played a major role—also economically—in our later story. Although less sophisticated than musical theatre and orchestras, military bands were the means that the sovereign had to procure himself background music in his open-air parties, inspections, and banquets. Indeed, the first composition of this type (a military march) was due to Lully himself and dates back to 1658 (*First march of the musketeers for oboes and drums—Première marche des mousquetaires pour hautbois et tambours.*)[8]

The manufacturers who had managed to escape from this vicious circle, either by buying part of their freedom to practise, or by disguising their business in another way, saw their discomfort increase at the turn of the eighteenth century. The enlightened class from that period joined the protests against such deterministic economic policies as criticism over corporations continued. A liberal creed, which criticized exclusive privileges and other monopolies, began to take form, especially regarding basic necessities. The strain put the central authorities under pressure, which then implemented certain regulatory initiatives—for example, tax controls—to reduce these differences. However, the treasury's measures were clearly ineffective given that a lot of information could be disguised; furthermore, the system was arbitrary and there were so many exceptions that the task was extremely complex. Other significant intermediation attempts were the creation of the Trade Office (*Bureau de Commerce*) in 1722 and later on (1762) a royal initiative (*Déclaration royale, concernant les privilèges en fait de commerce*) that sought to limit the privileges that had become in some cases lifelong or hereditary.

In any case, it is assumed that, by the end of the eighteenth century, these old-fashioned statutes were done away with and gave way to a society in which equality between citizens—and traders—become effective. Nonetheless, it is worth adding that the French Revolution can and should be seen as a change in the elites: the control of the aristocracy and the high clergy was replaced by the power of the capitalist bourgeoisie, who was made up in part of artisans who had become rich, those who had the aforementioned very exclusive regulations and who would go on to become the middle class.

---

[7] Laurence Depambour-Tarride, 'La création de l'Académie royale de Musique. Théorie et pratique de l'absolutisme français', in Huegues Dufourt and Joël-Marie Fauquet, dirs, *La musique et le pouvoir* (Paris: Aux Amateurs des Livres, 1987), 33–5 and Agnès Terrier, *L'orchestre de l'Opéra de Paris: de 1669 à nos jours* (Paris: Éditions de la Martinière, 2003), 11–22.

[8] Thierry Bouzard, *Les usages musicaux dans l'armée française de 1815 à 1918* (Thesis, Amiens, Université de Picardie Jules Verne, 2016), 188–90.

In other words, the Late modern period politically formalized an already existing economic and social reality, which ended up making the model of feudal political power obsolete. On this side, the social and economic change was prior to the Revolution, that is, to the political change.[9] However, part of the traditional and opaque character of the musical instrument makers' sector was still present in the mid-nineteenth century, as we shall see later on.

Nevertheless, France's transformation into an industrial and capitalist society is a complex issue. This restructuring entailed major and sometimes chaotic transformations in the tapestry of a country that was still purely agricultural. Undoubtedly, the overpopulation in the countryside facilitated the beginning of industrial activities and the rural exodus for the cities was not significant if we compare it with that of Britain. Since the end of the Napoleonic wars, French economic growth was somewhat constant, especially with regards to small industry. This development saw a social disturbance at the end of the century's twenties which culminated in the Revolution of 1830. However, and from a practical point of view, this disruption did not affect the regularity of that effective take-off following the most acute crisis of 1848.

If we examine each issue separately and contextualize the setting, we could say that, although after Napoleon the economic situation was completely disorganized, decisive steps were reached in the previous years. Additionally, the first symptoms that a modern industry was taking shape started being felt in a protectionist environment where an attempt was made to stimulate heavy industry and the textile sector enjoyed the absence of English competition. Regarding musical instruments, the French government's shielding in customs also impacted on imports in artistic sectors that were deemed key, such as organs and especially pianos. The high taxes on British products were not only effective in the early years of the nineteenth century or during the continental blockade ordered by the Emperor in 1806, but also after the Restoration. The situation remained this way until the free-trade policy with England sanctioned by Napoleon III in 1860, known as the *coup d'État douanier* (Cobden-Chevalier Treaty), led to a considerable easing of the levies on British products.

Another fundamental aspect was that Paris continued to be the sounding board of the entire state and the driving force for exports during the take-off of the French Industrial Revolution. One of the most thriving branches in that

---

[9] Barrington Moore, *Social Origins of Dictatorship and Democracy. Lord and Peasant in the Making of the Modern World* (Boston: Beacon Press, 1966), 40–69.

first period was furniture items, which had obvious similarities in terms of common technical and procedural particularities with piano manufacturing. This concerns woodworking processes that used power saws, lathes, milling machines, and, of course, steam engines that put those machines and gears to work. Therefore, piano workshops and industries were the first to receive these crucial manufacturing processes to make their frames, tops, keys, and hammers in a faster and more mechanized fashion. In the realm of brasswinds, we observe constant growth throughout those first thirty years of the nineteenth century. In the trade almanacs of that time, we found three business dedicated to metal in 1805, 11 in 1820, and 20 in 1830 out of a total of 88, 143, and 288 companies dedicated to music in those times.[10] The number continued to grow and, leading up to the year the confrontation began (1847), we count 38 brass manufacturers. This steady increase was mainly due to three reasons. The first (and fundamental) was the business opportunities created by bands, not only military—which were the great majority—but also civilian, and which promised extraordinary dividends for the years to come. The second cause, as already mentioned, was the ease, speed, and cost-effectiveness of manufacturing in brass, thanks to the new transformation procedures of metallurgy. The third reason, also crucial to attracting more clients, was founded on an exclusively technical issue and linked to the execution in this type of instruments, namely, the discovery and subsequent widespread use of pistons or air channelers. The *valve era* had arrived in France (initiated in Germany c.1814–16)[11] and with it the race towards the impulse and diffusion of valves in brass instruments. Thanks to these mechanical devices, it was possible to achieve, among other things, greater ease, speed, and precision in playing.[12] These improvements were not only welcomed in bands, but also in orchestras and operas, where the most influential composers of the time (Spontini, Rossini, Meyerbeer, Berlioz, Verdi, Wagner…) gave them their approval.

---

[10] By way of comparison, Lyon had at the beginning of the century (1808) fourteen instrument makers of all kinds, to which we must add seventeen more if we take into account self-employed workers, *luthiers*, and bell founders. Denis Watel, 'Luthiers et musiciens à Lyon en 1808–1809 d'après les recensements de population', *Larigot* 49 ([February] 2012), 24 and 27.

[11] Günter Dullat, *Metallblasinstrumentenbau: Entwicklungsstufen und Technologie* (Frankfurt: Bochinsky, 1898), 147–55.

[12] Before the use of valves, most brass aerophones were restricted to tones provided (naturally) by the series of the physical-harmonic phenomenon and determined by the length of the tube. Therefore, in order to produce further notes, the performers had to resort to conflicting and risky procedures—e.g. putting their hand inside the bell of the instrument, or resorting to expertly 'bending' or twisting the notes—or resort to awkward and uncertain structural procedures or devices, namely drilling holes in the body of the instrument, including keys, attaching pieces of pipe (crooks), etc. Of course, one could also use sliding fittings—the principle of today's trombone—that is, the movement of one tube within another tube to change the basic harmonic series.

Indeed, the years coinciding with the July Monarchy and the Second French Empire proved to be a golden age for innovation and creativity in this type of industry and, especially, its coveted market. According to official data, brasswinds were billed at 1,620,000fr [francs] in 1847 and, just thirteen years later, they almost doubled that profitability to 3,185,000fr. In addition, taking into account that the number of entrepreneurs had remained stationary—there were barely forty employers in 1860—the relative performance was much higher.

Nineteenth Century French Industrial Property Laws

As previously mentioned, the newly capitalist industrial model based on free competition brought about by the French Revolution needed regulations to sustain it, especially in its economic and productive aspects. Finding that legal path was not easy at a time of such aggression and tension, since it had to satisfy both those who did not want corruption and favouritism to perpetuate itself, and those who trusted that their inventions and efforts would be protected by a fair system. However, this regulation was so imperative and urgent that, in only a few months, the French Assembly passed the first (1791) of what are known as the major laws (the second is from 1844) on industrial property.

The first of those rules endured throughout the Revolution, the Empire, the Restoration, and the July Monarchy, and also served as a reference and model for those countries that France occupied and influenced. The immense influence of that text is perfectly justified since, for the first time in history, the liberal property right over inventions and new means of production was codified in writing, abolishing any arbitrariness in the granting, enabling the means for authors to protect themselves and, very importantly, with the intention that the market would dictate the success of the novelty. The other provision (1844)—which was essentially an update and expansion of the previous one in line with the new industrial standards—also prevailed in the last years of Louis-Philippe's reign. Furthermore, not only did it continue in force during the Second French Republic, the Second Empire, and the entire *Troisième République*, but it lasted until the dawn of the Fifth French Republic (the 1960s) when the definitive shift towards a European patent law forced a break with legal practices from the previous century.[13] Beyond

---

[13] Of course, the regulation of 1844 was later supplemented by other minor provisions, such as that of 21 October 1848, stating that the law would be applicable in the colonies and their disputes settled in

the astonishment or oddity that these long-standing regulations may have caused, the laws of 1791 and 1844 show the importance they had for the economic and capitalist system of the time. None of the various French political regimes from those 150 years dared to repeal them or even question them because they clearly favoured growth.

Given the importance of both regulations, English translations are provided in the appendices of this book. Although, if we briefly review and compare their cardinal points, it should be pointed out that the 1791 law still showed a certain uneasiness with the new system and perhaps an excessively protectionist attitude towards entrepreneurs. Thus, the first article of that text dictated that any discovery or new invention in all genres would be the 'property' of its author; in the second epigraph, this privilege was also granted to real (i.e. useful) improvements to existing manufactures. The most substantial of the following items was that no prior examination was required—that is to say, that no government or technical commission would assess the virtues of the advance—and that the privilege could be exclusively obtained for five, ten, or fifteen years, except if imported, in which case the time remaining in the other country would apply. On the other hand, and in case of conflict, the patent would be invalidated if the inventor concealed or hid the means by which he had crafted the product, if he did not detail them sufficiently, or if there were contradictions in the declaration. The document would also be revoked if the invention had already been published, if it took more than two years to be put into operation or if there was the same time lag in production, and, lastly, if the owner registered the same invention abroad. The application had to include the 'exact description of the principles, means, and processes', as well as the related designs and, once approved, the Government granted a title under the denomination 'patent for invention (*brevet d'invention*)',[14] which, legally, protected that discovery and granted private and time-limited exploitation rights.

The second normative (1844) was in direct agreement with the first and was born with the aim of better adapting to the rampant capitalist context. Both laws also agreed that the document could be freely consulted by anyone interested, that is to say, it was considered as a source of information so that further progress could be made on at the frontier of that technology.

their respective judicial courts; 5 June 1850, ditto for Algeria; 31 May 1856, concerning the transportation of patented objects into the territory and their display at exhibitions, etc. Alain Beltran, Sophie Chauveau, and Gabriel Galvez-Behar, *Des brevets et des marques: une histoire de la propriété industrielle* (Paris: Fayard, 2001), 31–9.

[14] The French prefer to use the word *brevet* (article 1 of the regulation of 25 May 1791) to refer to a patent because this last word had already been used by Pierre d'Allarde referring to a kind of annual tax that gave the right to exercise freely a profession or trade.

However, and unlike the first regulation, article 1 of the second law referred to the fact that any new invention or discovery would confer the exclusive right of its enjoyment on its author, but without explicitly mentioning the word 'property'. The second item added that only 'new industrial products', 'new means', or 'the new application of known means for obtaining an industrial result or product' would be protected. This wording confirms that less protection was awarded to the authors and, above all, exemplifies the practical approach—purely capitalist, at the whim of market forces—to which we referred earlier.

Regarding fees, those interested in applying for a patent had to pay 100fr every twelve months, which was a relatively affordable sum and, of course, more appropriate than that dictated by the 1791 law. Under the latter, inventors had to pay in one lump sum—or pay half at the time of application and the rest over the following six months—for the coverage lasting five, ten, or fifteen years (300fr, 800fr, and 1500fr respectively). Therefore, they had to bear the initial cost of implementation and not knowing whether their product would be profitable.

An interesting aspect of the second law—as suggested earlier—was that it allowed for the possibility of extending the duration of the patent by five more years (article 15). These types of exceptions were very controversial and complicated, as they had to have the rank of law, that is, be in a hierarchical and normative position immediately inferior to the Constitution (or Constitutional Charter, as the case may be) and, needless to say, overcome some rocky and tense parliamentary procedures until receiving approval.

Lastly, it is worth noting that the patent began to be effective from the day of the deposit—and not from its administrative approval—another characteristic of 1791 jurisprudence. We will soon see that this is not a trivial detail, as legal and punitive actions to make profits or erode rivals (raids) were squeezed to the last day.

Nineteenth Century French Justice System

Although the subject of debate is simple wind instruments—metal components and tubes welded or mechanically joined, that is, a technology not at all deep—the application of the law became complex due to the number of actors involved. The protagonists themselves, the Government, the Army, the press, an academic or wise institution, certain influential figures, etc., exerted pressure (more or less subtle) on the judges. In order to foreground the discussion, we offer here a brief review of the functioning of the French justice system, which will be expanded throughout the book as needed, since the legal battles also drew on the Civil, Criminal, and Procedure Codes.

Roughly speaking, French individual of the mid-nineteenth century had six avenues to litigate depending on the nature or substance of the conflict, namely Peace (*Justice de paix*), Commerce (*Tribunaux de commerce*), Military (*Justice militaire*), High Court of Justice (*Haute-Cour de justice*), Accounts (*Cour des comptes*), and Ordinary (*Justice ordinaire*). The first was presided over by a non-professional judge and sought to untie minor common conflicts. The second, also supervised by a lay mediator, resolved disputes between merchants up to a certain sum of money (1500fr). The third had its own legal battery and martial courts, and was totally on the margins due to idiosyncrasies. The fourth, which was re-established in the Second Republic—previously, in the Restoration and with Louis-Philippe, its functions were exercised by the Chamber of Peers—investigated crimes, attacks, and plots against the head of state or the Government itself, and did not allow any appeals. The fifth, of a clearly administrative nature, ensured the accuracy of public accounts, income, and expenditures. And finally, the sixth artery, which we identify with the common judicial order—today it is called the *ordre judiciaire*—was the one that arbitrated conflicts and private interests between individuals (civil) or imposed sanctions on the perpetrators of infractions or crimes (penal).

As we can guess, the litigations discussed in this book—and most of the complaints from individuals and businessmen—were channelled through this last, gigantic two-headed jurisdiction on which it is necessary to point out two core aspects. First, that French law was (and still is) administered by the Ministry of Justice (or *Chancellerie*, as it is popularly known in its original form), but what is unique to the events described in this book is that the Government intervened or positioned itself in legal action. This meant that, once the arguments of the parties had been exposed, the Administration—through the prosecutor's office—also expressed its preferences, although ultimately later the (impartial) court was the one to decide. (In France, justice was and is, with some exceptions, collegiate, i.e. the sentence is decided by several judges.) In other words, that, relying on itself in the general interest, the Executive could modulate the application of the law and support the thesis of one or the other contender. This power became even more interesting when there was a criminal prosecution, since one only has to imagine the strength of the public prosecutor's opinion in a punitive and more serious procedure.

The second point was the principle of double instance, that is, the possibility of appeal. That is to say that, in the event of a disagreement and so that there were as few errors as possible in human decisions, the legal

Table 0.1 Common French judicial system in civil and criminal matters during the July Monarchy, the Second Republic, and the Second Empire, with an approximation to its present-day equivalent (2023)

Legal Degree	French Political Regime	Civil Jurisdiction	Penal or Criminal Jurisdiction
High jurisdiction (or control of power)	July Monarchy Second Republic Second Empire Modern	Court of Cassation Court of Cassation Court of Cassation Court of Cassation	Court of Cassation Court of Cassation Court of Cassation Court of Cassation
2nd grade (or level)	July Monarchy Second Republic Second Empire Modern	Royal Court Court of Appeal Imperial Court Court of Appeal	Royal Court Court of Appeal Imperial Court Court of Appeal
1st grade (or level)	July Monarchy Second Republic Second Empire Modern	Court of First Instance Court of First Instance Court of First Instance Tribunal *Judiciaire*	Court of First Instance Court of First Instance Court of First Instance Tribunal Criminal (*correctionnel*) Tribunal *de police*

Compiled from, among other sources, *Almanach Royal et National pour 1847* (Paris: Guyot et Scribe, 1847), 374–6, 385, and 404, *Almanach National de la République Française pour 1848–1849–1850* (Paris: Guyot et Scribe, 1850), 346–8, 357, and 376, *Almanach Impérial pour 1853* (Paris: Guyot et Scribe, 1853), 365–7, 378, and 397; and <https://www.justice.gouv.fr/justice-france/cours-tribunaux> (accessed 4 August 2023).

system offered another court to review the sentences issued by a forum composed of fewer professionals with lesser professional office (*lumière*). However, the regulations still allowed the contingency of presenting another objection before the Court of Cassation (*Cour de cassation*), the interpretive apex of the entire French legal system. A case of this type was (and still is) the one that interposed before the highest court and ultimately (*en dernier ressort*) against final rulings in which laws, legal doctrine, or some essential guarantee of the process were infringed. Therefore, this forum did not rule on the subject matter of the disputes; although, in practice, at least in a field like the one discussed in this book, we will discuss whether it really was the case that it did not go beyond matters of content. In any case, when the high court ruled (and found the claim justified, because if not, the process would logically end there), it also generally forwarded the summary to a second-level legal forum (different from the one from which the protest had originated) so that the matter could be debated again, but evidently taking into consideration the guidelines that Cassation had established.

It goes without saying that the procedural costs increased not only due to the permanence support of the process itself, but also, and very significantly, when moving up the system. In the case that concerns us—with more than two decades of confrontation and constant ups and downs—they must clearly have been very high. On the other hand, it should also be borne in mind that the dispute persisted through three different political regimes (July Monarchy, Second French Republic, and very significantly, Second Empire), so that the names of the courts changed with the governments too, although for practical purposes their functions remained basically the same. Obviously, it will have already been inferred, the structure was hierarchical and complex, although it can be simplified (Table 0.1) omitting some exceptions and variants that will not occur in our way.[15]

Sources: Patents and *Factums*

This book interweaves economic, legal, political, and cultural contents, which obviously implies drawing on complex and very diverse sources. On the other hand, the court case also drew commentary from influential people who disseminated their opinion through various media, channels, or in important forums—for example, in the press; or through the official and unofficial reports that emanated from the national and international Exhibitions of the time. In reality, such behaviours and declarations were part of the dramatization of Romanticism which included an eternal and recurrent struggle between the new and the routine; and, although they provide certain complementary and useful data, they must of course be examined critically, since it is sometimes very difficult to differentiate between the news and publicity. Besides, most of these characters engage in the dialectics not only for the purpose of helping one of the contenders, but rather for self-promotion, under the guise of having certain kinds of knowledge. Of course, the (ruthless) bourgeois environment in which the action takes place is very slippery, as reality is easily confused with fiction; or scenarios are exaggerated. But in any case, it is the patents themselves and some derivatives of the legal process, namely the *factums*, that require greater caution.

A patent allows the appropriation (creation or discovery) of information that can be applied (leveraged) in production processes. This contract with the state empowers the author to enjoy competitive advantages limited in

---

[15] For example, that of dispensing justice to serious crimes (such as murder) which evidently belonged—and belong—to other criminal branch of the common judicial order—in French, *Cour d'assises*—and in which (fortunately) none of the brass manufacturers were involved.

time when his reward and benefits are proportional to the value the (theoretical free) market assigns to the invention—that is, fundamentally, to the laws of supply and demand. Likewise, a patent is a competitive tool in the sense that if various competitors are looking for a technical solution to a specific problem, only the first one to find it and adequately codify it will have the right to exploit it. Thus, this makes it a legal tool that provides enormous legal security, which, at first glance, might seem sufficient to endorse any product, improvement, or procedure. In addition, it can be used in both directions, that is to say, defensively (it allows dating and proving the origin and ownership of that technology) and offensively (as evidence to denounce usurpers). However, in practice, the patent does not have to be decisive or ensure professional success, being reduced to an instrument of imperfect protection and, substantially, just another component of the capitalist economic system of which it is a part.

To add to the complexity, some patents from the first Industrial Revolution require treatment due to the very novelty of the system and they did not always contain feasible or even real products. In addition, some inventors and entrepreneurs consciously wrote them in an inaccurate or cumbersome way to obtain a certain competitive advantage—thus reserving future lines of development—or they chose to keep certain key information to themselves. By playing with these ambiguities and double standards, patents take on a special meaning, since they illustrate the true (or feigned) intentions—they are pieces of the strategy—of these businessmen.

Connected to patents and the course of judicial confrontations were French *factums*, a sort of pamphlets that were paid and printed by the parties involved in a legal action in order to defend themselves, refute, or attack his opponent. These judicial reports or allegations usually contained, among other things, the exposition of the facts—according, obviously, to self-interest—supposed fragments of original rulings, and (pseudo)legal reasoning that sought not only to influence and pressure judges, but also external agents adjacent to the process, for example, an advisory institution and the experts or other influential specialists themselves. Of course, they were not the official minutes or records of a trial—the system had its secretaries—and they did not even emanate from the legal presiding authority, but from the individuals themselves or their representatives, that is, from their lawyers. These scripts were drawn at the expense of the interested party, so they did not involve a publisher, although they did have the name of the printing company that had produced them. Although they could be sent to the sentencers—with no obligation to be read—the dissemination was, as we have said, intentionally propagandistic; they sought to correct public opinion. Hence, they are considered as atypical sources, not used by legal historians due to their high bias, but useful here due to the amount of information they contain (also a lot of repetition, trifles, and literary crutches) if we know how to drive correctly, a purpose which has certainly been prioritized in this book. In the absence of the official reports and minutes of those legal battles, these false dossiers—some seventy related to the confrontation in question—offer us an on-the-ground vision and complementary to the official version.

Morphology and Components

This is not a music book, nor does the reader need to have any musical knowledge to understand and, we hope, enjoy it. In fact, none of the lawyers for the litigants, prosecutors, or judges involved were musicians, nor did they have any prior musical knowledge. Indeed, it is almost better to immerse oneself in the book without being a musician or playing a brasswind, as it would prevent certain preconceived ideas from undermining one's response or perception of the issue that is purely technical and legal in nature; although, as we have stated several times, the real battle was on the economic level.

Furthermore, we face the issue of how to name and classify this family of instruments, as we currently use the words brasswinds or brass instruments to refer to artistic wind tools made of any material, not necessarily brass. Likewise, and in apparent opposition, the term woodwind also does not require wood to be the constituent element and, for example, the flute and saxophone are included in this group even though they are made entirely of metal. Such names are certainly misleading but are tolerated for historical and practical reasons.[16] Anyway, as one may have already inferred, our approach has brass as a material for the construction of musical instruments. It is, in fact, the core element of the book because it harmonized very well with the new technologies implemented in the Industrial Revolution, causing the value, accessibility, and profitability of its derivatives—musical instruments—to multiply.

It is also worth remembering that these sound tools have and accumulate certain charged meanings over time depending on who they are associated with or who they serve, and they usually enjoy certain associations in

---

[16] See, among others, Anthony-C. Baines, *The Oxford Companion to Musical Instruments* (New York: Oxford University Press, 1992), 42–5 and Murray Campbell, Clive Greated, and Arnold Myers, *Musical Instruments. History, Technology, and Performance of Instruments of Western Music* (New York: Oxford University Press, 2006), 149–58. 'Lip-reed instruments', 'lip-vibrated instruments', or 'labrosones' are modern alternative terms for 'brass instruments' or 'brasswinds'.

certain languages and/or situations. Thus, for example, and using some simple metaphors, it could be said that the strings (the violin family) are the core of the orchestra; or that the organ elevates us to another level due to its close connection with church music. Brasswinds are portable and, in addition, they can offer considerable volume, that is, they work very well outdoors and as signalling instruments. These properties have been used since ancient times and the ancestors of these instruments were used to announce the presence or arrival of leaders and authorities—also religious—give gravity to ceremonial moments of pomp and circumstance, loss (funerals), or accompany and guide armies in battle. The idea is that brasswinds have been constantly associated with power and war, a heritage that has been active over the centuries and was certainly not entirely lost during the nineteenth century.

The litigation in question began when a group of businessmen and builders of wind instruments headed by Raoux, Gambaro, and Halary—whom we will get to know gradually throughout this book—filed (1846) a civil lawsuit against Sax claiming that the invention patents that supported his musical instruments were illegitimate. Specifically, that complaint sought to revoke two of his documents, namely, the patent [no. 2306] of 13 October 1845 for 'A musical instrument called a saxotromba, whose construction, by means of light modifications, can be applied to saxhorns, cornets, trumpets, and trombones (*Instrument de musique, dit saxotromba dont la construction au moyen de légères modifications peut être appliquée aux sax-horns, cornets, trompettes et trombones*)' and, the other, the invention patent [no. 3226] of 21 March 1846 for 'A system of wind instruments called saxophones (*Système d'instruments à vent, dits Saxophones*)'.

Obviously, both titles obeyed the 1844 law, but the saxotromba patent was dependent on another previous patent by Sax, [no. 15364] of 13 June 1843 for 'A system of chromatic instruments (*Système d'instruments chromatiques*)' that, presumably, protected such saxhorns. But, unlike its siblings, this patent was subordinated to the 1791 regulation. Therefore, and for practical purposes, the judicial debate was articulated around these three documents that, fundamentally—but in a somewhat slippery way—protected three instrumental concepts on which it is convenient to provide some brief and simple morphological notions.

Everyone today knows the saxophone, either because of its connection with jazz, music bands, or because it is linked to some unique characters of the American collective imagination that have made it popular, for example, Lisa Simpson (from the popular animated series) or the former US President Bill Clinton. In fact, it is a seemingly easy instrument to build, as it is essentially a (fairly) conical brass tube coated with a key system that is played through a mouthpiece. The keys are mechanisms with plates that open or close the holes that the instrument has throughout the body; and the mouthpiece is a kind of chamber or hollow piece to which a single reed is attached (Figure 0.1).

It is more complicated to describe what the saxhorns and saxotrombas were, but we will establish some basic and common concepts that characterize them. Firstly, they are made up of several cylindrical and conical tubes (with a predominance of the latter) made of metal joined together. Second, they have valves, that is, mechanical devices that regulate the passage of air and allow it to travel through another portion of the pipe called slide or valve slide. Thirdly, they are put into operation—blown—with a mouthpiece completely different from that of the saxophone (without a reed either) and which is cup- or funnel-shaped. In reality, this element (the mouthpiece) is the one that receives the first element that enters into vibration (the performer's lips), an oscillation that immediately passes to the injected air, converting it into sound and that is later amplified and modulated ('takes' shape) along that pipe to the bell or final part of the instrument (Figure 0.2).

These members or technical specifications may seem very exclusive or specific to brasswinds, but, in fact, they were derived from the Industrial Revolution itself that had previously been implemented in other more common and larger productive sectors. In this sense, it is not necessary to remember that certain technologies were applied much further—in a more far-reaching way, one could say—than was their initial purpose. For example, we could refer

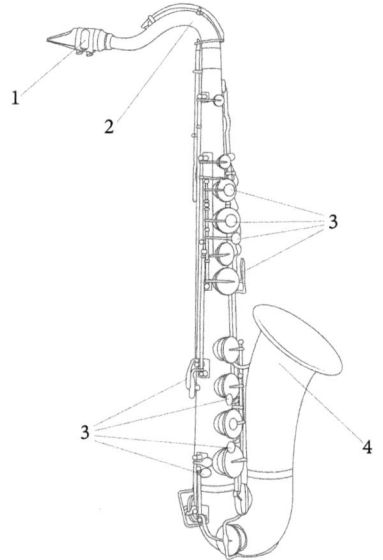

Figure 0.1 Saxophone main components: (1) mouthpiece; (2) neck; (3) keys; (4) bell

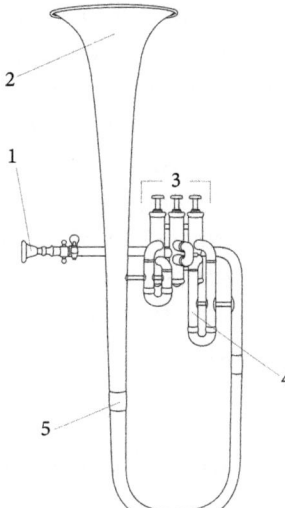

Figure 0.2 Saxhorn/saxotromba main components: (1) mouthpiece; (2) bell; (3) valves; (4) valve slide; (5) ferrule

to the development of precision machinery, like Henry Maudslay's screw-cutting lathe. This lathe cut metal very precisely and guaranteed reliability and strength, perfect for cutting tubes and components of different diameters and their attachments to steam engines and other enabling mechanisms. The principle was versatile, since the rotation movement (revolution) could result in machining, threading, perforation, rolling, smoothening, sharpening, etc. while maintaining precision and opening the door to mass production. All of these procedures and their extrapolations did surely have a nuclear influence on the development and proliferation of brass instruments and their parts, that is, to their tubes and valves. The latter mechanisms that regulate the flow of air and the number of constituent elements (buttons, springs, stops, boxes, shock absorbers, perforations, discs, unions, etc.) require precise fitting to guarantee correct and coordinated movement, in addition to perfect tightness of the air passages.[17] Some of their action principles and parts were indeed inspired by (or, better said, they took technology from) technical advances and constituent elements of very disparate areas, like plumbing, ironmongery, or the pipework and pistons of steam engines.[18]

---

[17] Jeremy Montagu, *The Industrial Revolution and Music* (Oxford: Hataf Segol Publications, 2018), 1–13, 119–23, and 137, Reine Dahlquist, 'Some Notes on the Early Valve', *The Galpin Society Journal* 33 (1980), 111–24, and John-Q. Ericson, 'Heinrich Stölzel and Early Valved Horn Technique', *Historic Brass Society Journal* 9 (1997), 63–82.

[18] Edmund-A. Bowles, 'The Impact of Technology on Musical Instruments', The Cosmos Club, *Cosmos Journal* (1999), article available on the Internet at <http://www.cosmosclub.org/journals/1999/bowles.html> (accessed 4 February 2022) and Christian Ahrens, 'Technological Innovations in Nineteenth-Century Instrument Making and Their Consequences', *The Musical Quarterly* 82: 2 (1996), 332–9.

Anyway, and apart from technical issues, the context described in this book is halfway between the new exercises of power that the bourgeoisie imprinted on (the business of) nineteenth-century culture and, on the other hand, the advantages and new realities opened up by the Industrial Revolution. The technical advances in metalworking and new production systems that were implemented in that century opened the door to a massive and standardized performance of brasswinds that promised substantial economic benefits to the best positioned. Although that hegemony was fought in court, the one who read the whims and the evolution of capitalism best would be the real winner.

Outline of the Chapters

As mentioned above, the book explores the issue from a legal viewpoint, since it allows us to pivot effectively to other areas such as culture, politics and, above all, economy, where the battle and the substance of this whole story really lies. The legal viewpoint is also useful in providing flashbacks to what the brasswinds market was like before that conflict broke out as the contenders constantly evoked past times or events. Also, during the development of the main contents, we will be spreading other practical tools and references to have a more specific, complete, and faithful contextualization; for example, what was the instrumental composition of the military bands at each time, the professional background of the main people involved and—of particular relevance for this book—how the price of the instruments oscillated as capitalism and the technical advances of the Industrial Revolution progressed. Incidentally, in order to analyse prices and to give the reader as accurate an idea as possible of whether the instruments were expensive or cheap, we will convert current prices into constant prices, because it is intuitive and stands the test of time better.

We have two main parts based on the character of the legal action, namely defence or prosecution. The first followed civil proceedings (six chapters), whereas the second, longer and more intricate, followed criminal proceedings, so the latter consists of eleven divisions. The pages of the first chapter present the basis of prosecution and defence in a civil court of the first instance in Paris. The plaintiffs—organized in a sort of lobby—tried to prove formal defects and lack of novelty in patents, and also to show the danger to French wind instrument manufacture and trade if these documents were to condition the greater part of that market and the army bands' instruments requests. On the other side, the defence lawyer described his client as a serious industrialist, a lover of progress, and a victim of the jealousy and greed of stagnant Parisian manufacturers. The interesting thing about this first episode lies in the purging of those conflicting statements (there was a lot of dramatization) and, most significantly, from beginning to connect more substantial underlying elements: who was actually behind that reform, what was achieved by it, or how a monopoly was legitimized in a capitalist framework of the theoretical free competition.

Once the arguments of the concurring parties had been set out, it was the turn of the public prosecutor's office, which showed a (very explicit) preference for Sax and his patents. However, despite this promising assessment, the Court (6 April 1847) postponed its verdict until a report was drawn up by a commission of experts (*lumières*) who could testify whether the patents and the resulting instruments were legal and truly new. That technical dossier and its controversial authors—a composer, a retired military engineer, and a popularizer (*vulgarisateur*)—provide us with the remaining contents of the second division.

The *Rapport d'expertise* (favourable and in line with the prosecutor's thesis) was recorded in November 1847, so that the proceedings were awaiting the Court to reconvene and (predictably) rule in favour of the defendant. In February 1848, however, the Revolution broke out and with it the collapse of the July Monarchy and the resurgence of the Republic. Among the six members of the provisional government that shaped the new model of government was *Maître* Marie, the lawyer who represented the interests of the rival manufacturers. In this impasse until the case was resumed, much happened, including the redefinition of the instrumental palettes of the walking and mounted bands—of course, without the instruments object of controversy— and the appointment of said lawyer as Minister of Justice. The trial was resumed in August 1848, and the same chamber struck down the first patent (saxhorn) and completely invalidated the second (saxotromba), which was key to the strategy. Only the saxophone was exonerated, but to little avail, since it had been removed from the military bands of the new republican government. The judges did not value the experts' report either, considering it as professional encouragement, but in no case as legal support for a patent 'to exercise a monopoly'. Chapter 3 develops the whole episode and focuses on the details and resources that made possible that abrupt change of judicial and economic course: the market had once again been liberalized. However, that ruling was not enough for some who wanted a harsher punishment, and not fair enough for the other, so both sides appealed.

In reality, it was the losing party that took the initiative to appeal, and the other party joined in by lodging an incidental appeal. In any case, that move meant escalation to the second level of jurisdiction, i.e. the Court of Appeal, which entailed more time and effort. The pages of Chapter 4 analyse the substance of those debates and, above all, how the political and economic landscape changed again, including the approval of an authoritarian constitution, the electoral triumph of the established Party of Order, and industrial promotion initiatives such as the organization of a National Exhibition in 1849. Oddly enough, it was at this event that the defendant and his brasswinds won the first and only prize awarded to wind instrument makers, which challenged the legal ruling that had dismissed these products. However, this and other informal pressures did not succeed in getting the Court of Appeal (16 February 1850) to disassociate itself from the sentence that the lower court had rendered in 1848 and continued to consider those brasswinds illegitimate.

The *Cour d'appel*'s ruling meant a new judicial setback for the defendant, and the months went by as the temporary validity of the disputed patents was consumed. For all practical purposes, this also prolonged the impunity of his opponents to continue to manufacture and sell brasswinds freely. However, Sax did not give up and appealed to the Court of Cassation. The situation was not simple, quick, or inexpensive, as the complaint had to go through the *Chambre des requêtes* (Requests or Petitions) which filtered the cases that were well formulated and had legal substance so that the *Chambre civil* could then rule and, ultimately, decide. While this process was going on, the prince-president Louis-Napoléon Bonaparte continued to climb the ladder of power, while restricting liberties and infiltrating like-minded agents into the Administration and other institutions. For his part, Sax's former allies (the cultural elites) took up positions and adapted to the new context that was to come. And, interestingly, on 28 April 1851, just three days before the opening of the first Great Universal Exhibition in London, the Chamber of Petitions allowed the defendant's complaint to proceed. From a business point of view, this safe-conduct not only allowed him to go to England in peace but also bought him time until the final trial was resumed almost two years later. During this interval, France experienced a coup d'état and a plebiscite (Louis-Napoléon Bonaparte definitively seized power and re-established the Empire). Sax experienced some paradoxical moments, such as receiving one of the highest prizes in London while going through his first bankruptcy. However, the new military leadership had already established ties with him (in December 1852, a military music concert with high-ranking officers of the Empire had been held in the businessman's factory) and were hatching a marketing and public opinion campaign (including the press) in his favour in order to relaunch him. The fifth chapter develops and contextualizes all these events, which ended in an unsurprising way (February 1853) with the appeal lodged three years earlier being considered as lawful and referred to another second-degree court.

The Imperial Court of Rouen received the summary on which it should rule following the interpretative line that Cassation had established, which foretold the victory of the accused and the restitution of his patents. Moreover, Napoleon III had already made his preferences clear by naming Adolphe Sax 'Manufacturer of the Military Household of His Majesty the Emperor' even though justice had not ruled yet. Chapter 6 contains the most significant arguments of the parties—accusations reappeared that an exclusive and forbidden commercial concession was affecting several entire families of brasswinds—and, above all, those of the prosecution, which were the reasons that the government put forward to allow such an advantage. Among the most interesting and original to justify the contradictions of those documents was an analogy with Columbus' egg, who, it is said, made a bet with some nobles that he would be able to make an egg stand without help or external elements. The argument was that Sax only departed from the construction guidelines he supposedly obeyed when there was no other choice, for example, when splicing pipes with different properties; just as Columbus slightly cracked the base of the egg to raise it. The final outcome of that trial came in June 1854, when the Court definitively rejected the motions of nullity and objections to the patents of the accused, who would also be compensated with 10,000fr. Beyond this victory, we will explore other interconnected parallel planes, such as the reasons why the Emperor and the military leadership supported this company and granted it—not even two months after the final trial—a large part of the exclusive supply of brasswinds for the Imperial bands.

The second part of the book opens with the early (December 1854) initiatives of Sax to seize instruments, ledgers, and machinery from several of his competitors—including Halary and Raoux, who had previously pursued civil proceedings against him—claiming that they were allegedly unlawfully manufacturing and selling brasswinds that stemmed from his saxotromba patent. However, those first raids turned out to be null and void in subsequent trials, not for lack of grounds, but for a different reason. To operate in accordance with the law, the raider had to have previously deposited a security, be a French citizen, or have a resident's permit; but Sax had not done the first, he was of Belgian origin, and had not bothered to apply for the third. Through clumsiness or lack of foresight (or, rather, tremendous impatience and galloping ambition) he wasted his first attack and put the other manufacturers on their guard. However—and here lies the kernel of

Chapter 7—the political and media outlets had already bet on him and could not afford to let him fall, so a second wave of much more aggressive and effective seizures were organized to cover up the fiasco (botched) of the first. These raids were not only to take place at the headquarters and workshops of the companies that allegedly copied him, but also at the site of the newly opened Parisian Universal Exhibition (May 1855), the first international one organized by France. This raid implied public humiliation and the branding of his rivals as pirates. (Of course, this time the raids were considered legal because Napoleon III had signed an imperial decree admitting the residence application of the interested party.)

One of the entrepreneurs concerned was Pierre-Louis Gautrot, the most important wind instrument maker in France and probably in the world at that time. We will explain why he was the strongest—he had understood better than anyone else the paradigm shift in the sector and was already implementing key procedures to become more competitive, for example, by relocating part of his workshops to Château-Thierry, a town ninety kilometres from Paris. The substance of Chapter 8 lies in the fact that this confrontation was with a builder who had more resources and was more intelligent than the previous ones. (Moreover, the former minister Marie reappeared as his representative.) Given that winning the case was very complicated, Gautrot's strategy was to delay the process in order to financially undermine his rival, who had not yet recovered from the bankruptcy he had been dragging on since 1852. Moreover, knowing that he was more solid, he only had to hang on, as the main patent blocking most of these instruments (saxotromba) would soon fall into the public domain (1860). Indeed, the dispute became heated—blocking of economic provisions, different interpretations of the statute of limitations, etc.—and the case went several times to the Courts of Appeal and Cassation. Hence, one of the judge-counsellors of the Imperial Court of Amiens said that they were facing 'the most relentless fighting spectacle between makers' which seemed 'to revive at every hearing'. However, these procedural ups and downs ceased when the two contenders reached (1859) a financial settlement of more than half a million francs and Gautrot accepted an (abusive) licensing agreement for as long as the saxotromba patent was active.

The following is undoubtedly one of the most interesting chapters, as it contains the unprecedented episode in which late modern France passed a state law for a private individual to enjoy a five-year extension to prolong the validity of his patents—the saxotromba, which would expire in 1865 instead of 1860, and the saxophone (1866 instead of 1861)—and, ultimately, for that entrepreneur to continue to enjoy a double monopoly. Although this was a contingency provided for in the legislation (article 15 of the 1844 law), it was remote because it required strong involvement of the Executive, approval by the Council of State, passage through committees, procedures, and debates in both the Parliament and Senate, and ratification by the Emperor. Needless to say, to embark on such an initiative, one had to have not only well-founded reasons but also contacts in the upper echelons of politics. Moreover, such an exception was highly controversial in a system of theoretically free competition; and, in this case, the stakes were enormous, with huge amounts of money and almost total control over the instrumental palette of the French army bands and the growing number of civilian bands. (To all this must be added the potential extra benefits of the free-trade agreement that Napoleon III also sanctioned in 1860, which facilitated the export of brasswinds to England.) Although under an imperial regime, Chapter 9 captures and transcends the reasons for and against such a concession, as well as the debates—and sharp commentaries—of the representatives of the French people and sovereignty.

The confrontation between Sax and Gautrot seemed to have ended in 1859 with a financial and a commercial agreement in the form of a licence. However, this could not be further from the truth, especially for the latter, who had to endure five more (unexpected) years of close surveillance and lost profits. However, there was still one final significant episode between them that embodies the struggle for control of the French brasswinds market. Sax, convinced that Gautrot was not respecting the agreed contract, inflicted a raid on him. This action, which might not come as much of a surprise, was orchestrated on the eve of the expiry of the saxotromba patent, i.e. on 12 October 1865. In addition, the treacherous seizure took place simultaneously at the Paris factory and its Château-Thierry branch. Of course, this action opened a new case between the two, which lasted seventeen months and escalated once again to Cassation. Chapter 10 recounts this episode in which we will also explore this and other business strategies to undermine rivals at any cost.

Chapter 11 focuses on Gustave Besson, another of Sax's fiercest and most vicious adversaries, who also suffered his raids early (1854) and often (four in 1857 and another in 1858). This entrepreneur is interesting not only because of his inventiveness but also because he designed ad hoc machinery that brought maturity (he was possibly the less obscure manufacturer in his procedures), fluidity, and competitiveness to the market, which made him a constant target for his enemy. Of course, we will narrate those confrontations—which also reached the Court of Cassation—but, more importantly, the focus will be on Besson himself and how well he fought against the monopoly situation he suffered. Like Gautrot, he also realized early on the shift of the business towards the civil market and used novel and advanced commercial strategies, such as adapting advertising to this new consumer, organizing popular demonstrations, giving more years of guarantee, approaching municipal and public institutions, and even expanding abroad. As early as c.1855, it was recorded that he had already established in the UK (London)—where the firm became famous—and protected new inventions there.

Besson's was one of the eighteen companies (Gautrot, Tournier, Goumas, Buffet *jeune*, Buffet-Crampon, Beaubeuf, Isbert, Jacob, Halary *père*, Belorgey, Martin *frères*—Jean-Baptiste and Félix—Roehn, Raoux, Drouelle, Florent, Battut, and Halary *fils*) that Sax confronted at the same time and in the same case. These firms defended themselves declaring that the Belgian entrepreneur was misusing his saxotromba patent in an abusive and arbitrary manner. On the other hand, the chronicles reported the virulence of these proceedings and commented that 'no other [manufacturer] had ever had to endure such a long and fierce struggle against adversaries so powerfully allied and so persistent in reproducing the same theses of attack and defence'. This sentence encapsulates part of the substance of the twelfth chapter, as it confirmed that these confrontations were very intense. It also attests to the corporate and associative character of the rival builders—some of them sharing blood ties, as will also be detailed—and that they insisted (in vain) again and again on the same arguments, namely, the lack of novelty of the saxotromba. However, they managed to introduce a new subjective element into the legal debate (the originality of the saxotromba's timbre), which further convoluted (and prolonged) the issue. To act in a more substantiated and technical way, the tribunal asked for an expert opinion which noted obvious flaws in the patent sketches, but recognized that they provided that 'special sound', adding incongruities to this whole affair which was also escalated to Cassation.

All the entrepreneurs we have introduced so far were based in Paris, but, as the century progressed, the Industrial Revolution spread and, above all, an extraordinary business was perceived, more and more factories appeared in other parts of France. Precisely, Chapter 13 focuses on one of them, that of Charles Kretzschmann, based in Strasbourg, and who, for the sake of complexity, was in partnership with Besson. In fact, he was one of the witnesses that Besson provided; after he testified, he also became a defendant and consequently had his instruments and account books seized. This section develops this episode and the web that had been woven to maintain the monopoly—the case was escalated twice to Cassation—and to dissuade the increasingly numerous (and competitive) brasswinds manufacturers in France.

Chapter 14 reconnects us with Besson and his very high resistance (*résistance très-vive*) to prove that the saxotromba patent was false and that Sax was abusing his position. To this end, Besson sent two letters to the Parliament at the time when the extension of those documents was being processed (1860) and which gave wings (and information) to the deputies opposed to said extension. In addition, he printed three *factums* with serious recriminations against his rival, such as that of being a speculator and providing false information. Before the law passed to the Senate for ratification, Besson sent another letter there—also with a *factum* reply to give it more public impact and repercussions—with similar accusations, imploring justice, and that the Upper Chamber should look after the collective interests. Sax sued him for defamation and that lawsuit was successful, resulting in his rival being fined 2000fr and sentenced to two months in prison. However, Besson evaded imprisonment by transferring his business to his wife and fleeing to London, where he had a branch of his company. Of course, once that law was passed by the Senate—and with it the renewal to continue persecuting his rivals—Sax inflicted a gigantic raid on *Madame* Florentine Besson before 1860 was over. What is interesting about this already intense chapter is to analyse its components, especially the information Besson provided, or why *Madame* Besson was found to have brasswinds from regiments that did not resort to the monopolist.

The following pages discuss the vicissitudes of the persecution of Sébastien Drouelle (a manufacturer of valves), which lasted more than nine years and was escalated to the Court of Cassation three times. The complaint was based on the fact that this businessman was illegally manufacturing valves and other loose parts (e.g. bells) for the saxotromba. One of the defence's arguments was that these valves were in the public domain—as well as being single parts—and, more interestingly, that some of his customers were licensees of Sax. This episode has a very accurate account of exactly how that raid unfolded (an event that is worthy of special attention) and what it uncovered, for Drouelle employed twenty-five people and his books were very reliably kept. These records showed that he traded with a plethora of builders, some of whom were well known—Michaud, Besson, Darche, Distin (British, so it can be confirmed that Drouelle's goods had also crossed the Channel), Labbaye, Courtois, Labitte, Jahn, Henry et Martin, Roehn, Halary, Raoux, Rivière, Coeffet, Michon, Peffer, Roth, Key et Cie, Mongin, 'and others whose list would be too long'. Thus, the more substantial contents of Chapter 15 explore some of the aspects that made the business more competitive—e.g. outsourcing or exploiting workers—and also the enormous amount of money it moved.

There was one more onslaught on 20 March 1866, the exact day before the saxophone patent expired. Sax inflicted a final simultaneous raid that would target the establishments of Gautrot, Halary, Millereau, Leroy et Goumas, Buffet *jeune*, Jules Martin, *Madame* Besson, Barbu father and son, Massabo, Kroll, the Martin brothers, Couturier, and Gaubert, most of them based in Paris, but others from Lyon or Lille. Remarkably, some of these firms had been licensees and therefore clients of his in relation to the saxotromba (Gautrot, Halary, Millereau, Jules Martin, and Couturier—these five at least), so there might have been some deference and/or warning towards them before proceeding with that aggressive seizure. However, the bellicose Belgian businessman reported them for trading in minor products that made it possible for the saxophones to sound (mouthpieces, ligatures, reeds, pads, etc.) or even for repairing them. Those attacks were declared null and void—even in the Court of Cassation (August 1867)—although Sax was determined to demonstrate the 'greed of those counterfeiters' and that he was battling 'alone against a redoubtable league that didn't withdraw before anything'. Chapter 16 explores that episode, the end of such a vast and exaggerated monopoly—further sustained by public authorities and other factual forces—the excessive ambition of some entrepreneurs, and more interestingly, the pressure to adapt to an increasingly large, complex, and competitive market. These pages also develop the last outcome, namely, the rise of a consumer society around this type of instruments. For this last period—which coincides with the first part of the Third French Republic—we do not have the same precise macroeconomic data as those of the middle of the century, but we have other direct and indirect references that confirm a great civilian affection for brasswinds and other very suggestive economic, political, and cultural factors.

Finally, the book's conclusion reviews, transcends, and rearticulates the significance of the largest judicial battle in culture and industrial property in nineteenth-century Europe. The turbulent process that French brasswinds manufacturing and marketing sector went through resulted in a modern understanding of this type of instruments that not only affected France later on but was also reflected in other countries. These last pages are also a reminder that brasswinds are simply products of the Industrial Revolution, namely the development of metallurgy and new technologies applicable to brass, but under the ubiquitous cover, evolution, and rules of the capitalist system, one of the latter being the codification of these advances and progressions through the patent system. Like other consumer goods, brasswinds were and are at the mercy of the economic interests and tastes of the bourgeois liberal society.

PART 1
DEFENCE

1
Chimeras, Tall Tales, and 'Joke-Horns' in the First Instance

Presentation of the Bases of Prosecution and Defence

The battle began when a group of instrument makers[1] filed a double civil suit against Adolphe Sax concerning the invention patents behind many of his instruments made of brass. The first notice was served in March 1846 and involved the patents from 1843 (*système d'instruments chromatiques*) and 1845 (*saxotromba*), while the second (November 1846) attacked the saxophone, whose patent had been filed just eight months earlier.[2] The complaint was based on the laws on invention patents, which established a range of fines of between 100fr and 2000fr (article 40 of the 1844 law), in addition to damages. The dispute was heard by a civil court of First Instance in Paris and proceeded in accordance with the prevailing legal procedure framework.[3]

The initial hearings were held in January 1847 and the plaintiffs' lawyer (*Maître* Marie) made a key point to the court in his first intervention: 'It is the whole of French [instrument] manufacturing that is at stake and asks for your protection.'[4] This request for intervention and assistance was needed, according to the lawyer, because the brasswinds market was becoming an

---

[1] According to a later *factum* (1860) by Adolphe Sax, Raoux was the president, Halary *père* [senior or father] was the treasurer, and then he cited Buffet *jeune* [junior], Gautrot, and Gambaro, whom we presume were members of the board. *Conclusions motivées pour Adolphe Sax, professeur au Conservatoire impérial de musique, demandeur en condamnation pour contrefaçon et défendeur en nullité et déchéance de son brevet du 13 octobre 1845, contre les Sieurs Besson, Raoux, Halary, Buffet jeune, Buffet-Crampon, Tournier, Goumas, Martin frères, Beauboeuf et Victor Jacob, inculpés de contrefaçon, défendeurs. Tribunal de la Seine, 6me chambre correctionnelle. M. Gislain de Bontin, Président. M. Mahler, juge suppléant, faisant fonctions d'Avocat impérial* (Paris: n. ed., [Impr. N. Chaix,] n.d. [March 1860]), 2.
[2] *Affaire Sax. Arrêt de la cour de cassation. M. Adolphe Sax, d'une part; MM. Raoux, Halary, Gautrot, Buffet Jeune et Gambaro, d'autre part* (Paris: n. ed., [Imprimerie H. Simon Dautreville et Cie. Rue Neuve-des-bons-enfants, 3,] 1854), 2.
[3] The French judicial system in the nineteenth century was based on numerous texts that were supplemented and adapted by other laws and instructions. However, a particularly important text was the law of 20 April 1810, on the Organization of the Judiciary and the Administration of Justice (*loi du 20 avril 1810, sur l'Organisation de l'Ordre judiciaire et l'Administration de la Justice*), where the main lines of the forums of appeal (art. 1 to 11), first instance (art. 34 to 44), and the role of the public prosecutor (art. 45 to 47) were drawn.
[4] Archive de la Bibliothèque-musée de l'Opéra, 'Dossier d'artiste. Adolphe Sax', *Affaire Sax. Audience du 1 Janvier 1847*, 1.

'exclusive privilege, a monopoly' in the hands of Sax, whom the claimants also accused of having registered patents that 'had no legitimacy' and 'were not true inventions'. Moreover, the lawyer accused him of plagiarism because he based the saxhorn system on the *Bass-tuba*, a brasswind owned by a German conductor and inventor (Wilhelm-Friedrich Wieprecht) and widely known in that country.[5]

Marie also pointed out that the patents had formal defects, had been disclosed prematurely, and lacked novelty, especially in those involving valves (1843 and 1845), as such mechanisms were commonly used in Germany and France.[6] In addition to mentioning Wieprecht again, the lawyer relied on the *clavicor* (French patent [no. 8962] of Jean-Auguste Guichard of 22 May 1838) and on the work of the renowned French horn player Joseph Meifred, which he had published seven years earlier.[7] With regard to the saxophone, he added that it was 'more of a fraud than [Sax's] valve and slide (*coulisses*) instruments' and that 'it had nothing new'. According to Marie, that musical device was another invention of *Herr* Wieprecht called the *Batyphone*.

On the other hand, Marie also complained about the recent regulations about musical instruments issued by the Ministry of War in August 1845, which further exacerbated all these problems. This lawyer had no qualms about publicly singling out General Marie-Théodore de Rumigny as Sax's lender and 'important protector'. Rumigny was a key figure in this first stage not only because he presided over the jury of a band competition at the Parisian Champ de Mars that preceded (April 1845) and inspired the new instrumental arrangement, but also because he was a direct advisor and aide-de-camp to King Louis-Philippe d'Orléans.[8]

---

[5] The *Bass-tuba* or *Chromatische Baß-Tuba* was patented in Prussia on 12 September 1835 by Wieprecht, although the author acknowledged the collaboration of another Germanic builder (Johann-Gottfried Moritz). According to that document, this deep, predominantly conical-pipe brass had a four-octave register, was intended for use in bands, and had a 'special' design that allowed for volume control and the production of a strong, powerful, and beautiful timbre. Clifford Bevan, *The Tuba Family* (Winchester: Piccolo Press, 2000), 513–19.

[6] Archive de la Bibliothèque-musée de l'Opéra, 'Dossier d'artiste. Adolphe Sax', *Affaire Sax. Audience du 12 Janvier 1847*, 2–5.

[7] Just as Wieprecht worked with Moritz, Meifred was assisted (c.1827) by Labbaye—another professional builder—to further improve and amplify these new developments. Both parties benefitted from this collaboration. Martin Mürner, 'Meifred und die Einführung des Ventilhorns in Frankreich', in Daniel Allenbach, Adrian von Steiger, and Martin Skamletz, eds, *Romantic Brass. Französische Hornpraxis und historisch informierter Blechblasinstrumentenbau. Symposium 2* (Schliengen: Argus, 2016), 223–9.

[8] Rumigny (1789–1861) had made a military career and achieved important successes in the campaigns in Prussia, Austria, Russia, and France, rising early to the rank of colonel (1814). During the Restoration, he was sidelined, although the Duke of Orleans rehabilitated him and made him his adjutant (also a count and awarded him the fourth grade, Grand Officer, of the Legion of Honour in 1833). From then on, the king entrusted him with important matters, such as restoring order in the western departments where he aggressively crushed the republican supporters. Germain Sarrut and Edme-Théodore Bourg, *Biographie des Hommes du Jour*, vol. 2 (Paris: Henri Krabbe, 1836), 400–1. He was also involved in politics (deputy

On 16 February 1847, the turn of reply and defence opened for *Maître* Chaix-d'Est-Ange, Sax's lawyer. He began his speech by presenting his client's professional career as an instrument maker, pointing out that he was Belgian[9] and had moved (1842) to France encouraged by the support from certain intellectuals and musicians such as Jobard (director of the Museum of Industry in Brussels), Buteux (first clarinet at the Paris Opera), Carafa (professor at the Paris Conservatoire and member of the Institut), or Halévy (composer).[10] In this first intervention, Chaix-d'Est-Ange portrayed Sax as a serious industrialist, a proponent of progress, and at the same time, a victim of the greed and jealousy of the Parisian manufacturers, who in his opinion represented routine and stagnation: 'there are two industries in front of you, the old and the new, routine and progress'. The lawyer went on to stress the decline of French brasswinds production before Sax arrived in France, which the influential Gaspare Spontini—arguably the foremost authority in the field—had previously pointed out.[11] According to Chaix-d'Est-Ange's sources—which he claimed came from the Ministries of War, Finance, and Commerce—the manufacture of brass wind instruments, once widely exported throughout Europe and the New World, 'was now dormant'. Consequently, economic

from 1831 to 1837) and became a general in 1840. When the monarch was overthrown, Rumigny fled with him to England, but later returned to France with a private profile. Adolphe Robert, Edgar Bourloton, and Gaston Cougny, dirs, *Dictionnaire des parlementaires français depuis le 1er mai 1789 jusqu'au 1er mai 1889*, tome 5 (Paris: Bourloton, 1891), 228.

[9] Sax was born on 6 November 1814 in the small Belgian village of Dinant. His father (Charles-Joseph) was a carpenter and cabinetmaker, but his passion for music led him to turn to the manufacture of wooden aerophones. The family soon (1815) moved to Brussels so that this business venture could expand and thrive. After initially making flutes, serpents, and clarinets, Charles-Joseph also began to produce brass instruments. After the outbreak of 1830, the Belgian government also relied on him to supply the various military bands and fanfares. The young Sax took an active part in his father's business and became immersed in the enthusiasm surrounding it. Moreover, he also began to gain recognition as a musician and clarinettist, although the most significant aspect of this early period was the patenting of his first invention in 1838, a new bass clarinet that would mark the beginning of his career. That instrument brought him much praise and positive criticism, and he used it as a covering letter in the most important musical circles of the kingdom. At the same time, his entrepreneurial side (and ambition) grew considerably, and in 1841 he entered the Belgian Exhibition of Industry with very high aspirations. However, he was awarded second prize by the jury, much to his chagrin, as he felt he was far superior to his rivals and was hoping for first place. This fact, presumably anecdotal, served as an excuse for him to leave Brussels and set out in 1842 to conquer his real aspiration, Paris.

[10] According to the chronicle of that introduction, Chaix-d'Est-Ange read out other eulogistic (*flatteuses*) letters from Sivori, Rossini, Liverani, Count Albert de La Ferronays, Donizetti junior, 'etc'. *Le Droit. Journal des Tribunaux*, 18 March 1847, 268–9.

[11] *Gazette des Tribunaux*, 26 and 27 April 1847, 645. Spontini (1774–1851) was a highly valued musician at the time. A native of Ancona (Italy), the promising young musician moved to Paris in 1803, where he found the protection of the imperial family and of Joséphine herself, who made him a court composer. His first successes in the form of lyric tragedies came with *La Vestale* (1807) and *Fernand Cortez* (1809). Spontini achieved important management positions and married (strategically?) (1811) Céleste Érard, the niece of Sébastien Érard, the famous harp and piano builder. After the fall of Bonaparte, he was given shelter in the Bourbon court, who rewarded him with naturalization. However, internal tensions (and/or the possibility of earning more money) made him move to Berlin in 1820, where he served as royal Kapellmeister in the capital and also had important administrative responsibilities.

transactions were no longer favourable to the French, and instruments had to be imported from the German states.

Chaix-d'Est-Ange also noted that Sax suffered a whole ordeal of personal and professional slander, humiliation, and scorn; labelling, for example, his instruments as *blagues-horns* (joke-horns). 'The unhappy Sax, rich in hopes, but poor and short of funds', found himself in a much crueller situation than he had expected in his first years in Paris, and which almost made him sink.[12] The lawyer narrated with clear emotional intent that Sax had to pawn the two medals he had won at the national exhibitions of Belgium 1841 and Paris 1844 for a derisory 35fr. Faced with such the desperate situation of 'a man struggling against everything, and even against hunger', he had 'no choice (*dernier appel*)' but to turn to General Rumigny as a last resort. Chaix-d'Est-Ange confessed that the high political and military official was so impressed (*touché*) that he lent him 1800fr and his secretary another 500fr.[13] (The lawyer failed to mention that the Belgian businessman's company was a limited partnership divided into ten shares of 4000fr each as of 12 December 1842, which represented a more than respectable sum.)[14]

Subsequently, Chaix-d'Est-Ange made known the contents of two letters attacking General Rumigny that the rival makers had sent to the Minister of War in the days before the Champ de Mars competition. The lawyer read the part of the protest in which they accused Rumigny of favouritism and of wanting to grant the 'monopoly of military music to a foreigner'. Furthermore, Chaix-d'Est-Ange dismissed as untrustworthy the sophistry of those businessmen who predicted that the instrumental change would 'kill a national

---

[12] This testimony seems to be (partly) true, as the press (*Revue et Gazette Musicale de Paris* [*RGMP*], 31 December 1843, 445) lamented much that Sax was enduring this situation when he had barely been living in France for a year. However, the *RGMP* also balanced this antagonism with the support of certain personalities (Meyerbeer, Spontini, Berlioz, Kastner, and Rumigny, among others) who had shown interest in his instruments. Another slightly earlier publication (*Revue et Gazette des Théâtres*, 3 December 1843, 2–3) and with such an explicit headline as 'Mr Adolphe Sax and his opponents' called for calm and suggested that the matter should not be discussed beyond musical circles. However, it was more of a manifesto and was accompanied by testimonies of support from Castil-Blaze, Berlioz, Halevy, Kastner, Federico Ricci, Meyerbeer, Adolphe Adam, Ambroise Thomas, and Carafa.

[13] While the loans were not exorbitant, Rumigny and his secretary were very generous with the Belgian maker: for comparison, at that time eating out cost 1.25fr and a bottle of quality wine was 2fr. Getting around Paris by omnibus was not too expensive (only 0.30fr), although moving by car would cost 1fr (*cabriolé*) or 1.5fr for extra comfort and shelter (*fiacre*). A tailor-made suit with a choice of fabric costed 30–45fr, and the best seats at an opera performance (*premières loges de face*) could be had for 9fr. [No name] Teyssèdre, *Conducteur général de l'étranger dans Paris* (Paris: Garnier Frères, 1842), 12, 14–16, 256, 260, 262, and 282.

[14] Archives de Paris, D31 U3 [112] [no. 1127], 19 July 1843, no title [*Registration of the formation of the company Sax et Cie.*], n.p. [1–2]. In April 1844, the company proposed a new issue of 250 and 500 franc shares for which an interesting 10% annual interest was offered (*RGMP*, 7 April 1844, 128). However, according to one of Sax's hagiographers, the competition boycotted this market launch by making potential investors believe that they were going to buy these shares at a very high price (50%). Oscar Comettant, *Histoire d'un inventeur au dix-neuvième siècle. Adolphe Sax, ses ouvrages et ses luttes* (Paris: Pagnerre, 1860), 60–4.

industry and drive 12,000 workers into beggary'. The lawyer pointed out that, according to his estimates, 'the manufacture of brass instruments in France, or rather in Paris, where almost everything was made, did not employ more than 200 or 300 workers'.[15] Chaix-d'Est-Ange ended his speech by reporting that Sax had already planned to sue those who were raiding his patents, but his opponents pre-empted him and initiated this process.

The above-mentioned developments were intertwined with less visible economic and political aspects. The band battle on the Champ de Mars in April 1845 that both Marie and Chaix-d'Est-Ange often referred to[16] can be described as an attempt to invest certain instruments with legitimacy in the context of French military bands, which were supposedly in decline.[17] In 1827, such bands were composed of twenty-seven members (from the original twelve) of whom up to nine could be *gagistes* or 'professional' civilian musicians[18] hired by the regimental boards of administration. The rest would be soldiers with (presumed) musical skills. This type of ensembles eventually lost their peculiar financing mechanism (the funds came from part of the salary withheld from the officers and the musicians were paid under the counter)[19] and (in 1828) were to be sustained with public money, but evidently under military administration.[20] That regulation (which also

---

[15] The official number of salaried brass workers in Paris in 1847 was 499. *Statistique de l'industrie à Paris résultant de l'enquête faite par la Chambre de commerce pour les années 1847–1848* (Paris: Guillaumin, 1851), 181 and 817–18.

[16] Military band competitions in France were popular and festive events that had their first antecedents at the dawn of the nineteenth century. However, it was not until 1827 that a modern competition was held, bringing together various social sectors. Thierry Bouzard, *Les usages musicaux dans l'armée française de 1815 à 1918* [Chapitre 2. L'âge d'or des musiques militaires (1815–1919)] (Thesis, Amiens, Université de Picardie Jules Verne, 2016), 208–12 and Patrick Péronnet, *Les ensembles d'instruments à vent en France 1700 à 1914: Pratiques sociales, insertions politiques et création musicale* [Volume 2. Le Triomphe d'Apollon 1815–1870] (Thesis, Paris, Université de Paris-Sorbonne (Paris 4), 2012), 22–5.

[17] See, among others, *Journal des Débats*, 1 April 1845, 1–3, *RGMP*, 27 April 1845, 134–5 and 28 September 1845, 316–19, Georges Kastner, *Manuel général de musique militaire à l'usage des armées françaises* (Paris: Firmin Didot Frères, 1848), 251–329, Albert Perrin, *Réorganisation des musiques régimentaires en France* (Mézières: Lelaurin-Martinet, 1851), 3–4, 11–14, and 42, Comettant, *Histoire d'un inventeur*, 99–114, Edmond Neukomm, *Histoire de la musique militaire* (Paris: Baudoin, 1889), 50, or Patrick Péronnet, 'Saxons et Carafons: Adolphe Sax et le Gymnase musical militaire, un conflit d'esthétique', *Revue belge de Musicologie* 70 (2016), 45–63.

[18] These were backup musicians with certain aptitudes and/or musical training, including Conservatoire-trained ones. In the absence of a better job or in addition to their official job (being a player, for example in a civilian orchestra or belonging to a theatre), these musicians earned extra money by being hired by the military commanders to make their artistic ensembles sound better. A decree of Louis-Napoléon dated 10 March 1852 prohibited these temporary hiring practices. *Journal militaire officiel*, [no exact date, first half of] 1852 [no. 10], 193.

[19] For information on the salary of one of these musicians, see Christophe Rostang, 'François Georges Auguste Dauverné et les trompettistes de l'orchestre de l'Opéra de Paris au XIXe siècle', *Larigot* 26 Spécial ([June] 2014), 56–73, which lists not only his regular income, but also his other remuneration—fixed and occasional—and expenses between 1838 and 1847.

[20] '*Journal militaire officiel*, 1er semestre, 1er janvier, p. 5', cited in Bouzard, *Les usages musicaux dans l'armée française*, 233–5.

restored cavalry music) did not specify the proportions between the types of instruments, so it is easy to guess that this would be at the discretion of the director or other superior, in addition to the availability of personnel and/or the instrumental material available for lending.[21] In any case, it is more than likely that, within this heterogeneity and leaving aside pure signal music (*céleustique* or sound signals to transmit orders),[22] clarinets were the most numerous instruments, although there were also oboes and bassoons, French horns, and trombones. Likewise, ophicleides—a kind of brass aerophone with keys and predominantly conical—and cornets became increasingly common.

These instruments were not exactly cheap, and in the first third of the nineteenth century small fortunes were paid for good clarinet (280–300fr), a flute (250fr), an oboe (270fr), an English horn (220fr), a bassoon (400fr), or a French horn (300–500fr).[23] It should not be forgotten that these musical tools were still handmade or semi-crafted products, and it is on this basis that one could argue for part of their high price. For example: for the price of a clarinet we could go to thirty premières at the Opéra and sit in the best seats, get 600 tickets for Séraphin's Chinese shadows in the Palais Royal, or enjoy the fantastic dioramas on the Boulevard Saint-Martin about 120 times. One flute would give a Parisian enough to treat himself to 125 plentiful dinners with a little wine in a small restaurant. An oboe would more than pay for a monthly full board during the winter at the lavish Hotel Meurice's City of London in rue Saint-Honoré, and the money spent on an English horn was equivalent to having a luxurious private car (*voiture de remise* or glass coach) at one's disposal for thirty days; a well-furnished flat could be rented for more than

---

[21] Kastner noted that a grand infantry band (*grande musique d'infanterie*) of 1825 was composed of 2 flutes, 2 piccolo clarinets, 4 oboes, 12 clarinets, 2 trumpets, 4 French horns, 6 bassoons, 2 trombones, and 2 contrabassoons (36 musicians in total). The numbers seem inflated; in any case, this would be an exceptionally large band. Kastner, *Manuel général de musique militaire*, 188.

[22] Roland Hervé, 'La Céleustique. La transmission des ordres par signaux sonores dans les armées françaises', *Revue historique des armées* 279 (2015), 5–12 and Péronnet, *Les enfants d'Apollon*, 40–1.

[23] Constant Pierre, *Les facteurs d'instruments de musique: les luthiers et le facture instrumentale: précis historique* (Paris: Sagot, 1893), 377–9 and Jérôme-Adolphe Blanqui, *Histoire de l'exposition des produits de l'industrie française en 1827* (Paris: Renard, 1827), 219.

Clair Godfroy's flutes in that last year were in the 155–400fr range depending on the number of keys (four to nine) and the type of wood (ebony, for example). His thirteen-key clarinets ranged from 180fr to 500fr, although he also had a lower-range model (*système simple* of six keys) for 50–60fr. Tula Giannini, *Great Flute Makers of France: The Lot and Godfroy Families, 1650–1900* (London: Tony Bingham, 1993), 90–2.

In the second largest city in France (Lyon), we find slightly cheaper examples labelled as 'military instruments', namely clarinets and bassoons with six keys (35fr and 120fr respectively), French horns with crooks (*tons*)—external tubing to change key—for 115fr (or an improved version for 150fr), trombones for 60fr, ophicleides, or *basses d'harmonie* for 130fr, trumpets or bugles [sic] with seven keys for 75fr, or with crooks for 50fr. Péronnet, *Les enfants d'Apollon*, 208. The same page also notes the value of the 'Religious instruments', among others, a serpent with three keys and ivory embouchure for 95fr or its contrabass version in A♭ and eight keys for 160fr.

three months, not far from the centre, for what a bassoon would cost. The money for a French horn would pay for a one-year stay for an elderly person in one of the best rooms at the Asile Royal de la Providence, 50 rue de la Chaussée-des-Martyrs.[24]

During the July Monarchy, Louis-Philippe closed down the King's Military Household, but not the ceremonial music and other ostentatious royal displays, which were taken over by the bands of the National Guard.[25] In reality, this ceremonial model of state was overlapping and mutating into a less serious, more civil, and shared environment, that is to say, more festive and distracting. The bourgeoisie had their salons and gatherings,[26] but they also went down to the streets, parks, and gardens more and more frequently to enjoy a concert around one of those military bands that also attracted other people of more humble status in a festive and peaceful setting for all. These significant groups from the capital were guided by an instruction (*ordonnance*) sanctioned by the king on 1 April 1838.[27] Basically, this regulation dictated that each of the twelve musical ensembles of the legions of the Paris National Guard would be composed of *gagistes* (25–30 people) and amateurs (soldiers), and would not exceed 45 troops. However, the ordinance said nothing about the instrumental palette, so this would be at the discretion of the commanders. In any case, we know that clarinets were still the backbone of these formations, although French horns, trombones, and ophicleides (a trio the French call *cuivres clairs* [bright brass]) still retained a relative importance, followed by bassoons and trumpets.[28] In fact, the ensembles were somewhere between a dying classical model (based on pairs of the traditional octet: two oboes or flutes, two clarinets, two French horns, and two bassoons)[29] and a rising one more typical of Romanticism, with brass instruments ready to take over certain positions.

As might be expected with the upheaval of the Industrial Revolution, the prices of these instruments diminished somewhat; or rather, they began to diversify. Precisely from the 1830s onwards, what in French are called *instruments de pacotille*, i.e. musical instruments of inferior quality or

---

[24] Edward Planta, *A new picture of Paris* (London: Samuel Leigh, 1827), 88 and 97; and *Galignani's new Paris guide* (Paris: Galignani, 1830), xiv, xlix, liii, 381–2, 437, 467, 541, and 561–2.
[25] Bouzard, *Les usages musicaux dans l'armée française*, 213–17.
[26] Laure Schnapper, 'Entre le théâtre et salon: les premières salles de concert parisiennes au XIXe siècle', in Laure Gauthier and Mélanie Traversier, dirs, *Mélodies urbaines, la musique dans les villes d'Europe (XVIe–XIXe siècles)* (Paris: Presses Universitaires de la Sorbonne, 2008), 201–20.
[27] Jean-Baptiste Duvergier, *Collection complète des lois, décrets, ordonnances, règlements et avis du conseil d'état*, tome 38 (Paris: [Duvergier?] 1839), 155–6.
[28] Planque, *Agenda musical ou indicateur des amateurs, artistes et commerçants en musique de Paris, de la province et de l'étranger* (Paris: E. Duverger, 1837), 82–8 and Péronnet, 'Saxons et Carafons', 50.
[29] *Revue musicale*, 16 November 1833, 331.

made without much care, and whose price was in accordance with this characteristic, began to gain strength and commercial viability. This trend was particularly noticeable in string instruments, and for example, in 1834, a certain Nicolas, from Mirecourt (Vosges department) claimed to employ 600 workers and to manufacture more than a million artistic bowed instruments a year. The highest price for one of these was no more than 60fr and a violin could be bought for as little as 2.5fr. On the side of the woodwinds, Martin, from La Couture (a village in the department of Eure, only eighty kilometres from Paris), employed twenty people in the intensive manufacture of flutes, clarinets, flageolets, etc.[30] Evidently, those violins had nothing to do with those made by a Paris luthier like Vuillaume (who employed eight workers and produced 150 instruments a year) and for which he asked no less than 200fr.[31] Nor did Martin's flutes, which could be around 30fr (or those of the Hérouard brothers, also from La Couture),[32] look much like those of Tulou, Godefroy, or Bréton whose price would be at least 250fr or 300fr.

Brass, however, lagged a little behind in this respect and there did not exist such a blatant practice of releasing trumpets, trombones, or basses at such reduced prices. Guichard may have been the first in 1839, as the report of the Exhibition of that year records that he presented several instruments and his new *clavicor*, and that 'a large number of them were already being used successfully in military music'.[33] These notes suggest that this veteran entrepreneur was in charge of an important factory and that he supplied brasswinds at a good price, or at least that he offered several quality versions of the same instrument. However, the definitive proof comes from the 1844 Exhibition, where it was confirmed that Guichard employed 210 workers and made a profit of 700,000fr per year,[34] a figure which was probably exaggerated to gain publicity or to attract investors.

---

[30] *Rapport du jury central sur les produits de l'industrie française en 1834*, tome 3 (Paris: Huzard, 1836), 295 and 298–300.

[31] *Exposition des produits de l'industrie française en 1839. Rapport du jury central*, tome 2 (Paris: Bouchard-Huzard, 1839) 351 and *Rapport du jury central sur les produits de l'industrie française en 1834*, tome 3, 294–5. Good imitations (300fr) of a violin by an Italian master, whose originals could cost between 8000fr and 10,000fr in those years, were also very expensive. [Gustave-Augustin] Quesneville, dir., *Revue Scientifique et industrielle*, tome 1 (2nd series) (Paris: Louis Colas, 1844), 426–9. A little later in time (1855), 600fr were paid for a Vuillaume cello, cheap compared to the Stradivarius (between 12,000fr and 25,000fr). L[éon] Brisse, *Album de l'Exposition Universelle*, tome 3 (Paris: Bureaux de l'Abeille impériale, 1856), 424.

[32] In 1844, the Hérouard brothers employed forty workers to mass-produce wooden aerophones. *Exposition des produits de l'industrie française en 1844. Rapport du Jury Central*, tome 2 (Paris: Fain et Thunot, 1844), 565. See also Emanuele Marconi, dir., *La Couture-Boussey. Regards sur la facture instrumentale* (La Couture-Boussey: Éditions du Musée des instruments à vent, 2022), 19.

[33] *Exposition des produits de l'industrie française en 1839*, tome 2, 360–1.

[34] *Exposition des produits de l'industrie française en 1844*, tome 2, 559.

Although these numbers were inflated, they also reveal that a substantial market for brasswinds had come into being and offered spectacular profitability; and, not least, someone was buying that merchandise. It is clear that the clientele base could not only be professional musicians (whether *gagistes* or not) who belonged to the Opera, Conservatoire, or other theatres; moreover, high-performance instruments are typically not bought on a recurring basis. For its part, the bourgeoisie preferred to continue to invest as one of their first choices in a piano which not only served to entertain their salon evenings, but also as an ornamental piece of furniture, an example of good taste among their peers, and a vehicle of prestige in the service of consolidating their social status. Nor is there any evidence yet that groups of workers and amateurs were taking up brass; the hobby was still in its infancy. (Moreover, it is not clear that the range of prices was too wide either). Therefore, if Guichard amassed that amount (or a similar one), it must have been because of orders from a very willing buyer: the military bands.

This is the background against which the band competition on the Champ de Mars (April 1845) took place, with only two proposals competing: Sax's and that of his opponent's—he was probably forced to take part as such—Michel Carafa.[35] In reality, this blatant instrumental restructuring was to take place without any public demonstration. But, in order to distance itself from the criticism and avoid a certain degree of responsibility, the Ministry of War and its representative (Marshal Jean-de-Dieu Soult) organized the competition, in which the same commission, with General Rumigny as chairman, would nevertheless continue to arbitrate. This is where the two communiqués that Chaix-d'Est-Ange read to the court, the second signed by thirty-four makers,[36] come in. Incidentally, the heading of the letter read exactly 'all the builders of military musical instruments in France', which was hyperbole, and perhaps also evidence of the vanity that characterized these Parisian businessmen.[37]

---

[35] Michel (Michele-Enrico) Carafa (1787–1872) was a French composer of Italian origin who enjoyed considerable influence on the musical scene in Paris. A friend of Cherubini and Rossini, he was one of the musical representatives of the Institut (1837), worked as a teacher at the Conservatoire from 1840, and was director (1838–56) of the *Gymnase Musical Militaire*. See, for example, Michel Brenet, *Les musiciens célèbres: La musique militaire* (Paris: H. Laurens, 1917), 93–4 and 99–100.

[36] PROTESTATION [sic] *de tous les Facteurs d'Instruments de musique militaire de France, adressée à Monsieur le Ministre de la Guerre, sur la Commission nommée pour l'examen des nouveaux instruments* (Paris: n. ed., [Typographie et Lithographie de A. Appert,] n.d. [1845]), n.p. [1–2].

[37] Lyon had nine music makers, at least three of whom (Dubois et Cie, Muller, and Rivet) were dedicated to aerophones and whose signatures do not appear on the 1845 protest. *Annuaire général du commerce, de l'industrie, de la magistrature et de l'administration* (Paris: Firmin-Didot frères, 1845), 1202.

The winner of the tournament was Sax, and his model was to serve as a reference for the Ministry of War to decree (19 August 1845)[38] some very controversial artistic reforms, as many instruments were protected by patents of Sax himself. In addition, other wood- and brasswinds were labelled with the words 'système Sax', giving visibility or priority to his particular version of that instrument or, directly, to his shop. Two examples of saxotromba were also included in the mounted ensembles, even though it was not patented at the time the regulation appeared (10 September 1845). The underlying issue was that, in order to comply with the law and to be able to sell regulatory instruments to the military formations, i.e. to participate in the money flow, the French manufacturers had to come to a forced and unwanted agreement with Sax.

This decision also implied that the *Gymnase Musical Militaire* in Paris— a sort of music academy for soldier-musicians, which Carafa himself had directed since 1838—had to adapt (buy) the new instruments. The manufacturers of woodwind aerophones were also affected, as the traditional oboes and bassoons were completely eliminated. Frédéric Triébert, a regular supplier of the latter instruments, demanded compensation for the cancellation of the contract previously signed (11 December 1844) between his company and the Ministry of War. This protest went all the way to the Council of State during the Second Republic and was rejected.[39]

Chaix-d'Est-Ange accused the plaintiffs (Raoux, Gambaro, Halary, 'and partners [*et consorts*]') of acting collegially. The lawyer asked with calculated sharpness if they were still living in the times when guilds and corporations managed production and trade in the cities (*Est-ce que nous sommes encore au temps des maitrises, des jurandes? Est-ce qu'il y a des corporations de métiers?*).[40] This idea was fundamental and one of the solid bases of the defence, since the Revolution and the new legislation had eliminated those privileges and the French enjoyed a capitalist industrial model based on free competition. These statements demonstrate the degree of sensitivity with which technical knowledge was handled and reinforced the role that patents would play as tools of information and commercial strategy in a field of intersecting economic interests.

---

[38] *Journal militaire officiel*, [no exact date, second half of] 1845, 197–8. (The regulations also stated that the replacement would be made as the old instruments were phased out of service, which could be interpreted as a measure to avoid a major outlay at the outset and/or to allow time for the builders concerned to reach agreements). In any case, the Minister of War ordered that the regiments of the 45th Line and the 9th Dragoons should immediately be provided with the new instruments. Comettant, *Histoire d'un inventeur*, 209–10.
[39] *Journal militaire officiel*, [no exact date, first half of] 1848, 155–6.
[40] *Gazette des Tribunaux*, 26 and 27 April 1847, 645.

Chaix-d'Est-Ange then covered the contentious documents on which Marie had noted a lack of novelty, premature disclosure, and formal defects. Regarding the latter, the lawyer argued that the technical specifications his client had written were sufficient and that, in any case, they should be interpreted not by ordinary people, but by men of the trade and skilled in the field (*homme de l'art, du métier*). The first patent of 1843 (*système d'instruments chromatiques*) protected 'adaptations [extra tube couplings] to the valve slides to ensure the tuning of the instrument when it changes key [or musical tone] (*Adaptation de coulisses aux cylindres pour assurer la justesse de l'instrument quand on change de ton*).[41] He [Sax] also reserved the right to produce other types of slides with internal springs, which the player could move by pulling a rod with his finger. The aim was to produce bent (slipped?) sounds without changing the usual fingering (*Coulisses rentrantes et sortantes au moyen de ressorts et mises en jeu par le doigt pour produire les sons coulés, sans changer le doigté connu*).[42] Another improvement was made explicit which sought to suppress the angular curvatures—to make them as round as possible—of some pipes and slides so that the sound would not come out blurred (*Suppression des angles ou des courbes trop heurtées qui dénaturent les sons*).

However, as much as Chaix-d'Est-Ange tried to shield his client with the claim that these and other explanations should be interpreted by professionals and builders, the patent file is (intentionally?) vague, abstruse, and complex.[43] Evidently, it is still too early to assess the whole matter, but the wording of the patent and the intangible nature of certain aspects of

---

[41] These *adaptations* to the valve slides are marked with the letter 'i' in designs no. 2 and 3 of the patent. The instrument could change key by means of different crooks or pipe segments (designs no. 12 and 13 of the patent) that would be coupled between the mouthpiece and the main tube of the instrument. (In any case, crooks—usually coiled—were widely known and used in the past, especially on the French horn. In addition, they can also be attached at some point along the length of the main tube, not necessarily between the mouthpiece and the main tube.) Notwithstanding, the *adaptations* seem very risky because the complementarity, balance, and execution of the harmonic series would be seriously affected.

[42] This contribution is represented in designs no. 7, 8, and 9 of the patent. (Designs 8 and 9 represent a section or cut-out of these mobile slides and in which the springs are marked with the letters 'c' and 'e' and the rods with the letters 'b' and 'f'. Design no. 7 has one of these slides inserted, namely the one depicted in design no. 8.)
No physical specimen of this type has survived, but the idea (albeit with the springs out) had already been explored by the Prague-born Vaclav Sámal (1842). Bohuslav Čížek, *Instruments de Musique* (Paris: Gründ, 2003), 174–5. However, the Musée des Instruments de Musique of Brussels holds (inv. 2009.029) a 'cornet compensateur' by Sax with an external spring allowing glissando [gliding, sliding, or slipped] sounds (*sons glissés*), which could be close to the original type of the patent. My deep thanks to Géry Dumoulin for bringing this instrument to my attention.

[43] Among other discomforts, Sax used the word *ton* to give substance to pitch (intervallic distance), key (musical tone), and pipe extension—whether referring to a slide, a valve slide, or a crook. He also used the word *coulisse* in a generic (slide) or particular sense (extra tube couplings on the slide itself), as well as *cylindres*, which sometimes refers to the valves themselves and sometimes to the slides coming out of those valves.

this subject (for example, the sound itself) leaves considerable room for interpretation, as well as the degree of depth and/or focus of the study. In any case, and surely to mask these gaps and inconsistencies, as well as to underline the novelty of these advances on brass, Chaix-d'Est-Ange once again used a very interesting and accurate apostrophe. The lawyer asked how it was that they, 'the makers [of wind instruments] of all France', the 'most accomplished in the practice of this art', 'without the approval (*concours*) of whom it was impossible to adopt any modification', the 'heroes', did not put this invention into practice earlier.[44]

The lawyer also gave a second argument in favour of the authenticity of his client's ideas, recalling that three years earlier (1844) Sax had received one of the two silver medals in the brass section at the French National Exhibition. Chaix-d'Est-Ange also noted that the jury had Gaspare Spontini as its advisor,[45] who recognized these products as 'new'. What is interesting here are not so much Spontini's words, but rather the fact that the national and international exhibitions were another stage and parallel arena where the legitimacy of those instruments were also be judged. The number of prizes won and how the information emanating from them was used (twisted?) would be part of the contenders' arguments. The silver medal won by Sax was not for his saxophone or his alleged saxhorns or saxotrombas, but for a trumpet with piston valves, a bugle, and a *clavicor*.

Chaix-d'Est-Ange went on to explain to the court the saxotromba, the second of the patents under discussion. The lawyer briefly introduced what brass instruments were and what they were used for, noting also the recent and ground-breaking application of valves on them. However, he added that they needed to be further developed and that his client was committed to solving

---

[44] 'On prétend que l'invention était connue depuis bien longtemps et pratiquée en Allemagne. L'invention était pratiquée en Allemagne! Vous la connaissez donc nécessairement; vous êtes tous les facteurs de France, les gens les plus habiles dans votre métier, les plus consommés dans la pratique de votre art, sans le concours desquels il est impossible d'y apporter une modification, vous eu tenez la clé, vous eu êtes héros. Comment! Vous savez ce qui se fait à vos portes, il n'y a pas à en douter, cette invention connue depuis longtemps en Allemagne ne pouvait être inconnue de vous, et vous ne la pratiquiez pas? Si vous ne l'avez connue et pratiquée, c'est qu'elle n'existait pas en Allemagne, car vous n'acceptez sans doute pas l'impérieuse supposition d'avoir voulu mettre la lumière sous le boisseau'. *Gazette des Tribunaux*, 26 and 27 April 1847, 645. The last phrase of this speech (*mettre la lumière sous le boisseau* [putting the light under the bushel]) was to accuse them of being clumsy or shady; in the first case, they had not achieved the solution, and in the second case, they would have preferred to hide it rather than disclose it.

[45] The official report does not mention this composer, nor are the members of the jury known. The commission of the music section (included in the precision instruments section) was composed of Pouillet, Delamorinière, Gambey, Mathieu, Oliver, Savart, and Baron Séguier. The second and sixth were assigned to it (they were the *rapporteurs*), but they were assisted by specialists (musicians) such as Auber, Habeneck, and Galay [sic]. *Exposition des produits de l'industrie française en 1844*, tome 1, xxxvii, xl–xli and tome 2, 529–30. The first was the director of the Conservatoire, the second an important violinist and conductor, and the third was Jacques-François Gallay (1775–1864), professor of natural horn (from 1842) also at the Conservatoire. Spontini must therefore have been an assistant advisor.

problems with ergonomics and manoeuvrability. He gave the example of conventional French horns where the player held the instrument by the bell with the right hand and used the fingers of the left hand to press the valves. It was, according to him, an instrument that was not at all effective in military music. Sax had therefore created a family of instruments that could be held comfortably while standing and moving, i.e. also on horseback and with one arm. In addition to this advantage, Chaix-d'Est-Ange said that the saxotromba bells were movable or rotatable, i.e. they could be turned in the same direction, thus creating, he claimed, a homogeneous mass of sound.

The saxotromba's document did mention possibility of holding the instrument between the musician's side and arm, which also had (supposedly) other beneficial properties for the performance and physical safety of the rider: 'the rider no longer has to fear that his horse, by raising its head, will strike the instrument and break his teeth or bruise his face'. However, the text did not say anything about moving or rotating bells, only that these terminations were in an elevated position and 'slightly inclined from left to right'. It is far more challenging to identify other utilities in Sax's chaotic, tangled, and ambitious contribution, as it intended to simultaneously protect a system, an instrument, and families of instruments.

Regarding the system itself, we assume that this alleged set of interrelated procedures or principles applied too to the other instruments mentioned in the patent statement (saxhorns,[46] cornets, trumpets, and trombones). In addition, such a system would allow the adoption of crooks (external tubing segments of different lengths to transpose the instruments to other keys); or, alternatively, a fourth valve (which would give access to a new pipe run) could be attached to them to make them deeper. Apropos of the instrument itself, Sax did not provide any description or specification; rather, he referred us to the section of the designs where these instruments and their components were drawn. And, he justified the family concept by saying that all the deep and treble members had the same fingering ('played in the same way') and that the sound would come out of the bell only, that is, they would not wear keys and there would be no holes drilled in the body of these instruments.

Finally, Sax strategically used the patent for the saxotromba (1845) to update and revitalize the previous one of 1843 (saxhorns), which was about to expire, as he signed it to last for five years. In this regard, the Belgian

---

[46] It is quite clear that the (commercial) name *saxhorns* was adopted after the instrument was marketed. That appellation does not appear in the first advertisement for his company (*La France musicale*, 24 September 1843, 316) three months after the registration of that patent. The Belgian maker used generic names to refer to them on the basis of a common formal paradigm (*bugle à cylindre* [bugle with valves]) or register (*Ténor-Basse*, *Basse*, and *Contre-Basse*).

manufacturer again addressed the (alleged) problem of the angles of the slides and tubing, stating that he would recycle some of the valves (*cylindres*) that appeared in the 1843 document, and that he reserved certain formal provisions that also appeared there, for example, that of an instrument with the bell facing forward instead of upwards. Nonetheless, the 1845 patent envisaged that saxhorns would use the 'saxotromba system'—referring to figures 6, 8, 9, 10, 11, and 12—with the bell upwards. However, he also pointed out that saxhorns had wider proportions (*proportions*) than saxotrombas and that it was necessary to differentiate between an E♭ saxotromba and an E♭ saxhorn with the saxotromba system (figures 1 and 10 of the document). Not even in his final summary—by the way, only one sentence—did he clarify this tremendous confusion; he also reminded that his invention 'comprises not only the individual instruments shown in the attached drawings, but also and above all the different families of which they are members'.

After the defence of Sax's two main brasswinds, Chaix-d'Est-Ange strove to demonstrate the reality and originality of the saxophone, claiming that its 'manufacture had such delicacy, such nuances of proportion' that only its inventor could achieve.[47] This exaggerated praise was intended to lend a certain weight to an instrument that was not yet well understood and had only just begun to be marketed.[48] The lawyer also read out the extract from the report of the 1845 band competition so that the court could hear that the saxophone had 'truly incomparable power' and 'lent itself very well to sweet or grandiose effects'. Moreover, 'it could be used with equal advantage (*avantage*) for solos or as part of an ensemble'. In any case, the introduction of this instrument capitalized on its intensity, versatility, timbre, and blend. Of course, Chaix-d'Est-Ange fought the accusation of premature disclosure (the saxophone was patented eleven months after the Champ de Mars tournament to which it was entered) on the grounds that it was normal to test a product before registering it, especially for musical instruments.

The second lawyer speaking for the complainants, *Maître* Etienne Blanc, took the floor at the session of 23 February 1847 and harshly attacked the Belgian maker. Once again, he brought up the sham (*simulacre*) of the Champ de Mars competition, and again made direct attacks on General Rumigny. The lawyer pointed out that 'the patents in question were supported by a [military] ordinance of adoption' and 'completely unrelated to [the legitimate reasons linked to] the novelty of the instruments'. He also highlighted

---

[47] *Gazette des Tribunaux*, 26 and 27 April 1847, 646.
[48] *Le Ménestrel*, 13 June 1847, 3–4.

the audacity of Sax who, despite his advantage, imposed his name on the musical instruments, leading the potential buyer in a well-established direction: his own shop. In this vein, Blanc warned of the 'monopoly' towards which the market was heading, where the strongest would set the prices. By way of example, he pointed out that Sax sold for 150fr the same instrument that his adversaries had for 90fr.[49] Therefore, if the defendant had his way, the customers and the War Administration would lose the most. The rest of the industry would also suffer consequent bankruptcies, and it would not be possible to secure the instrument endowments needed by the Ministry in case of large orders or insolvency of the sole supplier. Blanc demanded the revocation and invalidation of these patents—without compensation—which, if validated for external reasons, were to fall into the public domain and under a different nomenclature. The lawyer concluded the hearing by claiming that the manufacturers were trying to circumvent this vicious circle—a *double privilège*, he said—which had been created in favour of Sax so that 'the monopoly would not be perpetuated in his hands'.

Blanc left some flanks uncovered (significant orders or insolvencies could be solved by expropriating the product or granting licences), but, in essence, he was telling the truth: Sax's instruments were very expensive (Table 1.1). His first advertisement (*c*.1845–7), in which he of course mentioned his victory on the Champ de Mars, also claimed that his products were superior to the old ones and that they were protected by patents. However, he made it clear that he would not take advantage of that situation and would base his prices on careful manufacturing. Furthermore, Sax's guarantee extended for eight months, which was rather short, especially considering the high cost of these supposedly high-quality instruments.

The tone of the second pamphlet (1847) was less enthusiastic and more serious, indicating that Sax was under pressure from the other makers. On the cover of this leaflet he emphasized the superiority of his instrumental palette and that it was endorsed by official regulations. Sax again warned that his genre was protected by patents that allowed him to set specific prices (*établir des prix particuliers*), but that he did not want to set them above the standards of good manufacture (*cours ordinaire d'une bonne fabrication*). He also stated that he had succeeded in economizing on manufacturing labour, which meant that he could now offer a substantial discount (*réduction notable*), while giving a two-year guarantee and not an eight-month guarantee as in the previous flyer.

---

[49] *Le Droit. Journal des Tribunaux*, 18 March 1847, 269.

Table 1.1 Price of the saxophone, brasswinds, and percussion instruments of the manufacture Sax et Cie for the infantry and cavalry regiments according to the new organization of 1845

Instrument or type of instrument	Price
Saxophone	300fr
Piston valves cornet (*pistons*)	125fr
Three-valve cornet (*cylindres*) (Système Sax) [sic]	125fr
Valve trumpet (*cylindres*) (Système Sax) [sic]	125fr
Three-valve trumpet (*cylindres*) (Système Sax) [sic]	125fr
Three-valve trombone (*cylindres*) (Système Sax) [sic]	150fr
Three-valve French horn (*cylindres*) (Système Sax) [sic]	150fr
Trombone	90fr
Three-valve trombone (Système Sax) [sic]	150fr
Ophicleide	125fr
Small saxhorn in E♭	100fr
Saxhorn in B♭	110fr
Saxhorn in A♭ to replace the French horn (*pour remplacer le cor*)	125fr
Alto saxhorn in E♭	150fr
Saxotromba in E♭ to replace the French horn (*pour remplacer le cor*)	150fr
Alto Saxhorn in E♭ to replace the French horn (*pour remplacer le cor*)	150fr
Baritone Saxhorn in B♭	175fr
Four-valve Saxhorn in B♭	200fr
Contrabass Saxhorn in E♭	200fr
Bass drum	85–110fr
Snare	50–70fr
Cymbals	75–110fr

Compiled from *Manufacture d'instruments de musique. Adolphe Sax et Cie. Rue Neuve-Saint-Georges, no. 10* (Paris: n. ed., n.d. [c.1845/7]), 2–3.

The reduction in the price of most products was no more than 10fr or 15fr (20fr in the case of deep saxhorns),[50] which was still inaccessible for many, and presumably also significantly undermined the budget that the War Ministry had for the purchase of this type of material. Most significantly, however, the saxophone remained at 300fr, which suggests that Sax was still skimming the scoop of his upstart and/or that there were problems somewhere along the assembly line. In any case, it was not an affordable price even for individuals with some money to invest in such expensive devices born in a (closed) military environment. Saxophones and other brass were also prohibitively expensive for workers, even for those who worked on relatively well-paid industries, who could earn around 4.36fr a day. (The average wage

---

[50] *Nouveau prospectus d'Adolphe Sax et Cie. Manufacture d'instruments de musique. Rue Neuve-Saint-Georges, no. 10* (Paris: n. ed., n.d. [1847]), 1–4.

per working day for an adult male worker in Paris in 1847 was 3.80fr, while that of women could be around 1.63fr, and even less for children.[51] Of course, as will be discussed later, in the provinces these figures were almost halved.)

Marie took the floor in a later appearance and bluntly called Sax a 'speculator'. He also scorned him for being the darling of the press and for the influential Hector Berlioz's outspoken support for him in his column in the *Journal des Débats*.[52] He also again railed against Rumigny, the 'confirmed protector of Adolphe Sax, who travelled with his instruments, recommended them to all the [military] boards, to all the directors; he imposed them on one and all, and used his tremendous influence to rescind the previous agreements that existed with the former manufacturers'. After publicly denouncing a French army general and aide-de-camp to the king of corruption and coercion, Marie lashed out at Georges Kastner. Kastner was a musician and theoretician of Alsatian origin who was trying to make his way and exert a certain influence on the artistic life of competitive Paris, and who acted as secretary to the Champ de Mars commission. The lawyer wondered: 'Who is Kastner? He is the capitalist at the head of the *maison* Sax. Kastner is a rich man, a son-in-law of Boursault,[53] a former bookmaker (*fermier des jeux*), who has found in this fortune the same adventurous spirit that was at the origin

---

[51] The wages of adult male workers in brass instrument factories at this time ranged (depending on their professional category and assignment) between 2.25fr and 8fr; the majority (71%) were between 3fr and 5fr. This gives an average of 4.36fr per day (*à la journée*) which represented the fourth best option in terms of earnings, after the piano, organ, and luthier sectors. The worst paid were the woodwind and accordion workers. *Statistique de l'industrie à Paris (1847–1848)*, 49–55, 183, and 817.

[52] Up to that date (1847), Berlioz's most notable mentions of Sax in that newspaper were, namely that of 12 June 1842, when he described one of the prototypes of the saxophone; that of 1 April 1845 ('On the reorganization of military bands'); that of 29 of the same month and year ('Military band competition at the Champ de Mars'); and that of 14 February 1847 ('New Adolphe Sax Concert Hall'). Later, he would also appear (12 October 1847) in an entry entitled 'Sax and his instruments'. However, we think that Marie was referring to the entry of 8 October 1843, 'Musical trip to Germany', which proved to be premonitory. In his characteristic bombastic style, Berlioz said that Sax was enduring 'persecutions worthy of the Middle Ages and reminiscent exactly [sic] of the deeds and gestures of those of the enemies of Benvenuto, the Florentine chiseller'. The composer was referring to his 1838 opera *Benvenuto Cellini*, and particularly the moment in which the protagonist is under pressure and has to fulfil a task. Berlioz noted that the Belgian maker was suffering numerous setbacks, namely the abandonment of good workmen, the theft of plans, accusations of insanity, attempts at confrontation; to the point that, he said, 'with a little more audacity, they would murder him'. The composer concluded by underlining the animosity of those rival businessmen ('Such is the hatred they exercise'), whom he dismissed as 'having invented nothing'. *Journal des Débats*, 8 October 1843, 1.

[53] Very illustratively, Berlioz himself confirmed the numerous financial resources of this intellectual during a visit to his house in Strasbourg: 'we stopped for two days in Strasbourg at the home of Mr Kastner, who had invited us to visit his rich and beautiful property. Mr Kastner is a learned musician-theorist; he married the daughter of Mr Boursault [Léonie-Amable-Albertine], and consequently has an immense fortune'. Pierre Citron, dir., *Correspondance générale [de Hector Berlioz]*, tome 5 (Paris: Flammarion, 1989), 586–8 [Letter 2308 sent by Berlioz on 5 September 1858 to his uncle Félix Marmion].

Citron informs us in a footnote that Kastner's father-in-law was Jean-François Boursault-Malherbe (1750–1842) and confirms the gambling houses, as well as a famous collection of paintings.

See also Adrien De la Fage, *Quinze visites musicales à l'Exposition Universelle de 1855* (Paris: Tardif, 1856), 182 and *Le Ménestrel*, 29 December 1867, 36–7.

of all his money, ready to seek investments (*cherchant à commanditer*) and profits in all the enterprises that come his way. It is he who finances Sax, it is he who has his money in Sax's company; Sax's business (*maison*) is his.'[54]

After all these serious accusations, Chaix-d'Est-Ange came to his client's defence and tried to clean up General Rumigny's image by arguing that the commission was composed not only of himself, but also of two other colonels and the entire music section of the Institut (Auber, Adam, Halévy, Carafa, Spontini, and Onslow).[55] And, 'as if this were not enough', he also pointed to the expertise of Séguier and Savart—the former an aristocratic and influential intellectual, the latter a veteran military engineer—'the most competent men in the world in mechanics and acoustics'[56] (and who will come up again in our speech). The lawyer recalled that the Champ de Mars tournament was also witnessed by an audience that cheered Sax's instruments. In any case, and seeing how heated the debates were getting, Chaix-d'Est-Ange read aloud two letters from General Rumigny and Kastner defending themselves against accusations of 'intrigue and complacency'. In the former, dated 8 March 1847, the high command formally denied seeking profit in any way and acknowledged that, 'by giving his support to Adolphe Sax, he had no aim other than of providing the French regiments with the best instruments'. Furthermore, he confessed to having lent him money in those past moments 'of anguish to prevent him from succumbing to mediocrity and envy'.[57] And, after further declarations of support for the Belgian businessman, Rumigny warned that he did not rule out suing and prosecuting those builders if they continued to slander his name and question his honour.[58]

While we do not entirely rule out a financial interest on Rumigny's part, this high-ranking military commander had another, more calculated motivation

---

[54] *Gazette des Tribunaux*, 26 and 27 April 1847, 646.

[55] The Institut was a consultative institution established in 1795 and supported by public funds (in reality, it was a prolongation of the old *Académies* that had been closed by Robespierre). Its main mission was to watch over knowledge and promote it, although they also judged informally (and decisively, because of the tremendous influence they had) any discovery or advance that was brought to their attention. At the time (1845), the Institut was divided into five sections, namely *Académie Française*, *Académie royale des Inscriptions et Belles-Lettres*, *Académie royale des Sciences*, *Académie royale des Beaux-Arts*, and *Académie des Sciences morales et politiques*. Music (or rather, composition) was part of the fourth branch along with other creative disciplines. The Institut was under the direct *et spéciale* protection of the King, evidence of the monarch's interest in associating with the intellectuals of his time, who were compensated with an annual salary of 1500fr. (Vacancies were supposedly filled from among those nominated by each of these sections, although those chosen nevertheless had to be approved by the king). See, among others, *Almanach Royal et National pour 1847*, 796–809 and *Galignani's* (1845), 72–5.

[56] See also Kastner, *Manuel de musique militaire*, 253–4.

[57] A few years later, Sax himself again acknowledged this help in one of his most ardent defences. *Note pour Monsieur Adolphe Sax contre Monsieur Gautrot: tribunal correctionnel de la Seine: sixième chambre* (Paris: n. ed., [Imprimerie Charles de Mourgues Frères,] 1856), 34–5.

[58] *Gazette des Tribunaux*, 26 and 27 April 1847, 646 and *RGMP*, 23 May 1847, 172–3. Kastner's letter was shorter and more direct, stating that he was never interested in Sax's company or any other.

for supporting the Belgian inventor. Sax was the perfect bishop to weaken and punish those instrument merchants who were beginning to conspire against the Orleanist monarchy and were sympathetic to the Republican cause, as we will discuss in the following chapters. Although we obviously cannot be certain, we think that the contacts with the French diplomatic leadership and more than likely promises of business on French soil were initiated from Belgium. Indeed, the French Ambassador in Brussels when Sax was considering moving to Paris was Marie-Hippolyte Rumigny, the general's brother and another staunch supporter of Louis-Philippe.[59]

After these two statements, and again validating the opinion of the commission of Champ de Mars, Chaix-d'Est-Ange insisted on that the saxhorns, saxotrombas, and saxophones were novel and legitimate. The lawyer concluded his argument in a combative tone and claimed the sum of 50,000fr in damages (*dommages-intérêts*) from the plaintiffs. According to him, the rival makers had not respected the 'exclusive right' which the law granted to his client to produce and trade his instruments. He also added that the claimants had been engaged in copying and selling those products for one year without the express authorization of the owner.

---

[59] Henry-Thierry Deschamps, *La Belgique devant la France de juillet: l'opinion et l'attitude françaises de 1839 a 1848* (Paris: Les Belles Lettres, 1956), 28–30.

2
'Let Him Calm Down' and the Judgement of the *Lumières*

The Position of the Prosecutor and the Technical Report

Although the visible part of the conflict revolved around the alleged validity of patents, the underlying issue was different. In reality, the battle was over the supply and provision of wind instruments to military bands, which were very lucrative and willing customers. Bands were also to become a model and direct reference for civilian and other popular ensembles such as the *fanfares* (fanfare bands, i.e. groups composed mainly of brass).[1] The complaining makers knew that if Adolphe Sax won the case, he would control for at least fifteen years most of the brass palette and the saxophones, which were still not very significant. A military musical infantry regiment of fifty players had to have at least nineteen of his own compulsory instruments—saxhorns, saxophones, and other 'système Sax' specimens—while a cavalry group of thirty-six players would contain at least twenty-nine.[2] This represented 38% and 80% of the total instrumentation of these ensembles, to which we must add other possible benefits from the remaining unprotected brass- and woodwinds.[3]

In any case, brass was the key and this period (1840–60) coincided with a spectacular development in its manufacture and innovation, far surpassing woodwinds (Figure 2.1). While at the beginning of the century (first twenty years) there were only two patents dedicated to brasswinds, the following four decades saw an almost exponential growth (7, 15, 33, and 122), which was also reflected in dividend yields (Figure 2.2). It was precisely at

---

[1] Jean-Yves Rauline, '19th Century Amateur Music Societies in France and the Changes of Instrument Construction: Their Evolution Caught between Passivity and Progress', *The Galpin Society Journal* 57 (2004), 236–7.

[2] [Lieutenant-Colonel] Belhomme, *Histoire de l'Infanterie en France*, tome 5 (Paris: Henri Charles-Lavauzelle, n.d. [1893–1902]), 282 and Adolphe de Pontécoulant, *Organographie. Essai sur la facture instrumentale*, vol. 2 (Paris: Castel, 1861), 274.

[3] However, despite relying on official data, we must also look at the actual situation, i.e. whether there was indeed an effective and rapid implementation of these reforms. The chronicle of a great concert of several military bands at the Hippodrome de la Place de l'Etoile in 1847 noted the anarchy [sic] that reigned in these ensembles and the low level of the musicians. Kastner, *Manuel général de musique militaire*, 322–3.

'Let Him Calm Down' and the Judgement of the *Lumières* 51

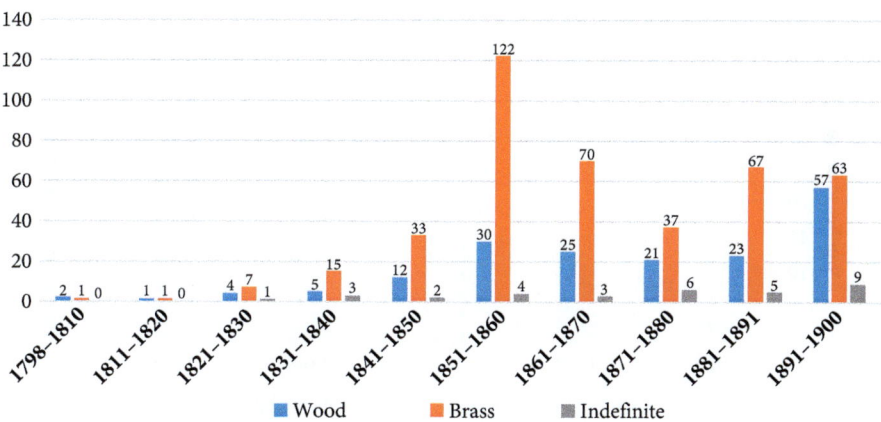

Figure 2.1 Evolution of the number of patents and certificates of addition—the values in the graph represent this sum—for all aerophones during the nineteenth century in France

Note: Sometimes, makers took advantage of the cheapness of registering a certificate of addition (20fr) to protect an improvement or advance that had little to do with the parent patent and was supposed to be nascent.

Compiled from Malou Haine, *Les facteurs d'instruments de musique à Paris au 19e siècle* (Brussels: Université de Bruxelles, 1984), 396.

this time (1847/48) that the Chamber of Commerce led a survey to find out the real turnover of all the Parisian companies. Surprisingly, there were 373 firms engaged in the manufacture of musical instruments in Paris, of which 38 dealt with brass, which came in fourth place—in terms of quantity—behind organs (40), accordions (62), and manufacturers of pianos or their components (197). Brasswinds managed to generate a considerable annual turnover of 1,620,500fr, which is almost 10% of the profits of all musical disciplines.[4] However, the projection of these businesses promised an extraordinary future in the short term. Looking at the same picture thirteen years later (1860), the brasswinds represented a comfortable third in terms of the number of firms (40)—out of a total of 358 businesses—but moved 3,189,620fr.[5] This figure does not seem very significant compared to the previous one, but it is very revealing when we realize that the number of patrons remained almost stationary and the economic return was almost double.

Resuming the court battle and after three months of hearings with conflicting statements, the parties heard the prosecutor's report. De Guajal considered that 'Sax's patents should be maintained and protected' and urged

[4] *Statistique de l'industrie à Paris (1847–1848)*, 757, 817, 823, and 833.
[5] *Statistique de l'industrie à Paris (1860)*, 751–4.

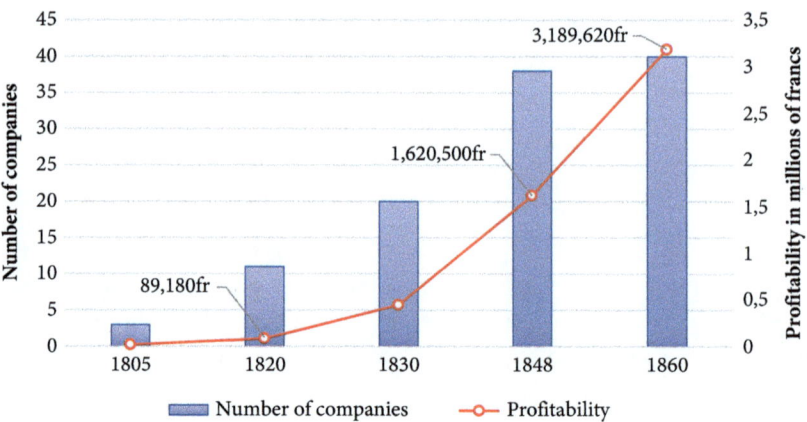

Figure 2.2 Growth of brasswinds companies and their profitability

Note: To calculate the values for 1820, we have taken the section on national exports of 'French horns (*cors*), *serinettes* [or small mechanical barrel organs], serpents, trumpets, and trombones', cymbals (*cymbales*) and, lastly, 'basses, Turkish crescents (*chapeaux chinois*) [or indirect blown idiophones made of metal], and bass drums (*grosses caisses*)' expressed in Haine, *Les facteurs d'instruments de musique*, 48–55 and 403. Unfortunately, there is no data we can use for 1805 and 1830, not even approximate as above, so we have not noted any figures at these levels and have only followed the trend.
Compiled from *Statistique de l'industrie à Paris (1847–48)*, 817 and *Statistique de l'industrie à Paris (1860)*, 751.

him to calm down (*qu'il se rassure*), as he was in France and that country gave value to foreigners who brought 'useful inventions' and 'protected acquired and legitimate rights'. However, despite this reassuring assessment, the court commissioned on 6 April 1847 a technical report to be drawn up by a commission of experts (*lumières*) in order to shed light on the patents at stake and the resulting instruments.[6] This working group was to be composed of Spontini, Savart, and Halévy, but the former excused his absence because of prior musical engagements with the King of Prussia; or, perhaps, he preferred

---

[6] Precisely, the court instructed these three experts 'to examine and compare [Sax's instruments] with the German instruments, that of Périnet, the *clavicor*, and the *Batyphone* which are opposed to them, in order to know whether Sax's processes were patentable, suitable or not for execution, and whether they have been previously worked out'. Furthermore, they should determine 'whether [these artistic devices] were sufficiently described in the patents; and if so, whether they were [truly] new or, on the contrary, constituted nothing more than mere changes of form; and whether, as to substance, they were already [knowledge] in the public domain'. *Gazette des Tribunaux*, 26 and 27 April 1847, 646.
Étienne-François Périnet was an instrumentalist (trumpet and cornet) and maker who was highly valued at the time. On 3 October 1834, he signed a five-year patent 'for attaching a third piston [valve] to the cornet'. However, his most interesting contribution was protected four years later (28 October 1838), precisely for improvements to the cornet pistons, but applicable to other brasswinds. In it, Périnet tried to soften the angles that the column of air had to pass through when traversing these valves and tubing. This refinement inspired the naming of a type of valve known today as the 'Périnet piston' or 'Périnet system'. Géry Dumoulin, 'The Cornet and Other Brass Instruments in French Patents of the First Half of the Nineteenth Century', *The Galpin Society Journal* 59 (2006), 80–2 and 85–6; and Maxime Chagot and Christian Chagot, 'Cornets modèle Halary et premiers pistons Périnet', *Larigot* 63 ([April] 2019), 6–25.

to distance himself from this thorny issue.⁷ His replacement was Nicolas Boquillon, 'a distinguished physicist and librarian at the Conservatoire des Arts et Métiers'.⁸

Boquillon earned a living as a journalist, translator, and technician at this distinguished French institution. He was also an inventor and patented certain discoveries of his own, such as his 'regulator of the flow of elastic fluids under all pressures' (20 June 1839).⁹ Even though we have no significant references to him prior to the present trial, he was one of the reporters covering the French National Exhibition of 1844 in which some of these instrument makers and Sax himself took part. Although we cannot say it openly yet—there will be more than obvious facts later—Boquillon felt sympathy for Sax from the very beginning. His report of the 1844 Exhibition dedicated four long paragraphs to describing his instruments and advances, while he dismissed his opponents (Raoux and Guichard, gold and silver medallists, respectively) with only one paragraph.¹⁰ However, Boquillon picked up two very significant details about the latter two entrepreneurs, noting that Raoux 'retained the long and arduous process of hammering (*longue et pénible fabrication au marteau*), but his instruments were in demand (*recherchés*) and their price compensated for the scarcity in the volume of production'.¹¹ Of Guichard, he said that he supplied instruments 'in considerable quantities at lower prices'.¹² This information therefore confirms that the quasi-artisanal practices and chain manufacturing coexisted in the making of brasswinds. (Guichard also made very well-finished exemplars.)

The second specialist was Nicolas Savart (1790–1853), not his younger brother, the famous physician, physicist, and acoustician Félix Savart, who

---

⁷ In any case, according to a later chronicle and a *factum*—*Le Droit. Journal des Tribunaux*, 27 September 1854, 930–1 and *Lettre adressée à M. le Président de la 4e chambre du tribunal de 1re instance de la Seine par M. Spontini. [Cour d'appel. 3me Chambre. Présidence de M. Poultier. Rôle du vendredi. M. Berville, avocat-général]* (Paris: n. ed., [Imp. de Appert,] 1850), 6—, Spontini must have sent a letter to the president of the Tribunal before leaving for Germany acknowledging that Sax's instruments were forgeries. The prosecutor wondered why the revered composer had changed his mind—if indeed he had, for he also said that Spontini only signed it, he did not write it—giving rise to conjectures of authenticity or rather of having been put under pressure (*l'homme d'affaires a passé par là*). In any case, the representative of the public prosecutor's office exonerated him for allowing himself to be dragged into this act of weakness [sic], also emphasizing his senility. (In 1847, Spontini was already seventy-three years old and would die four years later in Italy.)

⁸ Pontécoulant, *Organographie*, vol. 2, 280 and *Almanach National pour 1851* (Paris: Guyot et Scribe, 1851), 188.

⁹ [J-M.] Quérard, *Le Quérard: archives d'histoire littéraire, de biographie et de bibliographie françaises: complément périodique de la France littéraire* (Paris: Le Quérard, 1855), 347.

¹⁰ Quesneville, *Revue Scientifique et industrielle*, tome 1 (2nd series), 426–9.

¹¹ No period catalogue has been preserved in which to find out what the French horns of the fighting Raoux might have cost, but an estimate based on another of the reputable brass manufacturers (Halary) would suggest that these specimens would cost no less than 360fr or 400fr. Pierre, *Les facteurs d'instruments*, 377.

¹² Quesneville, *Revue Scientifique et industrielle*, tome 1 (2nd series), 426.

died in 1841.[13] Both brothers were born into a family of military engineers who were scholars of mathematics and physics. According to a reliable source,[14] Nicolas had a vocation for the exact sciences (he studied at the prestigious École Polytechnique)[15] and worked as a lieutenant-colonel at the *École royale du génie* in Mézières, a commune in the north of France. Later, when he retired to Paris, he devoted himself to continuing the research on acoustics and music that his brother had begun.[16] Savart also acted as a reporter at the French National Fair of 1844 and, curiously, confused and/or identified the saxophone with the contrabass clarinet, giving it very generic compliments.[17] In any case, everything suggests that Nicolas Savart was also to prove a favourable critic for Sax. In this respect, we can cite a statement (1839) by [Félix] Savart in which he asserted that '[Charles-Joseph] Sax, [Adolphe's father] knew the law of vibrations in an infallible way'.[18] Incidentally, those words were taken up by François-Joseph Fétis, a Belgian intellectual with a great deal of power in music and journalism, who lived between Brussels and Paris; he will reappear in the course of this book.

The third expert was Fromental Halévy, one of those composers who urged Sax to leave Belgium for France. A professor at the Conservatoire (1827), he enjoyed considerable media clout and influence, as well as royal connections.[19] Although with Boquillon or Savart one might expect a certain neutrality, Halevy had already openly sided with Sax from the beginning, not only as an instrument maker, but also as a clarinet player.[20] Sax's first

---

[13] Félix Savart served as a doctor in the Napoleonic campaigns and after the war devoted himself to physics and acoustics. He later worked with Jean-Baptiste Biot studying the magnetic field created by an electric current, and they jointly enunciated the Biot-Savart Law. In 1827 he was elected a member of the Académie des Sciences and the following year he taught physics at the Collège de France. He invented the so-called 'Savart wheel', which was intended to measure the frequency of a sound. As early as 1819 he wrote his *Mémoire sur la construction des instruments à cordes et à archet* and tried to apply his results by creating a 'rational' violin (1817) with a trapezoidal shape, which was not well received by performers.

[14] [M.?] Blanc, *Mémoires de l'Académie Impériale de Metz* (Metz: Académie de Metz, 1855), 585–96.

[15] At the time, the École Polytechnique was one of the military institutions (*Écoles*) where the commanders and officers who would later join the engineering corps of the land and sea armies were trained for two years. The curriculum of that school included subjects related to hydrography, bridges and mines, armaments (*poudres et salpêtres*), telegraphy, and even tobacco. See, among others, *Almanach Royal et National pour 1847*, 751–3.

[16] Blanc, *Mémoires*, 595.

[17] *Exposition des produits de l'industrie française en 1844*, 562.

[18] [François-Joseph Fétis,] 'Rapport de M. F. Fétis sur les travaux de M. Sax père', in *Bulletin de l'Académie Royale des Sciences, des Lettres et des Beaux-Arts de Belgique*, tome 18, first part (Brussels: Hayez, 1851), 565. See also François-Joseph Fétis, *Biographie universelle des musiciens*, tome 7 (Paris: Firmin Didot Frères, 1866), 413.

[19] At that time (1847), Halévy was honorary director of the Musique—we understand chamber or court music—of Her Royal Highness the Duchess of Orléans and the Princess Royal. *Almanach Royal et National pour 1847*, 833 and 840.

[20] *Revue et Gazette des Théâtres*, 3 December 1843, 2–3.

advertising leaflets included extracts from original letters from Halevy (11 August 1842 and 3 November 1844) in which he offered him his support and declared his devotion to him as the most skilled maker.[21] Paradoxically— or perhaps not so much—Halevy only used Sax's instruments on a single occasion during his lifetime (*Le Juif errant*, 1852).[22] This is very similar to the case of Berlioz, who, despite his press coverage of the Belgian inventor, did not produce an opera that featured his new and supposedly interesting brasswinds (nor the saxophone) in the orchestral pit. (*Les Troyens* of 1856/8 summoned several saxhorns, but at a specific moment and on stage.)

Once these technicians (*lumières de l'art*) had been presented, it can be anticipated that the report would be entirely favourable to Sax. Two of them had already pronounced in his favour in the competition of the Champ de Mars (1845) and, obviously, they did not retract in the second examination. The tribunal that chose them was aware of that first assessment, but now (1847) they were urged to deal specifically 'with the difficulties of which the present dispute was the subject', the only explanation the judges put forward for re-selecting these experts. It is difficult not to perceive a certain bias in that choice, which might otherwise have been (partially) resolved if other or more surveyors had been selected.[23] It was only logical to expect that these three experts would have reaffirmed themselves and that their decision would have further validated Sax. It is therefore not unreasonable to think that there was some interference between the executive and the judiciary, in addition to the pressure exerted by the Army, which was indirectly involved in the case, and by the press, which was also favourable to the Belgian inventor. Although we cannot prove this assumption at this point, we will soon see that the court's interpretation of the same matter under the same laws in the time of the Republic—only a few months later—could diverge considerably.

The technical dossier was divided into seven parts. The first five were devoted to saxhorns and saxotrombas on which no qualification were

---

[21] *Grande Diminution Provisoire de Prix. Manufacture d'instruments en cuivre et en bois fondée en 1843. Adolphe Sax et Cie, rue Neuve-Saint-Georges, no. 10* ([Paris: n. ed., n.d. [1848]), 2 and *Adolphe Sax & C*^{ie}*. Manufacture d'Instruments en cuivre et en bois. Fondée à Paris en 1843. Rue Saint-Georges no. 50* ([Paris: n. ed., n.d. [1850/51]), 2.

[22] Ignace De Keyser, 'Adolphe Sax and the Paris Opéra', *Brass Scholarship in Review: Proceedings of the Historic Brass Society Conference, Cité de la Musique, Paris, 1999* (Bucina: The Historic Brass Society series) 6 (2006), 144–6 and 165–6.
Fétis gave an extensive account of the performance (*RGMP*, 16 May 1852, 153–4). See also *Le Ménestrel*, 25 April 1852, 1–2.

[23] None of these three experts—four if we count Spontini—were among the 'experts usually [sic] called upon by the court' when advice was needed. *Almanach Royal et National pour 1847*, 914.

spared regarding their originality, proportions, and behaviour as a family of instruments.[24] The sixth defended the novelty of the saxophone and its independence from the *Batyphone* due to obvious structural differences (the latter was a kind of bass clarinet and therefore had cylindrical tube) and consequent sonorous responses. To embellish the truth (which completely dismantled one of the prosecution's attacks), the experts pointed out that the saxophone had a particular curvature (*courbure particulière*) which the author called 'parabolic cone'. The experts concluded (seventh part) that all these musical tools were new and the changes in shape provided possibilities that the old instruments did not have. Furthermore, they insisted that 'the conditions of the instruments described or represented were perfectly patentable' and that any person in the profession could, 'once the validity of the documents had expired', produce those instruments with the same guarantees as their original inventor.[25]

The *Rapport d'expertise* was deposited at the registry of the court on 2 November 1847,[26] so that Sax was unofficially—it was not a sentence—ahead of his competitors. In addition, another achievement he celebrated that same month was his appointment as head of the fanfare and external musicians of the Opera (*chef de fanfare responsable des musiciens externes à l'Opéra*).[27] In reality, this post was not very important from an economic point of view because it consisted of providing brasswinds on time when the works demanded them (the orchestral pit has space limitations and on stage they would be used accidentally), but it was undoubtedly very strategic for his interests.[28] However, one should not lose sight of the fact that the upheavals of 1848 were barely three months away. Social discontent and economic

---

[24] *Affaire Sax: rapport d'expertise par Messieurs F. Halévy, N. Savart et N. Boquillon, experts nommés par le tribunal civil de la Seine (4e chambre), par jugement en date du 6 avril 1847, dans le procès en déchéance intenté contre les brevets Sax, par MM. Raoux, Halary, Gautrot, Gambaro, Buffet, etc., délégués des facteurs français* (Paris: n. ed., [Imprimerie Edouard Proux et Cie,] 1848), 10–58.

[25] *Affaire Sax: rapport d'expertise par Messieurs F. Halévy, N. Savart et N. Boquillon*, 64–6.

[26] *Le Droit. Journal des Tribunaux*, 27 September 1854, 928.

[27] <https://www.nakala.fr/nakala/data/11280/01026c93> (accessed 4 August 2020).

[28] It is more than possible that Sax got that new job by currying favour (1842?) with the renowned François-Antoine Habeneck, violinist, composer, founder of the Société des Concerts du Conservatoire and, very importantly, orchestral director of the Opera (1821–46). (He was also a violinist in the Royal Chapel and was part of Louis-Philippe's Chamber Music.) Comettant, *Histoire d'un inventeur*, 13–14.

This source also points to a strategic connection with Édouard Monnais (1798–1868). Without drawing too much attention to himself, this civil servant, intellectual, and playwright had a tremendous influence on the administrative decisions that would favour (and in a very decisive way) Sax. Although trained as a lawyer, he was also an amateur musician (violin) and devoted his career to managing the most important French theatres. His professional rise began in 1836 when he got a post at the Ministry of the Interior, soon after which he became commissioner of the lyric theatres in Paris and, in 1839, he co-directed the Opera with Henri Duponchel until 1847. He was also one of the advisors to the teaching committee of the Conservatoire and a regular contributor and critic to the *RGMP*, writing under the pseudonym Paul Smith. See, among others, Edmond-Antoine Poinsot, *Dictionnaire des pseudonymes* (Genève: Slatkine Reprints, 1971), 408.

problems (pauperism and unemployment) had already taken hold in certain districts of Paris, provoking unrest among the working masses and reflections among a section of intellectuals. The political situation was extremely tense and François Guizot's prohibitions were a wedge that caused the Orleanist monarchy of Louis-Philippe to fracture definitively at the end of February 1848.

The 'Citizen King' was undoubtedly an indirect protector of Sax. The first time they came into contact was at the Exhibition of French National Industry of 1844, when Louis-Philippe—probably led by Rumigny—visited the instrumental section. According to the press, the sovereign was very pleased to learn of Sax's new instruments, which were 'destined to bring about a revolution in military bands and orchestras', and congratulated him personally. Incidentally, the same report mentioned a performance by the Distins, a British brass quintet (a father and his four sons), for the royal entourage, with whom the monarch conversed at length in English (*s'est long-temps* [sic] *entretenu, en anglais*).[29] The synergy between Sax and this famous group of musicians is very interesting because it encapsulates several characteristic components of modern ways of doing business. According to the chronicle of one of the Distin brothers, this family of artists was on tour in Paris, but they also made time to visit the city and attend other concerts as listeners. It was at one of these concerts that they met an accompanying performer playing a brasswind instrument made by Sax that caught their attention. 'The next morning' they went to meet this new manufacturer. From that moment on they adopted his instruments and achieved, according to Kastner, 'immense success'.[30] From then on they were also Sax's sole agents in London (1845) until the early 1850s.[31] However, that business partnership fractured when the Distins embarked on an entrepreneurial venture by manufacturing and distributing instruments on their own account.[32] (The British Isles also promised tremendous business in brass manufacturing, especially for them, who were already well-known as performers.) Of course, one

---

[29] *RGMP*, 2 June 1844, 195 and *La France musicale*, 2 June 1844, 173–4.
[30] *The New York Times*, 7 August 1881, 10 and Kastner, *Manuel de musique militaire*, 248–9.
[31] Trevor Herbert, *The British Brass Band: A Musical and Social History* (New York: Oxford University Press, 2000), 171.
[32] The Distins supplied the British Army between 1851 and 1862, and employed fifty workers. Later, after unsuccessful investments, they sold their factory (1868) to Boosey and moved to the USA where, with new partners, they tried to revive a business that did not succeed. William Waterhouse, *The New Langwill Index* (London: Tony Bingham, 1993), 90–1. See also Eugenia Mitroulia and Arnold Myers, 'The Distin Family as Instrument Makers and Dealers 1845–1874', *Scottish Music Review* 2: 1 (2011), 1–17 or Ray Farr, *The Distin Legacy: The Rise of the Brass Band in 19th-Century Britain* (Newcastle: Cambridge Scholars, 2013), 117–69.

of Sax's hagiographers (unrealistically) dismissed this practice as piracy—those patents were not yet protected in England—and even accused them of smuggling illicit material into the islands for resale there.[33] Be that as it may, the British quartet—one of the brothers died in 1848—and its individual members continued to appear from time to time in the French music press. A very explicit headline ('The Distin family and the saxhorns in Germany') reported that the group had performed in front of kings, aristocrats, chapel masters, and 'notables' of several important cities.[34] However, an interesting development came about in 1849, when the media reported that the Distins had given a successful concert—literally, 'made a splash'—in New York in front of 3000 people with the Sax's brass.[35] Another magazine picked up the story (including also explicit publicity for the instruments and their maker) and added that the tour would then continue to Canada.[36] The important thing about these tours was not the music or the praise, but the fact that this group of musicians spread the word *saxhorn* throughout the West,[37] which came to refer to many other brass instruments with little or no relation to the supposed original. For all practical purposes, this served to establish the name of the instrument and give celebrity to its maker.

Returning to Louis-Philippe, and to provide further evidence of his support for Sax, we can look at the run-up to the band competition at the Champ de Mars. The press implied the monarch's predisposition towards the musical duel, and even seemed to be campaigning in his favour. According to the *Revue et Gazette Musicale de Paris* (*RGMP*), the Belgian inventor must have met with the Minister of War beforehand and offered several samples of his instruments, and the latter expressed his satisfaction to the king. The sovereign wanted to know about them first hand and invited Sax to the palace where three pieces were performed in the presence of the entire royal family, who were delighted. Sax talked to the monarch about the manufacturing processes he used, and the king was very pleased. Louis-Philippe also congratulated Fessy (the band's conductor), and Arban and Kresser, the principal performers. Finally, and to embellish the story a little more, it was said that, 'as the King was leaving the hall, [he] re-entered and asked the Minister of

---

[33] Comettant, *Histoire d'un inventeur*, 53–5.
[34] *RGMP*, 19 April 1846, 125 and *Le Ménestrel*, 26 April 1846, 3.
[35] *Le Ménestrel*, 1 July 1849, 3.
[36] *La France musicale*, 29 July 1849, 236 and *Journal des Débats*, 21 August 1849, 2.
[37] The 'Maineville [Ohio] Sax Horn Band' (c.1860), as the side of the carriage on which it is mounted explicitly states (Cincinnati Historical Society's photograph), was one of the first brass ensembles to be formed in the USA under that special designation. Margaret-Hindle Hazen and Robert-M. Hazen, *The Music Men* (Washington/London: Smithsonian Institution Press, 1987), 87.

War that one of the previously performed fragments be played; a wish which was immediately granted [sic]'.[38]

After that battle, and with Sax's instruments now established in regulation, the king went on to praise the new palette brought to life in the formation of the 9th Dragoon Regiment.[39] The monarch also acknowledged the 'superiority' [sic] of the military musical ensemble of the 45th Line Regiment which had been designed by the Minister of War and which brightened up his dinner at Neuilly, on the outskirts of Paris. According to this chronicle, Louis-Philippe was struck by the charm (*charme*) 'of an instrument whose timbre was totally unknown to him' and which turned out to be the saxophone. It was undoubtedly important that this instrument began to receive its share of publicity, but it is even more significant that these statements were made in the midst of the proceedings we are recounting and when the experts' report was still being drafted.[40]

However, as we said, Louis-Philippe was forced to resign as head of France on 24 February 1848; with him disappeared a covert ally of Sax. The Republic had been reborn and with it a very ambitious political and social programme (universal male suffrage, abolition of slavery, freedom of the press, abolition of the death penalty, the right to work, freedom to strike, etc.) which, in practical terms, constituted an impasse in the judicial debates. Among the members of the provisional government who devised this project were such famous names as Lamartine, Arago, Louis Blanc, and Albert. But, in addition to them, there were also two lawyers, Ledru-Rollin (the famed democrat or radical republican) and *Maître* Marie, the lawyer who represented the interests of the rival makers.[41]

Alexandre-Pierre-Thomas-Amable Marie de Saint Georges (Yonne, Auxerre 1795–Paris 1870) became the first Minister of Public Works in the provisional government of the Republic.[42] The initial climate of enthusiasm after that tense February 1848 became very complex in the following three months. Marie's oppressive post of responsibility had to deal with the enormous problem of unemployment and the National Workshops, which

---

[38] *RGMP*, 2 March 1845, 70. The chronicle notes that Sax brought an ensemble of ten brass players, namely two trumpets and eight sax-horns [sic] (1 soprano, 2 tenor-contraltos, 2 tenors, 1 bass-tenor, 1 bass, and 1 contrabass).

[39] *RGMP*, 22 March 1846, 95.

[40] *Journal des Débats*, 12 October 1847, 2. This report signed by Berlioz also stated that Louis-Philippe was visiting Amiens and congratulated the conductor of the 9th Hussars Regiment for the good result of his ensemble 'with Sax's instruments'.

[41] See, among many others, *Actes officiels du Gouvernement provisoire dans leur ordre chronologique: arrêtes, décrets, proclamations, etc. Revue des faits les plus remarquables précédés du récit des événements qui se sont accomplis les 22, 23 et 24 février 1848* (Paris: Barba/Garnot, 1848), xi, xvi, and 2.

[42] Félix Bourquelot and Alfred Maury, *La littérature française contemporaine 1827–1849*, tome 5 (Paris: Delaroque, 1854), 279–80.

were proving unproductive and ruinous, as well as centres of even more revolutionary and subversive political propaganda. Not even the elections to the National Assembly (23 and 24 April 1848), in which the moderate republicans had won comfortably, succeeded in turning the tide, and a 'hidden' Louis-Napoléon Bonaparte was already a member of parliament (4 and 5 June) on the occasion of the by-election to the constituent National Assembly thanks to his results in four departments (Seine, Yonne, Charente-Maritime, and Corsica). Before that, however, Marie had left office on 11 May 1848, handing over the baton to Ulysse Trélat, who also failed to avoid the fierce clashes of the following June. Nevertheless, Marie remained at the head of the government after the latter date, as he was one of the five members (along with Arago, Garnier-Pagès, Lamartine, and Ledru-Rollin) of the Executive Commission (*Commission du Pouvoir exécutif*) set up by the National Constituent Assembly, which appointed ministers and exerted executive authority while a constitution was being drafted. However, General Louis-Eugène Cavaignac took in June of the same year full executive powers and was to preside over the Council of Ministers.[43] The former Minister of War and now de facto dictator returned to Marie to offer him a ministry more in line with his professional career, that of Justice.

---

[43] Jean-Chrétien-Ferdinand Hoefer, *Nouvelle biographie générale*, tome 33 (Paris: Firmin-Didot, 1860), 735–6.

3
Judicial Setback or 'Nothing Patentable'

Change of Regime and Procedural Course

Sax's trial, which had been frozen at the end of 1847, was resumed in July of the following year. This was in a totally different political context (the Second French Republic) and with a Minister of Justice who had previously been the lawyer for the plaintiff, i.e. the brasswinds manufacturers. His replacement was *Maître* Liouville, while Adolphe Sax continued to be defended by Chaix-d'Est-Ange. The type of court (a court of first instance) and the chamber (*4e Chambre*) were the same, although—as is to be expected—the *Chancellerie* changed the prosecutor (Berriat-Saint-Prix first and then Sallé).[1] In any case, it was now time to assess the technical report that the Chamber had commissioned from experts, and whose conclusions completely validated the patents in question, which foresaw the dismissal of the accusatory claims. However, the Court, on 19 August 1848,[2] partially annulled the first of these patents (saxhorns), a title that had in fact already fallen into the public domain. The evaluation recognized the originality of the spring slides (*coulisses à ressort*), but criticized the technical contribution that rounded off other tubes, arguing that the proposal 'rested on nothing more than a change of form' and therefore did not constitute a patentable invention. The Court was aware that this decision contradicted the experts' report, a dossier that it had interpreted as a testimony of professional encouragement (*médaille d'encouragement*) and in no way as 'legal support for a patent, nor as a right (*titre*) to exercise a monopoly'. The judges were even clearer and more categorical with regard to

---

[1] According to a *factum*, the president of the chamber was Hallé and the two judges accompanying him were Thomassy and Fagniez. *Dispositif du jugement rendu le 19 août 1848, par la 4e Chambre du Tribunal de première instance de la Seine, entre MM. Raoux, Halary, Gantrot* [sic], *Buffet et Gambaro, tous facteurs d'instruments de musique, agissant en leurs noms personnels, et encore comme délégués de tous les facteurs d'instruments de musique en cuivre de Paris et de la France, demandeurs, et M. Adolphe Sax, facteur d'instruments de musique en cuivre, défendeur* (Paris: n. ed., [Impr. Appert fils et Vavasseur,] n.d. [1850]), 8.

[2] *Extrait des jugements du Tribunal civil de 1re instance de la ville de Paris du 19 août 1848 et de la Cour d'appel du 16 février 1850* (Paris: n. ed., [Impr. Veuve Dondey-Dupré,] n.d. [1855]), 2 and *Almanach Royal et National pour 1847*, 910–16.

the saxotromba patent (1845), as they found it 'impossible to share the opinion of the experts'. Furthermore, they held that 'there was nothing patentable, [whether] in [the] means [of manufacture], in the [industrial] application, or in the results obtained'. And, finally, they concluded that 'this system of instruments and orchestration was devoid of any serious character of originality'.[3] Nevertheless, the judgement acquitted the saxophone completely. It may be that this gesture was intended to achieve an (impossible) technical tie between the parts, or that there was simply nothing to object to because the saxophone was something truly new and legitimate. Sax's claim for 50,000fr in damages was also dismissed, although the costs of the trial were to be shared equally.

Before the ruling was read out, the instrument makers had already moved ahead in another way. The Ministry of War of the (now) republican government repealed the instrumental reforms that Marshal Soult had previously (and with Louis-Philippe) authorized in 1845. A specific instruction dated 21 March 1848 banished the two saxophones, twelve saxhorns, two bass clarinets, and other 'système Sax' instruments (two trumpets and a trombone) from infantry bands (Table 3.1). Not even a month had passed since the proclamation of the Republic, which shows how keen some individuals were to change that instrumental palette and the effective contacts with the current executive.

The reconversion of the cavalry instruments on 18 May 1848 was even more substantial because, paradoxically, it did not put an end to Sax's instruments—or, at least, to his disposition—but rather changed their name and consequently their exclusive use of products that were supposedly not his (Table 3.2). In this sense, the regulations made it explicit that those artistic tools should return to the 'generic denomination they should never have lost' and that they would regain 'their true name'.[4] However, this haste, and above all, the apparently original and exemplary move may have been one of the biggest mistakes that those manufacturers made. Clearly, Sax was to suffer an immediate and severe financial punishment, but his ideas, or rather the board on which he laid them—an inevitable and vertiginous invasion of brass—remained latent. It is still too early to draw conclusions, but it is already possible to see how the executive branch took sides, pressured the judiciary (which should allegedly be independent), and determined public and private economic courses.

[3] *Annales de la propriété industrielle, artistique et littéraire. Année 1857*, tome 3 (Paris: Au Bureau des Annales, 1857), 212–13.
[4] *Le Moniteur de l'Armée*, 10 June 1848, 5 or *Journal militaire officiel*, [no exact date, first half of] 1848, 291.

Table 3.1 Comparison of the instrumental palette for infantry bands according to the 1845 (pro-Sax) and 1848 (republican) regulations, as well as their (theoretical) nominal correspondence arranged in parallel

1845 Provision	1848 Provision
1 piccolo in C	1 piccolo in C
	4 oboes
1 piccolo [or sopranino] clarinet in E♭	1 piccolo [or sopranino] clarinet in E♭
14 clarinets in B♭	14 clarinets in B♭
2 bass clarinets in B♭ (*système Sax*) [sic]	
	4 bassoons
2 saxophones	
2 cornets with two valves (*cylindres*)	2 cornets with piston valves (*à pistons*)
	2 regular trumpets (*ordinaires*)
2 trumpets with valves (*à cylindres*) (*système Sax*) [sic]	2 trumpets with valves (*à cylindres*)
	2 regular (*ordinaires*) French horns
4 French horns with three valves (*cylindres*)	2 French horns with piston valves (*à pistons*)
1 small (*petit*) saxhorn in E♭	
2 saxhorns in B♭	2 chromatic clarions [bugles] (*clairons*) in B♭
2 saxhorns in E♭ (alto) [sic]	
3 saxhorns with three or four valves (*cylindres*) in B♭	2 chromatic basses (*basses*) with four valves (*à 4 cylindres*) in B♭
4 contrabass saxhorns in E♭	2 chromatic contrabasses (*contrebasses*) with four valves (*à 4 cylindres*) in E♭
1 trombone with valves (*à cylindres*) (*système Sax*) [sic]	
2 trombones (*à coulisses*)	3 trombones (*à coulisses*)
2 ophicleides	2 ophicleides
5 percussionists (*instruments pour la batterie ou petite musique*)	5 percussionists (*batteries*)
[Total: 50 people]	[Total: 50 people]

Compiled from *Le Moniteur de l'Armée*, 10 September 1845, 2 and 20 April 1848, 4.

It was precisely at this time that Sax's third advertising leaflet (1848), entitled 'Large Temporary Price Reduction (*Grande Diminution Provisoire de Prix*)', was issued. In it, Sax commented that his business was enduring unjust attacks from a number of rival manufacturers who wanted to usurp and rename his instruments. Faced with such an offensive, he had to cut the prices of his merchandise by more than 40% of the initial valuation in order to be able to compete 'with piracy (*contrefaçon*) and shoddy (*pacotille*) instruments'. In addition, and in order to gain credibility in the eyes of public opinion, he enclosed excerpts from letters—some of which dated—that

Table 3.2 Comparison of the instrumental palette for cavalry bands according to the 1845 (pro-Sax) and 1848 (republican) regulations, as well as their (theoretical) nominal correspondence arranged in parallel

1845 Provision	1848 Provision
2 band trumpets (*d'harmonie*)	2 band trumpets (*d'harmonie*)
4 trumpets with valves (*système Sax*) [sic]	4 trumpets with valves
2 saxhorns in E♭	2 chromatic clarions [bugles] (*clairons*) in high E♭
7 saxhorns in B♭ (1 solo, 3 first, and 3 second)	7 chromatic clarions [bugles] (*clairons*) in B♭ (1 solo, 3 first, and 3 second)
2 saxhorns in A♭ to replace the French horns (*cors*)	2 chromatic clarions [bugles] (*clairons*) in A♭
2 saxhorns in E♭ to replace the French horns (*cors*)	2 chromatic clarions [bugles] (*clairons*) in E♭
	2 *clavicors* in E♭ (tenors)
2 saxotrombas	
2 cornets with piston valves	2 cornets with piston valves
1 trombone with three valves (*système Sax*) [sic]	1 trombone with three valves
3 trombones (*à coulisses*)	3 trombones (*à coulisses*)
3 saxhorns in B♭ (baritones) with three valves	3 chromatic basses (*basses*) in B♭ (baritones) with three valves
3 saxhorns in B♭ with four valves	3 chromatic basses (*basses*) in B♭ with four valves
3 contrabass saxhorns in E♭	3 chromatic contrabasses (*contre-basses*) in E♭
[Total: 36 people]	[Total: 36 people]

Compiled from *Le Moniteur de l'Armée*, 10 September 1845, 2 and 20 April 1848, 4.

several influential composers, conductors, musicians, and manufacturers (Berlioz, Carafa, Halevy, Kastner, Rossini, Liverani, Meyerbeer, Marschner, Niedermeyer, Ricci, Schollmieyer, Spontini, Ambroise Thomas, and Charles Fink) had sent him over the previous years in support of the originality of his proposals. Most of these testimonies lack substance, as they are more akin to opinions of encouragement and professional stimulation. However, some of them have several significant details that deserve our attention.

For example, Spontini (20 January 1844) acknowledged having visited the Sax's factory and attended a demonstration concert. The seasoned composer (he was sixty-nine years old at the time) highlighted among all the contributions the *bugles à cylind. (Saxhorns), les clarinettes basses et soprano, ainsi que le Saxophone*, which would produce 'excellent effects' in 'dramatic' music, namely opera; but especially (*et plus encore*), in military music. These words would confirm more or less innocently (since the legal battles had not yet begun) that Sax's principal brass instruments were improvements or progressions on the widely known bugles (we understand, aerophones with conically dominated tubing). Kastner, in another similar candid statement, said something similar when he spoke of 'refinements' made to the bass clarinet, 'as well as the bugle (*ainsi qu'au Bugle*)'. Similarly, and sharing the same perception, Ambroise Thomas pointed out that the 'Bugles and valved trumpets [of Sax] had an indisputable superiority for the homogeneity (*égalité*) and tuning (*justesse*) of their sounds'. On the other hand, Spontini's letter complained about the slow rate of progress in France in comparison with the German states. This statement could also reflect the French brasswinds industry, which was perhaps perceived as hindered and undermined by the interests of certain manufacturers who did not want to accept the change of scenery and the new productive and economic system.

Regarding the price reduction, Sax stressed that he had had to make 'such a financial sacrifice (*pareil sacrifice*)' out of the deeply held belief that any musician who tried his instruments would prefer to pay a little more for that quality and avoid a substandard instrument from a competitor. After this testimony, which revealed that his instruments were not affordable and that did not have a well-defined price range for each individual instrument, he went on to recall his increasingly out-of-date victory at the Champ de Mars, the medals at the Belgian and French Exhibitions of 1841 and 1844, and the successful complete instrumental regenerations in several foot and cavalry regiments. The advertising brochure also featured for the first time the silhouettes of its main instruments (Figure 3.1).

Significantly, this was a pivotal point in the development of events because the market was once again liberalized, which meant that any instrument could be manufactured and sold to army bands—or any other customer— without any problems. The government had neutralized Sax's patents and placed them in a kind of purgatory pending possible judicial developments. (Both sides intended to appeal.) However, even if Sax won in court, he could not count on a victory (or even on survival) in the business world. The instruments on which he claimed ownership were no longer used in the military, and/or would not be called what he wanted them to be. If we turn to iconography to verify the new economic practices—there are hardly any physical instruments from that period and they are difficult to date,[5] not so in advertising—we find specimens with certain morphological analogies with

---

[5] Eugenia Mitroulia, *Adolphe Sax's brasswind production with a focus on saxhorns and related instruments* (Thesis, Edinburgh, University of Edinburgh, 2011), 128.

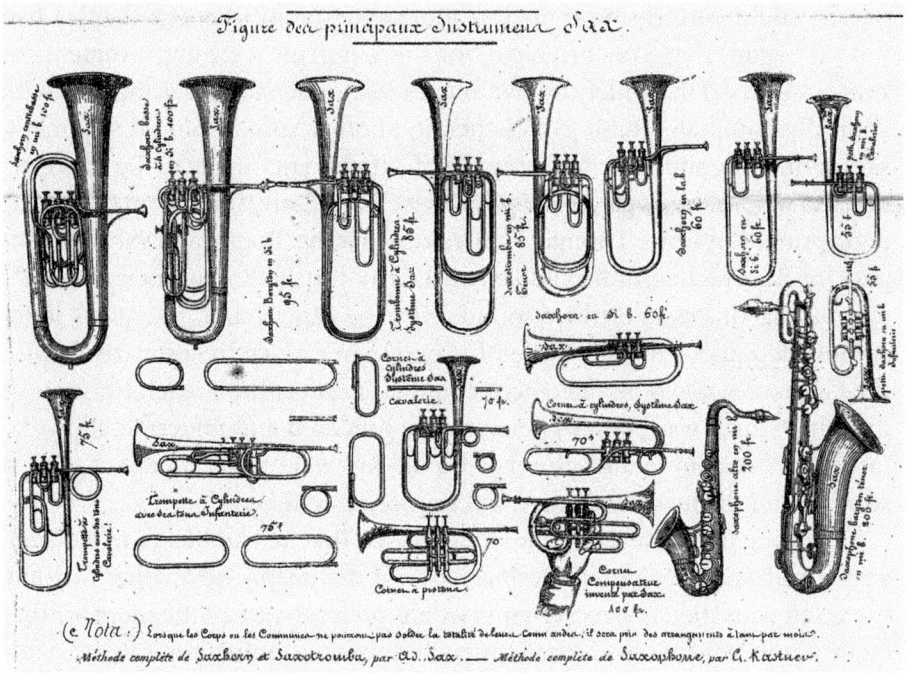

Figure 3.1 Earliest drawings of Sax's instruments for sale

Grande Diminution Provisoire de Prix. Manufacture d'instruments en cuivre et en bois fondée en 1843. Adolphe Sax et Cie, rue Neuve-Saint-Georges, no. 10 ([Paris: n. ed., n.d. [1848]), 4. With kind permission of Bruno Kampmann.

the designs of his patents. For example, the catalogue of Gautrot (a maker who will become very prominent in the second part of the book) showed chromatic clarions [bugles] (*clairons chromatiques*) in various forms, some of them with the valves parallel to the bell (Figure 3.2).[6] The Beauboeuf brothers (*c.*1850–3) also used generic words—*bugles, bugles chromatiques, altos, altos chromatiques, barytons, basses chromatiques*, etc.—to refer to such tools.

A comparison of the Sax and Gautrot catalogues also offers us an interesting price ratio (Table 3.3), as it was very difficult to compete with the latter's ophicleide, which could cost up to 55fr less. Sax sold trombones at 50fr, while his opponent sold them almost 60% cheaper. With valves, the difference increased even more, since if Sax's cornet costed 70fr, his competitor's could be obtained from 28fr. If we go into saxhorns or chromatic clarions [bugles], the difference was more than 50%, although it became smaller as

---

[6] *Manuf^{re} d'Instruments de Musique. Rue St Louis 64 au Marais. An^{ne} Maison Guichard. Gautrot aîné et Cie. Album & Catalogue 1850* (Paris: n. ed., [Impr. Plista,] 1850), 10 bis.

Table 3.3 Comparison of the prices of instruments made by Sax and Gautrot (c.1848–50)

Sax				Gautrot
Instrument or type of instrument	Price	Price		Instrument or type of instrument
Trumpet of orders (*d'ordonnance*)	18fr	9fr		Trumpet of orders (*d'ordonnance*) with slide (*à coulisse*)
Trumpet (*d'harmonie*)	50fr	25–50fr		Trumpet (*d'harmonie*) in A♭
Trumpet with valves	75fr	50fr		Trumpet with three valves
Cornet with valves (*à cylindres*) or piston valves (*à pistons*)	70fr	28–70fr		Cornet with three valves (*cylindres*), rotatory valves (*système rotation*), or piston valves (*à pistons*)
Trombone with valves	85fr	35–60fr		Trombone with three valves (*cylindres*) or piston valves (*à pistons*)
Trombone	50fr	20–22fr		Trombone
Ophicleide	100fr	45–60fr		Ophicleide
Small soprano saxhorn in E♭	55fr	25–35fr		Chromatic clarion [bugle] in F and E♭
Saxhorn in B♭ (or A♭)	60fr	30fr		Chromatic clarion [bugle] in C or B♭
		30–40fr		Chromatic tenor clarion [bugle] in C or B♭
Tenor saxotromba or saxhorn in E♭	85fr	40–50fr		Chromatic clarion [bugle] in F, E, E♭, or D
Baritone saxhorn	95fr	55–75fr		Baritone chromatic clarion [bugle] with three or four valves in C and B♭
Bass saxhorn in B♭ with four valves	100fr	70fr		Bass chromatic clarion [bugle] with four valves in E♭, D♭, and C
		75–90fr		Bass chromatic clarion [bugle] with four valves in C and B♭
		100–120fr		Bass chromatic clarion [bugle] with four valves in F and E♭
Contrabass saxhorn in E♭	100fr			
		100–120fr		Contrabass chromatic clarion [bugle] (*bombardon*) with four valves in C and B♭
Saxophone	200fr			

Compiled from *Grande Diminution Provisoire de Prix* [Sax, 1848], 1 and 4; and *Manuf^{re} d'Instruments de Musique* [Gautrot, 1850], 1–6 and 10–16.

the instruments became more deep. In any case, Gautrot's instruments were considerably cheaper, as 2fr was at the time a significant sum: one could sleep in guaranteed accommodation, rent a horse-drawn carriage for an hour, and even eat quite well in an average restaurant. For 8fr, one could get a seasonal subscription to one of the capital's newspapers and an extra 7fr would cover the costs of a funeral. Owning a saxophone was also a luxury, as 200fr could cover the annual maintenance of an elderly person at La Maison de Retraite or Hospice de la Rochefoucauld, or buy a couple of calves or eight sheep, or

Figure 3.2 Gautrot's 'chromatic clarions' from his 1850 sales catalogue

Note: Gautrot and Sax, like most other manufacturers, used different types of valves. However, at least in these early catalogues, they distinguished between *cylindres*, *pistons*, and *système rotation*. The first two types are what we would today call 'piston valves' and in which the valve loop is disengaged or engaged by the up-and-down movement of the piston within the casing that aligns the ports either with the main tubing or the valve loop. (In the third, evidently, the extra tubing is added by the turn of a rotor enclosed in an outer casing. We have not found examples of the latter in any of Sax's catalogues, but we have found examples in Gautrot's, for example, in this flyer, pages 2 and 2bis.) Nowadays, however, the two types of valves shown in these catalogues would be called 'Périnet valves' because the valve loops are arranged in such a way that the inlet tubing is positioned on a different level than the outlet tubing, or 'Berlin valves'—the inlet and outlet for the valve tubing are arranged on the same plane as the main tubing. The two instruments below in Figure 3.1 (*cornet à piston* and *cornet compensateur*) are examples of the former—because of an optical illusion it appears that the main tubing enters the piston from below, which would convert them into 'Stölzel [or Stoelzel] valves'—while the rest of the instruments (except obviously the saxophones) seem to wear the other type of valves. Many thanks to Géry Dumoulin for his advice.

Manuf^{re} d'Instruments de Musique. Rue St Louis 64 au Marais. An^{ne} Maison Guichard. Gautrot aîné et Cie. Album & Catalogue 1850 (Paris: n. ed., [Impr. Plista,] 1850), 10 bis. With kind permission of Bruno Kampmann.

pay a subscription to one of the exclusive circles, such as the Société des Amis des Arts for more than two years.[7]

Moreover, these commercial brochures also indirectly reveal something very important: both companies had the necessary technology to be able to manufacture this type of merchandise and applied appropriate procedures.

---

[7] *Galignani's* (1851), 5, 12, 14, 16, 49, 57, 121–2, and 129–30.

In fact, the press of the same year (1848) included two pictures of Sax's business. The first engraving (Figure 3.3) shows the workshop on the ground floor, a relatively large and well-lit working space with various machines and tools. The structure of the room is open-plan (except for the working equipment) and is supported by a framework of wooden pillars and beams, some of which were used to hang parts of unfinished instruments. In the middle of the picture, a flywheel press can be made out, which has a confined space between a framework of rods. This type of ramming device appears to be manipulated by the worker seated on a wooden stool with his back to us. The worker rotates the weights attached to the ends of the operating arms by

Figure 3.3 The most important tools, machines, and details of the workshop on the ground floor of Sax's factory (1848), consisting of a press (1), a screw clamp (2), mandrels (3), flywheel (4), strap (5), other wheels (6), guillotine (7), furnace (8), bellows (9), smoke expelling tube (10), ladders (11), and worker honing (12)

Compiled (numbers) from *L'Illustration*, 5 February 1848, 357.

means of a lever (which he is holding in his right hand) by which the plunger or multi-threaded bolt is lowered with sufficient force or pressure to cut or shape the metal at will.

Three interesting elements can be seen on the left of the picture. The first is the precision work of the two workers next to the window. The one practically facing the front is working on a bugle held by a screw clamp or fastening unit. The second significant object is the guillotine or metal shears behind the two workers. Evidently, this cutting device was used to cut the initial brass sheets from which the brasswind is made. (See its counterweight and outer handle, as well as some cuttings of unleaded brass sheets and small tools on the ground.) Finally, we call attention to the mandrels (solid metal cores) located on the three raised steps which were used as a mould so that the brass leaf could either be shaped according to specific measurements. (They are also used to eliminate imperfections or dents.) In the centre of the drawing and in the foreground, a worker seated in a circle is sanding, or more likely polishing the bell of an instrument with the liquids from the basins on his right. On the other side, a boy is also polishing one of the three piston valves cornets in front of him with his left hand. To the right there stands a brick wall, a bellows hanging from the ceiling, and a smoke exhaust pipe. Here there was probably a furnace or forge for heating the brass to make it more malleable, for soldering sheet metal parts, for joining also instrument parts—using other metals such as lead, silver, or tin as fasteners or splices—or for carefully bending the pipes and conduits of future brasswinds.[8]

But perhaps the most interesting element is at the back of the image, behind a prominent wooden pillar with four reinforcing branches. The eye can make out three wheels, one of which is quite large and probably required the power of a steam engine to operate. Although the huge pilaster hides the cistern or the air pump, the crankshaft from which the spokes (or arms) emerge is visible. The circumference of this enormous mechanism is accompanied by a strap which extends to the roller of the worktable on which a worker—located behind the mandrels—receives the energy necessary to operate his lathe, drill, or polisher.

However, the first brasswinds company in which the use of steam engines is explicitly mentioned was that of Gautrot in 1855,[9] an operation for which

---

[8] In order to bend a tube, the inside of the tube had to be coated with oil or some other non-stick material. The pipe was then filled with some solid form, i.e. sand, tar, resin, or liquid lead (which obviously had to harden before proceeding). By plugging the ends of the pipe and providing heat in the area of operation, the desired bend was achieved without deforming the section.

[9] *L'Illustration*, 21 July 1855, 43–5.

two other figures also exist. The article that introduced them spoke of an 'economy of labour which enabled products to be produced cheaply with an excellent finish, an important matter at a time when production [of brasswinds] was so advanced'. In the first of these (Figure 3.4) we see at the lower right those characteristic brass sheets referred to earlier. (It is obvious that these leaves—and some cylindrical tubes—were supplied by other external metallurgical factories that had the appropriate means to manufacture them.)[10] Next to them are some enormous scissors that would have been used for the guillotine we have seen in Sax's factory.[11] Moving to the left, we can see

Figure 3.4 View of a part of the workshops of the Gautrot *aîné* factory in the Marais district, Paris (1855) and its most significant elements, for example, brass sheets (1), scissors (2), hammers (3), drill or perforator (4), anvil (5), clamps (6), mandrel (7), bells (8), kettles or drumshells (9), furnaces (10), and tree stumps (11)
Compiled (numbers) from *L'Illustration*, 21 July 1855, 44.

---

[10] The Paris Chamber of Commerce survey of 1847/8 mentions several professions that would fit in with this type of supplier, namely *fondeurs* (foundry workers) or *lamineurs* (laminators) *et planeurs* (straighteners?) *de métaux*. *Statistique de l'industrie à Paris (1847–1848)*, 157–8. See also Cyrille Grenot, 'La facture instrumentale des cuivres dans la seconde moitié du XIXe siècle en France', in Daniel Allenbach, Adrian von Steiger, and Martin Skamletz, eds, *Romantic Brass. Französische Hornpraxis und historisch informierter Blechblasinstrumentenbau. Symposium 2* (Schliengen: Argus, 2016), 17–18.

[11] Taking Sax as a reference again, we can point out that other minor tools used by this type of makers: periwinkles (or winkles), a kind of hook twisted on itself (*bigorneaux*), blowtorches (*chalumeaux*), stretching bench (*banc à étirer*), anvils (*enclumes*), shears (*cisailles*), tongs (*tenailles*), elbows [?] (*tasseaux*), mandrels (*bouterolles*), lathes (*fraises*), bits (*forets*), hand drills (*vilebrequins*), tacks (*pointes*), burins

various tools, such as hammers, sharp objects, an anvil, and the usual screw clamps. In addition, we can make out at least two mandrels and several instrument bells piled up in the centre of the picture. To the right and also piled up, there are numerous cauldrons or shells that were probably intended to become the outlines of the bodies of percussion instruments, namely drums, bass drums, or snare drums. However, the most significant part of the image are the people in the background who are working in the small furnaces or forges, confirming that we are in the welding room.

With regard to the cauldrons or boilers identified in this drawing, it is worth recalling a very curious feature that we have already introduced: the metal cooking vessels, which some brasswinds manufacturers were still making in the mid-nineteenth century, for example Labbaye.[12] This family (Jacques-Charles, Jacques-Christophe, and Jacques-Michel) was one of the most important firms at the beginning and middle of that century, and supplied (at least from 1820) French horns, trombones, ophicleides, and many other aerophones to military regiments. Moreover, they were protégés of the King, as the epigraphs on their instruments state ('*Labbaye fils, brev.[eté] du Roi*'). Well-placed from the beginning and counting on the friendship of other weight manufacturers (Halary), they built-in collaboration with Meifred in 1827, as we have already noted, a French horn with pistons, probably one of the first uses of valves in France. However, after the explosive entry of Sax into the brass manufacturing scene, Labbaye was one of the makers who complained to the Minister (1845) and became involved in the dispute with Sax.

The other design from Gautrot's workshop (Figure 3.5) contains what is clearly a steam engine (right) enclosed by a gate and which would have driven numerous straps. Unfortunately, neither its composition nor its gears, which seem to be more forceful than those of Sax, can be seen. On this floor there are also at least two forges (one of them with a bellows on top) and even a coal storage area on the floor. Furthermore, from the work tables and the numerous screw clamps that can be seen, it can be inferred that we are in the area where the instruments were assembled, composed, or finished.

Focusing on Sax's workshop, the image of the first floor shows several interesting elements (Figure 3.6). The thirteen assembly lines or work tables are very significant because they confirm that division and specialization in the

(*poinçons*), pincers (*pinces*), etc., among many others. Archives de Paris, D11 U3, box year 1852, dossier 10,509: Faillite d'Adolphe Sax du 5 juillet 1852, *Inventaire. Matériel*, n.p.

[12] Pontécoulant, *Organographie*, vol. 2, 376.

Figure 3.5 The most important details of the ground floor of Gautrot's factory, namely steam engine and straps (1), forges (2), mandrels? bells? (3), bellows (4), coal storage area (5), assembly sections (6), clamps (7), and ladders (8)

Compiled (numbers) from *L'Illustration*, 21 July 1855, 44

production of instruments had been introduced to increase precision and speed. If we take a look at the foreground of the image and go from left to right, we can see workers who are working on the pavilions or bells, the workbench of those who work on the valves, those who splice or bore tubes, and a little higher up, another who seems to be polishing, who has a small lathe under the table.[13]

In the upper margin on the left-hand side, we can make out some wheels hanging from the ceiling, as well as some of the straps that would have powered polishing machines, sanding machines, lathes, etc. In the foreground,

---

[13] In any case, using the 1847/8 survey, we can confirm that the 499 metalworkers in Paris were distributed among 60 manufacturers (*facteurs*), 56 assemblers or fitters (*monteurs, ajusteurs et poseurs*), 32 polishers (*polisseurs*), 31 lathe operators (*tourneurs*), 30 cabinet makers (*menuisiers*), 27 bell makers (*pavillonniers*), 26 valve makers (*pistonniers*), 12 polishers (*ponceurs*), 11 key makers (*cleftiers*), 10 finishers (*finisseurs*), 9 workshop managers (*chefs d'atelier*), 7 people in charge of heavy duties (*hommes de peine*), 2 cooper workers (*cuivristes*), 2 painter-decorators (*peintres décorateurs*), and 129 without specific jobs (*sans dénomination spéciale*). *Statistique de l'industrie à Paris (1847–1848)*, 818. The rest (17) worked at home for an employer (*travaillant en chambre*), and there were 1 woman and 37 children between the ages of 12 and 16. (We will now go into this issue.)

Figure 3.6 The most significant details of the workshop on the first floor of Sax's factory (1848), namely a screw clamp (1), a hammer (2), a furnace (3), wheels (4), small tools (5), bells (6), and assembly lines (X)

Compiled (numbers) from *L'Illustration*, 5 February 1848, 357.

the clamps are clearly visible, and on the right-hand side there is another small furnace. Nearby, a hammer rests on a wooden base or log, indicating the existence of mandrels and more solid metal cores. On top of some of the work tables, and if we look more closely, we can see smaller tools such as tongs, awls, blades, brushes, etc. However, the most striking feature of the figure is the large number of workers, which is another indicator of the good health of this type of business. If we accept this drawing as reliable (it was customary to exaggerate the size of the spaces, machines, and the number of staff) and we add the numbers of staff from the other drawing (eleven), we count a total of eighty-six people. What seems clear is that he employed women[14] and, significantly, children (such as the two who are frightening a cat in the more open area of the room).[15] (In one of Gautrot's workshop drawings, four young boys are also clearly distinguishable on the left.) The

---

[14] Using a magnifying glass effect, we can make out three female silhouettes among the work tables, one at the second desk starting from the left, the next one under a larger wheel, and the last one behind the polisher (lathe) on the central table.

[15] See also *Sax Revolutions: Adolphe Sax's life* (Documentary in DVD). José-Modesto Diago (dir. and prod.) Exp. no. CA-217-14. Cádiz, 2014, 64 min: son. col., from 8:40 to 13:24.

point is that the brasswinds also reveal the existence of child labour in the factories and invite us to reflect on the conditions of the workers before labour regulations were enshrined and liberalism was forced to develop social legislation. (Moreover, as we shall see in Part 2 of the book, when competition between manufacturers intensifies, we shall see on whom the pressure to lower prices will fall.)

4
Appel-incident or Escalation to the Second Level of Jurisdiction
Challenge and Pressures on the Court of Appeal

Adolphe Sax and his lawyer (still Chaix-d'Est-Ange) decided to appeal the devastating judgement of 19 August 1848, which had damaged the saxhorns and annihilated the saxotromba, the latter being crucial to his commercial structure and the trial itself. It is not clear whether the manufacturers lodged their claim separately[1] or whether they joined the appeal of the party that had taken the initiative (*appel-incident*).[2] Nevertheless, there is no doubt that this was the way in which Raoux and his associates responded, making it known that they still had the advantage and they were not giving up either. Moreover, this adhesion could be used to develop new arguments that would definitively put an end to their enemy, who was obviously in a very delicate situation.

In any case, that move meant the escalation to the second level of jurisdiction, i.e. the Court of Appeal (*Cour d'appel*), which meant more seriousness, time, and financial drain. At that time (1848), France had twenty-seven such courts, and the one in Paris encompassed several departments. It was undoubtedly the most important and strategic in the State, the nucleus of the entire French judicial system, and the sounding board of classic French centralism (also) in this sense. Hence, when there was a change in the political system or a readjustment of the executive balances, the governmental leadership took it upon itself to nominate an Attorney General in line with its preferences.[3]

We do not know how many hearings took place in the higher tribunal, but we have located three *factums* which, although they do not provide substantial new information, confirm the positions of the disputants. In the first, Sax dissected his patents into five parts and complained that three points, 'the

---

[1] *Annales de la propriété industrielle*, tome 3, 1857, 213.
[2] *Le Droit. Journal des Tribunaux*, 27 September 1854, 927.
[3] *Almanach Royal et National pour 1847*, 386–7, *Almanach National de la République Française pour 1848–1849–1850*, 358–9, *Almanach National pour 1851*, 374–5, *Almanach National pour 1852* (Paris: Guyot et Scribe, 1852), 367–8, and *Almanach Impérial pour 1853*, 379–80.

most important ones' (the adaptation of the slides and the suppression of the angles of the saxhorns, and the whole saxotromba), had been annulled.[4] His rivals (second *factum*) basically claimed that the saxotromba 'was a three-valve brass instrument, conceived (*accordé*) in the key of E♭, [and] belonging to the *alto* family'. They also insisted that the word *bugle* was the generic name [sic] for this type of instruments and that they had been manufactured in Germany and France for many years with other designations (*alto-tromba* in E and *clavicor* in E♭).[5]

The third *factum* was a twenty-six page dossier in which Sax again explained his documents. As an encore, he synthesized the properties of saxhorns into three points. With regard to the saxotromba, he stressed the importance of the proportions (width of the tubing along its length) which he had adopted and its correlative affectation in providing a new timbre. (He also again exercised a marked opposition to the *clavicor.*) He further claimed that his new instrument had been created to replace the French horns in military music, fanfares, and above all, in dance music.[6] It is evident that an additional strategy of these pamphlets was to add new information to conform—often with dubious applicability and veracity—to theses which were already convoluted at best.

While this double appeal was being resolved and the necessary hearings were being held, the political landscape was about to change again. The (authoritarian) Constitution of December 1848 had given strong powers to the President of the Republic, and in the legislative elections of May the following year, the Party of Order triumphed. The trend was moving towards conservative positions as Louis-Napoléon was accumulating even more power. However, the key event for our story was to take place in the year that was about to begin. The National Exhibition of French Industry was held between June and July 1849 at the Grand Carré des jeux aux Champs Élysées where, out of a total of 4494 participants, 162 were related to music and fifteen of them were brass makers. Some of them (Raoux, Labbaye, Michaud, Gautrot, Halary, etc.) were involved in the judicial debates we are dealing with and would compete amicably among themselves, but also against Sax, who also took part. The 1849 Fair was therefore going to be less innocent than

---

[4] *Observation pour MM. Raoux, Halary et consorts, appelants incidemment, contre M. Sax, appelant principal* (Paris: n. ed., [Impr. Appert fils et Vavasseur,] n.d. [1850]), 1–2.

[5] *Note pour MM. Raoux, Halary et consorts contre M. Sax. Cour d'appel. 3me Chambre. Présidence de M. Poultier. Rôle du vendredi. M. Berville, Avocat Général* (Paris, n. ed., [Imp. de Schneider,] n.d. [1850]), 4.

[6] *Note pour messieurs les conseillers [de la troisième Chambre de la Cour d'Appel, 16 février 1850]* (Paris: n. ed., [Impr. Simon Dautreville & Cie,] 1850), 1 and 9–12.

might at first have been expected, as the winner would achieve an unofficial stroke of authority in this respect that could go beyond the judicial.

The judging panel in charge of music was composed of Armand Séguier, member of the Academy of Sciences and the Advisory Committee of Arts and Manufactures, who advised the Champ de Mars commission and was also on the jury of the previous fair in 1844; Pouillet, professor of physics at the Conservatoire National des Arts et Métiers; Mathieu, representative and member of the Académie des Sciences; Froment, maker of precision instruments; Peupin, 'representative of the people'; Pierre Érard, builder of harps and pianos; and Marloye, who made acoustic (*fabricant d'instruments d'acoustique*) and precision instruments.[7] The latter technician was rapporteur and responsible for all matters concerning the aerophones, since each examiner was in charge of a speciality (Séguier, for example, was in charge of the organs). Thus, in the 'General Considerations' of his report, Marloye began by noting that his section was advised by several professors of the Conservatoire and 'other distinguished artists' who had been kept anonymous so that there would be no leaks or preferential treatment.[8] Marloye also emphasized 'that, although the brass instrument manufacture had been at a standstill for a long time, it had taken an immense step forward in recent years. Mr Sax is the prime mover in updating (*en mettant au jour*) two families of instruments, saxophones and saxhorns (*clairons chromatiques*) [sic], as well as a large number of modifications made to already known instruments.'[9]

As we can guess from the fact that the reporter did not hesitate to use the word *saxhorns*, Sax was awarded the first and only prize (*Médaille d'or*) given to wind instrument makers (including woodwind makers), which certainly infuriated his opponents. The other participants who received a lesser reward were Raoux, Tulou, Labbaye, Michaud, Gautrot,[10] Halary, Buffet, Godfroy, Buffet-Crampon, Breton, Bartsch, Roth, Triébert, Adler, Courtois, Darche, Houze, Roehn, Thibouville, Gyssens, Coste, and Coeur.[11] The press picked

---

[7] *Rapport du Jury Central sur les produits de l'Agriculture et de l'Industrie exposés en 1849*, tome 1 (Paris: Imprimerie nationale, 1850), xiii -xv and xx; and *RGMP*, 1 April 1855, 103. Above them was the 'central jury' proper, chaired by Charles Dupin, a French mathematician, engineer, economist, and conservative politician who will also have space soon.
[8] Séguier noted in his dossier that not only teachers from the Conservatoire were involved as consultants, but also from the *Gymnase Musical Militaire* and other prominent musicians, such as 'Marmontel, Massart, Ney, Valin, Desmarest, Guffé, Dorus, Triébert, Gallais, Banneux, Dubois, Dantonnel, Grepo, etc'. *Rapport du Jury Central sur les produits de l'Agriculture et de l'Industrie exposés en 1849*, tome 2, 567–8.
[9] *Rapport du Jury Central sur les produits de l'Agriculture et de l'Industrie exposés en 1849*, tome 2, 593.
[10] The jury, however, congratulated Gautrot for the progress of his products, for withstanding foreign competition, and especially for 'the sacrifices he had had to make to continue to employ 150 or 200 workers since the revolution of the previous year'. *Rapport du Jury Central sur les produits de l'Agriculture et de l'Industrie exposés en 1849*, tome 2, 602.
[11] Pontécoulant, *Organographie*, vol. 2, 465–6.

up the news and was also full of praise for Sax, hailing him as France's foremost manufacturer. In addition, the editor stressed that, 'in the eyes of any impartial spirit', the Belgian entrepreneur had crowned his success with the saxhorn and saxophone families as major examples, and that, when his judicial worries were over, 'he could continue his work more calmly'.[12] However, Sax's joy did not end there, and that gold medal also brought him the Cross of Knight (*Chevalier*) of the Legion of Honour, the highest French honorary award.[13] In fact, fifty-one other people connected with the fair received the same distinction, two of them instrument builders, namely Cavaillé-Coll (organs) and, curiously, Raoux, who was awarded in this way for having come first at the 1844 Exhibition.[14] It is possible that, on the face of such peculiar recognitions,[15] the jury wanted to appear equidistant and neutral.

The medal award ceremony (coinciding with that of the Legion of Honour's accolade) took place on 11 November 1849 at the Palais de Justice, and, significantly, the organizers had Sax on hand to lend solemnity to the event with his brasswinds.[16] This last revealing detail suggests that the Administration and other political and cultural powers were firmly on Sax's side. In addition, in the last days of December of that year, a party was organized at the Théâtre-Italien to celebrate the prize-winners once again. In the presence of the President of the Republic (Louis-Napoléon), 'several works composed expressly for Sax's new instruments which had won first prize honours were played, including Fessy's fantasies on the *Huguenots* [by Meyerbeer] and *La Favorite* [by Donizetti]. The applause was unanimous and all the excerpts were greeted with warmth by the audience; Sax's success could not have been more complete (*le succès de M. Sax a été aussi complet que possible*)'.[17]

---

[12] *Le Ménestrel*, 26 August 1849, 1–2.

[13] *Rapport du Jury Central sur les produits de l'Agriculture et de l'Industrie exposés en 1849*, tome 1, xxxiv–xxxv and Theodore Zeldin, *Histoire des passions françaises (1848–1945)*, tome 3 *(Goût et corruption)* (Paris: Seuil, 1981), 301.

[14] *Le Moniteur Universel, Journal officiel de la République française*, 12 November 1849, 3630 and *Rapport du Jury Central sur les produits de l'Agriculture et de l'Industrie exposés en 1849*, tome 1, xxxiv–xxxv.

[15] Regarding the manners, but above all, the quantity and ease with which the French bestowed distinctions on each other, the revered pianist Felix Mendelssohn ironically recounted an event of his own. During a stay in Paris (1831) he visited several keyboard shops to sample their wares, starting with Herz's, where he discovered that his pianos were stamped 'Médaille d'or, Exposition de 1827', which impressed him (*cela m'imposa*). Subsequently, he visited Érard's shop, whose pianos bore the same inscription and, consequently, sapped his enthusiasm a little (*Cela diminua déjà mon respect*). And when he returned home, he realized that his own (a Pleyel) also bore the same mark, so he concluded that all male Frenchmen had, from birth, the right to wear the order of the Legion of Honour, and could only be deprived of it when they performed certain meritorious services. *Felix Mendelssohn. Voyage de jeunesse, Lettres européennes (1830–1832)* [compiled by Paul Mendelssohn Bartholdy, Karl Mendelssohn Bartholdy, and Rémi Jacobs] (Paris: Stock, 1980), 326.

[16] *Le Ménestrel*, 18 November 1849, 2 and *Rapport du Jury Central sur les produits de l'Agriculture et de l'Industrie exposés en 1849*, tome 1, xl.

[17] *RGMP*, 30 December 1849, 416.

Also, to round off the 1849 event, the October press printed a telling article entitled 'New challenge and new success (*Nouvelle épreuve et nouveau succès*)' signed by a certain Hohlweg. Of course, the article was dedicated to Sax of whom, 'everyone agreed, he had achieved an immense step forward in instrumental and especially brass manufacture'. The journalist praised saxophones and denounced pirates who tried to copy these products; but, more importantly, he noted that the businessman had invited numerous acousticians (*savants en acoustique*) led by Marloye, juror and editor of the report of the 1849 Exhibition, to a concert at his house. Also invited were distinguished composers, including 'Meyerbeer, Berlioz, Limnander, etc.'; other music teachers, virtuosos, and numerous amateurs 'to appreciate the new instruments of the indefatigable inventor'. Although the original source only specifies these three personalities,[18] a further source confirms that he received and would receive visits from more composers and musicians such as Halévy, Onslow, Adolphe Adam, Berlioz, Auber, Castil-Blaze, Ambroise Thomas, Kastner, Clapisson, Rossini, Vivier, Félicien David, Spontini, Fétis, Donizetti, Verdi, Georges Bousquet, Héquet, Léon Kreutzer, Niedermeyer, Ricci, Maurice Bourges, Henri Blanchard, Vieuxtemps, Sivori, Elwart, Messemacsckers, Massart, Chavée, the Batta brothers, Dorus, etc. Among the writers, essayists, or intellectuals (*écrivants*) mentioned were Théophile Gautier, Hippolyte Lucas, Prévost, Jouvin, Édouard Monnais, Azevedo, Henri Berthoud, Escudier, Roqueplan, Arago, Noël Parfait, Alphonse Royer, Brandus, E. Viel, Dardonville, Albert Cler, Altaroche, Heugel, Taxile Delord, Pommereu, Lovy, Louis Huart, Alphonse Karr, Pontécoulant, Jobard, Fiorentino, Achille Denis, Louis Desnoyers, Boquillon, Alphonse de Calonne, de Lavalette, Auguste Morel, Albéric Second, Duponchel, etc. On the political side, De Kisseleff (Russian Ambassador to France), General Fagel (Netherlands), Réchild Pacha (Turkey), Count Apponi (Austria), De Païva (Portugal), Baron de Guérick, General-Count Rumigny, General Moline de Saint-Yon, Marshal Soult, Admiral Mackau, Marshal Sébastiani, General Augareff (aide-de-camp to the Emperor Nicholas), Colonel du Génie Savart, Marquis Rumigny (French Ambassador to Belgium), Count Pillet-Will, Veli-Pacha, Baron Séguier, General-Baron Gazan, Viscount Kerckhore, De Varant (Turkish Minister), the Duke of Montpensier, the Crown Prince of Saxe-Weimar, the Prince Regent of Saxe-Coburg, Prince Gallitzin, the Prince of Ligne, the Prince of Montléar, the Prince of Chimay, the Prince of Württemberg, etc.[19]

---

[18] *La France musicale*, 14 October 1849, 322.
[19] Comettant, *Histoire d'un inventeur*, 79–80.

Appel-incident or Escalation to the Second Level of Jurisdiction 81

The list of all these important people and those who would still visit after 1860—Comettant's volume came to an end that year—shows that Sax's concert hall was not only used to organizing music-listening soirées, but above all, and very singularly, to articulate a whole social, political, and intellectual network that could help him to prosper in his business. One of these last visits was that of Emir Abd el-Kader (a Sufis who initially fought against the French in the occupation of Algeria and later became an ally of Napoleon III),[20] which was portrayed in the press (Figure 4.1). We cannot say too much about the appearance of that hall, but, to borrow again from Berlioz,[21] the space (newly inaugurated in 1847) would have seated 400 people, offered good visibility and sound, and was well decorated to boot. It was not suitable for a large symphony orchestra, but rather for a chamber ensemble. Finally, Berlioz mentioned that the hall could be rented for a moderate price (*prix de location fort modique*), which suggest that he was also advertising for the Belgian entrepreneur. In any case, and taking more reliable references from

Figure 4.1 Instrumental demonstration by Sax in the concert hall of his house
Le Monde Illustré, 2 September 1865, 160.

---

[20] See, among others, Claude Vigoureux, 'Napoléon III et Abd-el-Kader', *Napoleonica* 4: 1 (2009), 111–43.
[21] *Journal des Débats*, 14 February 1847, 1–2.

a little later,[22] it is more than possible that Berlioz exaggerated the size of the seating capacity, which, in reality, could be close to 150 (possibly less) people.

It is clear that Sax was committed to surrounding himself with influential individuals from all sectors of society to defend and sponsor these products and projects in various ways. Although we will gradually develop this idea (we are only just leaving 1849), we already have several examples in the political-military spectrum, such as the Rumigny brothers. In addition, and coinciding with the same dates, the elite of the now almost forgotten July Monarchy also made time in their diaries to visit this room and workshops. We are referring to two former wartime ministers, namely Jean-de-Dieu Soult and Alexandre-Pierre Moline de Saint-Yon. Of course, on the musical side, his greatest supporters at the time included heavyweights in the world of composition, such as Halévy, Berlioz, Meyerbeer, Donizetti, and even (occasionally, at least) Verdi, who had already cooperated with Sax to provide the brasswinds for his *Jérusalem* (1847). And finally, covering the propaganda flank, we find the managers of the three most influential music magazines in the country among the guests at his house, such as Louis Brandus (*Revue et Gazette Musicale de Paris*), Jacques-Léopold Heugel (*Le Ménestrel*), and Léon Escudier (*La France musicale*).

Undoubtedly, all these attachments of composers, positive reviews, contacts, and prizes made Sax the envy of an important and prominent group of people related to the music business. Also in connection with the 1849 Exhibition, the press (Pontécoulant) denounced that 'no sooner had Mr Ad. Sax set foot on French soil, he suffered numerous torments from the apathy towards his new ideas [on the part] of lethargic competitors'.[23] Henry Blanchard, another of the most influential chroniclers of French musical journals, went further, denouncing that saxhorns and saxophones 'had provoked the jealousy (*éveillé la jalousie*) of other manufacturers who have found no better means of curbing this artistic personality than by questioning (*contester*) his inventions and even tempting the loyalty of his workmanship (*et jusqu'à la perfection et la solidité même de sa main-d'œuvre*)'.[24] Of course, a dirty fight also took place between the makers and traders of musical instruments. Pontécoulant openly expressed in the press that the laurels and tokens of

---

[22] The inventory caused by the second bankruptcy of Sax (1873) noted that his concert hall was on the first floor of the building and contained ninety chairs, fifteen stools, and an organ case. There were also five bedrooms, a dining room, an office, a living room, another room, and a kitchen. Archives de Paris, D11 U3, box year 1873, dossier 17,524: Faillite d'Adolphe Sax du 6 août 1873, *Inventaire*, n.p.

[23] *La France musicale*, 5 August 1849, 240.

[24] *RGMP*, 12 August 1849, 253–5. The reporter added a metaphor denoting resistance (*bon cheval de trompette*) to 'obscure slanderers', and finally confirmed that the Belgian entrepreneur 'continued his upward march as a patient creator, inventor and perfector'.

support garnered by Sax had brought out of their daze a crowd (*foule*) of antagonists who did not enter into the dispute honestly (*qui n'entrent pas franchement dans la lutte*). Taking advantage of the rhetoric, he compared them to a boa that releases its saliva on what it wants to gobble up (*comme le boa jette sa bave sur ce qu'il veut engloutir*); likewise, his adversaries spread slander and incited his workers to boycott him (*on mutina ses ouvriers*) by destroying the items that were about to be finished, hiding (*enlevèrent*) the plans of the projects, or stealing the tools.[25]

Returning to the course of judicial events, we must bear in mind that the distinctions that Sax had obtained in 1849 could be understood as a kind of challenge or defiance to the judgement that had knocked out those instruments, as he had obtained prizes for something that, according to the magistracy, was not real and/or legitimate. However, on 16 February 1850, the Paris Court of Appeal (third chamber), under the presidency of Poultier, revalidated the ruling of the Civil Court of 19 August 1848, which had struck down the saxhorns and completely annulled the saxtromba.[26] Previously, the judges had received a letter from Baron Charles Dupin (president of the central jury of the 1849 National Exhibition)[27] dated 2 February 1850 in which he expressed his agreement with the opinion of that jury which had bestowed on Sax all its preferences and honours (*toutes les faveurs, tous les honneurs*) for his brilliant contribution to the field of musical instrument manufacturing.[28]

It is worthwhile to dwell on this last point and to look more closely at the use of political honours in mercantile activities or by acting as a prop in court cases. Evidently, Dupin's initiative was intended not only to add another statement to the case file, but also to put pressure on the Court of Appeal with the opinion of a powerful aristocrat and intellectual.[29] However, these interferences and reciprocal supports between the ruling elite and the artistic and economic initiatives are best noticed with the composers. Our first

---

[25] *La France musicale*, 5 August 1849, 240–1.

[26] *Annales de la propriété industrielle*, tome 3, 1857, 213.

[27] Pierre-Charles-François Dupin (1784–1873), baron from 1824, enjoyed a long career as a military officer (he studied at the École Polytechnique), politician (deputy and peer), state councillor under Louis-Philippe, and senator (1852–70). (He was also Minister of the Navy for three days in 1834). With increasingly conservative tendencies (he supported Louis-Napoléon during the coup d'état), he also gained respect as a naval engineer, mathematician, and economist; and belonged to learned bodies such as the Institut and the Conservatoire des Arts et Métiers. In 1840 he was already Grand Officer of the Legion of Honour. Adolphe Robert and Gaston Cougny, dirs, *Dictionnaire des parlementaires français depuis le 1er mai 1789 jusqu'au 1er mai 1889*, tome 2 (Paris: Bourloton, 1890), 493–4.

[28] Antoine Elwart, *Histoire des concerts populaires de musique classique contenant les programmes annotés de tous les concerts donnés au cirque Napoléon depuis leur fondation jusqu'à ce jour* (Paris: Castel, 1864), XXXII–XXXIII.

[29] An excerpt from that letter also appeared on the front page of the next commercial advertisements printed by the Belgian manufacturer. *Adolphe Sax & Cie. Manufacture d'Instruments en cuivre et en bois* [1850/51], 1.

example is Daniel-François-Esprit Auber, who shared a good rapport with the Emperor. Auber had been director of the Paris Conservatoire since 1842, the year he succeeded Cherubini, who had previously been his mentor and protector. The new head of the world's most influential official music education centre would occupy that office for the rest of the July Monarchy, the Republic, and significantly throughout the Second Empire. Louis-Napoléon and his advisors, aware of the power of such a position, quickly attracted him to their cause (perhaps Auber was also amenable) and as early as 1853 he was Director of Music of the Emperor's Chapel and Chamber.[30] We do not know what the specific duties or commitments of this post were, but the composer certainly endeavoured to maintain a friendly correspondence with their majesties, for example by creating music for intimate events such as the christening of the imperial prince.[31] A few months later, Napoleon III returned the gesture by inviting him, Meyerbeer, and Verdi to his lavish chateau at Compiègne,[32] just eighty-five kilometres from the centre of Paris.

At the same time, Auber was undoubtedly an ally of Sax and his circle of influence who, to a certain extent—he was another of those composers who never write a single note for saxophone—helped him. One quite obvious example was that at his suggestion, and with the approval of the Minister of State, he introduced Kastner, one of Sax's strongest supporters, as a 'member of the committee for musical studies at the Imperial Conservatoire of Music and Declamation.'[33] It was probably Kastner, a few months later and with the explicit approval of Auber himself, encouraged the introduction of a saxophone class and a saxhorn class for military students at the Conservatoire, which would also have Sax teaching in the former speciality.[34] The quid pro quo—to put it mildly—for these and other concessions was that the

---

[30] *Almanach Impérial pour 1853*, 47.
[31] *RGMP*, 22 June 1856, 202.
[32] *RGMP*, 26 October 1856, 346.
[33] *Le Ménestrel*, 1 February 1857, 3.
[34] *Le Ménestrel*, 14 June 1857, 3.

As a curiosity and reference, the annual salary of Sax as a teacher was between 1000fr (1863) and 1500fr (1864), out of a total budget of 20,000fr granted by the Ministry of War for these peculiar studies. The highest paid teacher for military students was Bazin (harmony) who was paid 2000fr, while Arban (saxhorn) and Dieppo (trombone) got the same as Sax. On the other hand, Alkan and Durand who taught solfège were paid between 600fr and 800fr. '[Archives of] S.H.A.T. [Service Historique de l'Armée de Terre à Paris-Vincennes or Service Historique de la Défense (SHD)], 1 M, 2016, pièce 245/293', cited in Jean-Pierre Rorive, *Adolphe Sax (1814–1894) Inventeur de génie* (Paris: Racine, 2004), 209. The salaries of the civil cloister (1860) were a little higher, namely, Auber, director, 8000fr; Berlioz, librarian, 1500fr; those of composition (Halévy, Carafa, Leborne, and Ambroise Thomas) 2500fr; the wind players: Dorus (flute) 1200fr, Verroust (oboe) 1200fr, Klosé (clarinet) 1500fr, Cokken (bassoon) 1300fr, Gallay (natural horn) 1600fr, Meifred (French horn) 1600fr, Dauverné (trumpet) 1600fr, and Dieppo (trombone) 1600fr. Constant Pierre, *Le Conservatoire national de musique et de déclamation. Documents historiques et administratifs* (Paris: Imprimerie nationale, 1900), 426.

Emperor's acolytes and people of great weight would preside over and tutor the Conservatoire at its most solemn events. At that time, for example, we find Count Walewsky,[35] Minister of State, presiding over the distribution of the prizes. In his speech to the learning community, he announced with great pomp that Napoleon III was going to raise Auber to the rank of Grand Officer of the Legion of Honour—the fourth in importance of the five that existed— which the public received 'with loud acclamations and numerous salutes and applause'.[36]

As the years went by and in such singular circumstances, the presence of high-ranking officials and military personnel became even more frequent and copious. Specifically, in 1864, the solemn distribution of the Conservatoire's prizes took place on Tuesday, 2 August under the presidency of His Excellency Marshal Vaillant,[37] Minister of Fine Arts and the Emperor's Household.[38] The high official and Louis-Napoléon's strong man was accompanied by a whole host of personalities, including Count Baciocchi, the Emperor's first chamberlain, deputy general superintendent of the theatres; Alphonse Gautier, state councillor, secretary general of the Ministry; Camile Doucet, director of the Administration of the Theatres; Lieutenant-Colonel Monrival, aide-de-camp to the Marshal; Delacharme, head of His Excellency's cabinet; General Mellinet, commander of the Seine National Guard; Ambroise Thomas and Louis Clapisson, members of the Institut; Édouard Monnais, imperial commissioner; Lassabathie, administrator of the Conservatoire; Émile Perrin, Édouard Thierry, De Leuven, and La Rounat, directors of the imperial theatres. It is clear that the Conservatoire—and its director—were permeable to interference from other professional and political quarters, and especially to the supervision and tutelage of Napoleon III himself. Vaillant's speech, 'interrupted by numerous and frequent bravos'

---

[35] Alexandre-Florian-Joseph Colonna Walewski, Count Colonna Walewski (1810–68) as he was known, was a son of Napoleon I and Countess Marie Walewska. He rose through the military, political, and diplomatic ranks, and managed to consolidate his questionable aristocratic status. Not without some friction, his cousin Louis-Napoléon included him in his government structure, first as a representative abroad and then in more important posts such as senator (1855), Minister of Foreign Affairs (1855–60), President of the Congress (1856), member of the Emperor's Privy Council (1860), Minister of State (1860–3), and President of the Assembly (1865).

[36] *RGMP*, 11 August 1861, 249–50.

[37] Jean-Baptiste-Philbert Vaillant (1790–1872) was one of Napoleon III's most trusted men who had previously fought with his uncle. His long-suffering but successful climb through the military ranks included such important political titles and posts as senator and Minister of various portfolios (War, the Emperor's Household, and Fine Arts), and the title of Count of Rome with hereditary effect, which Pope Pius IX conferred on him in recognition of the help he had given him in 1849. See, among others, Joseph Valynseele, *Les maréchaux de Napoléon III: leur famille et leur descendance* (Paris: chez l'auteur, 1980), 179 and Catherine Granger, *L'empereur et les arts: la liste civile de Napoléon III* (Paris: École des Chartes, 2005), 54–7.

[38] *Le Ménestrel*, 24 July 1864, 272.

acknowledged that 'a great and important reform, due to the liberal will and generous initiative of the Emperor', who was not in Paris at the time, but 'whose paternal attention (*sollicitude*) was never absent', was being carried out.[39]

Another quite obvious example of such perfectly calculated friendships was the case involving Gioachino Rossini. Although the composer of *Il Barbiere di Siviglia* or *Guillaume Tell* was practically retired, he still enjoyed huge media influence that was worth taking advantage of. Napoleon III sent the band of the Guides—we will talk about them soon—to entertain the composer at his villa in Passy, a gesture that the maestro fervently appreciated.[40] A few years later, the press reported that the Emperor's Household, through his minister Marshal Vaillant,[41] was going to elevate the composer to the rank of Grand Officer of the Legion of Honour.[42] The same source also reported that Berlioz was promoted to Officer (the second rank in the order) and that it was in fact another approach to this eccentric, if magnetic, composer. No doubt Berlioz's relationship with the royal couple was excellent and even quite profitable. The composer wrote a *Te Deum* in which he summoned 900 musicians in three choirs, orchestra, and organ to the church of Saint-Eustache to solemnize the festivities of the opening of the 1855 French Universelle Exposition.[43] The commercial viability of this score was undoubtedly complicated, so the Ministry of State bought ten copies of its edition. As if that were not enough, their Majesties the King and Queen of Prussia, the Queen of England, the King of Saxony, the Dowager Empress of Russia, the King of Hanover, and other members of European royalty and aristocracy also bought a few more.[44] In addition to this event, Berlioz was also engaged for the closing ceremony at the Palais de l'Industrie.[45] The programme was to include works by Handel, Beethoven, Mozart, and Gluck, among others, and one work—which was to be played last—by Berlioz himself. Specifically, this piece was *L'Impériale* for double choir and orchestra, whose libretto and music were nothing more than the counterpart of those contracts and other economic revenues that the composer was accumulating. In return, the international audience, with

---

[39] *Le Ménestrel*, 7 August 1864, 285–6.
[40] *Le Ménestrel*, 23 September 1860, 343.
[41] As a curiosity, this high-ranking official had rented box number 12 at the Opera for the whole week (Monday, Wednesday, and Friday). Louis Palianti, *Petites Archives des théâtres de Paris. Souvenirs de dix ans, du 1er janvier 1855 au 31 décembre 1864, et des six premiers mois de 1865* (Paris: Gosselin, 1865), 10.
[42] *Le Ménestrel*, 21 August 1864, 303.
[43] *La France musicale*, 15 April 1855, 119, 22 April 1855, 123, 6 May 1855, 140, and *RGMP*, 22 June 1856, 200. Berlioz used a sopranino saxhorn in the final *Marche* of this work.
[44] *Le Ménestrel*, 15 February 1857, 3 and *RGMP*, 3 May 1857, 150.
[45] *RGMP*, 28 October 1855, 339.

Napoleon III presiding, heard explicit (and repetitive) verses such as 'Dieu, qui protège la France, Veille sur son Empereur! [God, who protects France, watch over her Emperor!]' or, directly, 'Grand Dieu, veille sur l'Empereur! Vive l'Empereur! Vive l'Empereur! [Great God, watch over the Emperor! Long live the Emperor! Long live the Emperor!]'.[46]

---

[46] *RGMP*, 11 November 1855, 355. In addition to all the money invested in the composer, the Emperor (through the Minister of State) continued to reward him the following year for that cantata with 'a gold medal bearing the inscription *Awarded by the Emperor Napoleon to M. Hector Berlioz*'. *RGMP*, 14 September 1856, 298.

5
Persistance and Jump to *Cassation*
The Paradox of Winning an International Prize and Going Bankrupt

The judgement of the *Cour d'appel* of 16 February 1850 was another severe legal setback for Adolphe Sax, compounded by the fact that, as the months went by, the validity of the patents in dispute was slowly running out, and it was not frozen in the event of a legal action. Furthermore, it also prolonged the supposed impunity of his opponents to continue to manufacture and sell brasswinds freely. But the Belgian inventor did not give up and appealed to the Court of Cassation, the highest court in the French legal system. As has already been mentioned, this court had and still has the task of ensuring that the interpretation of the rule of law in a given matter is the same throughout the territory, i.e. to unify jurisprudence. This court was and still is unique, although at the time it was made up of three specialized chambers (civil, penal or criminal—*criminal*—and petitions—*Chambre des requêtes*).[1] The Court of Cassation of the Second French Republic was composed of a first president, three presidents, and forty-five other judges (*conseillers*) who were equally divided between the three chambers, although the first could rule any one of them. The resources of the public prosecutor's office were also significant, as the Attorney General was assisted by six deputy attorneys general advocates and other officials (chief clerk—*greffier en chef*—under-secretaries—*commis-greffiers*—etc., and no less than sixty other lawyers-consultants).[2]

Sax first escalated the case to this court and drafted his protest on two main points. The first pointed out the violation and false interpretation of articles 2 (what was considered an invention or discovery) and 30, point 3 (industrial applicability of a product) of the 1844 law with regard to the court ruling that had considered the smoothing of the angles in the saxhorns' slides to

---

[1] Today (2023), the French Court of Cassation consists of a social chamber, a commercial chamber, three civil chambers, and a criminal (*penal*) chamber.

[2] Adolphe-Pierre Tarbé, *Cour de Cassation. Lois et réglements* [sic] *à l'usage de la Cour de Cassation* (Paris: Roret, 1840), 349–51.

be insubstantial. The second (concerning saxotrombas) highlighted a similar tort based on articles 2 and 18 (the author's right to be the first to include improvements in the root patent) because the court had not recognized as patentable a change of shape illustrated in the designs and which produced new sounds. However, since the proceedings were civil—criminal proceedings were not necessary—the protest had to pass through the filter of one of the aforementioned chambers, the Petitions' one. After all, this chamber—which no longer exists as such today (2023)[3]—had the power to admit for processing those cases that were well formulated and in law, or at least had legal substance that was open to opinion, so that the civil chamber could then rule and ultimately decide.

While all this was going on and being processed, Louis-Napoléon continued to rise in power, while he suppressed universal suffrage and restricted the freedom of the press (May and July 1850). Despite this, the prince-president was popular with a large mass of the population including peasants, bourgeoisie, military, and even among workers. For his part, Sax and his allies (former sympathizers—some of them fervent—of the July Monarchy) were adapting to the new republican regime. His friends in the press such as the *Revue et Gazette Musicale de Paris*, took a back seat, and its director Deschamps d'Hanneucourt praised the benefits of (now) uncrowned government for artists.[4] Other characters directly changed their stance, as in the case of Halévy, either out of fear or, rather, in order not to lose their status and privileges. This composer who had been paid and enjoyed the benefits of being since 1841 director of the Chamber and Court Music of HRH the Duchess of Orléans, Princess Royal,[5] suddenly declared himself a staunch republican in a speech to the General Assembly of Artist-Musicians (an association of composers and people connected with music).[6]

Sax also had reason to be fearful and, to avoid trouble, he donated to the provisional government a complete set of instruments (*une musique complète*) for the first legion of the Mobile Guard (*Garde nationale mobile*). Even his workers offered their wages to the victims on the first day of work

---

[3] The law of 22 July 1947 abolished this screening procedure and it was taken over by the civil chambers themselves.

[4] 'The new Republic will also see in the musical art one of its greatest glories, one of its most powerful means of action. It will call upon and encourage artists; it will open up as wide a career as possible for them, and in this way it will accomplish, we firmly believe, one of the highest and most important missions of a government founded *by the people and for the people* [sic]'. *RGMP*, 27 February 1848, 65. A little further on, the same newspaper noted that the new Executive had organized a competition of military music. The chronicle underlined 'the incontestable progress' that this genre was achieving and, curiously, this time Sax was not mentioned. *RGMP*, 22 October 1848, 327–8.

[5] *Almanach Royal et National pour 1841* (Paris: Guyot et Scribe, 1841), 46–7.

[6] 'I was not a republican on 22 February. But what citizen today is not a loyal, sincere republican? Is not the Republic the last word in society?'. *RGMP*, 23 April 1848, 126.

on 28 February 1848 after the most serious riots.[7] Incidentally, as might be expected, the brass industry contracted during those months (102 of the 499 metal workers were laid off),[8] although Sax is supposed to have weathered the situation well, thanks to a loan from one of his investors.[9] Due to this dire situation, Fétis came to his aid from Belgium. According to a letter he sent to the French press, the theoretician and journalist was happy because the Belgian government had appointed him president of a commission to establish the new instrumental disposition of military bands, which would presumably adopt Sax's ideas, whom he praised for his courage and resistance. However, despite the fact that Sax had already advanced them a pilot ensemble (*en a envoyé une cargaison*), Fétis lamented the slowness and bureaucracy involved in such a matter.[10] (Evidently, Belgium's makers were also putting pressure on their government so that they could benefit from their country's money.)

In any case, although he won the gold medal at the French National Exhibition of 1849, it must have been a fateful time for Sax's business. The legal blow of 16 February 1850 also prolonged the competition in a completely liberalized market and without the arbitrariness of his patents. Consequently, he had to continue to contain the selling price of his products—in 1848 he said it was going to be a temporary decrease—as attested by the advertising leaflet he printed in 1850 or early 1851. That prospectus (the fifth of those that have survived) is stern in tone, and the reader can sense the effects of the economic and summary strangulation that was still looming over his company. The manufacturer tried to take refuge in his earlier achievements and recalled his crushing victory on the Champ de Mars five years earlier, but also charged against the shoddy instruments and piracy. He denounced that his patents were being assaulted (*atteinte à sa propriété*) and his enemies were pouring rivers of slander on him. To combat these attacks, he again aired those letters and testimonies of competent personalities who vouched for his work and products, including that of Charles Dupin. However, the most characteristic feature of that publicity is the invitation to 'amateurs and artists' to entrust him with orders; and he even appealed to 'men of the Church' to try the accompaniment of liturgical chant with his new baritone or bass saxhorns (also with the saxophone of those pitches) and to put aside the serpents and ophicleides.[11] The point is that Sax was timidly opening up the

---

[7] *La France musicale*, 12 March 1848, 79 and *Le Ménestrel*, 12 March 1848, 3.
[8] *Statistique de l'industrie à Paris (1847–1848)*, 181–2 and 817.
[9] Comettant, *Histoire d'un inventeur*, 388–403.
[10] *RGMP*, 29 October 1848, 334.
[11] The Christian faith was institutionally and economically strong in the middle of the nineteenth century. The French catholic clergy numbered 42,000 individuals, including 15 archbishops, 65 bishops, 176 vicars general, 661 canons, 3301 curates, 28,801 priests of branch churches, and 8500 seminarians. With

use of his products to amateurs, a clientele very difficult to reach with such high prices and without there being any real enthusiasm yet. At the other extreme—professional musicians—the situation was also very complicated, as his main instruments (the saxophone and the other brasswinds) lacked background, qualitatively valuable repertoire, and institutional support (they were not taught at the Conservatoire).

A further key date arrived on 28 April 1851, that is, barely seventy-two hours before the first Great Exhibition of the Works of Industry of All Nations of London opened. On that day, the Chamber of Petitions of the Court of Cassation (under the presidency of Mesnard) allowed the appeal that Sax had filed fourteen months earlier.[12] In practical terms, this sort of safe-conduct allowed him to compete with peace of mind in England; otherwise, it would have been untenable to present to the whole world instruments considered false and illegitimate by the highest French legal authority. However, from an economic point of view, his situation was very serious, as these instruments were not officially accepted in the French regimental formations—the republican regulations were still in force. A further problem was Sax's lack of liquidity which, above all, should not be revealed to public opinion.

But now it was time for Sax to visit Joseph Paxton and Charles Fox's Crystal Palace, an international meeting place to give shape and meaning to human progress through the twinning of commerce, industry, technology, science, and art. With all this supposedly fraternal and giving philosophy, national rivalries—which, in reality, took on more subtle overtones—were set aside for a moment, and an idealized image of triumphant capitalism was projected. On the other hand, the credit for these grand performances and showcases went to the prosperous middle classes, who were at all times aware of the publicity impact of such events.

Sax needed a clear triumph to shore up a possible procedural comeback—the opinion of the Chamber of Petitions invited optimism—and brought back from France an impressive display case with nearly eighty instruments,[13] the vast majority of them made of brass (Figure 5.1). A chronicler (Marie Escudier, co-owner with his brother of *La France musicale* at the time) highlighted this glass and oak container and played with rhetoric: 'a veritable little palace in the great palace of the Universe'.[14] Fétis later wrote for the *RGMP* and complacently expatiated on his compatriot's musical tools. We

---

an annual budget of 36 million francs, the salaries of the archbishops (15,000fr, although the archbishop of Paris was entitled to 40,000fr) and bishops (10,000fr), among others, were paid. *Galignani's* (1851), 127.
[12] *Annales de la propriété industrielle*, tome 3, 1857, 214.
[13] *Le Ménestrel*, 15 June 1851, 1–2.
[14] *La France musicale*, 18 May 1851, 156.

92 The Battle for Control of the Brass and Instruments Business

Figure 5.1 Photograph of Sax's stand at the 1851 London International Exhibition

Exhibition of the Works of Industry of All Nations 1851: Reports by the Juries on the Subjects in the Thirty Classes into which the Exhibition was Divided, vol. 2 (London: Spicer Brothers, 1851), 724 [RP-F-F25213-AL] [Photograph by Claude-Marie Ferrier?]. Rijksmuseum, Amsterdam.

are not interested in those compliments, but rather in the rather bold references to the ongoing process, with which there were indeed connections. Fétis took the Belgian inventor's side, denouncing 'those who longed for his ruin', and exposing rival manufacturers for making poisonous accusations, such as treating the invention of the saxophone as a chimera [sic] on the basis of inconsistent assumptions and criticizing something they had neither seen nor heard of. Subsequently, Fétis pointed to an earlier attempt to unseat it (being something 'impossible, impracticable, and fabulous') on the basis of analogies with Wieprecht's *Batyphone*, which he countered with a play on words (*batifolante plaisanterie* [Batifolante nonsense]). Further on, the influential columnist lamented that 'these things were said with impunity in a world of ignoramuses, who do not know what they are talking about; but in front of experts and competent judges, the illusion would soon be dispelled'.[15]

In fact, the international jury in charge of evaluating musical production[16] awarded Sax the Council Medal or first prize, ex aequo with three other French firms (Ducroquet, organs; Vuillaume, luthier; and Érard, pianos). On 10 August 1851 the news reached the French press, noting that 'our celebrated manufacturer' had recently been awarded 'unanimously' the highest prize.[17] Another French newspaper not only congratulated him, but also added that 'this brilliant success served to respond to the attacks and redress the injustices' he was enduring.[18] But, in reality, the English also won three first medals (Gray & Davidson, Hill & Son, and Willis, the three organ builders); four if we include Érard who competed for both countries because he had operations on both sides of the English Channel. In total, eight Council Medals were awarded in the music section, three each to France and England—an intentional tie?—Érard's, and one to Boehm (Germany).[19]

The official 1851 catalogue also contains other important details, such as the fact that some British and German manufacturers, such as James Gisborne of Birmingham, J-P. Oates of Lichfield, and Gottlieb Glier of Saxony, had already adopted the term *saxhorn* and that the word had therefore

---

[15] *RGMP*, 30 November 1851, 385–8.
[16] The evaluation committee consisted of then members: Sir H.R. Bishop, President and music professor at Oxford; Sigismund Thalberg, Vice President and pianist; W. Sterndale Bennett, professor at the Royal Academy of Music in London; Hector Berlioz from France; J. Robert Black, physicist from the USA; Chevalier Neukomm, organist, composer, and theorist from the Zollverein; Cipriani Potter, director of the Royal Academy of Music; Dr Schafhautl, professor of geology, mining, and metallurgy from the Zollverein; Sir George Smart, organist and composer of the Royal Chapel; and Henry Wylde, Doctor of Music and professor at the Royal Academy of Music. In addition, there were associated members: Rev. W. Cazalet, superintendent of the Royal Academy of Music; James Steward, piano builder; and William Telford, organ builder from Dublin. Peter Mactaggart and Ann Mactaggart, *Musical instruments in the 1851 exhibition* (Welwyn: Mac & Me, 1986), 79, 91, and 99–100.
[17] *Le Ménestrel*, 10 August 1851, 4.
[18] *RGMP*, 10 August 1851, 263.
[19] See, among others, *The great London Exhibition 1851: awards* (Paris: Brière, n.d. [1851]), 12.

entered the jargon of brass manufacture.[20] Nor should it escape our notice that the making and distribution of the saxophone was completely free in the British Isles, i.e. any company could manufacture (and even patent) it there without legal hindrance or replication of its author. We understand that, if this did not take place—there would be no problem to do the same in any of the German states or Austria—it was because there was no interest (demand) in the instrument. Sax did protect his threatened brass for the future in the United Kingdom (1859, 1862, and 1863).[21]

These last reflections lead us to focus briefly on the issue of industrial property in France and on the other side of the Dover Strait, especially to confront the number of documents protecting the creation of aerophones made of brass (Figure 5.2). Curiously, the French far outnumbered their northern neighbours in practically every decade, and it is also striking that no entries were produced there during the ten years preceding the 1851 Exhibition. However, after this international event, there was an explosion of applications in both countries, the largest in the whole of the nineteenth century. In any case, we must take into account other determining aspects, namely that the English preferred to import and that the regulation to protect an invention was more costly and cumbersome in the islands. The direct copying of continental and especially French models also played a role. Moreover, the number of patents does not correlate with the number of companies or the volume of production. In other words, anyone could make a trumpet or any other brasswind if he did not violate any special protected process or form; the issue was to be able to physically build it (i.e. technology and investors) and to have a clientele.[22]

There are only two points left before we close the first international exhibition in history. The first is that Sax did not avoid controversy either, since the

---

[20] *Great Exhibition of the Works of industry of all nations, 1851. Official descriptive and illustrated catalogue. In three volumes. Vol. I. Index and Introductory* (London: Spicer Brothers, 1851), 468 and *Vol. III. Foreign states*, 1105.

[21] *Patents for Inventions. Abridgments of Specifications Relating to Music and Musical Instruments. A.D. 1694–1866* (London: Tony Bingham, 1984), 300, 377–8, and 395.

[22] Roughly speaking, British inventors or entrepreneurs who wanted to obtain a patent had to follow the procedures dictated by the 'old' Statute of Monopolies of 1623, which had been updated and extended. Such protection could cost a prohibitively high £400, depending on whether the interested party wanted to cover the territories of the kingdoms of England—the most common, which would cost between £100 and £120—Scotland, and Northern Ireland. After the London International Exhibition, the British brought forward the Patent Law Amendment Act of 1852, which simplified the process somewhat and reduced the costs, which, in theory, would not exceed £180, payable in three instalments. Harold-Irvin Dutton, *The Patent System and Inventive Activity during the Industrial Revolution, 1750–1852*. (Manchester: Manchester University Press, 1984), 1–10, 34–5, and 62–3.

An invention patent in France cost 1500fr (fifteen years), considerably cheaper than on the other side of the English Channel, where £1 equalled 25fr. Even though the cost of living was lower in France—although Paris was a very expensive city—the economic difference and bureaucratic procedures still greatly favoured the French.

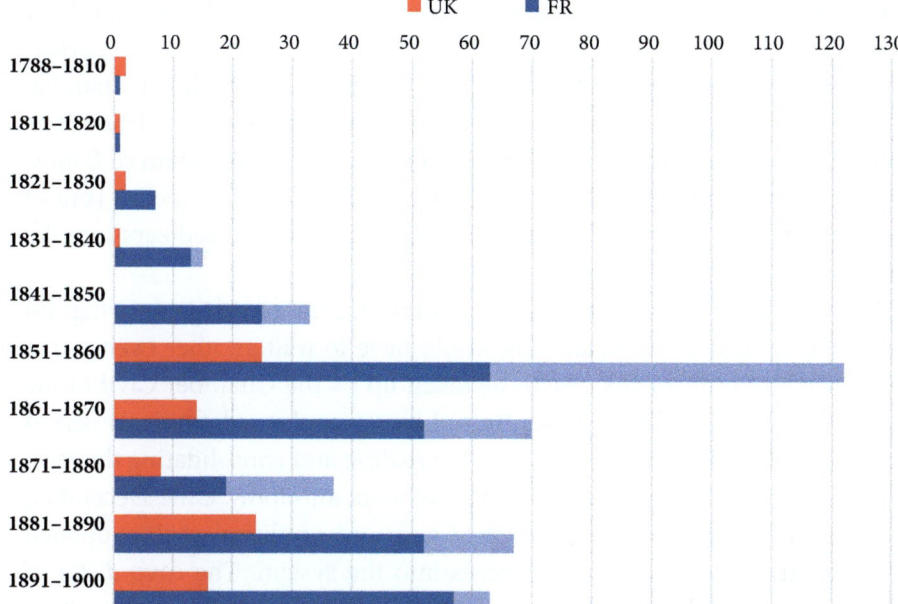

Figure 5.2 Comparison of the number of British and French patents relating to brasswind instruments registered during the nineteenth century

Note: British patents include those with provisional protection, that is, which did not give permanent protection, foreign patents—which we would call imported patents—and those filed by a British agent in association with a foreign inventor. In the French patents, we have added to the dark blue bar that represents the patents an extension of the same colour, but lighter, with the certificates of addition or complementary documents that complete the main one.

Compiled from Jack-L. Scott, *The Evolution of the Brass Band and its Repertoire in Northern England* (Thesis, Sheffield, University of Sheffield, 1970), 424–31 and Haine, *Les facteurs d'instruments de musique*, 396.

famous English maker Cornelius Ward (*c*.1796–1872)[23] lodged a complaint against him on the grounds that the metal bassoon that Sax had exhibited was in fact a duplicate of the patent that Ward had obtained in France. We will not delve into the similarities of those documents, but we would like to insist on the strength and thrust of the technical mastery of an artistic metallurgy that would also attempt to assault the woodwind classics, sometimes successfully (flute) and sometimes unsuccessfully (clarinet, oboe, or bassoon).

The second contribution comes from the report written by the jury, in which Sax's brass aerophones were highly praised. We are sure that Hector Berlioz had a great deal to do with it, for in the paragraph where the

---

[23] Ward set up on his own in 1836 after working with Monzani and Drouet. After making a name for himself among important clients, he copied the Boehm flute and registered his first patent for this instrument in 1842. Subsequently, his production was extended to bassoons. Waterhouse, *The New Langwill*, 421.

saxophone was expressly mentioned, it was literally cited in French (and not in English) that these new instruments had reached a high degree of perfection.[24] Nor did Berlioz forget to praise Sax in another (chauvinistic) parallel dossier commissioned by the French Ministry of Agriculture and Trade. The composer showered the saxhorns with compliments, spoke again of family, and recommended their use in military bands, still full of 'shapeless [brass] instruments with keys (*instruments à clefs*)' that hurt 'civilized ears (*oreilles civilisées*)'.[25]

That was an extraordinary publicity stunt, but the next legal hearing did not come as soon as expected. Sax would have to wait another twenty-two (painful)[26] months for his case to be taken up by the Chamber Civil of the Court of Cassation. During this time, Louis-Napoléon definitively seized power and devoted almost all of 1852 to creating and consolidating the legal levers that would allow him to manoeuvre with autonomy. On 2 December, the Empire was officially re-established and a new political context opened up, with the Empire infiltrating agents into the system. The *coup d'état* of the previous year had taken place without hostility, and the once exciting Republic was now perceived as an unstable regime, especially by a large part of the rural population. Moreover, the Army, mostly traditionalist and loyal in principle to whoever held executive power, had remained quiet and docile.

Sax's company could no longer stand the business pressure and declared bankruptcy (5 July 1852). The Commercial Court of Paris which arbitrated the debacle assessed his debt (*passif*) at 82,397fr,[27] which, while not an exorbitant amount, was quite considerable. This amount was more than double what the Belgian maker had invested at the start of the company in 1842; in other words, not only had he lost the initial money (40,000fr), but he had doubled it in losses. Those 80,000fr would have been enough to rent a small flat in Paris for more than forty-four years (at an average rent of 150fr per month), or to rent one of the coveted and busy little shops in the Galerie d'Orléans in the Palais Royal for twenty years. In the same place and seated in one of the *buvettes* (canteens or bars), we could drink 200,000 cups of coffee (at 0.40fr each) or go to the Opera 8000 times and get the best seat in

---

[24] Mactaggart and Mactaggart, *Musical instruments*, 102.

[25] Hector Berlioz, *Rapport sur les instruments de musique fait à la commission française du jury international de l'exposition universelle de Londres* (Paris: Imprimerie Impériale, 1854), 5.

[26] Sax was shocked by the news of the death of three of his brothers and the collapse (also professionally) of his father in Brussels, a manufacturer who was once considered (by the press in his country) the best in Europe. Natalis Briavoinne, *De l'industrie en Belgique: causes de décadence et de prospérité. Sa situation actuelle*, vol. 1 (Brussels: Dubois, 1839) 424–5.

[27] Archives de Paris, D11 U3, box year 1852, dossier 10,509: Faillite d'Adolphe Sax du 5 juillet 1852, *Bilan*, n.p. [1 and 3].

the hall (10fr per person). One could also pay eighty annual tuition fees at the prestigious École Polytechnique or buy space for 160 people at a rate of two square metres and in perpetuity in the Parisian cemeteries.[28] The official receiver (*syndic de faillite*) was surprised by the volume of business and losses that such an establishment could generate, but was in favour of reviving it ('an industry that is still capable of offering guarantees for the future') and seeking a solution through negotiation. Finally, a majority agreement (*concordat*) was reached on 17 September 1852 whereby Sax undertook to repay in full the capital owed to seventeen of his twenty-three creditors over the next eight years.

Herein lies one of the most interesting paradoxes of this type of bourgeoisie: Sax had won the only gold medal at the French Industrial Exhibition of 1849 and two years later was decorated—already at world level—also with the first prize in London; but, at the same time, he concealed a massive financial hole. The outward image did not match the real situation of a business that was in a state of disarray on all sides. It was a complex world of appearances and delicate balancing acts that would continue to grow and become even more complicated in the years to come.

The bankruptcy file provides us with other significant information. For example, on the side of the investors, there were several manufacturers, some of whom we already know (Labbaye) and others who will play a leading role in the second part of the book (Sébastien Drouelle, Darche, Belorgey, Thibouville Roussel, Massabo, etc.). Interestingly, the companies collaborated and supplied each other—a sign that the production system was mature—as we know that Drouelle was a valve specialist and Massabo only made reeds. Another interesting fact is that Boquillon (the expert who, together with Savart and Halevy, drew up the court report in 1847 validating Sax's patents) was also on the list of guarantors (500fr), which would confirm that he was not impartial.[29] The financing received from Edmon Viel (a librettist and critic-journalist who frequented the newspapers of the time) was considerably higher (9,371.89fr), but we have not highlight him for this reason, but because of an article of his from 1844. In addition to publicizing his depositary's instruments, this article questioned the 'old' players who were engaged in training and recruiting future performers, to whom they recommended

---

[28] Francis Coghlan, *The miniature guide to Paris and its environs* (London: Onwhyn, 1853), 53, 83–4, 86, 102, 129, and 157.

[29] Another sign of that continued support would come a little later, as Jean-Baptiste Singelée, one of the Belgian composers who would work for Sax's publishing house, dedicated (c.1861) his *Adagio et rondo, op. 63* for tenor saxophone and piano 'to Monsieur Boquillon'.

their own instruments. These behaviours were related to the instrument factories, which, as he pointed out, also had an interest in it; that is, they bought or financially compensated these teachers. Then came a sentence dedicated to these professors and industries: 'The fear of losing an acquired position, the awareness of their inferiority, and the certainty of not being able to sustain a struggle against a serious, enlightening (*éclairée*), and progressive rivalry.' Viel ended with another inflammatory statement: 'Innovation, liberty, progress; such is the motto that the new generation [referring to the young, vigorous, and promising Sax] has inscribed on its banner.'[30] It can therefore be confirmed that, as soon as he settled in Paris, Sax was perceived as a hostile and unbalancing agent for manufacturers who seemed to have the sector under control. In any case, it is perhaps no longer surprising to find Brandus (*Revue et Gazette Musicale de Paris*) also among the investors (1088.30fr), but Madame the *princesse* de Beaufremont not only because of the amount owed to her—the largest of all (30,013.17fr)—but also because she was the wife of Prince Théodore de Beaufremont Courtenay, lieutenant colonel of the cavalry.[31] This could be another indication that not all high military commanders were unmoved by the possibility of making money, even if it was, as in this case, by putting his wife in the title.

The inventory of Sax's estate from his bankruptcy file also reveals some curious details, for example, that the vast majority of the instruments specified were brass (cornets, clarions [bugles], saxhorns, etc.) and not woodwinds, which again demonstrates where the business lay. Furthermore, the trustee noted that he had machinery to be collected to the value of 3000fr in the prison of Melun, a town located sixty kilometres south-east of Paris. The point was that the Belgian businessman signed a contract on 10 January 1846 with the prison director by which the parties undertook to engage at least twenty-five prisoners in instrument-making work. The renting of the premises would be free, although Sax would have to supply it with the machinery, raw materials, and the rest of the tools needed. Evidently, the motive for this striking (and complex) decision was that labour was cheap, as the prisoners would work twelve hours for a wage of between 15 and 35 centimes franc, although after the first six months it could be as much as 50 centimes franc.[32] It certainly seemed like a good deal, as the average wage

---

[30] *L'indépendant*, 21 January 1844, 1–2.
[31] *Almanach de Gotha* (Gotha: Perthes, 1846), 159 and Nicolas-Viton De Saint-Allais, *Annuaire Historique, généalogique et héraldique de l'ancienne noblesse de France* (Paris: chez l'auteur, 1836), 198.
[32] Archives Départementales de Seine-et-Marne, [1] Y 178 [Maison Centrale de Force et de Correction de Melun. Travaux industriels des Condamnés. Instruments de musique. Documents concernant M. Sax], n.d. [10 January 1846], *Cahier des charges pour l'exploitation du travail des détenus dans la Maison Centrale de Force et de Correction de Melun*, n.p. [4].

for a worker in Paris was 3.80fr, and 4.36fr for a brass worker.[33] However, behavioural problems and theft surfaced,[34] which made the continuation of the prison operation unfeasible. Sax rescinded the contract, so he had to face disruption charges. This matter became protracted, and as on 29 October 1847 he owed 6633.31fr.[35] The penitentiary received half of this amount in January 1848 and the businessman managed to postpone the rest by leaving his machinery as a guarantee. On 10 October 1849 he was again asked for this money[36] which, if his implements were still there in 1852, he probably never paid.[37]

Nevertheless, before the end of that fateful year, Sax had time to weave a publicity machine that would enable him to revive his business and better position himself for the key trial that was soon to take place at the Court of Cassation's Civil Chamber. In this regard, the press reported that on Thursday, 30 December 1852, the band of the *Société de la Grande Harmonie* performed in the concert hall of the Belgian inventor's factory on rue Saint-Georges.[38] The event gathered 'an elite audience', including 'renowned composers (Meyerbeer, Berlioz, Auber, Halévy, and Ambroise Thomas) and 'several senior officers' such as Émile-Félix Fleury, colonel of the Guides Regiment and also First Squire (*Premier Écuyer*) and the Emperor's aide-de-camp.[39] The review made no secret of the fact that this was a model band for

---

[33] *Statistique de l'industrie à Paris (1847–1848)*, 49, 51–3, 55, and 183.
[34] Comettant, *Histoire d'un inventeur*, 173–81.
[35] Archives Départementales de Seine-et-Marne, [1] Y 178, n.d. [10 September 1849], *Doit Monsieur Sax*, n.p. [1].
[36] Archives Départementales de Seine-et-Marne, [1] Y 178, n.d., no title ['Letter from the Director of the Maison Centrale de Melun, addressed to the Citizen Minister of the Interior [sic] concerning a new deadline of four months for the Citizen Adolphe Sax [sic] to pay the debt of 3317.31fr in accordance with the terms of the act of 29 October 1847'], n.p. and ['Letter dated 10 September 1849 from the director of the Maison Centrale de Melun asking Sax to repay the debt of 3317.31fr'], n.p.
[37] Sax was not the only musical instrument maker to take up one of these supposedly beneficial initiatives for the reintegration of prisoners (and which, if successful, also had a strong impact on the competition). De La Fage, *Quinze visites musicales*, 101.
[38] *RGMP*, 2 January 1853, 7. In reality, this project had been in the making for a year and a half. According to the press (*Le Ménestrel*, 19 May 1850, 2–3 and *RGMP*, 19 May 1850, 171), Sax had created a new fanfare of fourteen players which would bear the name of *Société de nouvelle harmonie d'instruments en cuivre*. The germinal idea—on the other hand, logical for promoting one's own product—was still earlier. *La France musicale*, 11 August 1844, 248 and *Le Ménestrel*, 23 November 1845, 3. In any case, while still living in Brussels, Sax played bass clarinet in the *Société Royale de la Grande Harmonie* and in the *Société Philharmonique*. The first formation (which had its roots in 1811 or 1813) was composed of civilian and military personnel, and had the support of the monarchy, as well as the most influential bourgeoisie of the capital, which offered very interesting synergies for business. Édouard Jacobs, *Nomenclature des Sociétés musicales de la Belgique* (Antwerp: Van Merlen, 1853), 14–16.
[39] Fleury was one of the most solid defenders of the Bonapartist cause—he was a 'close adviser (*conseiller intime*)' of Louis-Napoléon—and suppressed resistance to the coup d'état. Later, he continued to climb the military career ladder, acquired diplomatic powers, attained the highest rank in the Legion of Honour (1859), and was appointed senator (1865) by *décret impérial*. Adolphe Robert, Edgar Bourloton, and Gaston Cougny, *Dictionnaire des parlementaires français depuis le 1er mai 1789 jusqu'au 1er mai 1889*, tome 3 (Paris: Bourloton, 1891), 10–11.

the aforementioned squadron 'organized under the care (*soins*) of the skilful maker' and *Le Ménestrel* explicitly stated that Sax was to be in charge of this new arrangement.[40] This shows that there had already been several private meetings (1851–2) between Sax and the military leaders of the time.[41] The third issue of the *Revue et Gazette Musicale de Paris* of 1853 spoke more openly about this matter, and the editors congratulated themselves on the successful New Year's concert with which this military musical ensemble had presented the Emperor. Moreover, they rejoiced that the government [sic] had chosen Sax for 'such a difficult and important mission'.[42]

It is worthwhile to dwell briefly on this new character and his regiment. The Guides had recently been formed (23 October 1852) as a sort of military unit or corps that merged two squadrons of the same name composed of general troops and four more of cavalrymen from the Dragoons, Lancers, and Hunters of Africa; a total of 1200 men.[43] The *chef de corps* (commanding officer) was Colonel Fleury, who had full powers to restructure the armed group and give it an aristocratic and very distinctive touch. In the officer's own words, that regiment was 'the finest cavalry corps in the Army' and would be commanded by 'officers chosen from among the elite'.[44] Within this set up, Sax would arrive to provide music and amplify with his instruments— not only aurally, but also visually—the impressive pomp and theatricality that was to envelop Napoleon III. Fleury was the architect who had to weigh the pros and cons—we shall understand more about this later—of helping (relaunch) Sax and associating him with the French leader's publicity apparatus. The pros outweighed the cons, and this initial support crystallized in the purchase of clarinets, saxhorns, saxophones, and saxotrombas for the artistic divisions of the Guides, both mounted and on foot. This adoption was a sort of vanguard, icebreaker, or vector of influence—the Guides also evoked the presence of the Emperor—while Sax's legal problems were being resolved in the courts, so that later these artistic tools would be passed on to the bulk of the military bands.

---

[40] *Le Ménestrel*, 2 January 1853, 4.

[41] In fact, on 10 May 1852, Sax's services were already contracted to provide instruments for some of the 1500 musicians belonging to the nineteen infantry and nine cavalry music corps led by Adolphe Adam at the ceremony of the Distribution of the Eagles—a ceremony in which Louis-Napoléon entrusted the new flags to the army commanders—on the Champ de Mars. Neukomm, *Histoire de la musique militaire*, 112–14.

[42] *RGMP*, 16 January 1853, 21–2.

[43] *Journal militaire officiel*, [no exact date, second half of] 1852 [no. 47], 212–15.

[44] Émile-Félix Fleury, *Souvenirs du général Cte Fleury*, tome 1 (Paris: Plon, 1897), 226. That formation orchestrated by Fleury was, according to him, the envy of foreigners and very spectacular: 'Nothing more beautiful and martial than the parade of these thousand horses, all bay, all in the same uniform! Nothing richer and more elegant than that uniform reminiscent of the Guides of the First Empire.'

It only took a few days (8 and 9 February 1853) for the civil chamber of the Court of Cassation under the presidency of Bérenger[45] to rule. The main actors in these hearings were Renouard[46] (judge counsellor—*conseiller*—who drew up the preliminary report), *Maître* Groualle (the manufacturers' lawyer), *Maître* Fabre (Sax), and the public prosecutor Rouland,[47] who issued conclusions that guided the judgement of the high court. Thus, the Tribunal annulled the ruling of 16 February 1850—which in turn had reiterated the decisions of the 1848 hearing—that had negatively impacted the saxhorns and totally dismissed the saxotrombas.[48] Bérenger and the other supreme justices thought the opposite of their lower-ranking colleagues. That is to say, while some had ruled that Sax's results were basically learned and professional merits, Cassation took it for granted that the Belgian maker 'had obtained new quotients, surpassing (*succédant*) other attempts which had not produced the same effects'.[49] Furthermore, and for the first time, a court acknowledged having been able to take into account the echoes coming from other fields,[50] which would expose its principle of independence and/or technical-legal approach. Likewise, with regard to the patent of 1843, its practical (industrial) application was considered to be infringed on the basis of articles 1 and 2 of the law of 1791, on which it originally depended, as was also indicated in the second item of the second regulation of 1844.[51] Similarly,

---

[45] Alphonse-Marie Bérenger (1785–1866) was an extremely brilliant student of law who also had an interest in politics. At the age of thirty he was already a member of the Chamber of Representatives for Valence, his native town, and at forty-two he was a member of parliament for the department of Drôme. Clearly of a conservative bent, he veered even further to the right over the years, calling, for example, for the rehabilitation of the hereditary title in the Chamber of Peers. He joined the Court of Cassation in 1831 and rose through the ranks until he became—Louis-Napoléon made him—president (1849) of the civil chamber. Adolphe Robert and Gaston Cougny, dirs, *Dictionnaire des parlementaires français de 1789 à 1889*, tome 1 (Paris: Bourloton, 1890), 263 and *Almanach National pour 1848–1849–1850*, 347–8 and 350.

[46] Augustin-Charles Renouard (1794–1878) had been, with Louis-Philippe in power, state councillor and secretary general to the Minister of Justice. Since 1837, he had been working as a counsellor to the Court of Cassation.
<http://www.inrp.fr/edition-electronique/lodel/dictionnaire-ferdinand-buisson/document.php?id=3519> (accessed 1 December 2022).

[47] Gustave Rouland (1806–78) had been a prosecutor at the Court of Cassation since 1847, although he was also interested in politics and was a Guizotine deputy. *Almanach Royal et National pour 1847*, 377. The government appointed him chief prosecutor of the Paris Court, probably in mid or late 1853. *Almanach Impérial pour 1853*, 380. Napoleon III later offered him the Ministry of Public Instruction and Religious Affairs (1856–63) and the post of Minister President of the Council of State (1863–4). He was then Governor of the Bank of France until 1878 (except for a six-month period when he was replaced by Ernest Picard) and, also at that time, he was a Bonapartist senator. <http://www.genea-bdf.org/BasesDonnees/genealogies/rouland.htm> (accessed 3 December 2022).

[48] [Désiré] Dalloz aîné, *Jurisprudence générale. Recueil périodique et critique de Jurisprudence, de législation et de doctrine* (Paris: au bureau de la Jurisprudence générale, 1853), 94–5.

[49] *Annales de la propriété industrielle*, tome 3, 1857, 214.

[50] 'Sax's special way of organizing the removal of corners [or angles] may have attracted the attention of experts, examination commissions and juries, and give him public endorsements'. Dalloz, *Jurisprudence générale*, 94–5.

[51] *Gazette des Tribunaux*, 16 February 1853, [1].

the saxotrombas (1845) received the protection of the hearing because they were essentially considered an unprecedent instrument, even if their inspiration came from a new combination of shapes and proportions of objects that were already known.[52] In addition, the charge of formal defects was also dismissed. As a result, the court referred the case—because it was closer to the Paris court and because procedural rules dictated it—to the Imperial Court of Rouen (Normandy), putting both parties back where they were in 1848, but validating that Sax's claims were consonant with the law and upheld.

Sax achieved a judicial (and publicity)[53] coup and put the rival manufacturers in check, but the final judgement was still to come. For this reason, and until the trial took place, he devoted most of his time and resources to reasserting and legitimizing himself in the eyes of the people. The press stayed on his side and, moreover, to align his interests with those of France itself.[54] The band of the *Société de la Grande Harmonie* continued to make public appearances[55] and participated in concerts that attracted important people, causing a significant positive impact. Particularly noteworthy was the one at the end of May at the Jardin d'hiver, where once again the press highlighted that there was 'an elite audience', naming Baron Charles Dupin, Baron Taylor, the prefect of the Seine (Berger), Jobard de Bruxelles, 'and a large number of generals, colonels, and officers'.[56]

The 'orchestre d'Adolphe Sax'—as the press called it directly—also gained daily favour thanks to initiatives such an event for the benefit of the victims of the fires in the seventh arrondissement of Paris in December 1853 or by collaborating with other associations.[57] Strategically, these home tours also reached the Conservatoire. Influential composers' pieces transcribed for band were performed in that high-profile institution, indirectly providing support for Sax's cause. One such example was Meyerbeer and his *Torchlight March* (*Marche aux flambeaux*).[58] It was precisely this composer who had acknowledged to the Emperor that he had the best band in the whole world (*Vous avez, Sire, la première musique d'harmonie du monde entier*).[59] Another

---

[52] *Affaire Sax. Arrêt de la cour de cassation. M. Adolphe Sax, d'une part; MM. Raoux, Halary, Gautrot, Buffet Jeune et Gambaro, d'autre part* (Paris: n. ed., [Imprimerie H. Simon Dautreville et Cie. Rue Neuve-des-bons-enfants, 3,] 1854), 10–11.
[53] *RGMP*, 13 February 1853, 55.
[54] *RGMP*, 1 May 1853, 164.
[55] *RGMP*, 20 March 1853, 99, *Le Ménestrel*, 20 March 1853, 3 and 15 May 1853, 4, and *RGMP*, 22 May 1853, 187.
[56] *RGMP*, 12 June 1853, 210–11.
[57] *RGMP*, 11 December 1853, 430, 18 December 1853, 440, and 25 December 1853, 447.
[58] *RGMP*, 11 December 1853, 431 and 9 January 1854, 8.
[59] *Le Ménestrel*, 11 December 1853, 1–2 and 25 December 1853, 1–2. That concert featured the *Société de la Grande-Harmonie*, but the reporters recognized 'the bulk of the Guides in its ranks' and this is where they took the opportunity to insert Meyerbeer's distinctive advertising wedge. In order to delve into the

of the Conservatoire's professors, Adolphe Adam, was also completely in favour of Sax, stating that he had been 'fighting with all his might for ten years to provide France with the best military music it could dream of'.

On the other hand, the *Société de la Grande Harmonie* was also interested in distinguishing itself in band and choral competitions, as they provided a certain level of prestige, such as the contest held at Fontainebleau, near Paris, on Sunday, 19 June 1853, where it won a prize.[60] Reviews outside the French capital were equally positive, as in Lille, where Sax's quadrille garnered 'bursts of frenzied applause, shouts, interruptions, and encores (*bis*) between each of the fanfare and full band pieces'. Léon Kreutzer, another staunch eulogist and author of this chronicle, stated that 'Mr Sax's system was perfect and complete, and wherever he went, his instruments and his music were judged to be the best'.[61] The media continued to publicize frequent interventions of the model ensemble and its relative military (Guides) led by Nicolas Mohr,[62] shamelessly cultivating and preparing the armed artistic terrain.

Before the end of 1853, Charles-Joseph Sax also re-emerged, trying his luck as a piano builder in Paris, a sector that moved huge amounts of money. The model of the keyboard instrument imagined by Adolphe Sax's father is not linked to our story, but it shows the number of individual supporters and the institutional backup[63] (also from Napoleon III)[64] that the family had. In addition, the press trumpeted the fact that the saxophone had already officially arrived in the United States in 1854 and received positive reviews.[65] In addition, the Imperial Household kindly offered its distinguished guests and European aristocracy (HRH the Prince of Saxe-Coburg) a guided tour of the workshops of Sax, as well as a concert in his concert hall with the emblematic Guides,[66] which gives us a very precise idea of how all these contacts and exchanges of favours were articulated. Specifically in this case,

---

intermingling and interplay between civilian and military formations, see Péronnet, *Les enfants d'Apollon*, 425–34.

[60] *RGMP*, 26 June 1853, 22–8.

[61] *RGMP*, 24 July 1853, 261–2.

[62] See, for example, *Le Ménestrel*, 26 June 1853, 3, 15 May 1853, 4, 22 May 1853, 4, 11 December 1853, 1–2, and 25 December 1853, 1–2, the latter for the benefit of the *Association des artistes musiciens* and on which the names of the performers were recorded.

[63] Charles-Joseph's new company issued a public sale of shares of 1000fr each, by which he sought to reach a share capital of three million francs. The supervisory board (*surveillance*) was composed of composers, musicians, intellectuals, and bankers such as Adolphe Adam, Hector Berlioz, Brandus, Félicien David, Georges Kastner, Léon Kreutzer, Massé, Giacomo Meyerbeer, Louis Niedermeyer, Ambroise Thomas, De Coislin, Jobard, and Pavie. *Bulletin financier* [of Paris], 29 July 1853, 4. (The company went bankrupt in October 1855).

[64] 'Recently, it was about the fertile (*fécond*) system applied to the piano by Mr Sax father (the Emperor wanted to hear the new piano at Saint-Cloud, and showed all his interest in the happy inventor).' *RGMP*, 12 June 1853, 210–11.

[65] *RGMP*, 15 January 1854, 22 and 22 January 1854, 32.

[66] *RGMP*, 12 March 1854, 89 and *Le Ménestrel*, 16 March 1854, 4.

the brief was to entertain a dignitary who was visiting Paris and who was said to be 'an excellent musician'. As a gesture of sympathy and complicity, Mohr had adapted an opera by the prince (*Casilda*) for military music, and his highness was very pleased; a feeling which he conveyed to the delight of HM the Emperor. The entire plenipotentiary entourage—which included General Roguet, the Marquis de Belmont,[67] and other high-ranking French and foreign representatives—was treated to more pieces such as the popular *Torchlight March* conducted by Arban, arguably the most famous trumpeter/cornetist of the day. Likewise, the event was attended by 'eminent men of letters and artists' including Meyerbeer and, significantly, Berlioz, who conducted his *Roman Carnival*, a piece that made up an audition 'which lasted no less than two hours'.

However, the gesture that unquestionably demonstrates such interference and favourable treatment is provided by the head of State himself. Louis-Napoléon Bonaparte appointed Sax 'Manufacturer of the Military Household of His Majesty the Emperor (*Facteur de la Maison Militaire de S.M. l'Empereur*),'[68] a title that the Belgian did not hesitate to print literally on his instruments (Figure 5.3). The Military Household was an integral part of the broader and more ambitious Emperor's Household (*Maison de l'Empereur*). The latter was inspired by the great royal courts of the *Ancien Régime*, but adapted to the demands and circumstances of a new time, such as proximity to the people, attraction of the elites, and attachment to the bourgeoisie. Moreover, Bonaparte set it up in the form of a Ministry with its own budget and civil servants.[69] It was not just a matter of embellishing and creating spectacular pomp at the sovereign's soirées and diplomatic gatherings, but rather of using a policy of cultivated image and propaganda.

---

[67] Christophe-Michel Roguet (1800–77), who also became a count, had a brilliant military and political career, rising from page to Napoleon I (1814–15) to general and aide-de-camp to the prince-president (1851), head of his Military Household, and senator (1852). On the other hand, Marie-Louis-Gabriel-Alfred-Stanislas Briançon-Vachon (1804–57), better known as the Marquis de Belmont, was a deputy (1855–7) and chamberlain to the Emperor. Robert, Bourloton and Cougny, *Dictionnaire des Parlementaires*, tome 5, 185 and tome 1, 248.

[68] *RGMP*, 7 May 1854, 154 and *Le Ménestrel*, 30 April 1854, 4.

As a curiosity, the head of the military section of the Emperor's Household at the time (1854) was Marshal Count Vaillant, and he was advised by a core team of twenty-four people including several major generals, brigadier generals, colonels (one of whom was Fleury), squadron commanders, captains, and a lieutenant. *Almanach Impérial pour 1854* (Paris: Guyot et Scribe, 1854), 53.

[69] The Minister of the Emperor's Household in 1854 was senator Achille Fould, who combined that post with that of head of the Interior (*État*). The Emperor's Household was run by 1440 people, namely the subordinates of the grand chaplain (*aumônier*) (16), the grand marshal (847), the grand chamberlain (79), the grand esquire or servant-at-arms (*écuyer*) (267), the grand hunter (*veneur*) (85), the grand master of ceremonies (13), those of the Empress Household (*Maison de l'Impératrice*) itself (22), and other officials (90). Xabier Mauduit, *Le ministère du faste. La maison de l'empereur Napoléon III* (Paris: Fayard [Kobo version]. 2016), 6 ['Annexes Statistiques'] and *Almanach Impérial pour 1854*, 50–6.

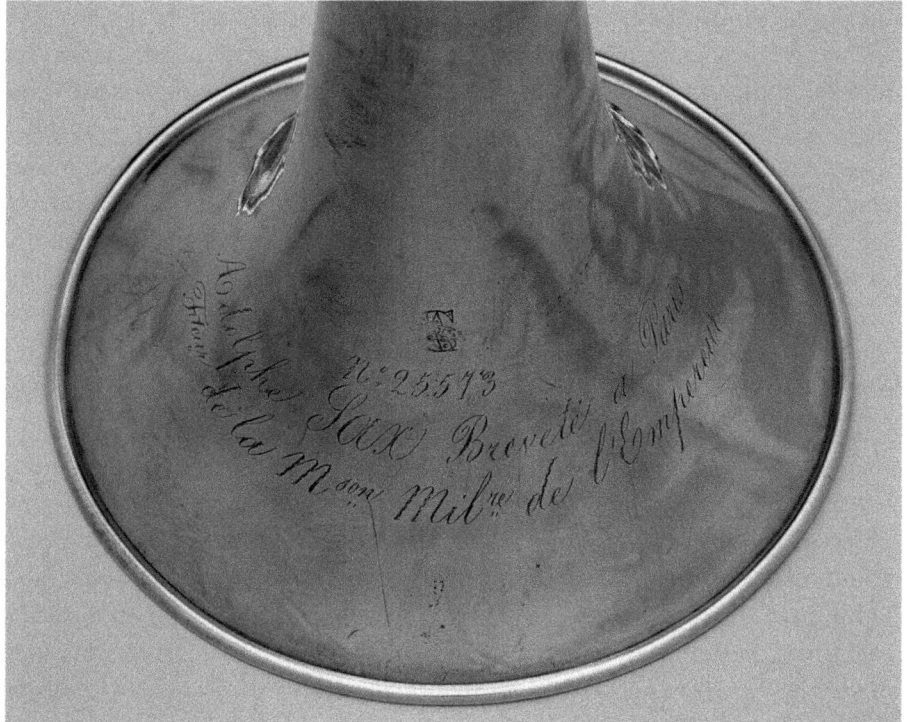

Figure 5.3 Bell of a Sax six-piston trombone with distinctive inscription 'F^{teur} de la M^{son} Mil^{re} de l'Empereur'
The Metropolitan Museum of Art, New York.

Crucially, with this honorary distinction, the Rouen court would find itself in the predicament of sanctioning something that the Emperor had recently taken under his protection.[70] There was a chance that the imperial court would not agree with Sax—or at least not completely—and would consider his instruments illegitimate. Additionally, Napoleon III also invested Raoux and Halari (Halary *père*) as his suppliers.[71] (Whatever happened, Bonaparte was going to win with little or no damage, although the real

---

[70] The press stated unequivocally that Bonaparte had not only wanted to give the Belgian maker a token of his confidence (*bienveillance*), but also of his 'protection'. *Le Ménestrel*, 30 April 1854, 4.

[71] *Conclusions pour Monsieur Raoux, appelant, contre Monsieur Sax, intimé. Cour impériale de Paris. Chambre des appels de police correctionnelle. Audiences des vendredi et samedi. M. Partarrieu-Lafosse, Président. M. De Vallée, Avocat général* (Paris: n. ed., [Impr. S. Raçon,] n.d. [1860]), 2, *Réponse de Monsieur Raoux aux conclusions motivées de Monsieur Sax* (Paris: n. ed., [Impr. S. Raçon,] n.d. [1860]), 2, and *Notice Historique sur la Manufacture d'Instruments de Musique de J. A. Halary* (Paris: n. ed., n.d. [c.1864]), 1–8. The latter information comes from a couple of *factums* and a sort of publicity pamphlet, but we have not been able to verify it with the official designation, although we have been able to do so from the epigraphy of some surviving instruments.

support was obviously for the Belgian businessman, and that of the others was part of a theatricalization.) In any case, this knot was legal and the judicial authority was supposed to retain (much of) its independence; but nothing could be further from the truth. Napoleon III de facto controlled this pillar of the state and infiltrated people sympathetic to the system into certain legal positions that completed this closed circle of power, including Bérenger who was specifically appointed by him. And since control had to be as broad and sophisticated as possible, culture and its legitimizing properties were not neglected. The quintessential artistic institution of the state, the Opera, was absorbed by the Emperor's Household. Curiously, the only legal representative of the commission in charge of the transfer was Chaix-d'Est-Ange.[72]

In view of the above, it is worth spending a few lines on the outstanding background of Gustave-Louis Chaix-d'Est-Ange, who was attached to traditional, monarchical, and especially imperial values, as there is no doubt about his attachment to the coup d'état of 1851. He was born (1800) into a family active in the legal profession—his father was a prosecutor at the Criminal Court in Reims and later worked as a lawyer in Paris. His mentor soon died, but the young Chaix-d'Est-Ange managed to carve out a promising legal and political career, for in 1831 he was already deputy for the department of Marne, a post he renewed for the periods from 1836 to 1842 and from 1844 to 1846. He must have been held in quite high esteem at the time, because he was *bâtonnier*—president or representative—of the bar association of the capital during the two-year period 1842–4. His effective career took off under Louis-Napoléon, with whom he rose through the ranks in meteoric fashion: member of the legal advisory council of the Emperor's Household (1855),[73] Attorney General of the Imperial Court of Paris (1857), state councillor (1858) and vice-president (1863) of this governmental body, senator (1862), president of the section for public works and fine arts, etc. He also reached the fourth level of the Legion of Honour in 1861, which made him one of the Emperor's best lawyers and public servants.[74] It is clear that recruiting him was a great success for Sax.

---

[72] *Le Ménestrel*, 9 July 1854, 1.

[73] This circle of power was composed, in addition to himself, of four other people who will be featured in the second part of the book, namely Rouher (Minister of Agriculture and Trade), Delangle (senator and president of the Imperial Court of Paris), and Pascalis and Pécourt (judges of the Court of Cassation).

[74] When Bonaparte ceased to be head of State in 1870, Chaix-d'Est-Ange retired to private life for good and died six years later. *Almanach Impérial pour 1855* (Paris: Guyot et Scribe, 1855), 96 and Adolphe Robert and Gaston Cougny, dirs, *Dictionnaire des Parlementaires*, tome 2, 24–5. As a curiosity, Chaix-d'Est-Ange also served on the administrative board of the Opera from at least 1841, which again underlines the support and advice of figures such as Habeneck and, above all, Monnais. *Almanach Royal et National pour 1841*, 767.

6
The Egg of Columbus and a Great Victory

The Denouement of the Civil Prosecution

The French Court of Cassation (1853) had entrusted the Imperial Court of Rouen with the arbitration of a case file in which seven years' worth of information had accumulated. In reality, however, only two issues remained in dispute. The first of these was whether the 1843 patent (saxhorns), which had already been validated for mobile spring slides (*coulisses mobiles à ressort*), should also be validated for the smoothing of angles in pipes. The second was entirely related to the authenticity of saxotrombas (1845). Nevertheless, the lawyers would squeeze out any past content that interested them, knowing the number of interconnections between unsound premises. The disputants were to be represented by *Maître* Dufaure (Sax) and, once again, by the former minister Marie (Raoux and the rest of the coalition of manufacturers)—Louis-Napoléon had evidently dispensed with his services as soon as he became president of the Republic in December 1848—who would also be joined by the Attorney General, Eugène Jolibois.

Jules-Armand Dufaure (1798–1881) was another prominent character in the French political scene in the nineteenth century. After studying law, in which he soon acquired a solid reputation, he entered politics (he was elected Liberal deputy in 1834), occupying a centrist position. He was appointed state councillor and obtained his first ministerial portfolio (Public Works) in the government of Marshal Soult (1839–40). Despite founding the Young Left (*Jeune Gauche*) with other politicians (Tocqueville, Corcelle, Rivet, and Billault), he did not join the banqueting campaign which aimed to wear down Louis-Philippe. On 13 October 1848, he accepted, for a little over two months, the office of head of the Interior (with General Cavaignac in power); and, a year later (from 2 June to 31 October 1849), he held the same office under President Louis-Napoléon, although he was not part of his cabinet after the coup d'état. At that time, he retired from political life and focused on his judicial career, although he would later return to the public arena as a member of the Liberal Union (*Union libérale*). Nevertheless, he continued to take part in legal proceedings (some defending people against the Emperor and even in the so-called 'Procès des Treize' in 1864).[1] During the Third Republic and as a moderate member of parliament, he was appointed Minister of Justice and Vice-President of the Council (February 1871–May 1873), repeating as Minister of Law in Buffet's cabinet in 1875. His political and professional successes continued in the following years (*arrêt* [judgement] Blanco, President of the Council, President of the Centre-Left party, immovable senator…).[2]

In the debates under discussion, Dufaure began his speech by presenting his client as a serious manufacturer, just as Chaix-d'Est-Ange had done in 1847. In addition to listening to all the professional merits of Sax—an outstanding clarinetist, winner of the Champ de Mars competition, and awarded in national and international exhibitions—the lawyer reminded the audience that it was for the benefit of France that he won all these prizes and distinctions. This was another of the emotionally charged considerations that had already been heard earlier and with which the favour and condescension of the tribunal was sought.

Dufaure knew that he had to present his client's theses very carefully, in a very didactic manner, and of course, in line with the applicable regulations (1791 and 1844). Dufaure therefore devoted the first few minutes of his speech to outlining the acoustic theory of wind instruments, leading up to the state of the valves at the time. According to Sax, these mechanisms still had three problems. The first, the still complicated passage from one note to another without interruption (*notes glissées*); the second, the inadequacy of the length of the valve slides (*tubes additionnels*) when one of the valves was pressed;[3] and the third, 'probably the most serious'—and the one that was ultimately to be assessed—concerning the curvatures of the tubes through

---

[1] See, among others, Rémi Dalisson, *Hippolyte Carnot 1801–1888: La liberté, l'école et la République.* (Paris: CNRS, 2011), 288–9.

[2] See, among others, Joseph Garnier, *Le droit au travail à l'Assemblée nationale: recueil complet de tous les discours prononcés dans cette mémorable discussion* (Paris: Guillaumin, 1848), 265–83, Trois publicistes [sic], *Profils critiques et biographiques des 750 représentants du peuple a l'Assemblée législative* (Paris: Garnier frères, 1849), 109–12, and Hoefer, *Nouvelle biographie générale*, tome 15 (1856), 60–1. For further biographical information, there is a monograph by Georges Picot (*M. Dufaure, sa vie et ses discours*) published in Paris in 1883.

[3] Dufaure gave specific figures and gave the example of a one-metre long tube instrument, where the slides of the semitone, tone, and tone-and-a-half valve slides measured 0.059 metres, 0.122 metres, and 0.189 metres. By pressing one of the valves, the acoustic properties of the other valve slides would be compromised and this 'inaccuracy' would appear. However, he acknowledged that for many people this irregularity would be imperceptible—barbarian ears (*oreilles barbares*) he called them—but that it would make a difference to musicians and seasoned artists (*la reproduction la plus nette, la plus délicate, la plus exquise des sons qu'un instrument doit produire*). *Le Droit. Journal des Tribunaux*, 27 September 1854, 927 and 929.

which the air passed, which were deemed too angular (*heurtées*), causing the loss 'of part of the smoothness and quality of the sound'.

On that point, Dufaure offered court three physical examples of this 'evolution': an instrument by Stölzel from 1813 or 1817 [sic], one by Périnet with the characteristics of his 1838 patent, and finally one by Sax. The lawyer made a complete tour of the tubing of the first in which he counted 'seven or eight angles and three bends' and it was therefore tremendously sharp. The second's channellings were more smoothed out, but several bends were still very steep. Cleverly, he quoted verbatim from Périnet's original patent—perhaps out of an excess of modesty—in which the author acknowledged that there was still room for improvement ('I do not pretend to believe that I have succeeded in giving them all the degree of perfection of which they are susceptible'). And finally, he showed his client's specimen whose curvatures, as we can predict, were even less aggressive.[4] This was a visible advance and effectively a new degree of improvement, namely, a consideration that fitted very well with the current regulations.

The opposing faction objected that Dufaure's arguments—and those supporting the saxotrombas—were, according to Marie, 'chimeras', that is to say, feigned, maximized, or purposely created reasonings on which the Belgian maker intended to build a 'monopoly', a term he intentionally repeated often, knowing how damaging it was perceived to be for the economy and industrial regulation. This intervention by the former republican minister was very engaging and contains one of his strongest and most profound theses. The lawyer argued that the premises underlying Sax's patents were not only erroneous and false, but also unnecessary. In other words, there was no irrefutable proof that the brass instruments were improved by these rectifications because the problems that Sax intended to solve and from which he had started, did not actually exist. Therefore, any potential industrial application derived from fictitious and poorly formulated approaches—not only in terms of content, but also in terms of form, which was also under discussion—would be automatically invalidated as a farce. This hoax took on bizarre overtones—Marie further argued—if, in addition, an exclusive and forbidden commercial concession was created on top of it, which, to add insult to injury, concerned several entire families of brasswinds.[5] Marie was obviously referring in a veiled way—as, under an authoritarian regime, he could get

---

[4] *Note pour M. Sax, appelant, contre MM. Raoux et consorts, intimés. Cour impériale de Rouen. Audience solennelle: 1re et 2e chambres réunies* (Paris: n. ed., [Impr. H. Simon Dautreville,] 1854), 8–9.

[5] In contrast, Sax's lawyer claimed that his client had been accused of being a protégé of the Orleanist monarchy (*La monarchie, disait-on, protégeait particulièrement M. Sax*), but when the republican government organized its National Exhibition (1849) and selected its jury, the examiners still gave the Belgian inventor as the winner.

into trouble if he did not choose his words properly—to the Army and other pressure and opinion groups, lobbies among which this time he did not cite any generals and certainly not the Emperor.

On the subject of 'myths' and 'fantasies', Marie devoted a similar attack at that hearing to the saxophone, an instrument that was not involved in the case, but which was certainly still present and connected to the rest of the musical instruments. According to Marie, that instrument 'had everything at once of the bassoon and the clarinet; [it was] a sort of monster [sic] which had no nature of its own and which really seemed to have no future (*et qui véritablement semblait ne devoir pas avoir d'avenir*)'.[6] This (happy) error of the legist contained, however, a certain truth, because the reasons with which Sax gave substance—and ultimately legitimacy—to his new upstart ('an instrument which, in terms of the character of its voice [sic], could be similar to string instruments, but which possessed more strength and intensity than the latter') were feigned. In a further view, the saxophone was also defended in a similar way, namely as a new combination of brass instrument but with the character of woodwinds;[7] an assumption that also appeared in Kastner's *Méthode de saxophone*. However, this statement of intent, which was apparently irrelevant to the context in which it was made, helped convey certain ideas which would then be beneficial on a commercial and sales level. Sax wanted the saxophone to find a niche in the complex market of instruments and in the quasi-impenetrable orchestral tradition by presenting it as a sound wild card or bridge (*une sorte de concordant, d'intermédiaire*).[8] Thanks to its ambivalent nature, it could allegedly be used in solo or accompanying roles (sound mass) in any kind of ensemble, whether outdoors (bands) or indoors (symphony or operatic music). Of course, this ambitious commercial ideology clashed with a more complex musical reality full of nuances and interests of all kinds.

Subsequently, Dufaure enlightened the court with a slightly more concrete clarification of what saxotrombas were. He explained that Sax had created a family of instruments that functioned as a homogeneous block (*ensemble homogène*) with affinities of timbre, fingering, and intensity (*puissance*). Likewise, Dufaure noted that these instruments encompassed a broad treble-bass tonal range in military bands similar to that of the string family in symphony

---

[6] *Le Droit. Journal des Tribunaux*, 27 September 1854, 929.
[7] *Note pour messieurs les conseillers*, 19–20.
[8] Georges Kastner, *Méthode complète et raisonnée de Saxophone [dédiée à Monsieur Ad. Sax]* (Paris: Brandus et Cie., Successeurs de Maurice Schlesinger et E. Troupenas et Cie,] s.d. [c.1845–50]), 1 and 22–7. Brandus was also the editor (c.1846) of the *Méthode complète pour saxhorn et saxotromba, soprano, alto, ténor, baryton, basse et contrebasse à 3, 4 et 5 cylindres suivie d'exercices pour l'emploi du compensateur* that Adolphe Sax himself wrote.

orchestras (violin, viola, cello, and double bass); or, 'better still (*ou, mieux encore*)'—he sought to clarify—with respect to the vocal spectrum (soprano, alto, tenor, and bass).[9] The lawyer also specified that those brasswinds were conical, and he stressed, it was the ratios (*proportions*) of width along the length of the tube that made them special and different, and by extension, their 'timbre, nature, [and] quality'. Moreover, he invited his opponents to read the references accompanying the drawings ('read the dimensions that accompany the drawings, and you will have the proportions according to which they [the instruments] should be built'), which, he pointed out, did not appear in the cylindrical artefacts, namely 'trumpets, cornets, etc.'. However, elsewhere in his speech, he also said that his client reserved the possibility of applying this principle—that of saxotrombas—to the old instruments, such as 'cornets, trombones, trumpets, etc.'.

Dufaure also commented that these instruments and improvements were intended for infantry and, 'above all, cavalry military bands'. The latter's musicians could also benefit from the fact that some of his client's brasswinds left the rider's right hand free to better direct the horse. Finally, he ended his argument by asserting Sax's right to claim that patent on the basis of that whole or ensemble, but also in respect of the details, 'particular structure, or design which he assigned to his instruments which he called saxotromba or saxhorn'. Although these arguments were confusing (perhaps intentionally), they are evidence of the Belgian maker's tremendous ambition to control and embrace a wide range of brass production.

Dufaure's exposition had left several flanks unprotected and Marie did not hesitate to attack in a very incisive and ironic way, saying that he had heard 'the most important discovery (*révélation*) in the world'. The ex-minister of the Republic charged that the proportions of the saxotromba tubing had to contain 'a mathematical law of proportion, according to which all brasswinds belonging to this family were to be organised and constructed'. Marie asked where such postulate was stated and developed, because, in despite of being allegedly central to and affecting the whole family, he found no trace of it in the title or in the text of the patent specification. He did recognize the existence of figures in some of the instrument designs accompanying the document, but these, he claimed, were also false. Marie and his clients had recreated the scale from those sketches—which was a rather naïve way of creating this supposed ratio—and had checked it against two of Sax's own instruments, concluding that the results made no sense. Moreover, interestingly enough, they found that the proportions of the instruments made by

---

[9] *Le Droit. Journal des Tribunaux*, 27 September 1854, 929.

the Belgian maker were nothing special and resembled those of the rest of the industry and other professional colleagues. All these manufacturers—including him—built these instruments in the same way, that is, with conical mandrels on which a brass sheet was folded and to which was then attached more conical (made in the same way) and/or other (cylindrical) tubing.[10]

Marie also lambasted homogeneity of timbre ('it is a pretence') and the left-hand position ('do you really think that this placement of the instruments on the left or right flank had not been found before Mr Sax?') as fallacies, and the same fingering as 'nonsense'. The lawyer argued that all valve instruments shared the same fingering—he said, sarcastically, that the Belgian maker had 'worked the miracle'—so he did not understand how it was possible to patent this property. Moreover, he pointed out that an instrumentalist could not switch from one brasswind to another because his embouchure was made to his usual instrument—that is, that a trumpeter would happily jump to a tuba or the other way round—a detail which, he mockingly commented, Sax forgot to record in his document.

It was now the long-awaited turn of the prosecutor Eugène Jolibois, who reasoned in much the same way as his colleagues of Cassation (1853) and Dufaure, but emphasized the important industrial value that any new invention had to have in order to be considered as such in the modern legislative framework (1844). In this respect, he pointed out that changes of shape which provided a new result and were not exclusively part of the ornamentation were perfectly patentable. Interestingly, he gave the example of upright pianos, which obviously had a specific function (to save space). The prosecutor applied the same formula to saxotrombas and considered them a legitimate result about which one could 'question their importance, but not their reality'. Jolibois also dismantled any presumption of prior authorship and said that Sax would lose the case if his opponents showed an instrument identical to Sax's, but not 'analogous or almost the same' as they had done up to that point. (We shall see later, when financial compensation and business kowtowing come into play, whether that precision is decisive.)

Jolibois used the metaphor of Columbus' egg to validate his argument and to dismantle Marie's complaint that the designs in the 1843 patent did not follow any pattern. The prosecutor said that the sketches in that document showed that figures 1, 4, 5, and 6 had perfectly rounded ducts, while those in drawings 2, 3, and 7 were less so. Jolibois stated that it was physically impossible to attach additional [tuning] slides (*coulisses d'accord*) to a circular tube, so Sax could not do so without adapting them: 'since he could not apply in

[10] *Le Droit. Journal des Tribunaux*, 27 September 1854, 929–30.

all its rigour, he proposed to get as close as possible to the circular line'. In this way, that theoretically beneficial lenticular contour was preserved and, to tie in with the analogy, the egg was broken a little and stood upright.

In short, the Belgian inventor had legally and correctly protected 'a special way of organizing' these conduits. Jolibois also dismissed the formal defect concerning the saxotrombas, considering the explanations in the wording to be sufficient, as well as the drawings in the annexes which, in any case, had to be interpreted by qualified persons (*langage des ingénieurs*).[11] With regard to this reference, we wonder whether Jolibois consulted any of the engineers close to him. In fact, he gave a speech in August 1854 at the Academy of Sciences, Fine Arts, and Letters of Rouen, which was presumably intended to deal with the work of children in factories, but which in fact touched on other, more general matters. Jolibois ended his lecture by proclaiming that 'never has there been a more favourable moment to raise one's voice and make one's legitimate wishes heard. Motivated by the greatest solicitude for the condition of the working classes, the Emperor's government will be able to overcome all obstacles, all resistance; He has the will, the strength, and the right, He will make the cause of humanity triumph!'.[12]

Returning to the case at hand, Jolibois also 'granted Mr Sax's claim for damages', underlining the fact that the coalition manufacturers had copied and produced his instruments without his consent during all those years.[13] The final outcome (see Figure 6.1 for the overview of this first phase) of these eight years of trials came on 28 June 1854. The first and second chambers of the Imperial Court of Rouen, presided over by Franck-Carré, ruled entirely in favour of Sax and definitively rejected the motions for annulment and objections raised by his opponents.[14] The press echoed the news, with *Le Ménestrel* rallying around the Belgian businessman, commenting that the

---

[11] *Annales de la propriété industrielle*, tome 3, 1857, 219–20.

[12] *Précis analytique des travaux de l'Académie des Sciences, Belles-lettres et Arts de Rouen pendant l'année 1853–54* (Rouen: Alfred Péron, 1854), 5–15.
Jolibois (1819–96) studied law and practised in Paris (1840–9). Once he had entered the magistracy, he was appointed Attorney General of Amiens, then of Rouen (which is the period we are currently discussing) and later of Chambéry (May 1861), prefect of Savoy (April 1863), and following that state councillor (December 1866). He almost became Minister of Justice (obviously with Napoleon III still in power), but the Third Republic reduced him to private life. He did, however, have a seat as a Bonapartist deputy before the end of his life. Robert, Bourloton and Cougny, *Dictionnaire des Parlementaires*, tome 3, 420. Of course, Bonaparte also awarded him the title of Knight of the Legion of Honour. *Bulletin des lois de la République française. XIe Série. Règne de Napoléon III, Empereur des français. Partie supplémentaire*, tome 10 (Paris: Imprimerie Impériale, 1858), 442.

[13] *Annales de la propriété industrielle*, tome 3, 1857, 220 and *Cour impériale de Rouen. Note pour M. [Adolphe] Sax, Appelant, Contre MM. Raoux et Consorts, Intimés. Note pour Messieurs les Conseillers* (Paris: n. ed., [H. Simon Dautreville et Cie,] n.d. [1854]), 26.

[14] Stéph. Cuënot, Th. Gelle and A. Fabre, *Journal du palais: recueil le plus ancien et le plus complet de la jurisprudence*, tome 1 (Paris: Bureaux de l'Administration, 1855), 443–4.

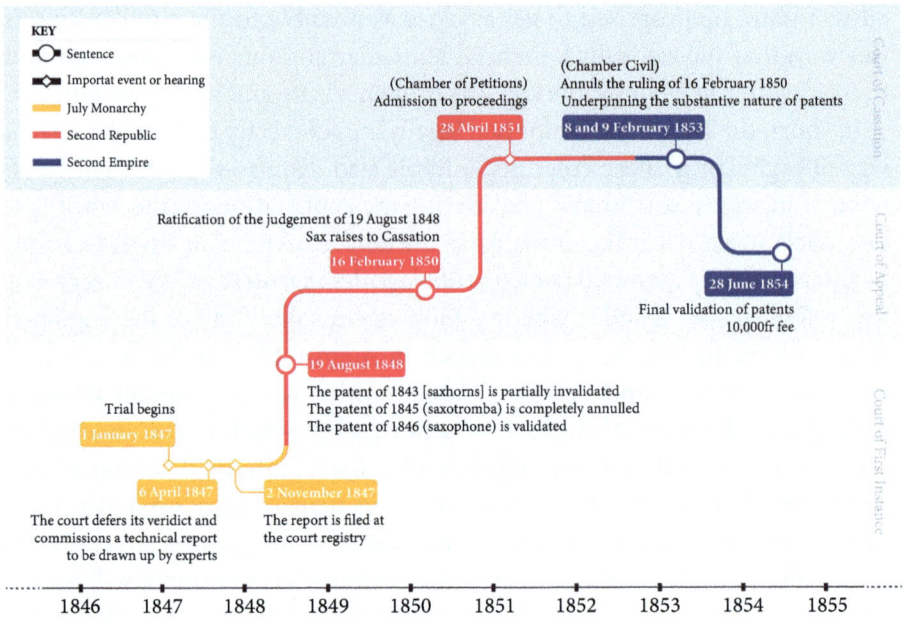

Figure 6.1 Timeline of the defence phase
Compiled by the author.

court decision enshrined his rights and restored 'his title deeds'.[15] For its part, the *Revue et Gazette Musicale de Paris* emphasised his overwhelming victory and that 'he had been proved right on all issues'.[16]

In addition, the imperial judge allowed Sax's claim for punitive damages and ordered Raoux and the other members of the coalition to pay him 10,000fr. Although exemplary, the fine was five times less than what the Belgian inventor had asked for and would barely cover 12% of what he owed the investors, not counting the costs of the court cases over the past seven years, interest, and other expenses. However, with this compensation money one could have lived in a furnished flat in the capital for more than eight years, eat lunch and dinner out 5000 times—or half that if one wanted to do so in a luxurious hotel with a restaurant—make about 130 trips from London to Paris via Calais in first class, or hire a two-horse (*fiacre*) or *coupé* (one animal) transport numerous times for 1.25fr a ride or 1.75fr an hour.[17]

---

[15] *Le Ménestrel*, 22 October 1854, 3–4.
[16] *RGMP*, 2 July 1854, 218.
[17] Francis Coghlan, *The Coghlan new guide to Paris* (London: Onwhyn, 1854), xxvii, 23, 60, and 62–4.

Of course, the rival manufacturers could have appealed to the Court of Cassation, but they did not do so, probably discouraged by such an overwhelming ruling and convinced that it would serve no purpose. It was therefore a case of resigning and readjusting while awaiting further developments. Precisely and immediately after that ruling—not even two months had passed—the Emperor decreed (16 August 1854) the composition of the bands of the Imperial Guard (*Décret impérial sur la composition du Personnel de la Musique des régiments de la Garde impériale*) according to a new arrangement.[18] From then on, eight saxophones (two sopranos, two altos, two tenors, and two baritones or basses [sic]) would return to the infantry bands, as well as fourteen saxhorns and three saxotrombas. Sax's brasswinds in the mounted regiments would also be rehabilitated (seventeen saxhorns and six saxotrombas).[19]

Self-evidently, the Imperial Guard was not the main body of the Army— besides, some of those instruments were already being used in the Guides— but it acted as a military body of reference for the rest of the military artistic groups. Moreover, the following year (5 March 1855), a *Décision impérial* appeared in which, 'in view of the good results obtained', the Minister of War (Jean-Baptiste-Philibert Vaillant) proposed to the Emperor (*j'ai l'honneur de proposer à Votre Majesté*) that the instrumental disposition of the Imperial Guard be replicated in the Line (*ligne*) formations,[20] which at that time numbered 100 regiments.[21] But, in addition, another regulation (*Note ministérielle*) of the following season (22 April 1856) called for the artillery squadrons to adopt the same palette of instruments as the cavalry music of the 16 August 1854 disposition.[22]

In other words, the ruling of the Imperial Court of Rouen not only rescued the instruments of the Belgian entrepreneur, but also set up a sort of legal defence for Sax to enjoy a monumental competitive advantage. In order to fully understand its implications, it is useful to gain a sense of the

---

[18] *Journal militaire officiel*, [no exact date, second half of] 1854 [no. 59], 282–92 or *Le Moniteur de l'Armée*, 16 September 1854, 2–3.

[19] The new regulations were reported in the press and also stated that the directors (*chefs*) of the music regiments 'would be appointed directly by decree of the Emperor'; and the sub-chiefs and the first-class musicians would be so by the Minister of War or his delegate (the commanding general of the Imperial Guard). *Le Ménestrel*, 1 October 1854, 3.

[20] *Journal militaire officiel*, [no exact date, first half of] 1855 [no. 11], 158–9.
However, this *Décision* sounds rather lax—more like a suggestion—it was subject to the availability of funds and did not require 'a general and immediate execution'. This suggests that Vaillant did not intend to support Sax so openly, although he was probably under pressure from other high commanders (Fleury).

[21] The Emperor decreed on 24 October 1854 that the twenty-five Light infantry regiments be reconverted into the 76th to the 100th ordinals of the Line units. *Bulletin des lois de l'Empire Français*, tome 11 (Paris: Imprimerie Impériale, 1854), 737–8. The Army (land and sea) was composed of some 558,000 men. Of these, 380,000 were infantry, 80,000 cavalry, 57,000 artillery, 8200 engineers, and 33,800 'other troops', including 25,000 gendarmes. *Galignani's* (1856), 66–7.

[22] *Journal militaire officiel*, [no exact date, first half of] 1856 [no. 15], 430.

Table 6.1 Price of instruments for a 55-person infantry band according to the 1854 provision

Instrument	Unit price	Total
2 flutes, big o small [sic]	110fr	220fr
4 piccolo clarinets (*petites clarinettes*)	225fr	900fr
8 clarinets (*grandes clarinettes sopranos*) in B♭	225fr	1800fr
2 oboes	150fr	300fr
2 soprano saxophones	160fr	320fr
2 alto saxophones	200fr	400fr
2 tenor saxophones	200fr	400fr
2 baritone or bass [sic] saxophones	225fr	450fr
2 cornets with piston valves or valves (*à pistons ou cylindres*)	115fr	230fr
4 trumpets with valves (*à cylindres*)	115fr	460fr
4 trombones, one of which bass	90fr	360fr
2 small (*petits*) soprano saxhorns in E♭	80fr	160fr
2 small (*petits*) alto saxhorns in B♭	85fr	170fr
3 saxotrombas in E♭	110fr	330fr
2 baritone saxhorns in B♭	120fr	240fr
4 bass saxhorns in B♭	150fr	600fr
2 contrabass saxhorns in E♭	150fr	300fr
2 deep contrabass saxhorns in B♭	250fr	500fr
1 bass drum (*grosse caisse*)	150fr	150fr
2 pairs of cymbals (*cymballes*)	100fr	200fr
2 drums (*tambours*)	80fr	160fr
TOTAL		8650fr

Compiled from de *Journal militaire officiel*, [no exact date, second half of] 1854 [no. 59], 282–92 and Antoine Elwart, *Manuel des aspirants aux grades de sous-chef et de chef de musique de l'armée* (Paris: Gérard, 1862), 82.

Note: Although the provision stated fifty-six instruments, the individuals (fifty-five) were distributed among one conductor, one assistant conductor, five first-class musicians, ten second-class musicians, thirteen third-class musicians, and twenty-five pupil-soldier-musicians.

size of the instrument-making business amounted to in those early years of the Empire. To appraise it, we can take to the model formation of the Imperial foot and horse Guards as a starting point, and find out the price at which the Army bought this equipment (Tables 6.1 and 6.2). The maker who managed to secure the complete supply for in those phalanxes would make a handsome profit of 8650fr and 4460fr per formation. We also know that in 1858 there were 192 *orchestres militaires*, 'without counting the fanfares of the foot Chasseurs, the Zouaves, and the Light infantry of Africa.'[23]

[23] Bouzard, *Les usages musicaux dans l'armée française*, 329–30 and Thierry Bouzard and Dominique De la Tour, 'Gagistes et tambours majors. Le statut du musicien militaire au XIXe siècle', *Revue historique des armées* 279 (2015), 68.

Table 6.2 Price of instruments for a 37-person cavalry band according to the 1854 provision

Instrument	Unit price	Total
1 small (*petit*) high-pitched (*aigu*) saxhorn in B♭	100fr	100fr
2 small (*petits*) soprano saxhorns in E♭	80fr	160fr
4 alto saxhorns in B♭	85fr	340fr
2 alto saxhorns in A♭	155fr	310fr
4 alto saxotrombas in E♭	110fr	440fr
2 baritone saxotrombas in B♭	125fr	250fr
4 bass saxhorns in B♭	150fr	600fr
2 contrabass saxhorns in E♭	150fr	300fr
2 contrabass saxhorns in B♭	250fr	500fr
2 cornets with piston valves or valves (*à pistons ou cylindres*)	115fr	230fr
6 trumpets with valves (*à cylindres*)	115fr	690fr
6 alto, tenor, and bass trombones	90fr	540fr
TOTAL		4460fr

Compiled from *Journal Militaire officiel*, [no exact date, second half of] 1854 [no. 59], 292 and Elwart, *Manuel des aspirants*, 82.

So, being very conservative—Sax was to grant several licences in 1855, as will be discussed later—and considering that he could get an average of 3000fr per regiment (nor was it obligatory to buy the flutes, clarinets, or percussion from him), the profits during that first half of the Empire could have exceeded 575,000fr. This amount—which, of course, other sources of income (the compensation of his licensees, other civil bands, professional musicians, the rent of his concert hall, his position as brass supplier at the Opera, etc.) would have to be added—seems more than enough to maintain and grow a business like his. If we want to measure this figure, we can point out that the annual salary of a minister was 100,000 francs, while a senator or deputy received 'only' 30,000fr. Other high salaries of civil servants, such as police commissioners (6000 francs), doctors (7000–10,000 francs), or university professors (2000–8000 francs) can also help us to understand that more than half a million francs. Other points of reference may be the income of the highest-paid religious authorities (vicars general and canons), which ranged from 2000fr to 4000fr, while the governor of the Hôtel des Invalides received a compensation of 40,000fr for his administration and the colonel-major in charge, 7000fr. From a more day-to-day perspective, omnibus rides were 0.3fr (0.15fr in the open), the daily rent for a room with guarantees started at 2fr, as did a dinner with a little wine. A comforting bath with hot water would cost 0.2fr—a little more (0.6fr) with certain comforts; the price of gas was not very high either (from 0.15fr and 0.30fr), and bread—controlled—was 0.15fr per pound (450 grams).[24]

In conclusion, Louis-Napoléon and his advisers had two alternatives on the table. The first was to favour a group of businessmen (Raoux and *consorts*) who controlled a certain amount of money and several hundred workers, which was not significant enough to create a real problem for him. The second was to support a foreigner (which was risky), but who enjoyed an astonishing standard of support from numerous intellectuals, engineers, and leading composers (Meyerbeer, Adam, Berlioz, Halévy...), which was a very strong propaganda asset. Napoleon III chose the second option, not because of Sax or the health of the French brass industry, but because of the power and possibilities that culture had over public opinion and the legitimization of positions,[25] in his case of representation. Moreover, as Louis-Philippe had done earlier, Bonaparte was weakening that sector of the business community which was not likely to be loyal to him or had previously sympathized with republican ideas. Good public contracts such as those at stake might shape the political preferences of these traders, but that purchased support did not weigh heavily enough for his money—the State's—to reach them. On the other side, by backing Sax, Napoleon III not only instrumentalized a key sector of art in his favour (music, and especially opera and its tremendous symbolic associations), but he could also better seduce the people (bourgeois and ordinary) with those military marches and the multifarious and brilliant brasswinds of the energetic Belgian maker. Moreover, these spectacular bands would also prove to be another tool with which Napoleon III could adorn himself and enhance his prestige among his subjects and occasionally on the international stage. Indeed, one of the first orders these new military musical ensembles received was to travel to England and act as ambassadors for the French people and their leader.[26] According to the press, the Emperor's Guides had just visited London at the invitation of the British government, receiving standing ovations at each of its performances.

---

[24] *Galignani's* (1856), 6, 11, 33, 48, 60–6, 76, 101, 120–1, 134, and 352.

[25] Joaquín Piñeiro, 'La música como elemento de análisis histórico: el barroco y el clasicismo en la crisis del Antiguo Régimen', *Aula-Historia Social* 17 (2006), 57–64, 'La música como fuente para el análisis histórico: la historia actual', *Historia Actual On-Line* 5 (2004), 155–69, and 'Nuevos caminos de investigación en la historia del tiempo presente: la música como instrumento de análisis histórico', *Tiempo Presente. Revista de Historia* 2 (2014), 67–77.

[26] See also Patrick Péronnet, 'Musiques militaires et relations internationales de 1850 à 1914: le cas français', *Relations internationales* 155: 3 (2013), 50.

The chronicle also noted their participation in a macro-concert with fourteen bands from the English-speaking world in Sydenham Park. Afterwards, they entered the palace alone, where they were surrounded by more than 30,000 people and performed *God Save the Queen*, and the English reciprocated with cheers such as 'Vive l'Empereur! Vive Napoléon! Vivent les Français!'.[27]

---

[27] *Le Ménestrel*, 5 November 1854, 4 and *La presse musicale*, 23 November 1854 [2–4].

PART 2

CHARGE!

7
Hasty Raids

A Fiasco and a Second Wave of Aggressive Seizures of Instruments, Ledgers, and Machinery

After more than seven years of defending himself, and with the crushing victory at the Imperial Civil Court of Rouen on 28 June 1854 behind his back, Adolphe Sax went on the offensive. The prosecution became a criminal one, namely, built on the assumption that a crime had been committed, which added severity to the process and allowed for harsher penalties. By virtue of article 47 of the law of 5 July 1844 and the power conferred on him by the saxotromba patent, Sax requested the confiscation of numerous brass instruments that other manufacturers were illicitly producing. The president of the sixth chamber of the Criminal Court (*correctionnelle*) of Paris authorized this, and gave the order for the bailiffs (*huissiers de justice*) and the police to confiscate on 29 December 1854 the goods in question from the factories of Besson, Halary, Raoux, Labbaye, David, Georget, and Deschamps.[1] Needless to say, the raids were a very aggressive and disruptive type of action—not only instruments could be seized, but also tools, machinery, and books of information and records—which would further damage the professional relations between the brass entrepreneurs. However, these manufacturers succeeded in having the raids declared null and void on the basis of the provisions of article 47 of that law. On the grounds that Sax was a foreigner (Belgian), he should have deposited a security (*dépôt de cautionnement*)[2] before proceeding with the raid. Therefore, the same Court, under the presidency of Gislain de Bontin and after having heard the pleadings of Liouville and Dufaure, ruled on 3 May 1855 against Sax and annulled the prosecution proceedings he had initiated; in addition, of course, he was forced to pay compensation and the costs of the trial (*dépens*).

---

[1] *Annales de la propriété industrielle*, tomes 1 and 2, 1855–6, 46–7. Beauboeuf may also have been attacked. *Conclusions motivées pour Adolphe Sax, professeur au Conservatoire impérial de musique*, 84.

[2] Such deposits are popularly known in legal jargon as *judicatum solvi* and were intended to enable the attacker (outsider) to pay the damages resulting from a possible defeat.

Although he afterwards offered to pay the guarantee, Sax lodged an appeal, which was immediately rejected.³ The businessman set out to obtain naturalization as a French citizen and it was then that the political and media support apparatus raised its head again. On 10 May 1855, Sax applied to the Ministry of Justice for naturalization, accompanied by a letter of support from Colonel Fleury, *Premier Écuyer* and the Emperor's aide-de-camp. However, this application underwent several complications, not only because of time, money, and bureaucracy, but also because Sax was still bankrupt, which glaringly clashed with the outstanding values that candidates were supposed to possess.⁴ In any case, Sax had squandered his first offensive attempt through clumsiness, impatience, or ambition, and had also put the other manufacturers on their guard.

In order to avoid bail in the second round—which seemed inevitable at this point—he could resort to obtaining a residence permit as an intermediate step towards nationalization. Two days after this first procedural setback (5 May 1855), Sax appealed to the mayor of the former second *arrondissement* of Paris, in the presence of his friend Georges Kastner (presumably his advocate), on the premise that he wished to settle and establish his residence in France. If approved, the application would grant Sax civil rights, which, for legal purposes,⁵ exempted him from paying the pre-confiscation deposit. Within three months, on 4 August 1855, the Emperor signed an imperial decree approving Sax's residence request.⁶ Importantly, in the event of necessity or conflict, the approval would apply retroactively if resolved in the affirmative.

Knowing in advance that the petition would be successful, Sax organized a second offensive on 25 and 26 May 1855. This raid took place not only in the workshops and factories of the companies that allegedly copied him, but also within the grounds of the newly opened Paris Universal Exhibition of 1855.⁷ This offensive generated new legal cases, involving a new character,

---

³ *Annales de la propriété industrielle*, tome 3, 1857, 223.

⁴ [Auguste] Valette, *Explication Sommaire du Livre Premier du Code Napoléon et des lois accessoires* (Paris: Marescq, 1859), 14 and 34–5. As a curiosity, he would not have been naturalized either if he had married a French citizen, like his partner Louise-Adèle Maor (1830–60), with whom he already had a daughter (Anna-Emilia, b. 1853). The Code only provided for the acquisition of citizenship in favour of the woman, i.e. if the husband was French and the wife was from another country. In the case of Sax, the wife would adopt the nationality of her husband, i.e. Belgian.

⁵ Joseph-Adrien Rogron, *Codes français expliqués*, tome 1 [Code civil expliqué] (Paris: Videcoq/Alex-Gobelet, 1836), 5.

⁶ Malou Haine, *Adolphe Sax: sa vie, son œuvre, ses instruments de musique* (Brussels: Éditions de l'Université de Bruxelles, 1980), 180–1.

⁷ According to Sax, the irregular instruments could be identified through three signs: the overall shapes (*l'ensemble des formes*), the proportions of the tubes (*proportions des tubes*), and the way in which they

Michel Rivet.[8] Unfortunately for him, he could not cite article 47 in his pleading, so he based his defence on the insubstantiality (*non-brevetabilité*) of the saxotromba patent.[9] Rivet had not taken part in the previous civil case that culminated in Rouen (1854) and could therefore perhaps erect and sustain a renewed opposition.[10]

Sax and Rivet clashed in at least six hearings (26 July and 1 December 1855; 28 February, 6 March, 27 March, and 17 April 1856). These hearings also showed the extent to which French musicians, conductors, and various French entrepreneurs and lessors on one side or the other were polarized. For example, Blanc (director of the music band of the 9th Artillery Regiment), Brick (Paris artist), Buffet (maker of wooden and brass aerophones), Cathodeau (instrument dealer with a shop in Mexico), Caulle, Chaumont, Dupire, Ersham (former labourer, now dealer in household goods), Fermet (head of the 7th Artillery), Girauld-Huget, Guérin (trumpet major of the National Horse Guards), Kretzschmann (instrument maker based in Strasbourg), Lagnier (*ex-maître* [schoolmaster?] in La Loupe, a commune in the Eure-et-Loir department in northern France), Lebrun (former artist, toy dealer), Louis-François, Libert (ex-music officer of the 8th Legion), Grin-Lachapelle (ex-trader in Chartres, now lessor), Mithouard (grower in La Loupe), Sassaigne (manufacturer of valves and keys for instruments), and Texier (lessor) supported Rivet, arguing that there was nothing new in Sax's instruments and that prior to his patent (1845) they were freely traded.[11] Rivet reinforced this idea on 27 March 1856 by arguing that the characteristic alignment of the valves parallel to the bell of the instrument which made many brasswinds identifiable for seizing was widely known. In this respect, he

---

matched existing families (*étendue aux familles*). *Conclusions motivées pour Adolphe Sax, professeur au Conservatoire impérial de musique*, 10.

[8] Michel Rivet (b. 1805) was a Lyonnais maker who was active between 1839–70s. In 1840 he employed six people. Waterhouse, *The New Langwill*, 330, Pierre, *Les facteurs d'instruments*, 347, and Denis Watel, 'Facteurs d'instruments et luthiers a Lyon en 1840', *Larigot* 52 ([July] 2013), 17.

[9] *Annales de la propriété industrielle*, tome 3, 1857, 223. Rivet and his lawyers (Félix Liouville and Parmentier) pointed out that Guichard's *clavicor* was patented in 1838 and that the *néo-cor* and the cornet in B with parallel valves were already being manufactured in 1840. *Mémoire pour M. Rivet contre M. Sax: contrefaçon: instruments en cuivre. Pavillon en l'air—pistons parallèles au pavillon: tribunal civil de première instance. 6e chambre: présidence de M. le président Dubarle: jugement à prononcer le jeudi 17 avril 1856* (Paris: n. ed., [Typographie et Lithographie Maulde et Renou,] 1856), 1–2, 43, and 62.

[10] According to Pontécoulant, this strategy was designed and paid for by Gautrot. Pontécoulant, *Organographie*, vol. 2, 318–20. See also *Nullité de brevet. Instruments et brevets Sax. Tribunal Correctionnel de la Seine, 6me Chambre. Affaire Rivet contre Sax. Documents* (Paris: n. ed., [Imprimerie de Mme Dondey-Dupré,] 1855), 4–10, 37–9, 41–52, and 59–72. Rivet and Sax were previously involved in a minor dispute (c.1850) when a military musician ended up in Sax's workshop to have his saxophone made by Rivet repaired. Pontécoulant, *Organographie*, vol. 2, 303–4 and *RGMP*, 25 August 1850, 285.

[11] *Nullité de brevet. Instruments et brevets Sax. Tribunal Correctionnel de la Seine, 6me Chambre. Affaire Rivet contre Sax*, 11–35 and *Conclusions motivées pour Adolphe Sax, professeur au Conservatoire impérial de musique*, 48.

invited the court to consult the reports of the 1844 Exhibition where several such examples were exhibited.[12]

On the other side, the testimonies in favour of Adolphe Sax included those of Arban and Weber (musicians of the orchestras-Sax [sic], Opera, and Opéra-Comique), Boquillon, Buhaut (conductor of a Versailles ensemble), David (maker of brasswinds), Dunkler (conductor), Klosé, Noel-Firmin Michaud (supplier of instruments to the *Gymnase* until 1854), Thibault junior (musician of the 65th Line Regiment), Thibault senior (conductor of that band), and Weber.[13]

These opposing positions and the number of statements from both sides bring two interesting takeaways. First, that not all military bandmasters (and perhaps not all of their managers either, which was why these individuals were allowed to act as prosecution witnesses) felt that the musical reforms that the government had enacted for military bands in 1854–5 were appropriate and/or just. Second, that some musicians and manufacturers who had previously worked together to develop interesting products were now on different sides, such as Conservatoire professor Hyacinthe-Eléonore Klosé and builder Louis-Auguste Buffet (Buffet *jeune* [junior]).[14]

However, the battle with Rivet ended on 24 April 1856, when the Paris Criminal Court, sixth chamber, under the presidency of Dubarle, ruled in favour of Sax. The grounds of the ruling also pointed out that the saxotromba patent prohibited the manufacture of a *basse à quatre pistons* (bass with four valves) which Rivet made in his workshops, at least without asking permission or reaching an agreement with his rival. In any case, the judges definitively validated the 1855 seizure and fined Rivet 200fr; he would also have to pay another 500fr in damages.[15]

The procedural episode with Rivet is not very substantial; what was really interesting was the raid in the middle of the Exposition and, above all, the Emperor's approval of Sax's residence request so that he could pursue his rivals. Clearly, Napoleon III—or, rather, the military powers that had orchestrated his propaganda apparatus—could not afford to let the Belgian

---

[12] The dossier of that fair did not include any specific description. *Exposition des produits de l'industrie française en 1844. Rapport du Jury Central*, tome 2, 558–60.

[13] *M. Rivet contre M. Sax: tribunal de police correctionnelle: 6e chambre: audience du 27 mars 1856: présidence de M. Dubarle* (Paris: n. ed., [Imprimerie de Mme V[euv]e Dondey-Dupré,] 1856), 2–55.

[14] Buffet *jeune*, with the assistance of Klosé, patented (1843) a novel key system for clarinet (and oboe) that would prove to be the dominant version of the instrument in France and later in many other countries. Both practitioners took inspiration (technology) from a Munich maker (Theobald Boehm) who had (1832) applied it to the flute earlier. See, for example, Ardal Powell, *The Flute* (New Haven/London: Yale University Press, 2002), 152–8, 168–9, and 316–18; and Albert Rice, 'The Early History of the Nineteenth Century Boehm-System Clarinet', *Musique-Images-Instruments* 13 (2012), 131–7.

[15] *Annales de la propriété industrielle*, tome 3, 1857, 227–8.

inventor fall. In fact, Sax's brass instruments were at the forefront of the whole operation, as suggested by the fact that his instruments accompanied the imperial procession (trumpets of honour of the Hundred Guards and the mounted band of the Guides) on its way to the opening of the International Fair on 15 May 1855 (Figure 7.1).

On the other hand, Sax did not avoid the controversy after the inauguration and the usual raids. Adrien De la Fage, an intellectual and regular contributor to the *RGMP*, denounced that the organization gave preferential treatment to Sax, who, despite not taking part in the first few days, was awarded 'an excellent and eye-catching display (*une place fort apparente*)'.[16] The fact of late registration or certain irregularities suggests that Sax was still in financial difficulties. In any case, the journalist was telling the truth, as several photographs have made it possible for us to locate his impressive stand with a very long trumpet tube (?) rising towards the ceiling of the great hall and very close to the Saint Gobain arch (Figure 7.2). Certainly some of the brass populating

Figure 7.1 'Opening of the Universal Exhibition of 1855. Imperial procession', colour engraving (1855?), anonymous. Musée Carnavalet, Paris

[16] *RGMP*, 4 November 1855, 341–2.

Figure 7.2 Great Hall of the 1855 Exhibition with the stand of Sax
Photographer unknown. © Victoria and Albert Museum, London.

this sideboard were used for celebrations and adjacent concerts, but they certainly were present in the first visit of Queen Victoria and Prince Albert to the Exhibition, who heard *God Save the Queen* with 'organ, piano, and fanfares-Sax [sic]'.[17] It may be that not only his instrumental workmanship, but also

---

[17] *Le Ménestrel*, 26 August 1855, 3.

these key interventions likely contributed to Sax's credit and played a role in his achievement of the *Grande Médaille d'Honneur* or first prize in his category, shared with Boehm (from Bavaria),[18] Cavaillé-Coll (organs), and Vuillaume (luthier), both for France.[19] Moreover, Baron De Brisse drew some interesting conclusions, pointing out the excellent results that had been produced in brass instruments during the last thirty years due to the progress of metallurgy and skilful (*savants*) builders. According to him, 'numerous wooden instruments have had to make way for their brass rivals in the orchestras of the theatres'.[20] Before the Emperor presented the medals, De Brisse also reports that the imperial entourage while on its way to the Palais de l'Industrie was again escorted by 'two squadrons of the Guides, their colonel [Fleury], and the music in the lead'.[21]

---

[18] De la Fage, *Quinze visites musicales*, 204.
[19] In total, 223 French makers were listed in the official catalogue; of which thirty (thirty-seven unofficially) were wind specialists and some (Besson, Buffet-Crampon, Gautrot, Martin, Thibouville, Courtois, Halary, Labbaye, Michaud, Raoux, etc.) won a first or second class medal, two levels below Sax. *Exposition 1855. Rapports du jury mixte international* (Paris: Imprimerie Impériale, 1856) 11–12, 19, and 657; and *Le Ménestrel*, 18 November 1855, 2.
[20] Brisse, *Album de l'Exposition*, tome 3, 1859, 414.
[21] Brisse, *Album de l'Exposition*, tome 1, 102–10.

8
Gautrot or 'the Most Relentless Fighting Spectacle between Makers'
Double Resistance and Exhaustion

The brief legal altercation with Rivet, to which there was no appeal, was followed by a more complicated and bitter trial that would last almost eleven years. This battle pitted Adolphe Sax against Pierre-Louis Gautrot, a much more ferocious enemy who probably bore some of the procedural costs of the coalition of manufacturers who took part in the earlier civil case.[1] Gautrot (1812–82) entered the musical instrument manufacturing business in 1835 thanks to Jean-Auguste Guichard, inventor of the *clavicor* (1838) and champion of French brasswind manufacture. The latter entrepreneur was able to recognize in 1837 the business acumen of Gautrot (who also eventually became his future brother-in-law) to whom he transferred in 1845—for the modest sum of 2000fr per year—full control of the firm, which was to be renamed 'Gautrot-*Aîné* [senior]'.[2] Originally, the workshops were located at the foot of Notre-Dame de Paris cathedral itself (6, rue Cloître-Notre-Dame),[3] but Gautrot moved them (1849–50)[4] to the Hôtel Voysin, a four-storey building at 60, rue Saint-Louis—later called rue Turenne—in the Marais district. It housed some 200 workers and also served as an official shop (Figure 8.1). Before the middle of the nineteenth century, this manufacturer officially accounted for 42% of the workforce (208 workers) in Paris, while Sax was at the head of an establishment of some seventy-six workers.[5] Gautrot claimed to export to New York, London, Madrid, Naples, etc. and his production was not only limited to brass, but also extended to

---

[1] *Dispositif du jugement rendu le 19 août 1848, par la 4e Chambre du Tribunal de première instance de la Seine, entre MM. Raoux, Halary, Gantrot [sic], Buffet et Gambaro*, cover.

[2] William Waterhouse, 'Gautrot-Aîné, First of the Moderns', *Brass Scholarship in Review: Proceeding of the Historic Brass Society Conference, Cité de la Musique, Paris, 1999* (Bucina: The Historic Brass Society series) 6 (2006), 121–5.

[3] *Exposition des produits de l'industrie française en 1839*, tome 2, 361–2.

[4] *Rapport du Jury Central sur les produits de l'Agriculture et de l'Industrie exposés en 1849*, tome 2, 602.

[5] The 1847–8 survey distributed the brass entrepreneurs by districts and we know in which districts both manufacturers operated. *Statistique de l'industrie à Paris (1847–1848)*, 817.

Figure 8.1 Interior view of the shop and/or warehouse of the Gautrot factory in the Marais district, Paris
L'Illustration, 21 July 1855, 45.

woodwinds, percussion, and stringed instruments.⁶ In 1855, he opened a second musical instrument production plant with another 320 employees in Château-Thierry, a town ninety kilometres from Paris. The Château-Thierry site had a quay directly on the River Marne, a tributary of the Seine and therefore connected to Paris, which was a very interesting logistical advantage. Gautrot was therefore one of the most important musical instrument makers at the time, not only in France, but in the world.

Gautrot lodged a complaint against the seizures of 25 and 26 May that Sax had instigated in his [Gautrot's] workshops and at the Universal Exhibition in Paris in 1855. The trial began on 26 December 1855 and the representatives were former ministers Marie and Dufaure. The fact that these excellent lawyers⁷ were hired again, at a considerable cost, for this

---

⁶ *L'Illustration*, 21 July 1855, 43–5.
⁷ 'At the end of each session, when the debates had strayed and it was time to conclude them, [Dufaure] would ask for the floor. In his possession, he simplified and reeled it in, surrounded it with interesting reasoning and wrapped it in his proofs as a spinner (*ménagère*) spins the spindle between her nimble fingers: he thus unfurled (*pousse*) his [argumentative] threads in all directions, grouped them together, intertwined them, and made a web so souple, so dense, that his adversary, trapped (*enveloppé*), was obliged to kneel down and admit defeat.' Robert and Cougny, dirs, *Dictionnaire des parlementaires français depuis*, tome 2, 454.

type of case, which might at first sight have looked rather trivial, reflects the intensity with which litigation and competition for control of a thriving market was actually being fought. Marie and Gautrot initially asked—to no avail—for the deposit described in article 47 of the 1844 law; they knew that arguing for the revocation of the saxotromba patent on the grounds of formal defects and lack of novelty was not a fruitful avenue. Therefore, they had to follow a different defensive strategy in the certainty that they would surely lose and would have to bear financial costs. However, as was to be expected, they emphasized again the lack of originality of the Belgian entrepreneur's constructive ideas, which they now considered as their own.[8] Gautrot pointed out that his *néo-alto* and *bombardon* met all the conditions of the saxotromba, including the parallel alignment of the valves in relation to the bell. Gautrot did not register any instrument called the *néo-alto* and which, by inference, it was a new version or model of *alto*, that is, a generic name for a brass instrument with a middle range (i.e. it is between the treble and bass). Nor has any physical specimen survived-or been identified, if it really existed.[9] The only source is iconographic and partial, and belongs to a *factum* that defended Rivet's positions (Figure 8.2).

Somewhat less contentious is the term *bombardon* which, technical details notwithstanding,[10] is likely to have given rise to ophicleides with valves, but without keys. Although they supposedly originated in Austria (1833) thanks to Wenzel Riedl,[11] what was relevant for the present case—the introduction and appropriation of the technology in France—was the fact that Guichard

---

[8] They also attempted to prove their superiority by comparing Sax's modest business with their own, as Gautrot allegedly made an annual profit of 800,000fr and had no need to engage with lesser competitors, unless he was provoked, as was the case here.

[9] Brass makers did not usually inscribe the name of the instruments or their tuning on the bell, but simply—if at all—the author, the brand name, or some distinctive mark. As a curiosity, the first Sax's saxhorn/saxotromba on which an identifying inscription appears is dated 1861, and from then on it became a slightly more common practice. <http://www.euchmi.ed.ac.uk/am/gdsl.html> (accessed 1 August 2023). Instruments from Sax's licensees—as will be discussed subsequently—usually had the term 'saxhorn' engraved on the bell and, in most cases, an appellation for the register such as *Basse*, *Contrebasse*, or *Baryton*. Bruno Kampmann, 'Licences accordées par Adolphe Sax à ses concurrents pour la fabrication des cuivres', *Larigot* 42 ([September] 2008), 10, 12, 14, and 17.

[10] Renato Meucci, 'The *Cimbasso* and Related Instruments in 19th-Century Italy', *The Galpin Society Journal* 49 (1996), 148–57 and 'Brass Bands and the Brass Instrument Industry in 19th Century Milan', in Tiroler Landesmuseen-Betriebsges, ed., *Wissenschaftliches Jahrbuch der Tiroler Landesmuseen* ([Innsbruck?]: Tiroler Landesmuseen-Betriebsges, 2010), 109–13. See also Baines, *The Oxford Companion to Musical Instruments*, 37 and Campbell, Greated and Myers, *Musical Instruments*, 170.

[11] Günter Dullat, *Fast vergessene Blasinstrumente aus zwei Jahrhunderten* (Nauheim: Dullat, 1997), 26–7 and Ignace De Keyser, 'The Keyed Ophicleide as a Paradigm in the Development of New Wind Instruments in the 1830s and 1840s', in *Vom Serpent zur Tuba (Entwicklung und Einsatz dertiefen Polsterzungeninstrumente mit Grifflöchern und Ventilen)*, [Proceedings of] XLI. Wissenschaftliche Arbeitstagung und 33. Musikinstrumentenbau-Symposium Michaelstein, 7. bis 9. November 2014. (Augsburg and Michaelstein: Wißner and Kloster, 2019), 69–81.

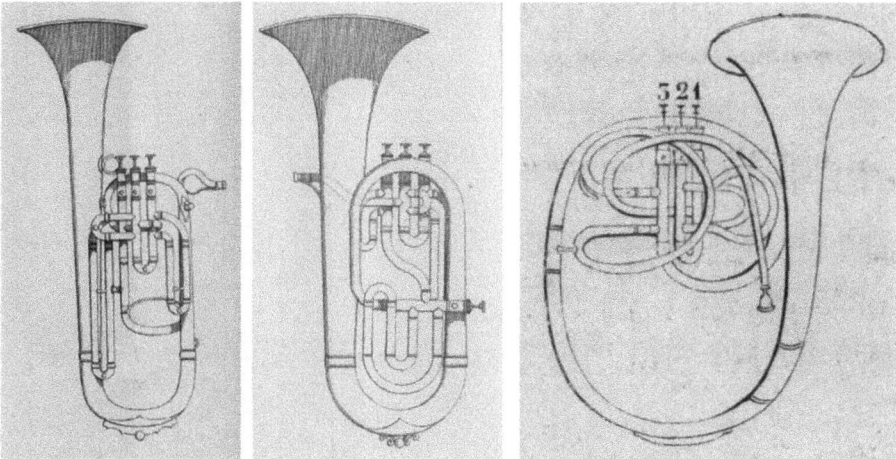

Figure 8.2 Presumptive E♭ *néo-alto* (left), B♭ Bass *bombardon* (centre), and a monster ophicleide (right)

Nullité de brevet. Instruments et brevets Sax. Tribunal Correctionnel de la Seine, 6me Chambre. Affaire Rivet contre Sax. Documents (Paris: n. ed., [Imprimerie de Mme Dondey-Dupré,] 1855), n.p. [planche no. 2] (BnF) (left and centre) and Kastner, *Traité général d'instrumentation*, 57 (BnF) (right).

patented an *ophicléide à pistons* (ophicleide with valves [or pistons]) on 29 December 1835 (Figure 8.3). That first model with the pistons perpendicular to the bell was tuned in E♭ and also had two more crooks to transport it to C or B. Informally, the name *bombardon* came to designate in France this type of long-tube brass—hence, bass—and predominantly conical with valves. Kastner (1837) gave them a new meaning ('Ophicléïde monstre', because they were rather large) and gave us two interesting designs, one of them with pistons parallel to the bell (Figure 8.2). According to the Strasbourg theorist, these specimens made 'all the passages with accuracy and rapidity, and had already been adopted in the French military bands'. He further noted that 'they could be considered as the double bass [string bass, in analogy to the string orchestra] (*la contrebasse*) of military music and were well established in the band (*musique d'harmonie*) where they were [or performed the function of] a perfect bass (*basse*) which we had always lacked [in France]'.[12] Gautrot's argument stemmed from somewhere along the process in which the bombardons developed and diversified—they took a multitude of different

---

[12] Georges Kastner, *Traité général d'instrumentation, comprenant les propriétés et l'usage de chaque instrument, précédé d'un résumé sur les voix, à l'usage des jeunes compositeurs* (Paris: Prilipp, [1836]), 57–8. Gautrot offered it in his advertising and it cost 90fr. *Manuf^re d'Instruments de Musique* [Gautrot, 1850], 16.

134 The Battle for Control of the Brass and Instruments Business

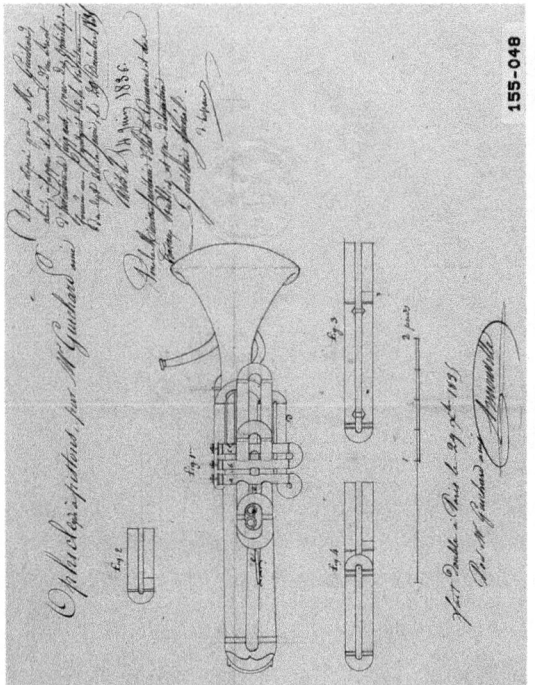
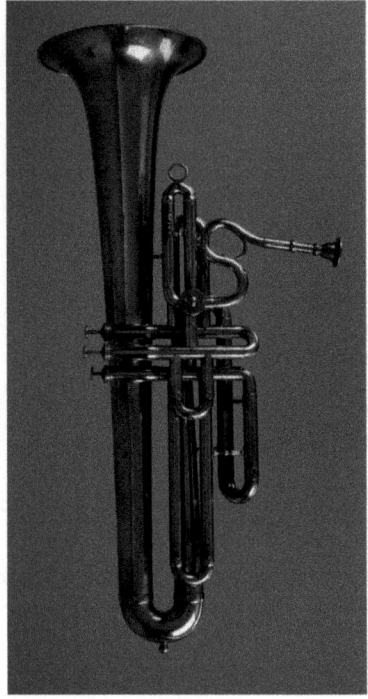

Figure 8.3 Guichard's original patent design for an *ophicléide [ophicleyde] à pistons* (1835) (left) and Gautrot's original instrument—E♭ ophicleide with pistons or bombardon, E.1450 (possibly third quarter of the nineteenth century) (right)

Patent [no. 6851] of Jean-Auguste Guichard of 29 December 1835 [for five years] for 'Ophicleides with valves (*des ophicléides [ophicleydes] à pistons*)', 7 (INPI) and Collections Musée de la Musique, Paris (Photographer: Thierry Ollivier).

forms—in France (and Europe),[13] including presumably the one that Sax had protected.

Gautrot also complained that he had been the victim of plundering and denounced the alleged slander Sax had cast on him. He was also surprised and mocked at his opponent's audacity in asking for 50fr compensation for each seized and allegedly forged instrument. But he was nevertheless open to negotiation and offered him a deal—ironically, he called it a 'sacrifice'— at the rate of 2000fr or 3000fr per month until the patents expired and on condition that he could freely manufacture any instrument. Gautrot's final

---

[13] Sax's father (Charles-Joseph) patented on 7 July 1842 in Belgium a 'New combination of valves for ophicleides and other bass instruments (*nouvelle combinaison de cylindres applicables aux ophicléides et aux autres instruments de basse*)'.

(and tempting) proposal was for 100,000fr, a sum which Sax refused[14] either because he considered it unfair or because he thought that delaying the lawsuit might yield greater financial returns. In any case, the situation was serious and the sums of money involved were increasing. Moreover, the financial offers implicitly admitted that the saxotromba patent had punitive authority.

In the absence of an agreement, the debates continued and Marie repeatedly brought up the word 'monopoly'. Moreover, he found a loophole in the Code of Criminal Procedure (*Code d'instruction criminelle*),[15] articles 637 and 638,[16] whereby certain offences, not precisely defined and among which Marie included counterfeiting (*contrefaçon*), were subjected to a three-year statute of limitations. Therefore, Gautrot, even accepting the case law less favourable to him, would only have to provide explanations for the instruments produced between 25 May 1852 and the day of the raid, that is, 25 May 1855. However, Dufaure stressed the 'enormous losses' [sic] that the illicit copying of the instruments had caused his client and the considerable profits that, particularly Gautrot, 'had amassed at the expense of this practice'.[17] The lawyer also highlighted that it was not a simple infringement of copied objects, but a case of 'mass production, made on illegal mandrels, and therefore giving rise to an successive offence (*délit successif*)'.[18] Dufaure also sought the court's sympathy and connivance by asserting that Gautrot had taken advantage of fifteen years of his client's work and research. He further linked him to the makers who initiated and prolonged the earlier civil case for the sole purpose of hindering prosecutions (*empêcher les poursuites*) and keeping him at bay (*le tenir ainsi en échec*) until the expiry of the patents.[19] A

---

[14] *Note pour M. Gautrot contre M. Adolphe Sax. Tribunal correctionnel de la Seine. 6me Chambre. Audience du jeudi. Présidence de M. Dubarle* (Paris: n. ed. [Imprimerie de Mme Veuve Dondey-Dupré,] n.d. [1856]), 1–7, 11, and 15–16; and *Note pour M. Adolphe Sax contre M. Gautrot: tribunal correctionnel de la Seine: sixième chambre* (Paris: n. ed., [Imprimerie Charles de Mourgues Frères,] 1856), 26.

[15] The *Code d'instruction criminelle* was the compendium of legal texts that determined the forms or procedures for prosecuting offences or crimes on the basis of justice, while the *Code pénal* was another set of regulations that defined or typified these infractions, as well as the punishment to be applied in each case.

[16] Rogron, *Codes français expliqués*, tome 2 [Code d'instruction criminelle expliqué], 310–15.

[17] Confirming Marie's data, Gautrot amassed 500,000fr of profit each year from brass. The rest of the profits (about 300,000fr) were made from wood, percussion, strings, and other accessories for instruments. *Note pour M. Gautrot contre M. Adolphe Sax. Tribunal correctionnel de la Seine. 6me Chambre. Audience du jeudi. Présidence de M. Dubarle*, 16. However, Marie also said that, despite these figures, Gautrot's net dividends were, 'in general, not very high'. Furthermore, he noted that the money his client earned from the brass with valves parallel to the bell—that is, Sax proprietary form—was at most one ninth (*un neuvième au plus*) of this total of half a million francs. The rest was made up of a 'heap of instruments all different, with perpendicular valves, with keys... (*Le surplus se compose d'une foule d'instruments tout différents, à pistons perpendiculaires, à clefs, etc., etc.*)'.

[18] In response to this accusation, Gautrot argued that the seized 'patterns, mandrels, or models (*patrons, mandrins ou modèles*)' could not only be used to make sax-instruments, but also for another type. *Note pour M. Gautrot contre M. Adolphe Sax. Tribunal correctionnel de la Seine. 6me Chambre. Audience du jeudi. Présidence de M. Dubarle*, 12.

[19] *Annales de la propriété industrielle*, tome 3, 1857, 229–30.

fiery and hyperbolic *factum* by Sax recounting the episode included annexes (*pièces justificatives*) with press entries on the matter and several letters that the Belgian inventor had managed to intercept from the coalition of manufacturers.[20] One of them was the agreement signed on 27 June 1854—the eve of the momentous civil judgement of Rouen that validated Sax—by which the manufacturers compelled themselves to continue to litigate and delegitimize their rival and his patents.

After at least two hearings on 17 and 24 April 1856, the latter coinciding with that of Michel Rivet,[21] the president of the sixth chamber of the Paris Court of First Instance (Dubarle)[22] ruled in favour of Sax on 12 June of the same year. According to the decision, Gautrot's guilt was proven and the confiscation that had taken place in the workshops of this maker and in the Palais de l'Industrie at the 1855 Exhibition was considered legitimate. Moreover, by applying articles 40 and 49 of the 1844 law, Gautrot would pay the maximum amount (2000fr) provided for in the regulations and the confiscated instruments would become the property of Sax, who would also be exempt from paying the costs of the trial. With regard to the prescription period— the most interesting aspect of the process—and considering that 'articles 637 and 638 of the Code of Criminal Procedure were generic (*généraux*), and that the statute of limitations also applied to piracy (*contrefaçon*) or any other crime [of a public or civil nature, not blood crimes]', Dubarle decided to open an investigation to find out the real extent of the criminal acts. To this end, and because 'the Court did not have the necessary elements to determine the amount', he considered it 'indispensable' [sic] to appoint a commission of three persons for this purpose, led by Boquillon. The other two specialists were to be Verre and Richardière, 'experts, accounting assistants (*teneurs de livres*)', who were ordered 'to collate the seized books, as well as other records, memoirs, correspondence, invoices, inventories, and those documents of the *maison* Gautrot', which were necessary to complete the report. Dubarle justified the scale of these enquiries by alluding to the

---

[20] *Note pour M. Adolphe Sax contre M. Gautrot: tribunal correctionnel de la Seine: sixième chambre*, 29–38. See also *Conclusions motivées pour Adolphe Sax, professeur au Conservatoire impérial de musique*, 91–5.

[21] *Note pour M. Adolphe Sax contre M. Gautrot: tribunal correctionnel de la Seine: sixième chambre*, 1–4.

[22] Dubarle had previously been one of the examining magistrates (at least since 1843) of the Paris Residing Court (*Petit parquet*) of First Instance and a member of the General Council of the department of Seine-et-Marne. *Almanach Royal et National pour 1843* (Paris: Guyot et Scribe, 1843), 873 and *Almanach Royal et National pour 1845* (Paris: Guyot et Scribe, 1845), 620. He was previously a lawyer at the Royal Court of Paris in 1830. *Revue encyclopédique ou analyse raisonnée des productions les plus remarquables dans les sciences, les arts industriels, la littérature et les beaux-arts*, tome 45 (Paris: Baudouin frères, 1830), 171. As an author, he published (1829) a history of the University of Paris where he highlighted in the preface of the book the 'public and honourable homage that one of the princes of the royal family has paid [to the University]', as his highness had entrusted the education of his children to this institution. Eugène Dubarle, *Histoire de l'Université de Paris* (Paris: Firmin Didot frères, 1844), xi–x.

complexity of the case, 'composed of a series of acts which are reproduced and interlinked; ... which are perpetuated and renewed at every moment' and which therefore constituted a successive offence; with the aggravating factor that Gautrot was 'both manufacturer and seller at the same time'.[23] The judge dictated that the exploration of the records should happen soon (1 October 1845), prior—by twelve days—to the date of the saxotromba patent. In addition, and while this uncomfortable audit of Gautrot's firm was being carried out, Dubarle fixed a provision of 50,000fr in favour of Sax on the basis of article 188 of the Code of Criminal Procedure itself.[24] This type of pre-resolutionary measures—which are another noteworthy aspect of these confrontations—was highly controversial, and the law dictated that it 'should only be applied in exceptional circumstances and with great circumspection'. Evidently, they could be very damaging and there was a possibility that the magistrate could be wrong and the innocence of the aggravated party could be proven in the end.

That ruling was perhaps more negative than expected, and Gautrot escalated it to Appeal. But, prior to that assault, Gautrot had obtained a preliminary hearing—*une audience spéciale pour statuer sur la question de provision*, noted the chroniclers Pataille and Huget—to decide whether to authorize or not a financial advance, which, to complicate matters further, he managed to win. On the basis of the replies of Marie for the appellant and *Maître* Allou for Sax, and the conclusions of the prosecutor Barbier, the court, on 13 August 1856, made the complainant pay for the costs of the trial and, what was worse for the latter, it released Gautrot from the obligation to pay 50,000fr.[25] The situation was now equal for both sides; or, rather, Gautrot gained time and managed to leave Sax momentarily without liquidity to relieve his pressing financial state. In any case, Gautrot's appeal was still pending and the two businessmen were to face for the first time a higher criminal court, namely the Imperial Court in Paris, for which Dufaure was recalled, while Gautrot was still entrusted to Marie. During several busy hearings that lasted until February of the following year (20 and 27 December 1856; 9, 17, 23, and 24 January 1857; 6 February 1857),[26] the strategy of the defendant focused on reopening the debate on the authenticity of the saxotromba patent (inconsistency of the document, lack of novelty, and premature disclosure), but, significantly, under the interpretative perspective of the jurisdiction in which they were at the time. Marie wanted to draw upon articles 46 and 48 of the 1844 law, which essentially allowed criminal courts to also discuss issues of

---

[23] *Annales de la propriété industrielle*, tome 3, 1857, 232–5.
[24] Rogron, *Codes français expliqués*, tome 2 [Code d'instruction criminelle expliqué], 96.
[25] *Annales de la propriété industrielle*, tome 3, 1857, 235–6.
[26] *RGMP*, 5 April 1857, 115–18.

patent substantiality.[27] This purported new approach and other dense legal ruses and aphorisms (e.g. the 'reus [in] excipiendo fit actor')[28] failed to convince the president (Zangiacomi) to reopen the debate on the legitimacy of the saxotromba patent in his ruling of 28 February 1857. The judge's basic argument for blocking this request was that the case met the conditions for the application of article 1351 of the Civil Code, namely that of the authority of *res judicata* (*l'autorité de la chose jugée*). This provision had a double effect: on the one hand, it confirmed a previous judgement—it bound the previous parties and courts on that point—and, on the other, it prevented the opening of a new avenue of confrontation on the same subject of litigation.[29]

The previous conclusions on 6 February 1857 of Attorney General Roussel[30] were very straightforward and supported the theses of the inventor of the saxophone. Among other corollaries, Roussel recognized that 'articles 30 and 32 [of the 1844 law] offered counterfeiters marvellous facilities [sic] to prolong debates almost indefinitely'. He also noted that article 42 only allowed the offender to be punished with a single penalty which could not exceed 2000fr for the offences as a whole, even if the damage caused was much greater. He also said that Sax had suffered numerous calamities and that his products were threatened by unfair competition.[31] Roussel also recalled the Belgian businessman's curricular merits, among which he was selected by the French Army to improve its military music. To accompany this honour, he read a letter from Rumigny in which the former aide-de-camp to Louis-Philippe claimed to have recognized Sax's potential ('a young manufacturer with a nascent reputation') when he moved to France. The prosecutor pointed to the existence of a defamatory coalition of manufacturers, with Gautrot as one of its main leaders, recalling also that this businessman had tried to sponsor Rivet to bring a new lawsuit against Sax. To intensify his denunciation, he added that Gautrot possessed the means to

---

[27] At the same time, the music press amplified this truculent judicial wrangling and published the rulings and appeals of the most important hearings of 1856 and 1857. See, for example, *RGMP*, 8 March 1857, 78 and 15 March 1857, 84.

[28] Marie was possibly seeking a relaxation in the rigidity with which the judge was punitively interpreting the authority of the saxotromba patent over other instruments, which was hindering and distorting the judicial assessment of the evidence.

[29] Rogron, *Codes français expliqués*, tome 2 [Code d'instruction civil expliqué], 448–50.

[30] Roussel had twenty-seven years of service and the Emperor would grant him the Legion of Honour in 1861. *Bulletin des lois de l'Empire Français*, tome 16, 1861, 293.

[31] Gautrot and Sax must also have been involved in economic complaints and arbitration in which the Paris Commercial Court had to mediate. Sax defended himself against accusations of unfair competition and asserted the weight of the law and his patents against his opponents. In addition to a few insults towards them ('impotent and envious'), he pointed to Gautrot as the head of the coalition of makers who were trying to ruin him and circumvent his property rights. Sax enclosed an alleged letter dated 10 June 1852 in which Gautrot urged all his colleagues to attend a meeting at his house in order to coordinate and battle better. *Tribunal de commerce de Paris. Audience du 8 novembre 1862. Concurrence déloyale. Sax contre Gautrot* (Paris: n. ed., [Imp. de N. Chaix,] 1862), 2–5.

counterfeit and copy illegally on a large scale (*Chez M. Gautrot, au contraire, la contrefaçon s'exerce en grand*). Roussel added his personal perception to his pleading by saying that Gautrot's attitude was 'an evil action, [sponsored in] a coalition directed, with unparalleled obstinacy, against an inventor full of merit'. Finally, he added that the defendant intended to 'take refuge in the statute of limitations and thus find impunity'. He therefore urged the court to punish him in the damages section with an exemplary fine commensurate with such a 'bold, persevering, and continuous' offence.[32] This determination of the prosecutor, but also the coverage and alignment of the trade press in favour of Sax, annoyed the rest of the manufacturers indirectly involved.[33]

However, Marie's arguments had led Zangiacomi to continue considering the advance of 50,000fr to Sax unnecessary until the investigations ordered by the judgement of 12 June 1856 had been completed. In reality, this decision was a success for Gautrot, who managed to delay his punishment while Sax suffered financially and strategically: there were only three years left for his main patents (the saxophone and the saxotromba) to enter the public domain. Moreover, Gautrot had introduced a new product on the market which, according to the most authoritative sources of the time and other more recent authors,[34] directly attacked the saxophone. Pontécoulant (1861) commented that Gautrot wanted to 'counterbalance the acceptance and vogue' of the latter instrument with a 'gross copy (*grossière imitation*)', which he called the sarrusophone[35] (Figure 8.4).

That new double-reed instrument with conical tube was protected on 9 June 1856 individually and as a family, one of Sax's key ideas for saxophones and saxotrombas.[36] Gautrot claimed that the participation of all the low, middle, and high models of the sarrusophone, the full range of the orchestra was covered, an approach—according to him—which had not worked before with the brass (*pour les instruments à embouchure les ressources étaient trop restreintes*).[37] Although he also said that its fingering was very similar

---

[32] *RGMP*, 5 April 1857, 115–18.
[33] *RGMP*, 22 March 1857, 94.
[34] Jeremy Montagu, *The World of Romantic & Modern Musical Instruments* (London: David & Charles, 1981), 60 and *The Industrial Revolution*, 115.
[35] Pontécoulant, *Organographie*, vol. 2, 513.
[36] The name sarrusophone was an eponym combining the Greek suffix with the surname of a distinguished French military musician, conductor, and decorated officer (Legion of Honour), Pierre-Auguste Sarrus (1813–76), who allegedly helped Gautrot develop this invention. José-Modesto Diago, 'Gautrot and His Sarrusophone Revisited: A Multidisciplinary Approach', *Journal of the American Musical Instrument Society* 48 (2022), 162–90.
[37] Patent [no. 28034] of Pierre-Louis Gautrot of 9 June 1856 [for fifteen years] for 'A musical instrument called Sarrusophone (*un instrument de musique dit: Sarrusophone*)', n.p. [1–2] (INPI). Gautrot would later sign a second patent on 20 May 1865.

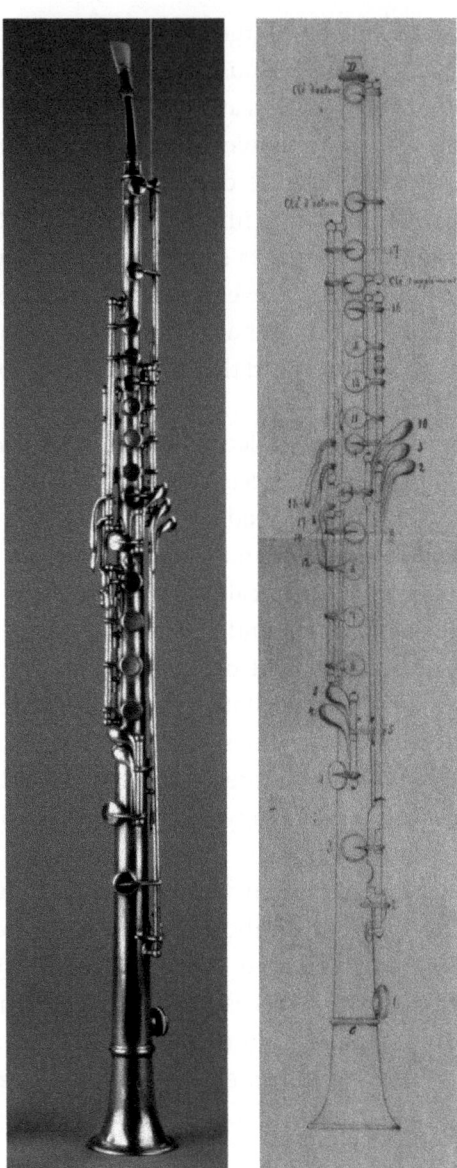

Figure 8.4 Gautrot-Marquet soprano sarrusophone (second half of the nineteenth century), E.1164 (left) and design of the Patent of the sarrusophone (1865) (right)

Collections Musée de la Musique, Paris (Photographer: Thierry Ollivier) and Patent [no. 67433] of Pierre-Louis Gautrot of 20 May 1865 [for fifteen years] for 'Improvements to the sarrusophone family (*perfectionnements apportés à la famille des sarrusophones*)', n.p. [12] (INPI).

to that of the clarinet (*presque semblable à celui de la Clarinette*)—which is rather uncertain due to the sound properties of the conical and cylindrical tubes—he avoided referring to the saxophone to avoid problems. We do not know how much the first sarrusophones costed, nor how many of them found their way into bands or orchestras in those early years; probably very few. The earliest Gautrot catalogue with the selling price dates from 1865. This advertisement proves that sarrusophones were cheaper than their (presumably) saxophone counterparts, enjoying a respectable discount starting at 40fr for a soprano and extending to 60fr for the baritone.[38]

Returning to the legal arena, Gautrot and his new lawyer (*Maître* Achille Morin), following their strategy of attrition and delaying the proceedings, filed an appeal in cassation on the basis of four theses (*moyens*), the first and the fourth twofold.[39] Gautrot's argument drew on various doctrinal sources[40] and sought to show that he had been the victim of various procedural irregularities and injustices. Furthermore, he insisted that he was right to reopen the debates on the form and substance of the saxotromba patent in a criminal forum.[41] However, Laplagne-Barris, president of the chamber, who had heard the conclusions of Attorney General Guyho, dismissed almost all his appeals on 8 August 1857. Without going into each of these explanations and their opaque deployment, the most substantial argument was that the magistrate considered the civil courts as the primary venue for the actions of patent revocation and loss. Article 34 of the 1844 law explicitly stated this, although he acknowledged that article 46 also stated that this could be done through the prosecutorial channel. However, as the matter had already been arbitrated in civil proceedings and the content, the actors, and the quality of these were the same, there was no room for Gautrot's complaint.

To further muddle the issue, the defence of Sax (*Maître* Paul Fabre)[42] did not manage to prevent his rival from obtaining a partial victory. The argumentation of the first part of Gautrot's fourth thesis convinced the court that the meaning of the term 'successive offence' had been distorted (*méconnu*) and that articles 637 and 638 of the Code of Criminal Procedure (prescription of offences after three years) had been violated. Laplagne-Barris

---

[38] *RGMP*, 27 March 1864, 104 and *Catalogue des instruments de musique de la Manufacture Générale de Gautrot aîné. À Paris, rue Saint-Louis (Marais, 60) et À Château-Thierry (Aisne).* ['80 rue Turenne', handwritten] (Paris: n. ed., [Imprimerie Édouard Blot,] 1865), 8, 10, and 12.

[39] *RGMP*, 12 April 1857, 125.

[40] The law of 1844, the Napoleon Code (or Civil Code), the Code of Criminal Procedure, and the law of 20 April 1810.

[41] *Mémoire pour M. Gautrot aîné contre M. Sax: cour de cassation: chambre criminelle* (Paris: n. ed., [Imprimerie de J. Claye,] 1857), 4–17.

[42] Paul Fabre worked as a lawyer at the Court of Cassation (at least from 1844), and was a former president of the order of the lawyers of the Council of State. Auguste Galopin, *Des voituriers par terre, par eau et par chemin de fer ou Traité théorique et pratique des transports* (Paris: Henri Plon, 1866), 5 and *Almanach Royal et National pour 1844*, 997. He was also involved in the legal advice for the construction of the Suez Canal. Ernest Desplaces, *Le canal de Suez, épisode de l'histoire du XIXe siècle* (Paris: Hachette, 1858), 280.

acknowledged that 'the more or less considerable manufacture of counterfeit objects could not be considered as a whole and reduced to a single offence'; i.e. he needed greater chronological accuracy ('each [of these offences] was subject to a different statute of limitations').[43] The president therefore annulled the judgement of 28 February 1857 in this respect and referred the case back to the Imperial Court of Rouen.[44]

Once again, Gautrot bought time and postponed his punishment while Sax's patents approached their expiry date. The final hearing in Rouen would take more than ten months (24 June 1858) and the chroniclers themselves (Pataille and Huguet) were surprised by the delay and the vicissitudes of this confrontation.[45] During this interval, the two manufacturers used the press—which was eager to amplify and fuel this heated dispute—to publicly throw numerous accusations at each other. The *Revue et Gazette Musicale de Paris* reproduced a letter from Sax, which he had previously sent from *Le Constitutionnel*. In it, he asked the editor-in-chief to correct certain 'inaccuracies' published in that newspaper about him and the trials he was holding in order to be able to defend himself against a large number of forgers acting collegially and maliciously (*la plus indigne des coalitions*). Sax stressed that the intention of his opponents was to prolong the case and wear him down by releasing numerous commercial prospectuses with illegal instruments, and also creating a public opinion campaign against him. However, the Belgian businessman already considered himself the winner because, although the Court of Cassation partially agreed with Gautrot, it judicially recognized him [Sax] as the victim of a *contrefaçon* on which the Imperial Court of Rouen was to determine only temporary details. In closing, he thanked his fellow manufacturers who, since the 1854 ruling, had recognized his rights.[46] (Sax was referring to his licensees, a matter which will be dealt with later.)

Gautrot's reaction did not take long, and he sent the same musical journal (*RGMP*) a first communiqué which must have been so long that they would not let him publish it.[47] He therefore wrote a second, shorter letter which, this time (1 November 1857), was indeed printed.[48] Gautrot accused the inventor of the saxophone of misleading or confusing (*égarer*) public opinion and preparing in his favour the debates that were about to take place at the Imperial Court of Rouen. Gautrot also demanded equal treatment by the media, as he considered that *Le Constitutionnel* and the *Revue et Gazette*

---

[43] *Annales de la propriété industrielle*, tome 3, 1857, 267.
[44] *RGMP*, 6 September 1857, 295 and *Le Ménestrel*, 13 September 1857, 4.
[45] *Annales de la propriété industrielle*, tome 5, 1859, 34.
[46] *RGMP*, 11 October 1857, 335.
[47] *RGMP*, 25 October 1857, 351.
[48] *RGMP*, 1 November 1857, 359.

Musicale de Paris had sided with his rival. He then launched a direct attack on the saxhorns, about whom he found numerous contradictions and described them as frauds. Relying on the *Manuel général de musique militaire*, the most important work by Georges Kastner—a stalwart (*panégyriste*) of Sax, Gautrot emphasized—he argued that his rival simply reformed the usual and customary bugles, that is, what all French and European manufacturers had been doing for a long time. Gautrot ended by complaining that it was 'precisely by means of this often-repeated subterfuge [i.e. renaming the immense range of brass instruments saxhorns] that Sax has led the public to believe that he was the inventor of a whole family of instruments which had revolutionized military music'.[49]

However, ignoring Gautrot's claim of impartiality, the *RGMP* published in the same issue (1 November 1857) an article of almost three pages—one of which took up half the front page—with the suggestive title 'Intellectual property from the point of view of morale and progress'.[50] The unidentified introducer of that entry (which might have been the editor of the journal), stated that 'our colleague [referring to the author of the essay, Oscar Comettant] and collaborator raised (*invoque*) an ensemble of arguments in support of his theses that become axioms'. That manifesto—which was also dedicated to Adolphe Sax—was previously a brochure that had to be recycled for the time to counter Gautrot's statements. Although the essayist's reasoning evidently did not point directly at him—rather, it had a general tone—the point of reference was undoubtedly Sax. From the presumed vulnerability of the situation as an inventor, to the parsimony of civil justice, Comettant deployed a whole string of considerations that seem to closely mirror what happened, also citing Jobard and Boquillon.

On the other hand, Gautrot left a very illustrative *factum* because, as a maker and specialist in brass instruments, he analysed the patent for the saxotromba. Gautrot concluded that the wording and description of Sax's document did not include anything about pistons parallel to the bell with which numerous allegedly illicit instruments were marked and seized; but that, in any case and taking the sketches as a reference, this provision existed in instruments prior to that patent, citing *clavicors* and German bugles. In addition, he said that some improvements were too naive and obvious—for example, the same fingering for family members—that there were obvious technical inconsistencies in the content regarding the length of the valve

---

[49] *Cour Impériale de Rouen. Faits et documents relatifs au procès entre M. Sax et M. Gautrot. Réponse par M. Sax aux notes fournies par M. Gautrot* (Paris: n. ed., [Imprimerie Centrale de Napoléon Chaix et Cie,] 1858), 4–15, 45–56, and 94–190.
[50] *RGMP*, 1 November 1857, 353–5.

slides and crooks for changing key, and that there were areas in the text that were 'impossible to know what they consisted of'. Nor was it lost on him that this document was a partial revival of the 1843 patent (the saxhorns) and that it had become obsolete after five years.[51]

The Imperial Court of Rouen was basically to decide on a thorny and abstract issue such as the extent of the damages and interests owed to Sax. Forestier presided over the chamber, and Deschamp and Chassan represented the opposing parties, with Jolibois mediating as Attorney General. The most substantial part of the chronicle of the confrontation—which still included echoes of the battle of the bands on the Champ de Mars in 1845—was the fact that Sax lowered his prosecutorial pretensions. (The judgement of 12 June 1856 had endorsed the start of the enquiries on 1 October 1845). The circumstances in which he found himself probably forced him to cede ground and to agree that the starting point would be set on 25 May 1852, that is, exactly three years to the day on which the confiscation had taken place. This cession unblocked the situation and scrupulously complied with articles 637 and 638 of the Code of Criminal Procedure. However, also at this hearing, Sax added a new claim and demanded that the enquiries should end on the day on which the present case was decided, which was to take place on 24 June 1858. That request—which the Court granted—was a new claim that (technically) did not conflict with the triennial forfeiture as it was a post 25 May 1855 offence. However, as we can imagine, this last plea was to be one of the reservations that Gautrot took advantage of to turn the situation upside down and file a new cassation appeal.

Without going into the details of the following trial, which are mostly derived from procedural details, the Court of Cassation admitted one of the four protests lodged by Gautrot and his new lawyer, *Maître* Rendu.[52] Relying on the alleged violation of articles 182, 183, 208, et seq. of the Code of Criminal Procedure and article 42 of the law of 1844, the president (Vaïsse) considered that 'the principle of two degrees of jurisdiction' between the courts of first instance and the imperial courts had been violated.[53] In other words, a higher jurisdiction (the Imperial Court of Rouen) had irregularly completed a judgement with new summary substance (the postulation of Sax to extend the enquiries up to that point) and which should have come from an ordinary curia (first instance). Therefore, Vaïsse, having heard the report

---

[51] *Explication des perfectionnements faisant le véritable objet du brevet pris par Monsieur Sax, le 13 octobre 1845* (Paris: n. ed., [Impr. Madame Veuve Dondey-Dupré,] n.d. [1858]), 6–13.

[52] *Mémoire pour M. Gautrot, demandeur en cassation de l'arrêt du 24 juin 1858, rendu par la Cour impériale de Rouen, au profit de M. Sax. Cour de Cassation, Chambre criminelle* (Paris: n. ed., [Impr. Le Normant,] n.d. [1858]), 1–19.

[53] *Annales de la propriété industrielle*, tome 5, 1859, 44–5.

of the counsellor (Legagneur) and the conclusions of the Attorney General (Martinet) decided on 21 August 1858 to annul the judgement of the Imperial Court of Rouen of 24 June 1858 and to validate the case until Gautrot appealed the decision of 12 June 1856 of the Criminal Court of Paris; that is to say, he undid the whole investigation in more than two years. Vaïsse also sent the case and the parties to the Imperial Court of Amiens for a new forum of appeal. Sax and his lawyer (again Paul Fabre) were to suffer a further defeat (to which the costs of the present trial would be added) and the necessary financial advance would have to wait.

The decisive trial at the Imperial Court of Amiens was to be held on Christmas Eve 1858, although it had at least two previous hearings (16 and 17 December). There were barely twenty months left until the expiry date of the fifteen-years period of exclusive exploitation of those patents (the saxophone and, particularly, the saxotromba that impacted several families of brass instruments). Gautrot's strategy was to endure and try to minimize the inevitable financial punishment. Councillor Le Royer du Bisson acknowledged in his speech of 16 December 1858 that this 'process was offering the most relentless fighting spectacle between makers (*le spectacle de la lutte la plus acharnée entre facteurs*)' which seemed 'to revive at every hearing'.[54] He therefore called for diligence and circumspection on the fundamental point of the debate, which was none other than to determine within which time limits the experts should work in order to calculate the compensation due to Sax. However, the details of the battle of the Champ de Mars, the victory of the sax-instruments, and their subsequent incorporation into the musical regiments were heard again. Nor did Gautrot's lawyer—again Marie—stick to the thematic contours intended by the counsellor.[55] The former republican minister focused his argument on the fact that the Rouen civil judgement of 1854 could not be considered the reference point in, ultimately, the criminal harassment of his client. Furthermore, he insisted that Sax's inventions—emphasizing those valves parallel to the bell that were doing so much damage—were not new. To demonstrate this, he offered the Court old instruments with the same characteristics and various testimonies from other makers, important musicians, and directors of military bands (Fermet and Jacottot). But he concluded by reminding the Court that, even if his client was

---

[54] *Annales de la propriété industrielle*, tome 5, 1859, 45–6.
The press spoke of a 'million (*myriad*) ever-renewing lawsuits', and reported that Sax was also facing an illness from which he seemed to be recovering thanks to the care of the Indian doctor Vries, with whom he had begun treatment four months earlier. *RGMP*, 19 December 1858, 422. On the health front—and to add an even more novel touch to his life—the Belgian inventor was to be cured of what was presumably lip cancer. *RGMP*, 20 February 1859, 61.
[55] *Gazette des Tribunaux*, 30 December 1858, 1280–2 and 31 December 1858, 1286–7.

found guilty, Gautrot would only have to give explanations for the events that took place in the three years prior to 25 May 1855, as the rest were definitively prescribed.

Unfortunately, the sources do not include the plea of Sax's representative, *Maître* Petit, or the conclusions of the public prosecutor's office, Bécot. However, it is clear that the Belgian maker gave in to his temporary claims in order to unblock the situation and not to enter into further contradictions with articles 637 and 638 of the Code of Criminal Procedure. In any case, the judgement of 24 December 1858 once again recognized the validity of Sax's documents as well as the raids that he orchestrated at the 1855 Exhibition and at the Gautrot premises.[56] It also recognized the authority of the Rouen civil trial of 1854 over the prosecution. And, importantly, it established the time frame in which Boquillon, Verre, and Richardière would work, which would be definitively fixed between 25 May 1852 and 12 June 1856 (the first judgment of a court of first instance that found Gautrot guilty).

Although his argumentative and legal resources were being exhausted, Gautrot again appealed to the Court of Cassation,[57] if only to postpone his inevitable punishment for a few more months. The claim drew on the same doctrinal sources as usual and was based on three points, the most solid of which was the controversial competence of the different legal courts.[58] The professional staff of this supreme forum (Legagneur, judge-counsellor and spokesman; Guyho, public prosecutor; and Fabre and Rendu, lawyers for the parties)[59] heard on 19 February 1859 the verdict of the president (Vaïsse) who, on this occasion, ended up rejecting all the complaints of the inventor of the sarrusophone.[60] Gautrot was thus left without any legal defence, while Sax, 'who had taken the necessary steps to begin the ordered investigation',[61] tried to subdue his adversary by lodging with the Court of Amiens—as can be inferred from the fact that it was from this court that the enforceable judgement to follow was issued—a claim for 250,000 francs pending the conclusion of the experts' report. To avoid the confrontation in court,

---

[56] *RGMP*, 2 January 1859, 6.
[57] *RGMP*, 9 January 1859, 14.
[58] *Annales de la propriété industrielle*, tome 5, 1859, 56–7. See also *Mémoire pour M. Gautrot, demandeur en Cassation de l'arrêt rendu le 24 décembre 1858, par la Cour impériale d'Amiens, au profit de M. Sax. Cour de Cassation, Chambre criminelle* (Paris: n. ed., [Impr. Le Normant,] n.d. [1858 or 1859]), 9–15.
[59] Gautrot issued a desperate *factum* complaining about Cassation's interpretation. He also accused his rival of extorting from them: 'Sax was not afraid to give his name [to the instruments], with the presumptuous and greedy idea of holding all rival industry as his tributary, or of hitting it, if it rebelled against this tribute …, with crushing condemnations in damages which would be a new wealth for him'. Gautrot also said that Sax had originally asked him for 1,500,000fr, i.e. 150,000fr for each year of piracy. *Dernières observations pour M. Gautrot contre M. Sax. Cour de Cassation. Chambre Criminelle. M. Legagneur, Conseiller Rapporteur. M. Guyho, Avocat général* (Paris: n. ed., [Impr. Madame Veuve Dondey-Dupré,] n.d. [1860]), 1–8 and 15–17.
[60] *RGMP*, 20 February 1859, 62 and 27 February 1859, 75.
[61] *Annales de la propriété industrielle*, tome 5, 1859, 208–9.

Gautrot made two firm offers (23,650fr first and then 50,000fr, payable in three instalments, the last one before the end of September 1859) which, as we can guess, Sax rejected. A new confrontation at the Amiens Imperial Court became inevitable and judge Poirel, at the session of 19 May 1859, ordered Gautrot to advance 150,000fr in two instalments (75,000fr within eight days and the rest one month after the first payment).

For the umpteenth time, Gautrot lodged an appeal with the Court of Cassation, essentially on the grounds of excess of power and false application of article 188 of the Code of Criminal Procedure.[62] However, although the sources do not report it, Gautrot and Sax had to hold several informal confrontations between May and July 1859. The brief ruling of the hearing on 8 July at the Court of Cassation—Vaïsse was still the president—stated that Gautrot had withdrawn (*désistement pur et simple*) all his protests, but that his appeal was nevertheless null and void (*nul et non avenu*); he was also ordered to pay the costs of this last procedural manoeuvre. The chroniclers also reported that, 'if their sources were correct (*si nous sommes bien informés*)', the two makers had reached an economic and business agreement which put an end to all their disputes. Gautrot's audit, which had been ordered by the Imperial Court of Amiens, would no longer be necessary. In exchange, Gautrot undertook to compensate Sax with 505,000fr, of which 200,000fr would be in cash and immediately (*comptant*). He also undertook to identify (*poinçonner*) from then on all instruments inspired by the 1845 patent that would leave his factories with a reference, of which Sax would receive a percentage.

This business agreement between the two builders was signed eleven days after the Court of Cassation had ruled against Gautrot and he had withdrawn his last appeal, namely on 19 July 1859. The contract comprised a total of six points. In the first of these, Gautrot acknowledged the authority of the court decisions that had been made up to that point and the legitimacy of the saxotromba patent. He also stated that he had successfully applied for a licence from his opponent for the said invention which would remain active as long as that title was in force. In the second article, Gautrot undertook to produce an annual profit in favour of his licensee of at least 15,000fr per year and, in the event that he did not exceed this amount, the difference would be borne by Gautrot himself. The control system to be followed by both makers was very detailed: Gautrot would start only by manufacturing the bell of each saxotromba on which he would engrave his anagram and serial number and, 'before mounting it on the body of the instrument, he would submit it to the

---

[62] *Annales de la propriété industrielle*, tome 5, 1859, 210.

control of Sax, who would add his own mark; committing himself [Gautrot] not to prepare the other parts of the instrument [e.g. the valves or the rest of the tubing] before this supervision has been completed'.

The third prerogative provided that the premium for each authorized instrument, whether sold or not, was 5fr, 7.5fr, or 10fr depending on the size. In addition, and in line with the above, any specimen of the same characteristics that Gautrot replaced, repurchased, or repaired—whether it was his own or came from another manufacturer—would also yield a commission of 3fr or 5fr to Sax. He also did not spare his control mark on these secondary specimens, which should be effective in less than twenty-four hours. The fourth and fifth clauses empowered Sax (or his representatives) to appear at any time (*quand ils jugeront à propos*) at Gautrot's workshops and premises to check his trading books and 'verify that the present agreements were being loyally exercised'. Any infringement detected would be penalized with the (staggering) sum of 500fr. The sixth and last point stated that any subcontracts, royalties, and double royalties that Gautrot orchestrated on the basis of the present contract would be his responsibility. Likewise, Sax could, 'when he considered it appropriate (*quand M. Sax le jugera nécessaire*)', elevate the present private contract to proof of cause (*formalité d'enregistrement*), that is to say, register it so that it could be used in legal offence.[63]

The conditions that Gautrot had agreed were extremely unfavourable to him. What is striking is the absence of neutral agents and, especially, the enormous permissiveness in the access to his documents and accounts, which would be endorsed by a fierce competitor. On the other hand, we will never know what the compensatory valuation of the inspectors appointed by the Court of Amiens would have been; nor will we know how long it would have taken them to prepare it, another important factor that came into play. It may be that Gautrot, by agreeing to this ludicrous agreement, avoided a greater sanction, or that he was threatened with imprisonment, which was a real contingency (articles 43 to 45 of the 1844 law), but one that had never been raised in the judicial proceedings up to that point.

In short, Sax obtained from this legal process a very generous compensation (505,000fr). It was also in the Belgian inventor's interest to reach a financial settlement as soon as possible, as he had not yet recovered from his first bankruptcy and the concordat was less than fourteen months away. Moreover, his final rehabilitation took more than seven months (23 February 1860),[64] suggesting that, despite the size of these sums and their potential

---

[63] Malou Haine, 'Les licences de fabrication accordées par Adolphe Sax à ses concurrents. 26 juin 1854–13 octobre 1865', *Revue belge de Musicologie* 34–5 (1980–1), 198–203.

[64] See, for example, *RGMP*, 29 January 1860, 38.

cures, the inventor of the saxophone was (and would continue to be) facing serious financial and managerial problems. On the other hand, the controversy over the saxotromba was also closed, as the licence of 19 July 1859 acknowledged the authorship of Sax. It is also possible that Gautrot's contractual bending of the contract was a different (and extremely painful) way of buying time. In reality, the inventor of the sarrusophone would only have to wait a few months—the patent for the saxotromba was due to expire on 13 October 1860—for the manufacture and marketing of brasswinds of that type to be fully released. Gautrot knew he was a better manager than his opponent, and had a greater volume of production and diversification.

9
Masterstroke

The Extension of Contested Patents

In parallel to the battle and negotiations with Gautrot, Sax concocted an exceptional legal move that could further strengthen his already advantageous position. Under article 15 of the 1844 law, he applied for an extension of the saxotromba and saxophone patents for a further five years. In other words, Sax wanted France to enact a law with state reach, but for private use, so that he could continue to trade exclusively in his two flagship products. Above such a law would only be the Constitution of 1852. It is clear that, in order to embark on such an initiative, he needed to have not only absolutely well-founded reasons, but also effective contacts in the highest political spheres. It was precisely the Executive and the Council of State itself that were going to defend before Parliament (*Corps législatif*) this awkward bill which, if passed in that chamber, would also have to be ratified by the Senate and sanctioned by the Emperor.

In the public eye, such exceptions were highly controversial because they seriously undermined the system of theoretically free competition.[1] Moreover, Sax's case was to be the second time since the French endowed themselves with intellectual and industrial property laws in 1791.[2] The first grant was made in 1856 to Jean-Auguste Boucherie of Bordeaux for a process for preserving and colouring wood.[3] However, the stakes for Sax were much higher, as the almost total control of the instrumental palette of metals that populated military bands was on the table. For this reason, and before the Belgian businessman's request could be processed, the Army went

---

[1] The chroniclers of those debates between Gautrot and Sax said that 'these extensions are so rare that they made history (*sont si rares qu'elles font époque)*'. Annales de la propriété industrielle, tome 6, 1860, 321.

[2] In fact, it would be the third time if we take into account (Huget and Calmels do not count it) that Napoleon I granted, by skipping all parliamentary procedures, a five-year extension for distillation procedures. *Bulletin des lois de L'Empire Français, 4e Série*, tome 20, 1814, 51–2.

[3] The law of 18 June 1856 extended the duration of the patent granted on 10 June 1841 so that its author would enjoy for five more years and exclusively those improvements of conservation—but not of colouring—on wood, that he would pay the fees of the current law (1844, not 1791), and that another related patent of his of 1854 would fall into the public domain at the same time as the parent document. Duvergier, *Collection complète des lois*, tome 56, 1856, 203 and *Annales de la propriété industrielle*, tomes 1 and 2, 1856, 229–37.

ahead—leaving it implicit which side it was on—and published on 26 March 1860 the new regulation which repealed the previous regulation of 1854–5, but maintained the patronymic Sax on numerous instruments (Table 9.1).

This legislative initiative and the exceptional nature of its achievement deserve a closer look at the preceding parliamentary procedures, deadlines, and debates.[4] The bill was registered on 26 June 1860[5] and its explanatory memorandum (*Exposé des motifs*) was presented by F. Le Play (speaker), Count E. Dubois, and F. Boilay (secretary), the three Conseillers d'État. According to the 1852 Constitution, the Council of State was a body with the function and power to discuss and draft public administration bills and regulations, as well as to defend them before Parliament and the Senate on behalf of the government itself. Of course, it also advised and counselled the Executive, especially with regard to the inception and drafting of regulations.

Table 9.1 Instrumental palette of the military bands (*Décret impérial* of 26 March 1860)

Infantry	Cavalry
2 flutes	1 small (*petit*) high-pitched (*aigu*) saxhorn in B♭
2 piccolo clarinets (*petites clarinettes*)	
4 clarinets (*grandes clarinettes*)	1 small (*petit*) soprano saxhorn in E♭
2 oboes	4 contralto saxhorns in B♭
2 soprano saxophones	1 alto saxhorn in A♭
2 alto saxophones	3 alto saxotrombas in E♭
2 tenor saxophones	2 baritone saxotrombas in B♭
2 baritone saxophones	4 bass four-valve saxhorns in B♭
2 cornets with piston valves or valves (*à pistons*)	1 contrabass saxhorn in B♭
2 trumpets with valves (*à cylindres*)	2 cornets with piston valves or valves (*à pistons*)
3 trombones	4 trumpets with valves (*à cylindres*)
2 contralto saxhorns in B♭	3 trombones
3 alto saxotrombas in E♭	
2 baritone saxhorns in B♭	
3 bass four-valve saxhorns in B♭	
1 contrabass saxhorn in E♭	
1 contrabass saxhorn in B♭	
1 snare or side drum (*caisse claire ou roulante*)	
1 bass drum (*grosse-caisse*)	
1 pairs of cymbals (*cymbales*)	
[Total: 40 people]	[Total: 27 people]

Compiled from *Journal militaire officiel*, [no exact date, first half of] 1860 [no. 14], 261–3.

---

[4] Duvergier, *Collection complète des lois*, tome 60, 1860, 368–70, Dalloz, *Jurisprudence générale*, [1st booklet, part 4] 1860, 124, and *Annales de la propriété industrielle*, tome 6, 1860, 321–58.

[5] *Le Moniteur universel*, 27 June 1860, 1.

Although it was divided into six sections, at the time its general assembly was composed of between forty and fifty people, and its representation, in the absence of the Emperor, was held by its president (and also minister) Pierre-Jules Baroche.[6]

The explanatory memorandum of the bill began with an introduction of the two instruments; firstly, the saxotromba, noting that it was a brasswind with novel features and that it had been constantly attacked by counterfeiters. Of the saxophone, it was remarked that it was a metal tube with keys and a single reed, that its construction was 'special' [sic], and that it had not yet found quality players, except in the last three years in which Sax had been a teacher of this instrument in a class attached to the Paris Conservatoire for military students. In addition, the professional merits of the Belgian inventor and the difficulties he had encountered in exploiting his patents were reviewed, with particular emphasis on the legal proceedings he had endured. For all these reasons, the Council of State, which had previously met on 12 June 1860, was in favour,[7] and submitted a bill for approval consisting of a single article with this extension for five more years for the two instruments.

From 2 July 1860, a commission in which different types of opinions were deliberately present studied the matter in detail before the discussion was broadened and passed on to the Lower House.[8] The working group consisted of seven people, namely Creuzet (chairman), Josseau (secretary), Aymé, Du Miral, Geoffroy de Villeneuve, Véron, and finally Nogent de Saint-Laurent (chronicler).[9] The dossier highlighted that Sax had barely had time to exploit these ideas and wielded arguments strong enough to warrant the granting

---

[6] *Almanach Impérial pour 1860* (Paris: Guyot et Scribe, 1860), 83–93 and Joseph-Adrien Rogron, *Codes français expliqués*, tome 2 (Paris: Henri Plon, 1863), 13.

[7] The music press also supported the request, commenting that 'everyone would applaud this act of consideration (*sollicitude*) by the government in favour of an artist whose merit and perseverance have been able to combat the tribulations'. *RGMP*, 15 July 1860, 262.

[8] *Le Moniteur universel*, 1 July 1860, 2 and 2 July 1860, 2.

[9] André Creuzet was a Member of Parliament from 1854 to 1870, but originally worked as a military officer (*garde du corps*). He was also an opponent of the Republic, mayor of Saint-Flour, and won his seat as an official candidate for Cantal. In 1870 he voted in favour of the war against Prussia. François-Jean-Baptiste Josseau was also an officialist supporter, but with a background in law and author of projects concerning agriculture. He sat in the hemicycle for thirteen years (1857–70) with the support of his fellow countrymen from the Seine-et-Marne department. Jacques-Gabriel Aymé de la Herlière had a similar legal background—he became an examining magistrate in the French commune of Neufchâteau—and supported the imperialist majority. Francisque-Rudel Du Miral was a lawyer and defended the interests of the state before the revolutions of 1848. However, he joined the candidacy of the prince-president in 1852 and won his seat from then until 1870 for his home region (Puy-de-Dôme), even becoming vice-president of the Chamber and a personal friend of the influential Rouher, Minister of Commerce. Ernest-Louis Geoffroy de Villeneuve enjoyed the 25,000fr annual salary of deputy thanks to a circumspection of the department of Aisne from 1852 until his death (1865), also defending the dynastic and political interests of the Empire. Louis-Désiré Véron (1789–1867) was the oldest and most eccentric of them all. And he certainly enjoyed a privileged economic position that he had amassed with pharmaceuticals—he studied medicine—then as a journalist, and finally as what we would call today a producer (*directeur-entrepreneur*) of the Paris Opera (1831–5), followed by other buying and selling businesses. He supported

of his request. Nogent de Saint-Laurent acknowledged the reluctance of the Consultative Committee on Arts and Manufactures (*Comité consultatif des arts et manufactures*), an institution which is likely was commonly consulted on matters of this kind. However, he pointed out that this body had not taken into account the special circumstances surrounding Sax. Moreover, the Council of State, including its president, as well as another of his peers and a key player in the whole affair, Eugène Rouher, *Monsieur le Ministre du commerce*, found the request favourable in this case.[10]

Notwithstanding, Their Lordships agreed (*Toutes les autorités qui ont eu à se prononcer au sujet*) that, in order to proceed in favour of such a cause, the applicant had to have introduced a considerable improvement in the field of industry or art; and, secondly, that circumstances of force majeure had not allowed him to make a profit. As regards the first condition, Nogent de Saint-Laurent underpinned the Sax's worthiness on the basis of four pillars. The first three were the victory in the battle of bands on the Champ de Mars (1845), the first prize at the 1849 Exhibition of French Industry (and consequent award of the Order of Legion of Honour), and also the highest decoration (*Council Medal*) in London 1851. The fourth, and most interesting, highlighted the tremendous impetus that Sax had given to French brass manufacturing. Before he arrived, France produced little and 'defective', and had to import from Bavaria, Bohemia, or Austria. Nogent de Saint-Laurent pointed out that Sax's transformations had led to a four-fold increase in the number of workers in this industry, and it was France who were exporting to the whole of Europe, including—he remarked—England and the German states.[11]

Concerning the circumstances of *force majeure*, Nogent de Saint-Laurent underlined the number of legal proceedings that Sax had endured in order to keep his patents afloat and punish his counterfeiters: 'he found himself in the presence of a veritable coalition, which at first succeeded well in absorbing his time and exhausting his resources'. At the same time, he noted that the profits from the construction of the new instruments had gone mainly into

---

Louis-Napoléon in his rise to the top and got his seat thanks to one of the Seine's circumspections. Jules-Henri Nogent Saint-Laurens (or Saint-Laurent) also belonged to the dynastic majority group for the Loiret region, although he was preceded by a brilliant career in the magistracy and in the always complicated *Cour d'assises*. He was also another who voted in favour of the war of 1870. Robert, Bourloton and Cougny, *Dictionnaire des Parlementaires*, tome 2, 22, tome 3, 428, tome 1, 130, tome 2, 478, tome 3, 155, tome 5, 568–9, and tome 4, 505.

[10] *Le Moniteur universel*, 3 July 1860, 2, 4 July 1860, 2, and 5 July 1860, 1. See also Duvergier, *Collection complète des lois*, tome 60, 1860, 369.

[11] Nogent de Saint-Laurent exaggerated those figures. At least in Paris and according to official data, the number of employees had not even doubled in the last thirteen years. *Statistique de l'industrie à Paris (1847–1848)*, 817 and *Statistique de l'industrie à Paris (1860)*, 751.

the pockets of their copiers. The courts had 'belatedly' proved him right and the Belgian entrepreneur was beginning to recover part of these profits in the form of financial compensation for damages from the main counterfeiters, which was an indirect reference to Gautrot. It was only since then, when the legitimacy of his patents was recognized, that Sax was able to negotiate licences for interested manufacturers and thus obtain a counterpart. In other words, out of the fifteen years that a patent normally lasted, the first thirteen were filled with 'moral suffering and financial disasters'. Finally, Nogent de Saint-Laurent noted that seven—without specifying who[12]—of Sax's former and main rivals 'were pleased' that their now colleague (*confrère*) was granted such a time extension.

In the end, despite the reluctance of some members of the committee, the majority (a total of five votes to two)[13] believed that Sax met the two conditions necessary for his documents to be extended. This was confirmed on 13 July 1860,[14] which gave him the green light for the bill to go to the plenary session of Parliament for its final discussion and vote, scheduled for the 19th of the same month. But on that day, Baron David said that there could be a procedural and substantive problem in combining in a single article the extension of two different patents protecting two different instruments, which put the whole process into risk.[15] (He was, of course, going to speak out against it if this inconvenience was not corrected.)[16] And, after a brief debate, and probably with the aim of winning over the group of parliamentarians who thought this way, Baroche asked for the discussion to be postponed until the following day (20 July) so that the draft could be redrafted, divided this time into two articles and assuming that this split would not change the substance of the future law. Of course, the opposition jumped on him and demanded that a new commission be created to evaluate it, to which Baroche refused, arguing that it was not a new draft, but the same one, and that the government would continue to request adoption in the same way. Thus, it

---

[12] According to a *factum*, they were Antoine Courtois, Halary, Labbaye, Gautrot, Auguste Buffet, Belorgey, and Lecomte. *Réponse aux observations soumises par Monsieur Besson aux membres du Corps législatif contre la prolongation de brevets demandée par Monsieur Adolphe Sax* (Paris: n. ed., [Impr. N. Chaix,] n.d. [1860]), 6.

[13] It is quite clear that Creuzet, Véron, and Nogent de Saint-Laurent voted in favour and Aymé against. Therefore, the opinions of Josseau, Du Miral, and Geoffroy de Villeneuve also had to be split in the same direction of two against one.

[14] *Le Moniteur universel*, 15 July 1860, 4.

[15] *Le Moniteur universel*, 21 July 1860, 2.

[16] This punctilious character, who was actually the son of Jérôme Bonaparte—Napoleon I's younger brother—made a career as a prominent military officer under General Cavaignac and later next to his uncle, whom he accompanied in the Crimean campaign. Later, he turned to politics, evidently on the side of the dynastic majority, and was one of those most determined to go to war against Prussia, although before that he was Minister of Public Works for a few days, from 10 August 1870 to 4 September 1870. Robert, Bourloton and Cougny, *Dictionnaire des Parlementaires*, tome 2, 275–6.

is likely that on the same day, or the morning of the 20th, someone went in search of Napoleon III—who must have been at the Palace of Fontainebleau, since the imperial decree, dated the 20th, came from there—so that he could approve the modification to the draft and its division into these two articles.

That same day, 20 July 1860, at 2 p.m., the final discussion resumed in the Lower House, which was to debate the extension of the saxotromba and saxophone patents. Baroche, Le Play, and Count Dubois took their seats on the bench reserved for government commissioners.[17] The President of Parliament (Count De Morny) received the bill from the Minister of State (Achille Fould), signed by the Emperor, and now consisting of two articles. The floor was first given to the head of the previous commission, Creuzet, who justified the harmlessness of splitting the bill into two separate articles. Aymé, however, argued against this, claiming that if the rules of procedure allowed such a thorny amendment, the Assembly could also remove it from the agenda. Another parliamentarian (Monier de la Sizeranne) urged his colleagues to return to the discipline of the meeting; but another opponent— Ernest Picard[18]—insisted that such a partition 'not only invited to vote against the bill, but also to fight it vigorously'. It was then that the Speaker of the House raised his voice to try to defuse the situation and convince His Lordships that this was not a political bill, but rather a matter of private interests with conciliatory or moderating intentions. Therefore, De Morny appealed to the presumed independence of legislators in order to avoid overly heated discussions and not delay the agenda.

The parliamentary debate resumed and Aymé returned to the fray, this time to play down the professional merits of the Belgian inventor. That deputy demanded extreme circumspection regarding the immense favour that Sax claimed for them, and recalled that not even his precedent (Boucherie) was granted; for Parliament only authorized a moratorium of exploitation on the procedure of wood preservation, but not on the aspects of colouring that he also originally claimed.[19] Aymé was annoyed at Sax's aggressiveness,

---

[17] *Le Moniteur universel*, 22 July 1860, 2–3.
[18] Louis-Joseph-Ernest Picard (1821–77) seemed to belong to the opposition, or at least he was a vector in the unofficialist sense. He was an excellent lawyer who always dabbled in politics, being a clear liberal (*à la façon de la bourgeoise orléaniste*), but with little sympathy for what happened on 2 December 1852. Nevertheless, he won his seat in 1858 from one of the independent parties and was one of the fiercest rivals of Haussmann and his ideas. He became known as the leader of the Open Left (*Gauche Ouverte*), as opposed to the more extreme supporters of that thought. He voted against the war with Prussia and accompanied Favre to Versailles in 1871 to negotiate France's capitulation. From 4 September 1870, he was a member of the Government of National Defence and Minister of Finance. After that time he held various public offices. Robert, Bourloton and Cougny, *Dictionnaire des Parlementaires*, tome 4, 620–1.
[19] *Annales de la propriété industrielle*, tomes 1 and 2, 1856, 229–37.

and expressed his frustration with how easily the courts authorized raids 'on the grounds that all the instruments were saxotrombas'. He asked what the 'exceptional' qualities of that instrument were and how to find them, as they were supposedly based on a simple change of shape that was also uncertainly applied to other brass. Aymé went further and was surprised that such a problematic artefact was even worthy of this kind of attention and that its author was asking for a five-year extension of exclusive exploitation. The politician concluded his assessment by reading the 1847 letter signed by Spontini and addressed to the president of the fourth chamber of the Paris Court of First Instance. Astutely, Aymé did not contextualize it and His Lordships heard that, in the opinion of the celebrated composer and musical authority of the time, 'Sax was a skilful copyist and not an inventor; his instruments are those of others with some changes in the outer forms and new names'.

On the government's side, Le Play countered his opponent's arguments and underlined the overwhelming value of Sax's research. Interestingly, he noted that the entrepreneur's 'misfortune was that he had to exercise his inventive genius within [the parameters] of an immaterial art [sound], where the products are not very tangible (*perceptibles*)'. Le Play did not spare compliments and flattery in favour of the saxotromba and the saxophone (which had been heard so often in the civil process), as well as underlining their value and behaviour as instrumental families. To close his speech, Le Play brought up Sax's curricular merits from the Champ de Mars competition to his last medal at the 1855 Exhibition to make it clear that the Belgian inventor had the majority of the scientific community on his side.

After several clashing retorts, Véron came out in favour of Sax and countered Spontini's negative criticism with a favourable one by Meyerbeer. Picard, however, recalled that the Italian composer had more credit in the field of brass bands because he had been conductor at numerous regiments for more than twenty years in Austria and Prussia. Picard stated that Sax's real purpose was to further swell his pockets, and scathingly pointed to the more than half a million francs he had received from Gautrot so that the House would be aware of such financial compensation. Picard also highlighted a business advantage as a supplier to the Imperial Guard that another of his colleagues (Belmontet)[20] extended to 'all the regiments of the Army'. The faction opposed to the project read a letter sent by Besson

---

[20] Louis Belmontet (1798–1879) was the son of a military officer of the First French Republic and, although he was trained in law, his passion was literature and poetry. A fervent Bonapartist—he published a biography in 1832 (*Le Buste, napoléonienne en vers lyriques*) praising Napoleon's recently deceased son and heir—he fought against the July Monarchy, and when he saw the possibility of Bonaparte's nephew becoming Emperor, he threw his resources into the cause. The people of the department of Le Tarn-et-Garonne gave him their support in 1852 to represent them in the Lower House, and he was re-elected three

that uncovered an insulting profit of 2,280,000fr net. The latter maker also pointed out that the licences had earned Sax another 300,000fr, and that he had not granted any for the saxophone, from which he made a 100% profit.[21]

Picard also warned that if the petition was finally approved and thus the 'monopoly' extended, instruments would cost twice as much and, more importantly, the Belgian manufacturer would still be somehow pressuring other manufacturers to license with him to avoid the risk of being raided. Nevertheless, Picard was open to extending the saxophone patent, but not the saxotromba's. The latter instrument and its documentation were a source of trouble that Sax interpreted as his privilege and interest to pursue his opponents. In a humorous and ironic way, the congressman said that when listening to an instrument endowed with saxotromba proportions, 'a dilemma presented itself: to listen to this new timbre, or not to listen to it (*on est placé entre deux écueils: ne la trouver jamais, ou la trouver toujours*). Therefore, when Sax appeared with a cohort of bailiffs (*cortège d'huissiers*) in the factories of his adversaries and told them what to seize, he would tell them 'everything: the objects made because they contain the voice; the metal, because it is destined to make the instruments that contain the voice; the mandrels, very expensive pieces because they are the means with which the instruments that give the voice are made'.

Nogent de Saint-Laurent called for the debate to be taken seriously (*Il faut rentrer sérieusement dans la question*) and to discern whether the merits of the Belgian entrepreneur and the circumstances surrounding the exploitation of his instruments were serious enough to extend the duration of these patents by five years. The spokesman stressed the importance of military music: 'it encourages (*soutient*), raises the morale of the soldiers, revives the wounded combatant; on the battlefields, marches bring to the men an enthusiasm which often becomes an irresistible force'. Nogent de Saint-Laurent also made it clear that all the financial resources that Sax had managed to raise were being consumed in the fight against piracy, and that this—and not his own incompetence—had led him to bankruptcy from which he had managed to emerge in January of the same year (1860) thanks precisely to the financial compensation of one of these copyists (Gautrot).

---

more times (1857, 1863, and 1869). Robert, Bourloton and Cougny, *Dictionnaire des Parlementaires*, tome 1, 248–9.

[21] Besson also reminded the legislators that justice had not always been unanimous and that doubts had always surrounded Sax's patents. *Observations soumises aux membres du Corps législatif contre la prolongation des brevets demandés par M. Sax* (Paris: n. ed., [Impr. de E. Brière,] 1860), 1–3.

The Marquis de Grammont disagreed and underlined Sax's lack of professional expertise for not having taken advantage of such a privileged position. The politician finally warned that, if these patents were to be prolonged, 'a real monopoly' would come into being. Baroche came to the defence of Sax, reminding the audience of the value of his work and his resistance against a coalition of manufacturers organized to set up a deposit to cover legal costs. The minister also assured that prices would not rise because they were set by foreign competition and that Sax would not abuse his position, as he said he had not done in the past.[22] Nogent Saint-Laurent added that 'Sax had granted the licences on the same terms to all those who had asked for them, and that [in the future] he would do so again to all those who asked for them', further stating 'that the conditions contracted with the assignees were moderate'.[23]

In an attempt at dismantling the arguments of Baroche, Picard recalled that Sax enjoyed exclusive supply to the Army from 1845 to 1848, and also from 1854 to that point (1860); and asked sarcastically whether this was really a complex situation for a businessman. Moreover, the argument of procedural calamities did not hold for him either, because it was Sax himself who took the prosecutorial initiative in 1854 and seized instruments and tools from his alleged copyists (*prétendus contrefacteurs*). Picard also emphasized that justice had not yet made its final pronouncement and that proceedings were still open (*n'a pas été définitivement résolu*).[24] However, the majority of the chamber was inclined to put aside all these issues and move forward, especially in the knowledge that the extension of a patent did not compromise any future proceedings and that, in any case, such an extension could be revoked.

At last, and certainly on the basis of sufficient information on the subject, the majority of the House wished to proceed to the vote, which was logically in favour of the Belgian maker by a comfortable margin of 141 votes in favour

---

[22] *Le Moniteur universel*, 22 July 1860, 4.
[23] Sax signed around twenty-five agreements to exploit the saxotromba from 1855 onwards. The conditions of these contracts were similar to those of Gautrot, but adapted to the labour force of each. For example, the number of instruments to be made by Halary junior could not be less than fifty per year, while Courtois committed himself to more than 100, but less than 400. As for the bonuses, Lecomte had to make at least 2000fr of profit every year, while Gautrot was not to go below 15,000fr. All of them seem to have in common that tight control by Sax who had to supervise each of the products and keep a parallel record system. Haine, 'Les licences de fabrication accordées par Adolphe Sax', 198–203 and Kampmann, 'Licences accordées par Adolphe Sax à ses concurrents', 9–17. In practice, however, the exact measurements and proportions of these aerophones (which the Belgian inventor was so concerned about in the past) were relaxed as long as he was paid the agreed royalties on a regular basis. The agreements abroad (England) were in favour of the Distin (c.1846–51), Rousselot & Co. (1851–2), and Rudall Rose & Carte (c.1853). Mitroulia, *Adolphe Sax's brasswind production*, 177, 244, 246, and 249.
[24] *Annales de la propriété industrielle*, tome 6, 1860, 335–58, *Le Moniteur universel*, 22 July 1860, 2–4, and Duvergier, *Collection complète des lois*, tome 60, 1860, 369–70.

and 72 against. Four days later, on 24 July 1860, the draft law was passed to the Senate, which did not raise any objections, and the law was promulgated on 1 August 1860.[25] Sax would have five more years to exclusively exploit the saxophone and saxotromba patents, a considerable triumph.

---

[25] *Bulletin des lois de l'Empire Français*, tome 16, 1861, 349–50.

10
With Malice Aforethought

Squeezing Out the Deadlines

The warlike saga between Adolphe Sax and Pierre-Louis Gautrot seemed to have ended with a double financial (505,000fr) and commercial agreement in the form of a licence (1859). However, nothing could have been further from the truth: the next five years were a false stalemate. The rivalry between the two entrepreneurs remained latent. Despite the Belgian inventor's overwhelming contractual superiority, Gautrot still had room to take advantage of his larger workforce and his two factories, especially the one in Château-Thierry, which could have made the difference.[1] Moreover, there are clear indications that the civilian and amateur clientele was finally building up and, in this niche, Gautrot was much better prepared.

From the point of view of distribution, the Château-Thierry works was interesting because of its direct connection with Paris by river (Figure 10.1), but the key matter was the 320 workers it employed on low wages. Although it is difficult to know the exact figures, it is possible to obtain an approximation from the fact that the boilermakers (*chaudronniers*) in Laon (department of Aisne) were paid between 2.5fr and 3fr in 1853, although if their employer provided food for them their wages could be as low as 1fr a day.[2] Engravings and photographs of the Gautrot factory on the banks of the river Marne and outbuildings with smaller windows suggest that not only did the workers eat there, but that it was also their place of residence (Figure 10.2). In any case, it is clear that Gautrot saved there (well) more than half of the salary that a metalworker could earn in Paris (5–6fr).[3] Incidentally, the rents in the French

---

[1] Gautrot was widowed by Aimée Fischer in 1851, and five months later he married Augustine-Desirée Marquet, a wealthy landowner with land in Septeuil (Yvelines department) and other real estate in Paris. Cyrille Grenot, 'La facture instrumentale des cuivres', 22–3 and 49.

[2] The national average wage for a worker engaged in this trade ranged between 1.79fr and 2.7fr without meals, and between 1.32fr and 1.8fr with meals. *Statistique de la France. Prix et salaires à diverses époques* (Strasbourg, Veuve Berger-Levrault, 1864), 18–19 and 200.

[3] Although the wages of the 725 brass workers ranged from 3fr to 10fr, more than half of them were paid between 5fr and 6fr (the forty-three apprentices were paid a maximum of 1.75fr). *Statistique de l'industrie à Paris (1860)*, 754. A small increase in these amounts was a real relief for these people, especially when it came to food. A meal in a cheap restaurant (*établissement de bouillon*) cost, namely bread (0.10fr), a bottle of wine (0.80fr)—if *de carafon*, less: 0.15fr; stews and soups (0.20fr), beef (0.20fr), roast

With Malice Aforethought 161

Figure 10.1 Factory of musical instruments by Couesnon (c.1900), formerly owned by Gautrot

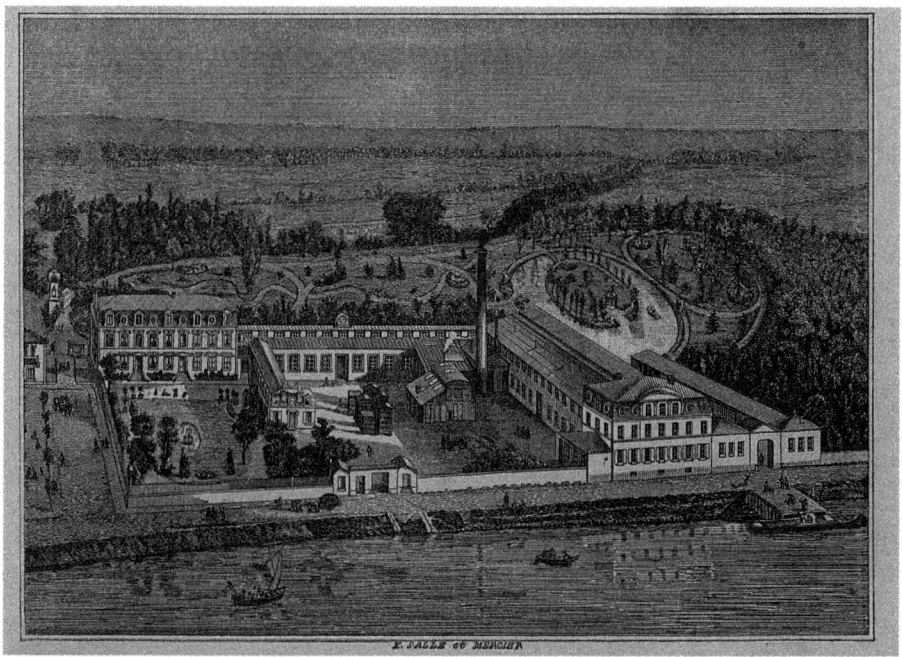

Figure 10.2 Bird's eye of Gautrot's Factory in Château-Thierry

Catalogue des instruments de musique de la manufacture générale de Gautrot Aîné, Durand et Cie, Paris, rue de Turenne, 80 et à Château-Thierry (Rennes: n. ed., [Typographie Oberthur & Fils,] 1878), [xv].

capital—although dependent on location and surface area[4]—were not exactly cheap and increased every year. Sax was paying (1860) around 9500fr for his exploitation in the rue Saint-Georges[5] and Gautrot (1872) 14,000fr for his in the Marais.[6]

In fact, offshoring was not new, and other manufacturers had already realized the advantages of moving the bulk of production to the provinces or to the outskirts of Paris, leaving a small branch or representative shop in the centre. For example, Jean-Louis Buffet (also known as Buffet-Crampon)[7] advertised in 1850 that he had opened a second factory in Mantes—still in operation today[8]—which at present is a commune in the department of Yvelines, fifty-seven kilometres from the Hôtel de Ville in Paris. However, the company retained its former location on the Passage du Grand Cerf, just a fifteen-minute walk from the Louvre (1.4 kilometres). Registering the business in the capital (for obvious reasons of promotion and differentiation), even if its main production plant was elsewhere, would explain (partially at least) why the most authoritative compilation of the time did not record the Château-Thierry operation and gave little weight to other proven production sites such as those of La Couture (winds) or Mirecourt (strings).[9] Indeed, Husson et Buthod was a Parisian firm (rue Greneta) whose advertisements in 1856 stated that it had factories in these two locations and offered not only wood- but also brasswinds.[10] It was also common from the mid to late 1840s for some instrument makers—such as the Martin brothers, also of La Couture—to maintain a small workshop in Paris so that instruments

(0.35fr), cooked dishes (0.50fr), fish (0.35–0.50fr), poultry and game (0.50fr), vegetables (0.20–0.30fr), salads (0.25fr), omelettes (0.35fr), and desserts (0.20fr). The prices went up in a restaurant (Grand Vattel): bread (0.5fr), soup (0.3fr), steak with potatoes (0.90fr), lobster with salad and mayonnaise (1.5fr), and a decent wine (1.5fr). For dessert, a rum-sweetened pancake—*omelette sucrée au rhum*—(1.5fr), and a coffee (*demie-tasse*) and a cognac digestif (*petit verre*) were between 0.4–0.65fr. *Stanford's Paris Guide* (London: Stanford, 1862), 15, 30, 41–2, 44, 47–8, and 50.

[4] Haine, *Les facteurs d'instruments*, 123.

[5] We have made this estimate knowing that the 1860 survey counted two brasswind industrialists in the district where Sax lived—he, and another who worked alone or with only one assistant—and that they both had a rent of 10,300fr. *Statistique de l'industrie à Paris (1860)*, 751. According to a later communication of his, the rent had risen from the initial 3000fr to 15,000fr as of 1864. *Le Figaro*, 1 July 1874, 3 and 4 August 1874, 1.

[6] In reality, the rent cost him 20,000fr, but he had subleased (*sous-loue*) a part of the building to a certain Schmoll for 6000fr. Archives de Paris, D1P4 [no. 1032, 1033, 1160, and 1161], [*Cadastres*], 'Saint-Louis, rue (4e), no. 32–112, 1852', n.p.; 'Saint-Louis, rue (4e) 1862, 1876, 1900', n.p.; 'Turenne, rue de (3e, 4e) 1862', n.p.; and 'Turenne, rue de (3e, 4e) 1876, 1900', n.p.

[7] Waterhouse, *The New Langwill*, 49–51.

[8] <http://www.buffet-crampon.com/en/our-story> (accessed 20 August 2023).

[9] *Statistique de la France. Industrie. Résultats généraux de l'enquête effectuée dans les années 1861–1865* (Nancy: Berger-Levrault, 1873). See also Jean-Marie Chanut et al., *L'industrie française au milieu du 19e siècle. Les enquêtes de la statistique générale de la France* (Paris: Ehess, 2000), database included in the CD-ROM.

[10] 'Catalogue Husson & Buthod 1856', rep. in *Larigot* 15 ([June] 1994), 4.

from the provinces could be finished in the capital by more skilled workers.[11]

In any case, it is clear that the Château-Thierry operation had some very interesting characteristics for producing low-cost products and targeting an emerging clientele. The market for *de pacotille* brasswinds that we sensed in the 1840s was gaining momentum, although it also had to go through some reluctance; or rather, it needed its own promotion (turning a potential flaw into a virtue) and time to establish itself. Clearly, there were poor quality instruments—and/or people who played very badly[12]—but the new construction procedures made it possible to maintain quality standards and at the same time greatly reduce production costs. Adrien De la Fage (1855) acknowledged that the new business model Gautrot was pursuing made sense and was viable. (Of course, there was also publicity in disguise, as De la Fage was an antagonist of Sax). This connoisseur commented that Gautrot produced 'quickly and with extreme precision [sic], which made it possible to offer a fairly good genre at reduced prices'.[13] Another journalist (Charles Robin) asserted—also in 1855—that Gautrot's modest cornets had nothing to envy in quality to those of other makers. Robin also stated that this entrepreneur had the honour [sic] of having created the model of cheapness (*bon marché*) in the sale of brasswinds.[14]

The price of brasswinds was essential to reach the more humble strata of the population, which gave rise to other very interesting spin-offs. For example, the initiatives of some employers to organize musical groups among their workers in the form of choirs,[15] fanfares, or bands. These projects were appealing and motivating for the workers, at the same time as the managers tried to ensure that their labour force did not get too distracted during the rest periods. Moreover, in this way, the social theories—so much in vogue at the time—of moralizing and educating the working classes through cultural activities were put into practice.[16] Obviously, these actions were not only philanthropic, for apart from serving the administrators to show themselves to public opinion as benevolent men committed to their fellow citizens,

---

[11] Haine, *Les facteurs d'instruments*, 87 and 98.
[12] *La France musicale*, 4 February 1855, 33–4.
[13] De la Fage, *Quinze visites musicales*, 177.
[14] Charles-Joseph-Nicolas Robin, *Histoire illustrée de l'exposition universelle* (Paris: Furne, 1855), 129-31.
[15] Wolff, for example, the director of the renowned Pleyel piano company, established a choral society comprised solely of his employees to foster among them a sense of brotherhood, camaraderie, and passion for music. Adolphe de Pontécoulant, *Douze jours à Londres. Voyage d'un mélomane à travers l'exposition universelle* (Paris: Henry, 1862), 139.
[16] Jean Quéniart, 'Les formes de sociabilité musicale en France et en Allemagne, 1750–1850', in É. François, ed., *Sociabilité et société bourgeoise en France, en Allemagne et en Suisse (1750-1850)* (Paris: n. ed., 1987), 144–5.

they also advertised their brand and instruments at concerts, gatherings, and competitions. Gautrot again provides us with the most descriptive example in our field (winds), for he selected thirty-six of his employees from Château-Thierry to form a brass band (*corps de musique*). In addition to hiring a teacher and providing them with a rehearsal room (*salle de répétitions*), he opened a savings fund (*fond de caisse*) for them, which he increased by paying them a small (*légère*) monthly stipend. This ensemble made its debut in 1857 in a public competition in Meaux (a town halfway along the road to Paris) where the band won a silver medal. This prize and a subsequent one in the same town led other proletarians to apply for admission to the band.

To join the music group, they first had to attend solfège classes four times a week for two hours. Then, if they had made sufficient progress, the applicants would continue to attend the class only once a week, but they would be provided with an instrument which required two more lessons and attendance at the dress rehearsal (*répétition générale*) on Sunday mornings.[17] It is striking that, after ten or twelve hours of daily work, the operators still had the strength to devote another 120 minutes to musical instruction.

However, the effort was worthwhile, as the (worker-)musicians enjoyed special consideration (*certaine considération*) and had an important position (*ils ont la meilleure place*) at the solemnities or festivities of the establishment. In addition, they were often hired for occasional performances at neighbouring agricultural fairs where they were compensated for their travel expenses. During the winter months, they gave benefit concerts (*au profit du bureau de bienfaisance*) and in the summer they also went out two or three times to participate in the patron saint's feast of a neighbouring village where they were always well received. Of course, also, 'once a month, on Sunday afternoon, they played in the square [of Château-Thierry] like the regimental bands.'[18] Pontécoulant again emphasized the sobering properties of music for these workers—'it amused, instructed, and uplifted their souls'—and the important work done by Gautrot which not only linked them in this way to his establishment, but at the same time was 'a means of avoiding or at least preventing

---

[17] Gautrot launched *L'Instrumental* in 1864, his distinct publishing project aimed at providing increasingly popular ensembles like bands and fanfares with their own literature, including arrangements, transcriptions, tunes, and operatic reminiscences. According to its proprietor, this publication featured 300 works, mostly inspired by motifs from operas adapted by 'eminent artists'. *Catalogue des instruments de musique de la Manufacture Générale de Gautrot aîné & Cie. À Paris, Rue Turenne, 80 (Ancienne Rue Saint-Louis) Au Marais et à Château-Thierry (Aisne)* (Rennes: n. ed., [Typographie Ch. Oberthur & Fils,] n.d. [1867]), iv.

[18] The press made reference to the 'excellent wind music of Mr Gautrot's factory' that had greatly contributed to the festivities of that town during the summer. *RGMP*, 8 July 1860, 246.

visits to the cabarets where the workers squandered (*engloutissent*) in one day the fruit of a whole week's work'.¹⁹

The above-mentioned false understanding between Adolphe Sax and Pierre-Louis Gautrot had a perfect staging at the most important world event of the time, The London International Exhibition on Industry and Art of 1862. Both entrepreneurs 'occupied the same magnificent and horribly expensive (*qui a coûté horriblement cher*) showcase'—in reality, there were two stands—but they were placed back to back (*côte à côte*). Pontécoulant also commented that, 'in spite of the numerous and loud trials', he did not find it strange to see these 'two former adversaries locked under the same glass' (Figures 10.3 and 10.4). This set-up pleased and satisfied him (*me charme et*

Figure 10.3 Sax's stand in The London International Exhibition on Industry and Art of 1862

Le Monde Illustré, 3 January 1863, 13.

---

¹⁹ Pontécoulant, *Douze jours à Londres*, 236–8. Later, the author also emphasized the paternalism and protection (insurance) that the employer provided for his employees. Gautrot was also supposed to encourage savings so that the most diligent workers could be provided with their own accommodation on his land. Adolphe de Pontécoulant, *La musique à l'Exposition Universelle de 1867* (Paris: L'art musical, 1868), 104–5. Needless to say, this astute entrepreneur also wanted to build loyalty and sedentarize a skilled workforce so that they would reject more lucrative job offers from other competitors, while retaining good trainers for the apprentices.

At La Couture (*c*.1865), there was also a similar initiative, promoted, it is believed, by the workers themselves. Marconi, *La Couture-Boussey*, 20.

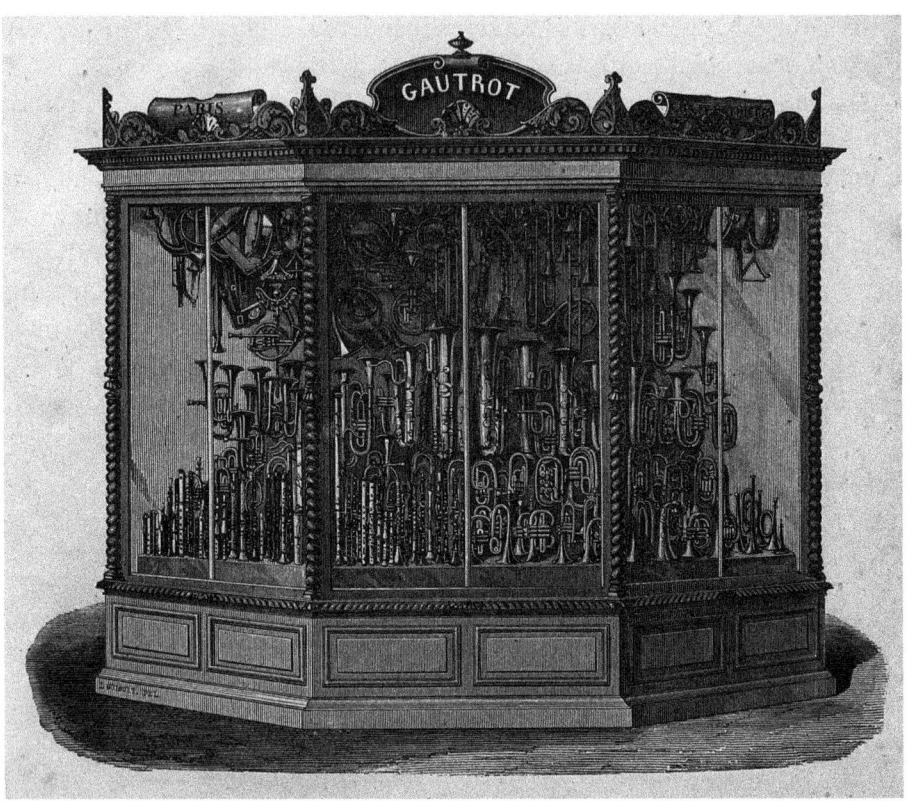

Figure 10.4 Gautrot's stand in London 1862 Fair
Catalogue des instruments de musique de la manufacture générale de Gautrot Ainé [1878], [xiii].

me fait plaisir) 'and proved that men of spirit and talent always end up understanding each other, which would be beneficial to [French] instrumental workmanship'.[20]

The reporter's words also invite reflection on the money spent on the presentation of these products and the importance given to the external image. Sax confessed to having spent 52,000fr on the occasion,[21] an amount that seems hyperbolic. However, the sheer scale of these sideboards (more than five metres)[22] and, above all, the copious amounts of brass they contained, shows that these makers spared neither expense nor imagination in order to differentiate themselves. Indeed, so-called fantasy instruments were becoming more and more common, i.e. instruments with disproportionate and

---

[20] Pontécoulant, *Douze jours à Londres*, 30.
[21] 'Archives nationales, F 21-4597, dr. 2, Conservatoire, Instruments de musique', cited in Haine, *Les facteurs d'instruments*, 148.
[22] *Le Monde Illustré*, 3 January 1863, 14.

striking shapes and volumes—or those with certain complications—but with doubtful or no commercial projection. The Belgian entrepreneur brought to London his immense *saxhorn-bourdon* (or subcontrabass saxhorn) of seventeen metres of tubing—which had already been used in 1851 and 1855—to attract attention and serve as a publicity stunt. For his part, Besson exhibited at the French National Fair (1849)—and also in 1855—his *trombotonar*, a 'gigantic bugle' [sic] more than three metres high.[23]

The brass business was dominated by intense competition and here Sax, despite his immense advantage, did not seem to stand out clearly. Lecomte (just created in 1859) claimed to employ more than 100 people in Paris and to use a steam engine, Courtois highlighted its prizes and its volume of exports abroad,[24] although that of Labbaye was higher (75%), which also boasted ancestry status (1661), as did Henry et Martin (1780). Husson et Buthod were quite diversified (brass, but also woodwinds, strings, and related items), and the Buffets (Louis-Auguste and Buffet-Crampon) were specialists in flutes and clarinets.[25] Also on the subject of the London Fair of 1862, Boquillon emphasized that the Belgian maker's contribution was, 'without doubt (*sans contredit*), the most brilliant and numerous of its kind'. However, he considered that the *maison* Gautrot 'was probably the most considerable in the whole world in the manufacture of almost all types of musical instruments'.[26] Pontécoulant summed it up perfectly: 'Gautrot makes very well and very fine (*Gautrot fait très-beau et très-bon*)'.[27] Moreover, the prize system, with only two distinctions (Medal and Honourable Mention), did not elevate the winners as much as in other occasions,[28] and Sax shared the first prize with other French competitors (the Buffets, Courtois, Godfroy, Henry et Martin, Labbaye, Husson et Buthod, Triébert, Thibouville, and, of course, Gautrot); and even with his brother Alphonse, who had also started making brasswinds.[29] Nor did his economic and business situations seem buoyant in the light of a brief (18 October 1864–31 August 1865) and fruitless partnership

---

[23] Charles Soullier, *Nouveau Dictionnaire de musique, illustré, élémentaire, théorique, historique, professionnel et complet à l'usage des jeunes amateurs, des professeurs de musique, des institutions et des familles* (Paris: Bazault, 1855), 324–6 and De la Fage, *Quinze visites musicales*, 145.

[24] To better know the intricate saga of the Courtois family, see Maxime Chagot and Christian Chagot, 'Courtois, la dynastie enfin retrouvée!', *Larigot* 54 ([December] 2014), 24–39.

[25] *Exposition Universelle de 1862 à Londres. Section Française Catalogue officiel publié par ordre de la commission impériale* (Paris: Imprimerie Impériale, 1862), 122–3 and 103 (Appendice).

[26] Ch. Laboulaye, dir., *Annales du Conservatoire Impérial des Arts et Métiers*, tome 3 (Paris: Eugène Lacroix, 1862), 221–6.

[27] Pontécoulant, *Douze jours à Londres*, 238.

[28] *International Exhibition 1862. Medals and Honourable Mentions awarded by the In International Juries* (London: George Edward Eyre and William Spottiswoode, 1862), iii, ix, and 219.

[29] Alphonse Sax was eight years younger than Adolphe and reportedly worked for him before becoming independent (c.1855–6). He promoted himself as a 'manufacturer-engineer in musical instruments', registered seven French patents, and led an all-female brass ensemble that gave concerts in Parisian salons.

with Goudot (manufacturer)[30] and Chantepie (former notary, who was to act as administrator of the new business). The disagreement meant that a cash injection of 100,000fr could not go ahead and, what was almost worse, brought the firm into disrepute.[31]

Yet, after five years of apparent calm, Sax, 'convinced that Gautrot was not respecting the agreement [of licence they had signed in 1859]', inflicted a raid on him which resulted in the seizure of numerous bells and sets of valves, as well as several instruments. The complaint was based on an offence of forgery and demanded financial compensation 'at the rate of 500fr for each object not chiselled (*poinçonné*)'.[32] This attack—perhaps not too surprising—was orchestrated the day before the patent for the saxotromba was due to expire (12 October 1865). In addition, the treacherous raid took place simultaneously in Paris and at the Château-Thierry factory, and initially resulted in the seizure of 305 bells, 214 sets of valves, and five complete instruments belonging to other manufacturers.

The sixth chamber of the Paris Court of First Instance resolved this bitter dispute on 9 February 1866. And, having heard the conclusions of the prosecution (Thomas), the president (Vivien) found Gautrot not guilty with regard to the bells because they did not strictly violate the second article of the licence agreed between the two entrepreneurs. However, he considered 131 of the 214 sets of valves and four of the whole instruments to be illegal, for which Gautrot was requested to pay a fine of 500fr each (total: 67,500fr); plus, obviously, the corrective of 2000fr that article 40 of the 1844 law stipulated. However, Vivien was not sure of the legality of the eighty-three valves that had been saved, so the court hired a technician (Eugène Surville) to examine them and submit a report that could be subject to the surcharge.[33]

Both makers lodged appeals. The representative of Sax (*Maître* Hébert) claimed a global compensation for his client of 196,500fr for a total of 393 elements that he considered fraudulent. On the other hand, Gautrot (*Maître*

His business debacle (1864) revealed that he owed money (over 80,000fr) to forty-three people including other brass entrepreneurs such as Drouelle (3459.95fr), Godefroy *aîné* (290.50fr), Labbaye (413.98fr), Buffet-Crampon (547.15fr), and Gautrot himself (924fr). Archives de Paris, D11 U3, box year 1864, dossier 2593: Faillite d'Alphonse Sax du 25 janvier 1864, *Rapport du syndic définitif*, n.p. and *Concordat*, n.p. See also Pontécoulant, *Douze jours à Londres*, 275 and 298–301; and Bruno Kampmann, 'Alphonse Sax vu dans L'Illustration', *Larigot* 37 ([May] 2006), 27–31.

[30] Goudot had been one of the entrepreneurs who protested against the Sax instruments and the commission that was to judge the military musical formations in the episode of the Champ de Mars in 1845. PROTESTATION [sic] *de tous les Facteurs d'Instruments de musique militaire de France*, [2].

[31] In the end, the three associates ended up in court in 1865. *Observations pour M. Sax contre MM. Goudot et Chantepie et M. Vidal, liquidateur de la Société dite Maison Adolphe Sax, Goudot et Chantepie* (Paris: n. ed., [Impr. E. Brière,] n.d. [1866]), 2–3 and 7–10.

[32] *Annales de la propriété industrielle*, tome 15, 1869, 313.

[33] *Annales de la propriété industrielle*, tome 15, 1869, 317–18.

Bétolaud) tried to formally invalidate the offence by arguing that the matter was being wrongly channelled through the criminal channel. Moreover, he argued that the seized items 'were merely infringements of the agreement of 9 July 1859' and therefore 'could not be considered as offences of counterfeiting'. However, the court—under the presidency of Saillard and acting as general prosecutor, Dupré-Lasale—ratified on 9 May 1866 the irregularity of these 214 valve mechanisms and two of the whole instruments for which Gautrot 'would pay a sum proportionate to the offence (*toute proportion avec l'importance réelle de ce préjudice*)'. The magistrate considered it disproportionate to pay 500fr for each one, especially as the instruments had not yet been put up for sale and given that they would pass into the hands of Sax as a result of the seizure. Saillard therefore valued at an average of 50fr (ten times less) per fault, making a total of 10,800fr, 'a sum that would be sufficient to repair all the damage'. The expert's work was also disabled.

The Court of Cassation received two appeals, although only Sax's was granted because Gautrot lodged his after the deadline (two days late). However, it did not help Sax to have arrived on time either, as the arguments he put forward, which dealt with procedural defects and injustices, were finally rejected on 23 February 1867 by the president (Vaïsse, again).[34] The chronicler (Pataille) acknowledged in his observations that he did not understand (and did not agree with) this ruling, as the criminal jurisdiction allegedly could not rule on a private commercial clause. He said that those chambers did not recognize before them as binding the contractual agreement between the two manufacturers and decided at their own discretion. Pataille wondered whether it would not have been appropriate (the right thing to do) to conduct the dispute through civil or commercial channels, since it was his patent, not the agreement (*c'est en vertu de son brevet et non de la convention qu'il agit*), that gave force to Sax's attack. In any case, the chronicler's bewilderment mattered little—incidentally, he showed his acuity in identifying the patent as a defining competitive tool; the decision of the criminal court was final and the inventor of the saxophone had to settle for 10,800fr indeed.

---

[34] Legagneur (counsellor) read the preliminary report, Clément and Groualle represented the parties, and Bédarrides acted as the Attorney General. *Annales de la propriété industrielle*, tome 15, 1869, 322–4.

11
Besson, a Brass Heavyweight Maker
Brave Competition and an Interesting Production Model

Gustave-Auguste Besson (1820–75) was another of Adolphe Sax's fiercest and most furious rivals. The son of an army colonel and apprenticed to Dujariez as a young man in instrument making,[1] he set up his own business at the age of eighteen or nineteen.[2] In reality, the enmity between the two manufacturers went back a long way. Besson was one of more than thirty businessmen who signed the March 1845 protest to the Minister of War against the bias of the commission in charge of determining the artistic model for the French *Armée*.[3] Although Besson did not take part in the civil case that led to Rouen 1854, it is possible that he supported it from less compromising positions. However, the direct confrontation between these two manufacturers erupted on 29 December 1854, when Sax inflicted on him a raid that was declared null and void.

The press at the time bore witness to and fuelled the animosity between the two entrepreneurs, which once again showed that there was a parallel battle in the public eye. On 4 November 1855, Adrien De la Fage attacked the new structure of music bands and their most characteristic instruments, namely Sax's brass. His article began with an apathetic comment—'Each to his own taste (*Chacun son goût*)'—and acknowledged that he liked civil music best, a preference which he reaffirmed over time. He also considered the brasswinds of the French military formations as 'instruments of doubtful luck' and advocated another model containing more types of flutes, oboes, clarinets, bassoons, and contrabassoons, 'so essential and so successful'. However, the

---

[1] Emmanuel-Jean-Marie Dujariez—apprentice at the beginning of Raoux senior—was another manufacturer of brasswinds who supplied military bands. His establishment was open from 1829 to about 1855. In 1831 he improved a French horn which was endorsed by the Conservatoire. Pierre, *Les facteurs d'instruments*, 339. Dujariez was another of these veteran makers who only worked brass with the hammer (*Il ne travaille le cuivre qu'au marteau*) and used traditional procedures: 'he uses no new process to shape his tubes into a long cone, to solder them, to bend them, to make them as polished on the outside as they are on the inside'. *Bulletin de la société d'encouragement pour l'industrie nationale* (Paris: Madame Huzard, 1831), 415–16.

[2] Waterhouse, *The New Langwill*, 29–30 and Grenot, 'La facture instrumentale des cuivres', 28–31 and 56.

[3] PROTESTATION [sic] *de tous les Facteurs d'Instruments de musique militaire de France*, [1–2].

Army was going for the 'insipid' and 'monotonous' combination of clarinets and brass; and used a curious metaphor to complain about the excessive popularity the latter were receiving: 'it is as if the improvements made to scissors concluded that knives have become useless'. However, he also implied that there were economic interests in the whole affair (*le bon de l'affaire*). He then referred directly to Sax's instruments about which he 'would have a lot to say'; but, as the closing of the Paris Exposition Universelle of 1855 was approaching, he preferred to hold his tongue. De la Fage did, however, point out Sax's subterfuge—referring to the nominalization of numerous brass aerophones with the word *saxhorn*—in order to gain the market and, in particular, 'the supply (*la fourniture*) of numerous regiments formed in recent years'. Finally, De la Fage openly took sides with rival manufacturers, citing Halary—'honour to veterans! (*honneur aux anciens!*)'—Roth[4] and, finally, Besson.[5]

A few months later (May 1856), an interesting and striking advertisement by Besson appeared in the *Revue et Gazette Musicale de Paris* with a suggestive headline: 'Complete regeneration of the military bands'. As well as his prizes and medals, the maker advertised that he supplied instruments to the Opera, the Conservatoire, the schools, but also to the French land and sea corps, the Brussels Guides, and the Imperial Guard. He also boasted that the leading artists of France, Great Britain, and Belgium used his products, implying not only that he had contacts abroad, but also that he had signed up great musicians. His brasswinds were of such quality that 'all counterfeiting was impossible (*toute contrefaçon est impossible*)', and he offered a six- to eight-year guarantee, which was very tempting.

This claim was a provocation intended for Sax—moreover, in a medium traditionally supportive of his—as it occupied and encroached on common interests. The situation grew in tension and intensity when, a few months later, the same newspaper announced that Besson was employing new manufacturing methods 'of the highest interest'. Furthermore, he proclaimed the principle that the sound of the instruments did not depend on the material used, 'but only on the proportions of the tubing (*de la combinaison de la perce*)', which he demonstrated with cornets made of plaster, paper, and

---

[4] De la Fage was referring to Charles Roth of Strasbourg, father of Jean-Chrétien (1816–81), who was to become another licensee of Sax. Waterhouse, *The New Langwill*, 336. See also Albert-A. Stanley, *Catalogue of the Stearns Collection of Musical Instruments* (Ann Arbor: University of Michigan, 1921), 97 and René Pierre, 'La saga des anges trompettistes ou les Facteurs d'instruments de musique à Strasbourg 1720–1920', *Larigot* 45 ([April] 2010), 23 and 'Jean Chrétien Roth (1816–81). Facteur de tous les instruments à vent à Strasbourg. Successeur de Dobner & Co et de Bühner et Keller', *Larigot* 49 ([February] 2012), 19–23.

[5] *RGMP*, 4 November 1855, 341–2.

brass.⁶ There was, of course, a publicity component to create excitement and grab the spotlight, but also what appeared to be some innovative ideas from a diligent entrepreneur. Sax could not tolerate such discloseurs and wrote a letter in which he was surprised that the magazine was giving so much publicity (*grand bruit*) to the alleged discoveries of this manufacturer when he had already disclosed this idea more than ten years ago. After a brief lesson in acoustics, he included statements from other experts and excerpts from court cases in which he defended this theory. He also named his supporters (Meyerbeer, Fétis, Berlioz, Kastner, Marloye, Foucault, Gavaret [Gevaert], Léon Kreutzer, Edmond Viel, Hernry Berthoud, Piquemal, Fiorentino, J. Weber, Dufaure, Duval, etc.) and shared at the end that he was convinced that certain people wanted to undermine him and copy his inventions [sic].⁷

The escalation continued when De la Fage reappeared in the following issue in support of Besson's research and advances.⁸ He also recalled that 'well over ten years ago' there were already 'countless (*infiniment*) people' who knew the principle of 'air vibrations in wind instruments', giving as an example the acoustic treatise of the German physicist Ernst Chladni of 1802. De la Fage concluded his intervention by expressing his desire for Besson's experiments and conclusions to be published in more detail and not as schematically as the medium had previously done. Sax's reply did not take long to arrive, and the following week he also asked for more space to explain himself better and try to close the matter, but not without first highlighting the contradictions (*points obscurs*) of Besson's supposed improvements, citing, for example, 'vibrations that escape into the interior (*vibrations qui s'échappent à l'intérieur*)'. However, he ended by appealing to pride and saying that his worth had already been sufficiently tested to give wings to his opponent.⁹

Although De la Fage's bias was blatant (and his publicity exaggerated), Besson would embody the best R&D of the time in brass. This diligent entrepreneur managed to reconcile and optimize simple and economical manufacture with a very good finish that included an improvement in the musical possibilities of the instruments without altering the technical habits of the musicians.¹⁰ De la Fage said that his client had studied the dimensions of the tubes in the brass to the nearest hundredth of a millimetre.¹¹ It is assumed that he transferred this level of precision to mandrels of his

---

⁶ *RGMP*, 3 August 1856, 251.
⁷ *RGMP*, 10 August 1856, 257.
⁸ *RGMP*, 17 August 1856, 265.
⁹ *RGMP*, 24 August 1856, 272–3.
¹⁰ Grenot, 'La facture instrumentale des cuivres', 28–9.
¹¹ *RGMP*, 4 November 1855, 343.

own design (*mandrins régulateurs*), which avoided any inaccuracies in the tube walls and which, above all, resulted in completely identical instruments. Of course, what was interesting was not the use of mandrels, but rather the development of their own tooling with which to produce brasswinds quickly, reliably, and cheaply, a very interesting property when moving towards the rationalization and standardization of instruments. These steel moulds were renamed (*système prototype*) and protected by a certificate of addition in July 1856, as well as an analogous device to keep the diameter of the tube unchanged during bending.[12] Although some of Besson's *mathématico-acoustique* [sic] assumptions in the document are more than questionable, his *système prototype* became the capital element of the company's branding for many years, even when his granddaughters (Marthe and Méha) inherited the business (1908–50).[13]

Gustave-Auguste Besson's advertisements continued to appear on a fortnightly basis in the newspaper. The *RGMP* also advertised small, positive chronicles of performances of his brass instruments, such as the one at the emblematic Herz Hall in July 1857.[14] In this sense, his popularity was increasing and his recurring commercial advertisement included the merits he was reaping, such as the 'Grand Medal of Honour' awarded to him by the Mayor of Paris on 29 January 1857.[15] It also stated that he had business and products protected in the United Kingdom (*Breveté de S.M. la Reine d'Angleterre*) and that he continued to give an extensive five-year guarantee. The following year (1858), Besson continued to climb the ladder and received the compliments of Marshal Vaillant—Minister of War at the time—on the occasion of a commercial exhibition in Dijon. Moreover, the *RGMP* commented that almost all the instruments in his showcase 'had been acquired by the amateurs of [the department of the] Côte-d'Or and neighbouring departments'.[16]

This last note contains more than meets the eye, as it confirms the definitive emergence of a new clientele with few economic resources, but increasing numbers and enthusiasm. Gautrot was competing with his *de pacotille* instruments, and Besson had also found a way to sell—at least partially—his wares, in spite of the preserve established by Sax. Thus, the middle years of

---

[12] Certificate of addition of Besson of 12 July 1856 on the Patent [no. 22072] for 'Improvements to all types of brass musical instruments (*perfectionnements aux instruments de musique de tous genres en cuivre*)' of 18 January 1855 [for fifteen years], 41–59 (INPI).
[13] 'Manufacture d'Instruments de Musique bois & cuivre F. Besson' [c.1910], rep. in *Larigot* 5 ([May] 1989), 20–8. See also Arnold Myers and Niles Eldredge, 'Brasswind Production of Marthe Besson's London Factory', *The Galpin Society Journal* 49 (2006), 43–76.
[14] *RGMP*, 9 July 1857, 263.
[15] *RGMP*, 11 October 1857, 335.
[16] *RGMP*, 19 September 1858, 314.

the Second French Empire were confirmed as the golden age for the brass industry. In reality, this period coincided with a larger process of industrial modernization that was affecting the entire state. Also, fortunately for the peasants, a certain agricultural prosperity was achieved, which partly alleviated hunger and poverty, although the many who moved to the cities in search of better work had to suffer the hardships of other exploitative work. On the other hand, many French cities were changing their *allure* (appearance) thanks to major urban renewal works.[17] The suburbs of Paris began to take on an industrial dimension, as did those of other major capitals such as Lyon and Marseille.

The *coup d'État douanier* (Cobden-Chevalier Treaty) that Napoleon III signed with the British also dated from this time (1860). This agreement with the UK meant free trade in goods, above all raw materials and most food products, but also included musical instruments.[18] The main objective was to seize the comparative advantage in favour of French products and of course to increase the number of customers. The new market could be of interest to the French brass manufacturers, for even though the agreement had not yet come into effect, their cross-Channel neighbours were their best customer (except for their own domestic market and the American continent).[19]

Within the tapestry of artistic Paris, this was a period of relative excitement and enthusiasm where musical events multiplied and revealed a bourgeoisie eager for social contacts in various spaces, not only in its salons or in the powerful and representative palace of the Opera. Among the most popular groups, genres, and venues were the choral societies and their popular competitions (*concours*),[20] the concert cafés, the rise of the dance halls, the revival of religious music, and so on. The military brass bands deserve

---

[17] In the case of Paris, two major axes were created, one along the Champs Elysées and the Seine, and the other across the Boulevard de Sebastopol from the *cité* to the railway stations. These reforms were used to combat unemployment and, at the same time, the large spaces and avenues would make it possible to maintain order and break up demonstrations more effectively. See, among others, Roger-V. Gould, 'Urban transformations, 1852–70', in *Insurgent identities: class, community, and protest in Paris from 1848 to the Commune* (Chicago: University of Chicago Press, 1995), 71–7.

[18] From 1861 onwards, any instrument (including pianos and organs) was left with only 10% customs duty in England—not 30% as was previously the norm. *Galignani's* (1868), 23–4.

[19] *Statistique de l'industrie à Paris (1860)*, 754. Another source with macroeconomic data from 1844 claimed that already in 1844 the UK was importing £12,000 (approx. 300,000fr) worth of musical instruments, and that 'the finest brass wind-instruments are imported'. William Waterstone, *A Cyclopaedia of Commerce, Mercantile Law, Finance, Commercial Geography, and Navigation* (London: Henry G. Bohn, 1844), 485.

[20] A musical almanac of the time reported that the most successful festival was the one organized in Paris in 1859 at the Palais de l'Industrie, with 172 choirs and bands from all over France taking part. *Almanach des orphéons et des sociétés instrumentales* (Paris: Pagnerre, 1863), 28–33. By 1867, France counted 3243 choral groups with more than 250,000 active members and benefactors. (The department of the Seine had 150 such musical associations.) This number continued to rise to around 10,000 at the beginning of the twentieth century. Paul Gerbod, 'L'institution orphéonique en France du XIXe au XXe siècle', *Ethnologie Française* 10: 1 (1980), 28 and 31; and Sophie-Anne Leterrier, 'Musique populaire et

special mention, as they had never before enjoyed such public admiration or popular appeal. As well as continuing to take part in parades and solemn parades, their other concerts in more convivial settings such as squares, boulevards, gardens, and parks were increasingly frequent (Figure 11.1).[21] These ensembles acted as a magnet, drawing people from different social classes together in an atmosphere of festivity, conviviality, and temporary leisure. The flowerbeds and open spaces were also decorated with statues, fountains, small greenhouses, and other urban furniture with a central element, namely the bandstand. These gazebos were to be one of the iconographic elements of the musical diffusion and sonorization of the nineteenth (and much of the twentieth) century not only in France,[22] but throughout the Western world and also in its colonies.[23] Music emanating from roofed

Figure 11.1 Concert of a military band in a grove in Versailles
Le Monde Illustré, 29 August 1868, 133.

musique savante au XIXe siècle. Du *peuple* au *public*', *Revue d'histoire du XIXe siècle* 19 (1999), article available on the Internet at <https://journals.openedition.org/rh19/157> (accessed 10 March 2023).

[21] The press advertised that Paris-based brass bands would play 'every day' except Sunday in the Tuileries gardens. *Le Ménestrel*, 3 May 1863, 175. A little further on, the *Garde de Paris* used to meet its listeners on Tuesdays in the Place Vendôme and on Saturdays in the garden of the Palais Royal. *Le Ménestrel*, 24 May 1863, 200.

[22] Péronnet, *Les enfants d'Apollon*, 458–70.

[23] See, among others, Trevor Herbert and Helen Barlow, *Music and the British Military in the Long Nineteenth Century* (New York, Oxford University Press, 2013), 154–95 or Suzel-Ana Reily, 'From

platforms had this power to culturally uplift the masses without, in fact, providing them with any real power or other tools that could be destabilizing for the regime. On the other hand, attendance at these concerts was free, which was the only possibility for many people to listen to music. Moreover, the repertoire was easy to digest (marches, polkas, fantasies, mazurkas, galops, waltzes, *pasodobles*, etc.); light, in every sense of the word. Operatic themes and reminiscences were also frequent but were evidently adapted and/or vulgarized so that the group and the performers could show off. The visual impact of the uniforms, and the brightness and size of some instruments set a new code of fascination to the amateur community; and, as the vast majority of those instruments were brass, their popularity was (and would continue to be) at an all-time high. Of course, the economic returns were commensurate, and in Paris alone, the brass companies were making more than three million francs a year. Furthermore, the 1860 survey also subdivided the manufacturers into profit groups, and in the case of brass there were five manufacturers amassing between 100,000fr and 200,000fr, and five others between 200,000fr and 500,000fr,[24] more than respectable figures (and evidence that there was not one—Adolphe Sax—dominant player).

Processions to *Encontros*: the Performance Niches of the Community Bands of Minas Gerais, Brazil'; Sylvia Bruinders, 'Soldiers of God: the Spectacular Musical Ministry of the Christmas Bands in the Western Cape, South Africa'; and Helena Simonett, 'From Village to World Stage: The Malleability of Sinaloan Popular Brass Brands', in Suzel-Ana Reily and Katherine Brucher, eds, *Brass Bands of the World: Militarism, Colonial Legacies, and Local Music Making* (London & New York: Routledge, 2016), 99–122, 139–54, and 199–215.

[24] *Statistique de l'industrie à Paris (1860)*, 751–3. Officially, Sax earned slightly less than 281,500fr.

12
Versus Eighteen . . . at the Same Time

Collective Confrontation 'against Adversaries So Powerfully Allied and So Persistent'

In fact, in 1858 Sax and Besson were already at loggerheads in court. However, Besson's was only one of the eighteen companies (manufacturers and retailers) that had been indicted, including such names as Gautrot, Tournier, Goumas, Buffet *jeune*, Buffet-Crampon, Beauboeuf, Isbert, Jacob, Halary senior, Belorgey, Martin brothers (Jean-Baptiste and Félix), Roehn [or Roëhn], Raoux, Drouelle, Florent, Batut [or Battut], and Halary son.[1] Almost all these businessmen were preceded by interesting professional careers—and also by very intense personal lives—on which it is unfortunately not possible to give many more details, for reasons of space. We already know Marcel-Auguste Raoux (1795–1871), who led the civilian persecutions that ended in the Imperial Court of Rouen 1854; moreover, he had studied the French horn and that he subsequently joined the Army, presumably as a military musician. Later, with the help of his father, he managed to climb the ranks and became a regular supplier to French military bands. His grandfather was an *Ordinaire du Roi*—a regular supplier to the king—a distinctive label that his descendants picked up (*Facteur d'instruments du Roi* or *Facteur de Cors [French horns] du Roi*) at the Restoration and under Louis-Philippe.[2] It is possible that the Raoux family enjoyed not only such protection and publicity, but also optimal marketing conditions to which it was easy to become accustomed. Also, that distinction and their own seniority added to their credentials in the bid for the top positions in the wind instrument building

---

[1] According to a *factum* by Sax, the raid on Buffet *jeune* took place on 14 September 1857, his relative Buffet-Crampon was attacked on 30 April and 14 December 1857, Tournier on 13 and 17 December 1857, and Beauboeuf on 13 December 1856, 30 April, and 14 December 1857. The Martin brothers had two corrections (30 April and 12 December 1857). Beauboeuf should have offered him a compensation of 10,000fr and asked for a licence. However, Sax 'did not take the bait (*ne fût qu'un leurre*)', considering that these were ruses to gain time and get rid of the evidence. *Conclusions motivées pour Adolphe Sax, professeur au Conservatoire impérial de musique*, 81–2, 84–5, and 88.

[2] A press entry commented that the president of the Philharmonic Society of Tours was going to give a French horn by Raoux father, 'the king of makers (*le roi des facteurs*)', to a musician (Vivier), an instrument that had once belonged to a king. *RGMP*, 9 June 1845, 191. See also Waterhouse, *The New Langwill*, 318–19.

community, and the Raouxs probably settled into that vantage point.[3] However, the economy was shifting away from these exclusive positions towards requirements based on the demand of a booming middle class; the other factors of the Industrial Revolution did the rest.

The case of the Halary family is similar in that it consisted of three highly regarded generations who were especially known for being the inventors of the ophicleide (1817, 1821, and 1822),[4] or at least for having patented it in France for the first time. Although it is not known whether the founder of the firm (Jean Hilaire Asté) was the grandfather or another relative, the business flourished and its products were highly valued. Moreover, they were pioneers in making metal clarinets and bassoons (1817 and 1818) and by 1823 they had the royal seal of approval (*Facteur de la musique du Roi*).[5] The continuator, Jean-Louis-Antoine Halary (Halari), better known as Halary *père* [father] (1788–1861), was one of Sax's fiercest antagonists in the earlier civil case. However, such animosity and the present criminal prosecution undermined his health and he died in 1861.[6] The son, Jules-Léon-Antoine (Halary *fils* [son]) and first prize for French horn at the Conservatoire in 1845, was less combative and signed a licensing agreement with Sax on 15 December 1859 to exploit the saxotromba.[7] The company—which in 1872 employed some thirty-five people, including children[8]—barely survived another year and was taken over by Coste & Cie, with Sudre as manager.[9]

François Tournier and Pierre Goumas worked for and were associates of Buffet-Crampon, with whom the latter also shared blood ties.[10] In 1849, the Beauboeuf brothers (Jules-Oscar and Lazare-Auguste), banker and manufacturer respectively, started a promising business of building wood- and brasswinds, which in the following years came up against the interests of Sax.

---

[3] Thierry Maniguet, 'La dynastie des Raoux, facteurs de « cors de chasse » du XVIIe au XIXe siècle', *Musique-Images-Instruments* 15 (2015), 226–42. Raoux ceded his business to Jacque-Christophe Labbaye in 1857 for an annuity of 2400fr, but Sax did not stop pursuing him.

[4] Dullat, *Metallblasinstrumentenbau*, 126–44, Jérôme Wiss, 'Essai sur la datation des ophicleides', *Larigot* 61 ([April] 2018), 8–15, and Jérôme Wiss and Bruno Kampmann, 'La Basse d'Harmonie de Sautermeister', *Larigot* 55 ([May] 2015), 3–11.

[5] Ralph-Thomas Dudgeon, *The keyed bugle* (Oxford: Scarecrow Press, 2004), 22–4, 148, and 267–8; and Pierre, *Les Facteurs d'instruments de musique*, 334–6.

[6] Waterhouse, *The New Langwill*, 156–7.

[7] According to a sort of publicity brochure, the company had its roots in 1768 and had achieved numerous professional and honorary successes, including being suppliers to Kings Louis XVIII and Charles X. *Notice Historique sur la Manufacture d'Instruments de Musique de J. A. Halary*, 1–8.

[8] 'Archives nationales, F 12-4726, Travail des enfants, 1872', cited in Haine, *Les facteurs d' instruments*, 25.

[9] François Sudre (1844–c.1912) trained with Edmond Daniel, then worked for Couturier in Lyon, in 1865 for Neudin, and finally became associated with Halary (1866), although by that time he was already an administrator at the Coste. Waterhouse, *The New Langwill*, 391–2. As a curiosity, he was another of the manufacturers who attempted to establish longevity through his *sudrophone* (patented in 1892), another brasswind that has not survived to this day.

[10] Pierre, *Les Facteurs d'instruments de musique*, 311.

This clash—Beauboeuf confessed that he had forged 1684 instruments—and the independence of his foreman (Roëhn), who set up on his own, ultimately dynamited the firm.[11] The latter maker, who trained in Besson's own workshops, seems to have entered into a licensing agreement with the owner of the saxotromba in the following years, and his name survived until the 1880s.[12]

The Martin *frères* society also enjoyed a relatively long existence (*c*.1840–1927). The family had a considerable number of branches and several of its members were linked by marriage to subjects of other famous clans involved in active music and wind instrument making, such as the Lot, Noël, and Thibouville families.[13] However, despite all this pretended pedigree and their presence at various French and British fairs,[14] the Martins did not achieve a preponderant influence or presence in the French instrumental scene. Nor did the other makers involved in the process (Victor Jacob, Isbert, Battut, Belorgey, Florent, and Drouelle)[15] play a decisive role, although we will deal with the last of these later.

Back in the legal arena, the chroniclers (Pataille, Huget, and Calmels) continued to be surprised by the bellicosity of these proceedings: 'the struggle has begun again more vividly than ever (*la lutte a recommencé plus vive que jamais*)'. Referring to Sax, they said that 'no other [manufacturer] had ever had to endure such a long and fierce struggle (*une lutte aussi longue et aussi acharnée*) against adversaries so powerfully allied and so persistent (*aussi puissamment coalisés et aussi persistants*) in reproducing the same theses of attack and defence'. Those words may not have been neutral, but they reflect the corporate and associative character of the rival makers and that their strategy would still be to demonstrate the lack of foundation in the saxotromba

---

[11] *Le Droit. Gazette des Tribunaux*, 20 April 1856, 394 and Haine, *Les facteurs d'instruments*, 306.

[12] Waterhouse, *The New Langwill*, 25 and 332.

[13] To find out more about the intricate Martin family, see Bruno Kampmann and William McBride, 'Martin frères and the Martin family: four generations of woodwind instrument makers', *Larigot* 22 spécial (1995), iv–viii. See also <https://www.luthiers-mirecourt.com/thibouville_genealogie.htm> (accessed 10 December 2022).

[14] Pontécoulant, *Organographie*, vol. 2, 405.

[15] Jacob was a reseller or middleman (*commissionnaire acheteur*) who was in the business of supplying merchandise of all kinds to American dealers. He was supplied by several French instrument makers, notably Beauboeuf. His lawyer's (Payen) defence was based on the fact that the law did not penalize this type of agent or third party insofar as Jacob was not aware (*sciemment*) of this irregularity and had always acted in good faith. His argument was also supported by an attestation dated 14 May 1860 with the signatures of other Parisian businessmen from whom he bought material and who belonged to various sectors such as textiles, arms, horse-drawn carriages, ironmongery, stationery, goldsmiths' shops, etc. *Cour impériale. Chambre des appels correctionnels. Note sur Victor Jacob prévenu de contrefaçon sur la poursuite de M. Sax. Audience du Vendredi 18 mai 1860. M. Parta[r]rieu-Lafosse, Président. M. Oscar de Vallée, Avocat-Général* (Paris: n. ed., [Impr. E. Allard,] n.d. [1860]), 1–7. Battut was a 'trader in Constantinople (*négociant à Constantinople*)', that is, also a kind of middleman or supplier for the Turks. *Conclusions pour Monsieur Raoux, appelant, contre Monsieur Sax, intimé. Cour impériale de Paris*, 2. We have not found anything from Florent, although he was probably, like Belorgey and Drouelle, a manufacturer of valves and spare parts.

patent. Particularly Besson, who 'was performing (*reproduit*) with renewed ardour and intensity (*une ardeur et une insistance*)', managed to introduce a new subjective element into the debate: the lack of novelty in the saxotromba's timbre (*la non-nouveauté de sa voix*).[16] During two hearings on 30 July and 13 August 1858, more than thirty opposing testimonies were heard, including those of the directors of certain military groups.[17] Moreover, not all the legions of the Paris National Guard were in favour of the standard instrumental model, such as Joseph Meifred's (third).[18] It was precisely this influential conductor, teacher, and collaborator of the Halarys who led some 200 military musicians from five bands in a single band to greet the Emperor on New Year's Day 1856, a performance which did not include any brass by Sax.[19] However, this anomaly (which did not go unnoticed) was quickly corrected and the National Guard corps was reformed by *Décret impérial* (12 March 1856),[20] leaving a contingent of 2423 and a single band composed of a conductor (Jean-Georges Paulus), five first-class musicians, ten second-class musicians, thirteen third-class musicians, and twenty-five pupils (*élèves*). Although the exact instrumentation of this ensemble was not specified, the *Garde de Paris* soon adopted saxophones and other brass instruments from the Belgian inventor, just as their counterparts in Light infantry and the Guides had done.[21]

For his part, Sax reiterated the originality of his work and that 'what gave the saxotromba its new voice were the proportions, the diameter'. In any

---

[16] *Annales de la propriété industrielle*, tome 6, 1860, 242–4.

[17] Besson's supporters were: Achard, manufacturer; Bartès, military musician; Blanchuissier; Bonnange, professor; Davinet, manufacturer; Depuille, lessor; Droz, Swiss manufacturer; Ehrsam, manufacturer; Gohin, manufacturer; Guérin, artist; Guchard [Guichard], manufacturer; Hanh, workman; Hérissé, notary; De Montivilliers, teacher; Hubart, workman; Hugo, artist; Jacoutot, bandmaster; Joly, manufacturer; Kretzschmann, Strasbourg manufacturer; Kunzé, *chapelier* [milliner?] and artist; Lacombe, manufacturer; Lebrun, quincallier; Libert, clerk; Meifred, Conservatoire teacher; Michiels, artist; Minod, Swiss manufacturer; Paul, teacher; Rodel [Rödel], valve manufacturer; Sassaigne, lessor and former maker of valves; Tolbecque, former brass band director; Vignier, musician; and Zoepffel, administrator (*économe*) of the small ensemble (*séminaire*) from Chapelle-sous-Rougemont. And for Sax: Rumigny, former general; Nicolas Mohr, director of the Guides; Klozé [Klosé], professor at the Conservatoire; David, instrument maker; Roënh, maker and ex-worker of Besson; Thibault senior, ex-conductor of the band of the 65th Line Regiment; Thibault junior, also musical leader of the Cuirassiers of the Imperial Guard; and Michaud, maker. *Défense de M. Besson contre M. Sax: enquête, contre-enquête et jugement avant faire droit rendu par le tribunal le 13 août 1858: tribunal correctionnel de la Seine (6ᵉ Chambre): présidence de M. Berthelin* (Paris: n. ed., [Imprimerie de H.S. Dondey-Dupré,] 1858), 1–6, 8–45, and 47–72.

[18] Planque, *Agenda musical ou indicateur des amateurs*, 82–8 and Joseph Meifred, *Quelques mots sur les changements proposés pour la composition des musiques d'infanterie* (Paris: Bureau de la France musicale, 1853), 5.

[19] *Le Ménestrel*, 30 December 1855, 3.

[20] *Journal militaire officiel*, [no exact date, first half of] 1856 [no. 13], 394–7.

[21] The band of the *Garde de Paris* would be renamed in the Third French Republic as the *Musique de la Garde Républicaine*, an ensemble that would gain respectability and prominence, including diplomatic duties. See, among others, Oscar Comettant, *La Musique de la Garde républicaine en Amérique, histoire complète et authentique* (Paris: Bouallay, 1894), 65 or Sylvie Hue, *150 ans de Musique à la Garde Républicaine. Mémoires d'un Orchestre* (Paris: Nouvelle Arche de Noé, 1998), 18–43.

case, the sixth chamber of the Court of First Instance of Paris decided on 13 August 1858 that an expert should verify the uniqueness of the instrument's timbre. The technician appointed for this purpose (Surville) was also to ascertain whether, among the confiscated instruments, there was any specimen—whatever its name—which, by its shape ('by their internal dimensions') or its voice, was sufficiently similar to the saxotromba to be considered a forgery.

After almost a year (and with the parallel victory of Sax against Gautrot at the Imperial Court of Amiens and the Court of Cassation on 19 May and 8 July 1859), the hearings against the coalition of manufacturers—including Besson's case—resumed. The sessions began on 5 August 1859 and continued in December (15, 22, and 29) of the same year and in January (5, 12, 19, and 26) and February (2, 9, 16, and 23) of 1860.[22] But before hearing the judges' opinions, it is worthwhile to look at the report commissioned from Surville, on which the interested parties were initially (October 1858–January 1859) invited to intervene. As might be expected, these confrontations led to discussions of interpretation and mutual accusations of adulteration and cheating. Sax complained that instruments provided by his opponents had been intentionally altered. On the other hand, Besson and Gautrot showed that the dimensions (measurement of the diameter of the tubes) that the Belgian entrepreneur had represented in the patent were not even accurate, since by following the scale and comparing the thickness of the tubes, they did not correspond.[23] For example, and with regard to design 1 of the patent (Figure 12.1), the reference of 0.070 metres near the bell was absolutely incongruent with the 0.024 metres dimension shown below.[24]

On this occasion—and unlike the Halevy, Savart, and Boquillon dossier in 1847—Surville did follow a methodology. The expert witness established seven external dimensions (inspired by those seven reference points provided by the patent designs)[25] to compare and characterize Sax's original

---

[22] *Tribunal de la Seine: 6e chambre correctionnelle: jugement rendu à la suite des audiences des 30 juillet et 13 août 1858, 5 août, 15, 22 et 29 décembre 1859, 5, 12, 19, 26 janvier, 2, 9, 16 et 23 février 1860. M. Gislain de Bontin et M. Mahler* (Paris: n. ed., [Imprimerie de E. Brière,] 1860), 1–14.

[23] The expert referred to these errors as follows: 'From this point of view, the Sax patent is at least open to criticism.' *Rapport de M. l'expert Surville, ingénieur, déposé le 18 février 1859 et dire de M. Sax.* (Paris: n. ed. [Imprimerie centrale des Chemins de Fer de Napoléon Chaix et Cie,] 1860), 17 and 23–7.

[24] The overall scale was also controversial—Sax only noted that the 'Instruments [were] at 25% per metre'—and it was clear that the high examples in that sketch ('Fig 12', for example) did not correspond in size to the low ones ('Fig 10'), which should have been drawn considerably larger.

[25] The measurement of tubes is still a very controversial topic today, although some authors have tried to develop a method. See, for example, Arnold Myers and Raymond Parks, 'How to Measure a Horn', *The Galpin Society Journal* 48 (1995), 193–9 and Arnold Myers, *Characterization and Taxonomy of Historic Brass Musical Instruments from an Acoustical Standpoint* (Thesis, Edinburgh, University of Edinburgh, 1998), 34–42 and 79–115.

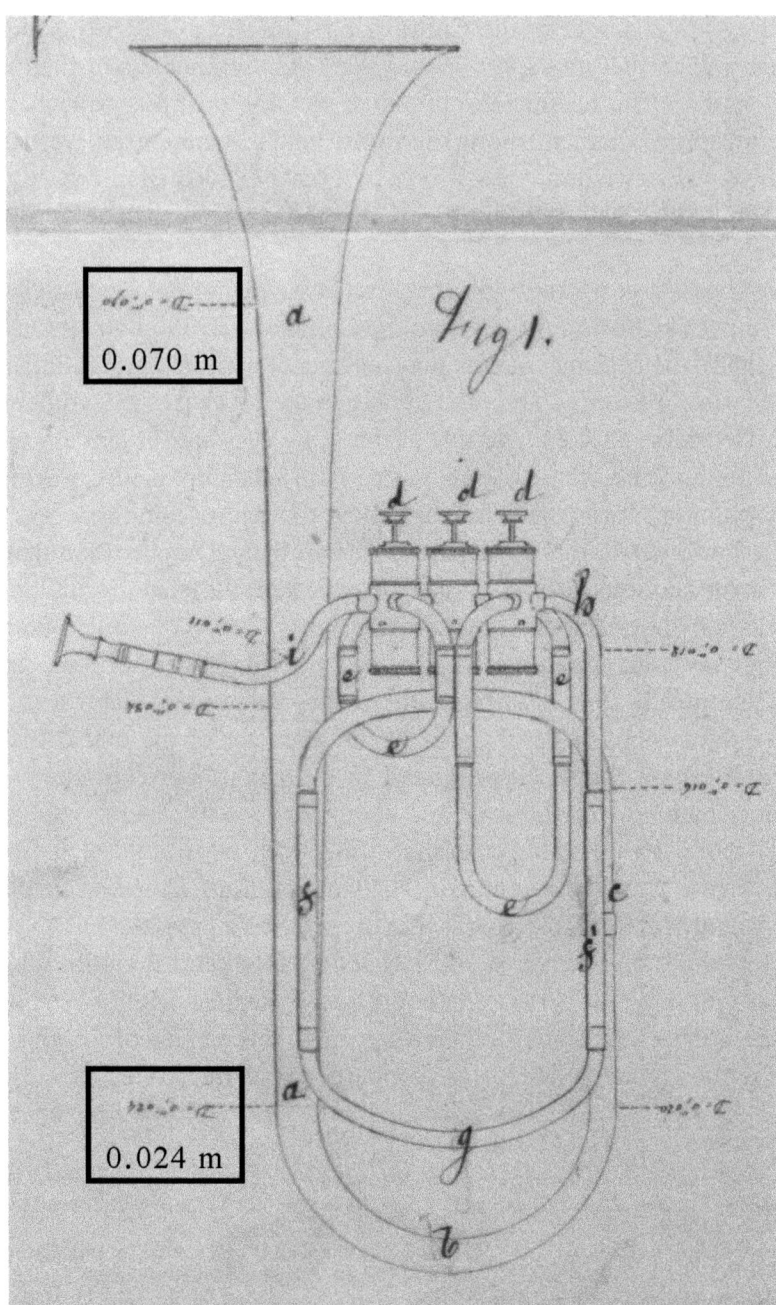

Figure 12.1 False correlation between the measured levels of the saxotromba patent

Compiled from Sax's saxotromba patent (1845) (INPI).

instruments with the seized and pre-patent instruments (four *clavicors*, two ophicleides, and one *néo-alto*)[26] (Figure 12.2). The header of the resulting table consisted of the parameter *Diamètres*, which actually refers to the type of instrument and its key; then *Pavillon*, to refer to the author of the instrument, as well as the number of the copy audited; and finally, numbered from 1 to 7, those levels that ran along the tube and were given in millimetres. The first row of contents represents the references of the official document of 1845 (the patent), the second a saxotromba provided by Sax (with the serial number 16,214 and with 1.95 metres of pipe length), and the third and following ones contain the measurements of several *altos* seized and the rest of the brass.

On the basis of his measurements and having called in even seasoned performers, Surville came to conclusions in favour of Sax. According to the expert—and (presumably) answering the first question that the judge had urged him—the saxotromba 'had a special timbre (*voix spéciale*), but common (*mais qu'elle leur est commune*) to the other instruments designated as

§ IV.

COMPARAISON DU SAXOTROMBA EN MI BEMOL AVEC LES INSTRUMENTS DU MÊME TON QUI ONT ÉTE SAISIS ET DÉPOSÉS AU GREFFE.

Voici le tableau des instruments en *mi* bémol saisis qui ont été mesurés contradictoirement avec les parties.

DIAMÈTRES.	PAVILLON.	1er	2e	3e	4e	5e	6e	7e
Saxotromba........	Brevet.	70	34	24	20	16	12	11
Id. *mi* b....	Sax.	60	33	23.5	18.5	16	12	11
Altos *mi* b.........	Besson 1er	61	36	27	22	20.5	13	12
Id. Id..........	Id. 2e	61	36	27	21.5	20	13	12
Id. *fa* et *mi* b....	Id. 3e	61	34	25.5	20	18	13	12
Id....	Id. 4e	60	34	25	20	18	13	12
Id.........	Id. 5e	62	34	25	20.5	17.5	13	12
Id. *mi* b..........	Halary 6e	66.5	35.5	26	21	19	11.5	11
Id.............	Id. 7e	68	35.5	25.5	21	20	11.5	11
Id. *fa* et *mi* b....	Id. 8e	66.5	33	25	20	18	12	12
Id....	Id. 9e	66.5	33	23	49	18.5	11.5	11
Id. *mi* b..........	Buffet 10e	68	34	26	22	20.5	12	12
Id...........	Id. 11e	64	34	25.5	21	17.5	12	12

DIAMÈTRES.	PAVILLON.	1er	2e	3e	4e	5e	6e	7e
Altos *fa* et *mi* b...	Beaubeuf 12e	58.5	33	24.5	19	18	12	11.5
Id. *fa* haut et *mi* b.	Gautrot 13e	61	32	24	18	15	12.5	11.5
Id. *mi* b..........	Guignon 14e	60	33	24	18	16	13	11.5
Id. Id...	Noblet 15e	68.5	37.5	29	24.5	20.5	13	11.5
Id. Id....... ...	Muller 16e	79	42	32	26.5	22	13.5	12
Alto en 8 *mi* b....	Gautrot 17e	52	30.5	22	17.5	16	12.5	12
Clavicor...........	Besson 18e	48	39	19.5	16.5	14	12	11
Id......	Id. 19e	59	30	21	17	16	13	11
Id.............	Id. 20e	60	34	29	22.5	19.5	12	11
Id.............	Id. 21e	65	38	31	26	22	13.5	11
Ophicléide.........	[illegible] 22e	72	42	30.5	24.5	20.5	13.5	12
Id............	Id. 23e	75	42	31	25	21	13	12
Néo-Alto..........	Guichard 24e	82	48	38	32	28	14	12

1° Considérons d'abord la première série composée de quatorze instruments qui forment la tête de ce tableau.

Il est à remarquer que non-seulement les dimensions des diamètres correspondants varient dans les instruments des différents facteurs, mais encore dans ceux d'un même facteur. **Ainsi dans les altos de M. Besson, dans ceux de M. Halary il existe, d'un instrument à l'autre, des différences dans les diamètres correspondants qui s'élèvent de 2 à 3 millimètres.**

Cela confirme ce que nous avions déjà dit de l'influence de la fabrication pour faire varier la grosseur des tubes, et aussi ce que nous avons fait observer que ces variations sont ordinairement assez peu considérables pour ne pas altérer d'une manière sensible le timbre des instruments, **puisque tous ceux-ci sont donnés comme bons pour remplir les parties intermédiaires des orchestres,** *ce qui fait supposer qu'ils ont tous la même voix.*

Nous ferons encore remarquer que les dimensions ne varient sensiblement dans ces instruments **qu'au premier diamètre, celui où le tube se raccorde**

Figure 12.2 Comparison of the E♭ saxotromba with the rest of the instruments of the same pitch (*altos*), including *clavicors*, ophicleides, and a *néo-alto* of the rest of the manufacturers

Rapport de M. l'expert Surville, 36–7 (BnF).

[26] The judge had told him that these dimensions were to be 'inside', but Surville, aware of the difficulty this would entail, took them on the outside because the difference was 'negligible'. According to him, the brass sheeting was the same for all these instruments and was only half a millimetre thick. *Rapport de M. l'expert Surville*, 9.

altos and *barytons*, which are used in conjunction [with saxotrombas] for the intermediate voices (*que l'on emploie concurremment avec les saxotrombas pour les parties intermédiaires*) of military bands. On the second question—whether forgeries had been produced—Surville thought that the proportions of the *altos* and *barytons* and other instruments taken were very similar to those of the saxotromba, which led one to believe that they were copies (*il y a toute raison de le croire*). Finally, Surville allowed a sort of final statement by the Belgian inventor (*Dire de M. Sax*) in which he added that the saxotrombas possessed a central timbre between that of the French horn (*cor*), the trombone, and the ophicleide; a subjective assessment which seems to coincide with that of the technician.

The judge, Gislain de Bontin, gave value to the report and ruled on 22 March 1860 in favour of Sax. However, some defendants withdrew early (Gautrot and Halary junior); and others had their assets restored for lack of evidence (Isbert, Roëhn, and Battut), prescription (Buffet-Crampon), or extenuating circumstances (licence of another manufacturer—Jacques-Christophe Labbaye) such as that of the Martin brothers. Halary senior had tried to circumvent Sax's rights by using a patent of his own dated 19 August 1856.[27] However, the judge ruled that this document concealed the same instrument (the saxotromba) 'with a simple inversion (*renversement*) of the bell'. Nor could Halary senior avail himself of the licence agreement between his son and the Belgian entrepreneur because the latter had expressly reserved his rights against him in the contract. Apart from the stubborn insistence on the unoriginality of the saxotromba,[28] the highlight of Besson's case was the intervention of Kretzschmann, one of the witnesses who testified on his behalf and who was to enter the scene with a bang. At the hearing of 30 July 1858, this instrument maker from Strasbourg had brought four instruments as background to the saxotromba. He referred to them as *ophicléides-alto*, featuring an upward-facing bell and parallel valves. He claimed that his father had crafted three of these instruments in 1839, and he had made one himself.[29] This testimony turned against him and Sax

---

[27] In fact, that patent [no. 24419] was dated 9 August 1855 and Jules-Léon Halary protected, for fifteen years, 'Parabolic cut bells applicable to musical instruments (*pavillons à coupe parabolique applicables aux instruments de musique*)' (INPI).

[28] *Affaire Sax: réquisitoire: Adolphe Sax demandeur en condamnation pour contrefaçon contre les sieurs Raoux, Halary, Buffet jeune, Besson, Buffet-Crampon, Tournier et Goumas, Beauboeuf et Victor Jacob, Martin frères et autres: tribunal de la Seine. M. Mahler. Audiences des 30 juillet et 13 août 1858, 5 août, 15, 22 et 29 décembre 1859, 5, 12, 19, 26 janvier, 2, 9 et 16 février 1860: enquête, contre-enquête et plaidoiries: audience du 23 février 1860: réquisitoire de M. Mahler* (Paris: n. ed., [Imprimerie centrale des Chemins de Fer de Napoléon Chaix et Cie,] 1860), 12, 33–41, and 60–8.

[29] *Quinze ans de procès!: M. Sax contre MM. Besson, Raoux et consorts: 1846–1860* (Paris: n. ed., [Imprimerie centrale de Napoléon Chaix et Cie,] 1860), 10–18, *Tribunal de la Seine: 6e chambre*

had these four instruments seized, which compromised him in the present case and gave rise to a new piece of litigation (to be dealt with later). The chronicle of those battles also reveals the numerous raids—five, from 1857 to April 1858[30]—that Sax orchestrated against Besson's factory, where not only allegedly corrupt aerophones were seized, but also trade books and very expensive construction material including eighteen mandrills. Besson's records (and those of other defendants) revealed that his clients included numerous military groups: 'on each page were repeated entries of supplies of musical instruments to all the regiments of the Army'.[31]

Although all penalties were roughly on the same scale (Raoux 1000fr, Halary *père* 1000fr, Buffet *jeune* 1000fr, Tournier and Goumas 500fr each, Beauboeuf 1000fr, and Victor Jacob 500fr),[32] Besson bore the brunt of the punishment. His fine was the highest provided for by the 1844 law (2000fr), in addition to the payment of three quarters of the costs of the trials and the expert's fees. As if this were not enough, Sax's rival had refused to hand over certain instruments in the last of the raids (22 April 1858), thus incurring a blocking (*séquestre judiciaire*) which, if not remedied immediately, would mean another penalty of 4000fr. In addition, the surcharge for damages in favour of Sax remained open, for which Gislain de Bontin appointed a commission (Boquillon, Verre, and Richardière) to calculate the amount.[33]

Knowing the character of those makers, it should come as no surprise that all the defendants—except Beauboeuf, who had probably already gone bankrupt or could no longer keep up with the pace—appealed. Sax, for his part, also lodged his own protest against all his rivals, without exception. Again, a cohort of lawyers, namely Senard, Larnac (Raoux),[34] Payen (Jacob), Blanc (Buffet-Crampon, Tournier, and Goumas), and Hébert, the

---

correctionnelle: jugement rendu à la suite des audiences des 30 juillet et 13 août 1858, 6–7, and *Conclusions motivées pour Adolphe Sax, professeur au Conservatoire impérial de musique*, 51.

[30] *Annales de la propriété industrielle*, tome 6, 1860, 251 and *Conclusions motivées pour Adolphe Sax, professeur au Conservatoire impérial de musique*, 7–9.

[31] *Conclusions motivées pour Adolphe Sax, professeur au Conservatoire impérial de musique*, 7–8, *Quinze ans de procès!: M. Sax contre MM. Besson, Raoux et consorts*, 3–4, and *Annales de la propriété industrielle*, tome 6, 1860, 253–4.

[32] *Tribunal de la Seine: 6e chambre correctionnelle: jugement rendu à la suite des audiences des 30 juillet et 13 août 1858*, 12.

[33] This report and the alleged compensation were to be a long nightmare for Sax. In an open letter of 1887, he said that the experts' report had not even been registered (*déposé*) and that he had spent 4000fr on the bureaucratic formalities involved. The businessman implored that this matter be resolved as soon as possible so that, before he died [sic], he could pay other people to whom he owed money, breathing 'a few hours of peace in a life consumed by unrest'. Why he did not collect that indemnity—Besson fled to London and died in 1875—will be developed later, but it remained unresolved the following year (1888). *La musique des familles*, 21 April 1887, 215–16 and 28 April 1887, 22–4, *Gil Blas*, 2 April 1887, 1, *Le Ménestrel*, 3 April 1887, 142–3, *La Justice*, 26 March 1887, [1–2], *Le Petit Parisien*, 28 March 1887, [2], *Journal des Débats*, 17 April 1887, [2], and *La Justice*, 20 January 1888, [3].

[34] *Conclusions pour Monsieur Raoux, appelant, contre Monsieur Sax, intimé. Cour impériale de Paris*, 1–2.

latter representing Sax, faced each other in six hearings in May 1860. It is worth noting the pleading of Besson's advocate (Senard) and that it contained 'a battery of no less than fifty-one reasons (*chefs*)' supporting his position. It is also noteworthy that Kretzschmann brought a lawyer from his own district (*avocat du barreau de Strasbourg*), *Maître* Kügler, to represent him. However, having heard the report of councillor Halton and the conclusions of the public prosecutor De Vallée,[35] the president of the chamber[36] ratified on 15 June 1860 all that had been ordered in the judgement of 22 March of that year; the only exception being that the fine for Buffet *jeune* was reduced from 1000fr to 500fr.

The clashes did not end there, as Raoux[37] and Besson lodged an appeal to the Court of Cassation, which, in practice, was only pursued by the latter. Drawing on doctrine from the codes of Civil Procedure and Forestier, as well as the law of 1844, Besson based his protest on two points. The first sought to demonstrate abuse of power in the seizure of the four brass presented by his colleague Kretzschmann, and the second related to the problematic and allegedly erroneous affiliation of saxotromba with these instruments. However, on 16 August 1860, the president (Vaïsse), after hearing the report of councillor Rives, the arguments of the lawyers Rendu and Fabre—for Besson and Sax respectively—and the opinion of the public prosecutor (De Marnas), decided to ratify the ruling of the previous chamber of appeal (15 June 1860). Moreover, the judge said that, 'far from having misapplied the articles in question, [the previous Imperial Court] had done a just diligence', thus effectively dismissing Besson's appeal in cassation and condemning him to pay the full costs of the trial.[38]

---

[35] *Affaire Sax: conclusions de M. l'avocat général Oscar de Vallée à l'audience du 26 mai 1860: Adolphe Sax demandeur en condamnation pour contrefaçon contre les sieurs Raoux, Halary, Buffet jeune, Besson, Buffet-Crampon, Tournier et Goumas, Beauboeuf et Victor Jacob, Martin frères et autres. Cour impériale. Chambre des appels correctionnels. Audiences des 11, 12, 18, 19, 25 et 26 mai 1860: plaidoiries* (Paris: n. ed., [Imprimerie centrale des Chemins de Fer de Napoléon Chaix et Cie,] 1860), 3–6.

[36] The name of the presiding judge is not known. *Annales de la propriété industrielle*, tome 6, 1860, 256–63.

[37] *Note pour M. Sax en réponse à la nouvelle note de M. Raoux* (Paris: n. ed., [Imprimerie de E. Brière,] n.d. [1860]), 1–4 and 6–10; and *Réponse de Monsieur Raoux aux conclusions motivées de Monsieur Sax* (Paris: n. ed., [Impr. S. Raçon,] n.d. [1860]), 1–3.

[38] *Conclusions motivées pour Adolphe Sax, professeur au Conservatoire impérial de musique*, 42 and *Annales de la propriété industrielle*, tome 6, 1860, 359–61. See also *Le Ménestrel*, 26 August 1860, 311 and *La France musicale*, 19 August 1860, 343.

13
Tentacles in Strasbourg

Competition from Outside Paris and in Other Ways

The four brasswinds that Kretzschmann exhibited before the Paris Court of First Instance in support of Besson (hearing of 30 July 1858) led to his indictment in the previous case and triggered a parallel lawsuit. Sax dragged this Strasbourg manufacturer[1] into the dispute by arguing that these instruments were forgeries of the saxotromba, so the patent holder acted accordingly and had the Court retain them.[2] Evidently, the Belgian entrepreneur did not (only) want to seize these *ophicléides-alto*, but to have access to all the 'material evidence to support his statements', i.e. Kretzschmann's books, which could further compromise him.[3] Kretzschmann tried to wriggle out of the web—the bailiffs had already appeared at his Strasbourg holding on 28, 29 March, and 19 April 1860—by arguing the incompetence of the Paris court to authorize and decide on searches and seizures outside the capital. However, that legal forum not only considered itself apt to do so and to arbitrate the present dispute, but also held co-responsible Besson—who was not in the courtroom and would not be present at the forthcoming hearings, but who was represented—for the criminal acts. Furthermore, in a second hearing held on the same day (26 July 1860), the judge (Gislain de Bontin?) fined each of the guilty parties 2000fr, to which he added another 2000fr in compensation for the four fraudulent instruments and another indemnity for what was revealed in Kretzschmann's books.[4]

---

[1] Charles-Auguste Kretzschmann (1818–88) was the continuator of the brass manufacturing firm that his father (Charles-Gottlob) had started in 1812 in the capital of the Alsace region. René Pierre, 'Charles Kretzschmann (1777–1842), de Markneukirchen à Strasbourg', *Larigot* 48 ([September] 2011), 20–3 and Pierre, *Les Facteurs d'instruments de musique*, 348.

[2] According to a Kretzschmann's *factum*, three of the brass (the ones his father had made) had been held at the court secretariat (*greffe*) since 1857, and the final seizure of the fourth one took place on 19 April 1860. *Note pour M. Kretzschmann, fabricant d'instruments de musique, demeurant rue Sainte-Hélène, à Strasbourg (Bas-Rhin) contre M. A. Sax, fabricant d'instruments de musique, demeurant rue Saint-Georges, 50, à Paris* (Strasbourg: n. ed., [Impr. G. Silbermann,] n.d. [1861]), 1–6.

[3] *Note pour M. Sax contre MM. Besson et Kretzschmann: tribunal correctionnel de la Seine: audience du jeudi; jugement par défaut du 26 juillet 1860 auquel Kretzschmann a formé opposition, et dont M. Sax demande au contraire le maintien; Besson prétendant, sans le justifier légalement, qu'il y a aussi formé* (Paris: n. ed., [Imprimerie française et anglaise de E. Brière,] n.d. [1860]), 2–24 and 28–9.

[4] *Annales de la propriété industrielle*, tome 7, 1861, 291–3.

The latter businessman appealed, but the president of the Imperial Court (De Guajal), after having heard the report of counsel Mongis, the speeches of the lawyers (Blanc and Hébert, the latter representing Sax), and the conclusions of the public prosecutor Barbier, confirmed, on 19 December 1860, *par adoption pure et simple*, the judgement of first instance. As was to be expected, Kretzschmann also appealed to the last level (Cassation) with a complaint based on three points according to which his procedural rights had allegedly been violated on the basis of the Civil Code, the Code of Criminal Procedure, and the law of 1844.[5] The president of the criminal chamber (Vaïsse), after hearing the report of councillor Nouguier, the plea of Michaux-Bellaire—Kretzschmann's representative—and in accordance with the conclusions of the public prosecutor Blanche, finally rejected most of their positions on 4 July 1861. However, the episode, which seemed to have ended here, took another turn. Kretzschmann found a loophole, namely that the Paris Court of First Instance exceeded its compensatory assessments of the judgement of the (second) hearing of 26 July 1860.[6] Cassation ordered it to return to the first level and opened a new artery for litigation, which rather postponed a chastisement that seemed inevitable.

The sixth chamber of the Criminal Court of First Instance of Paris, now presided by Melchior-Jules Salmon, recognized in its motivation of 6 February 1862 that the obstruction lay in ascertaining the nature and characteristics of the four instruments that had been intercepted. To this end, the judges relied on the report commissioned by the Criminal Court of First Instance—same chamber—to Surville on 13 August 1858. However, before ruling, Salmon stated that, although the authority of the saxotromba had been established in another forum in which Kretzschmann had not taken an active part, the legitimacy of the instrument had 'undisputed authority' over him and the present proceedings. The judge added that the defendant could not hide behind ignorance of cause either, as it was amply demonstrated that he and Besson had participated since 1846 in the coalition of manufacturers who sought the invalidity of Sax's patents.[7] Furthermore, he recalled that Kretzschmann had been a witness in the case between Sax vs Gautrot and Rivet in 1856 and was therefore aware of everything. Salmon also

---

[5] *Mémoire ampliatif pour M. Kretzschmann, fabricant d'instruments de musique, demeurant rue Sainte-Hélène, à Strasbourg (Bas-Rhin) contre M. A. Sax, fabricant d'instruments de musique, demeurant rue Saint-Georges, 50, à Paris. Cour de cassation. Chambre criminelle. M. Vaïsse, Président. M. Nouguier, Conseiller rapporteur* (Strasbourg: n. ed., [Impr. G. Silbermann,] n.d. [1861]), 6–14.

[6] *Annales de la propriété industrielle*, tome 7, 1861, 291–3 and tome 9, 1863, 116. Sax's lawyer is not known.

[7] *Quinze ans de procès!: M. Sax contre MM. Besson, Raoux et consorts*, 18.

included two intervened letters in his judicial decree. In the first (24 January 1846), Kretzschmann acknowledged that Sax had indeed modified the shape of some instruments and that, following the ministerial order, he [Kretzschmann] too had begun to make them. In addition, and very significantly, he commented that only five days ago he had received an order covering the entire [sic] band of the 6th Artillery Regiment of Douai, a French town in the department of Nord in the Nord-Pas-de-Calais region. The second (17 February 1846) was addressed to Halary, 'the treasurer of the coalition', and urged those manufacturers not to let their guard down with the likes of Sax and his allies: 'I find that with people like Sax and company, you can never be too careful.'

Disproving the other evidence and testimony on which Kretzschmann relied—including that of the customers to whom he allegedly sold the four instruments—the judge found that the four brasswinds were forgeries. Salmon also claimed that the instruments had been welded and reworked, which could have involved Besson or Kretzschmann himself in order to use them as evidence in his favour. In their efforts to prove that Sax's invention was already known in other countries, the two defendants would have to endure a new offence. The owners of the four instruments—three of which were from Switzerland—caused them to be accused of having introduced illicit goods into France, an action punishable by article 41 of the 1844 law, even if this had been done in support of one of Kretzschmann and Besson's theses.

Therefore, on 6 February 1862, the Court found Kretzschmann—and Besson—guilty and ordered them to pay a fine of 2000fr on the basis of articles 40, 41, and 49 of the 1844 law. It also declared valid the seizures that Sax had orchestrated and the confiscation of those assets in his favour and ordered him to pay (also Besson) a further 2000fr in damages and interest for the brass quartet. On top of that, there was the additional 1000fr uncovered by the audit of Kretzschmann's movements and records (*livres*) over the last three years and, finally, the costs of the trial. After that crushing judgement, Besson printed a fiery *factum* to complain again about the seizure of the four instruments and that Sax had no scruples in persecuting his Strasbourg colleague so viciously.[8]

---

[8] Besson again pointed out that the 1845 patent did not say a word about what was taken for granted, i.e. that the saxotromba had the bell up, pistons parallel to it, and a particular voice. *Pour M. Besson. Réponse à la Note publiée par M. Sax sur la saisie faite au greffe des quatre instruments intitulés Antériorités. [Tribunal de première instance de la Seine. 6ᵉ Chambre. Présidence de M. Salmon. Audience du jeudi]* (Paris: n. ed., [Impr. Renou et Maulde,] 1862), 2–5.

Naturally, Besson and Kretzschmann appealed. After the hearings of 8 and 15 May 1862, at which they heard the report of councillor Puissan and the arguments of *Maître* Favre (Kretzschmann);[9] those of 22 and 24 May, *Maîtres* Ferry and Hébert, representatives of Besson and Sax; and that of 7 June, when the conclusions of the public prosecutor (Dupré Lasale), and another reply from Favre were heard,[10] the trial was ready for appraisal. The judgement was read on 19 June 1862 under the presidency of the imperial judge De Guajal who, for the most part, found in favour of Sax. Besson and Kretzschmann tried to make some desperate arguments, the most obvious being that the four instruments should not be admitted into evidence because they were originally the subject of another case. However, the defendants succeeded in proving that two (and not three) were the brasswinds from abroad, namely those of Monsieur Blanc from Lausanne and Huguenin Virchaux from Locle (canton of Neufchâtel). On the other hand, De Guajal admitted that these were isolated items, i.e. unrelated to any industrial mass production, but—he emphasized—illegal and punishable. However, as regards the offence 'of piracy of which Kretzschmann in particular was accused', the judge acknowledged that, although the latter 'offered in his advertisement instruments practically identical (*en tout semblables*) to those of Sax, it had not been proved that [the accused] had executed this offer (*offre*)'. And, 'in the absence of any corpus delicti (*qu'en absence de tout corps de délit*), it was not possible to declare with certainty that [Kretzschmann] had incurred in this forgery', and therefore exempted him from paying the 1000fr in damages. However, De Guajal maintained the other charges and made him and Besson bear the costs of the present appeal trial.[11]

Besson and Kretzschmann completed their last remaining legal manoeuvre and appealed to the Court of Cassation. This forum finally resolved this conflict on 12 March 1863 under the presidency of Vaïsse who, after having heard the report of the councillor Caussin de Perceval, the arguments

---

[9] *Affaire Kretzschmann contre Adolphe Sax. Cour impériale de Paris (Chambre des appels correctionnels). Audiences des 8 et 15 mai 1862. Plaidoirie de Me Jules Favre pour M. Kretzschmann* (Strasbourg: n. ed., [Impr. G. Silbermann,] 1862), 1–71.

[10] Dupré Lasale also commented (*et pour tout dire*) that, after having won so many trials, it would have been 'generous' on the part of Sax 'not to pursue to the last extremity his defeated adversaries, and not to reduce them to this humiliation and make them come and lay at his feet the weapons that no longer served them'. *Affaire Kretzschmann contre Adolphe Sax. Cour impériale de Paris (Chambre des appels correctionnels). Présidence de M. De Guajal. Audience du 7 juin 1862. Extrait des conclusions de M. l'Avocat général Dupré-Lasale. Réplique de Me Jules Favre pour M. Kretzschmann* (Strasbourg: n. ed., [Impr. G. Silbermann,] 1862), 5–37.

[11] *Affaire Kretzschmann contre Adolphe Sax. Cour impériale de Paris (Chambre des appels correctionnels). Présidence de M. De Guajal. Audiences des 8 et 15 mai 1862. Plaidoirie de Me Jules Favre pour M. Kretzschmann. Audience du 7 juin 1862. Extrait des conclusions de M. l'Avocat général Dupré-Lasale. Réplique de Me Jules Favre pour M. Kretzschmann. Arrêt de la Cour du 19 juin 1862* (Strasbourg: n. ed., [Impr. G. Silbermann,] 1862), 108–16.

of the parties (Michaux-Bellaire and Léon Clément), and the conclusions of the public prosecutor Savary, dismantled each of the three arguments of Kretzschmann's representative. Combining the Criminal, Civil, and Criminal Procedure Codes, as well as the 1844 law,[12] Michaux-Bellaire tried to show that the four seized brasswinds could not be the object of the prosecution, nor were they sufficient evidence or grounds to support such a prosecution. However, the magistrate emphasized the criminal behaviour of Besson and Kretzschmann that other legal forums had already pointed out and continued to validate the attack that Sax had inflicted on them. Thus, the Court of Cassation continued to make the decision of 19 June 1862 valid and effective in all its details, which definitively confirmed a severe punishment, especially for Kretzschmann.[13]

The latter had revealed that the provincial operations were in the bidding on the brass market and that, more importantly, they put up fierce competition. During this process, Sax also argued that Kretzschmann was selling at 35fr less the saxhorns he sold for 140fr.[14] Pontécoulant added that Kretzschmann offered trombones at 80fr while his supplier (Gautrot) had sold them to him for 22fr; or of doing the same with valved cornets, which he put at 90fr while they had cost him a third of that value.[15] Obviously, Kretzschmann had the advantage of working outside the capital—and effective contacts in that part of the territory—and Gautrot had all his machines and the factory of Château-Thierry. However, the cheapness of those instruments also cast an obvious pressure on the workers themselves that came to light at this point. The Parisian workers published their own report (*rapport*) on the London Fair of 1862, as well as other related issues. Among the most significant, that volume contained the 'Social Aspirations' of those employed in the manufacture of wood- and brasswinds who united their voices to demand better work.[16] Those people complained that the competition between employers was stifling them, as their bosses put the pressure on them: 'the prices of rents, foodstuffs, and generally all basic necessities follow a progressive path and tend constantly to increase; the competition between

---

[12] *Mémoire ampliatif pour M. Ch. A. Kretzschmann contre M. A. Sax. M. Waisse, président. M. Caussin de Perceval, conseiller rapporteur. Me Michaux-Bellaire, avocat* (Strasbourg: n. ed., [Impr. G. Silbermann,] 1863), 8–28.

[13] *Annales de la propriété industrielle*, tome 9, 1863, 126–30.

[14] *Note pour M. Sax contre MM. Besson et Kretzschmann: tribunal correctionnel de la Seine: audience du jeudi; jugement par défaut du 26 juillet 1860 auquel Kretzschmann a formé opposition*, 28–9.

[15] Pontécoulant, *Organographie*, vol. 2, 613. It was also common for the great makers such as Gautrot to sell individual parts of the instruments, which were then assembled by provincial makers; or to sell them whole instruments without signing (chiselling).

[16] *Rapports des délégués des ouvriers parisiens à l'Exposition de Londres en 1862* (Paris: Chabaud 1862–64 [sic]), 878–85.

manufacturers inevitably falls on the worker and takes away a portion of his wages every day'. Of course, they demanded higher salaries and shorter working hours, arguing that they had neither the time nor the strength to pursue any training or instruction. They also reproached their employers for preferring quantity over quality and treating them like machines rather than rational beings. Implicitly, they also said that their jobs were in danger, as they were aware that some companies had already set up outside the capital where they could produce for less money. Finally, they compared themselves with their English comrades who, according to them, were in better conditions, and called for the 'creation of trade union or corporate chambers (*création de chambres syndicales ou corporatives*)' to deal with all these problems and to redress an untenable situation[17] (which would remain so for most of them throughout the nineteenth century).[18]

At the time of the next Exposition (1867), the employees of the piano factories of Paris complained that they would have to earn 2200fr per year for a family of four to live in dignity, distributed between rent (300fr), entertainment (300fr), heating and light (75fr), laundry (100fr), insurance—*société de secours*—(36fr), education (*école*) 'for a child' (70fr), and food 'without wine' (1100fr) and with it 219fr more.[19] If we count 320 days of work per year and if no unforeseen contingencies (unemployment, illness, dismissal, etc.), a father would have to earn about 6.90fr each day, far from the average which amounted to less than 5fr in Paris and 2.90fr in the provinces.[20] This was hindered by other daily difficulties, like the commute to work—it was unthinkable to afford accommodation in the centre—which demanded resources and time, which, of course, were not included in the usual ten or twelve hours of work per day.

In fact, the brass workers had previously tried to remedy their precarious situation. After the incidents of 1848, some of them formed the Fraternal Association of Workers (*Association fraternelle d'ouvriers*), which was

---

[17] The *Le Chapelier* law (14 June 1791) supplemented the contents of the Allarde decree of 2 and 17 March 1791 regarding freedom of enterprise, but punished workers' associations and strikes. It was not until 25 May 1864 that this regulation was repealed by the *Loi* Ollivier, although workers' delegations existed even before then. In 1868, the first Parisian Chambre *syndicale* of artistic employees (pianos and organs) was formed, and thirteen years later, one for winds. Haine, *Les facteurs d'instruments*, 263 and 289–93. See also Paul Leroy-Beaulieu, *Le collectivisme: examen critique du nouveau socialisme* (Paris: Guillaumin, 1885), 26. The first union of wind instrument workers outside Paris was probably that of La Couture, established in 1887. Marconi, *La Couture-Boussey*, 161.

[18] *Rapport du délégué des ouvriers en instruments de musique (cuivre) de la ville de Lyon à l'Exposition universelle de Paris en 1889* (Lyon: Association typographique, 1890), 12–15 and 17–18.

[19] Henry Fougère, *Les délégations ouvrières aux expositions universelles sous le Second Empire* (Montluçon: Herbin, 1905), 92 and '[Archives nationales] F 12-3112: Exposition universelle de 1867. Rapports des délégations ouvrières', cited in Haine, *Les facteurs d'instruments*, 244.

[20] Émile Chevalier, *Les salaires au XIXe siècle* (Paris: Rousseau, 1887), 42.

short-lived, but which came to present itself at the French National Fair of 1849. The General Association of Manufacturers of Brass and Wooden Musical Instruments (*Association Générale des Ouvriers facteurs d'instruments de musique en cuivre et en bois*) (1865) was initially led by Neudin and Sudre and managed to survive until *c.*1905 when it was absorbed by Couesnon. However, these workers' initiatives, which started with good intentions in relation to the improvement of labour conditions and their active participation in the management of the company, ended up being de facto a changing employers' company—in 1894, it was led by L. François Maitre; and in 1898 by the latter and a certain Fonclause—in which the profits were shared by its shareholders.

14
Transfer and Escape to London

Accusations of Defamation, High Resistance, and the Introduction of *Madame* Besson

This chapter focuses again on the parliamentary debates (summer 1860) which led to the extension for five more years of Sax's main patents (saxotromba and saxophone). The minutes of the committee of 13 July 1860 which preceded the parliamentary vote recorded the very high resistance (*résistance très-vive*) of Besson, who had sent them two letters (*notes*) expressing his total opposition to these documents being extended.[1] Obviously, Besson thus joined the dispute in order to torpedo the bill by advising the Belgian inventor's opponents, who also used this information to fuel the discussions in the plenary session.

These letters from Besson provoked a reaction from Sax in the form of a *factum*,[2] which shows a telling exchange. On the one hand, Besson accused Sax of employing dishonest business practices, such as inflating the price of his instruments and imposing [sic] licences on his competitors at the risk of being raided; he suggested that these were a series of quid pro quos which, together with the contracts with the Army, had brought in 300,000fr to his opponent. Besson also pointed to the excessive profit his rival had made from the sale of 38,000 brasswinds to date (2,280,000fr), a figure that Sax claimed amounted only to 21,000. Besson had made this calculation by estimating an average of 150fr per instrument, which, according to the Belgian businessman did not reflect the reality of 60fr either. He claimed that 'far from being a victim, Sax was a speculator' [sic] who reaped a net profit of 40% per instrument, to which the Belgian businessman objected that an honest seller only made a fifth of its value: 'everyone knows that a maker who today makes 20% net on sales considers himself very happy'. Significantly, Besson

---

[1] In reality, there were three letters. The third should have been received during the plenary debates in the Lower House. *Prolongation des brevets Sax. Observations sur le rapport fait au nom de la commission* (Paris: n. ed., [Impr. L. Guérin,] 1860), 1–3, *Observations soumises aux membres du Corps législatif*, 1–3, and *Brevets Sax. Motifs à l'appui du rejet du projet de loi* (Paris: n. ed., [Impr. E. Brière,] 1860), 1–6. See also *Annales de la propriété industrielle*, tome 6, 1860, 325.

[2] *Réponse aux observations soumises par Monsieur Besson aux membres du Corps législatif*, 3–5.

also blamed him for trading exclusively in saxophones—the Belgian inventor did not grant any licences for this instrument—on which he made a 100% profit. However, Sax retorted that he had only built 945 specimens up to that point and had had to incur many expenses to get it off the ground. Of course, Sax omitted the agreement of more than half a million francs compensation he had obtained from Gautrot, claiming that Gautrot had only given him 200,000 francs. Also on the revenue side, Sax pointed out that the licences with the other manufacturers had only yielded him 36,000fr to date,[3] and that the legal compensation for damages was only 10,500fr. Besson repeated several times the word 'monopoly', and underlined the abuse and dilation of the dominant position of a maker who had had and would be allowed to continue to enjoy 'the supply of the Imperial Guard, of the Cavalry (except three instruments which do not bear his name [cornets, trumpets, and trombones]), and of most of the instruments of other regiments'. However, Sax claimed that his factory had been 'not very prosperous due to the forgery undertaken by Besson and his associates (*adhérents*)', that he had had to satisfy 60,000fr of his bankruptcy liabilities, and that he had spent 300,000fr in 'bulky loans (*d'emprunts onéreux*)' to support his 'innumerable lawsuits'.

While both businessmen exaggerated their data and enlisted ambiguity in their favour,[4] which makes it difficult to determine how truthful these figures might be, it is worth trying to come up with an approximation of what it cost to produce a brass, how much they were actually sold for (including licensees), and what doing business with the Army was worth. To get closer to the former, we can take Sax as a source who, under pressure from Gautrot in his 1855–9 court case (excessive profits and overpricing of instruments), defended himself by detailing the cost-benefit ratio of a specific piece. This breakdown referred to a low saxhorn or low saxotromba (*d'un saxotromba ou d'un saxhorn basse* [sic]) and attempted to show that the price of his merchandise was justified (in this case, 200fr) and that he was only making an economic return of just over 25% (Table 14.1).

The specifications and concepts provided by Sax can certainly be regarded as rather high. We don't know how much a brass sheet cost at the time, but 15fr was a high sum, enough to sleep five nights in the splendid Hotel du Louvre in the rue de Rivoli, drink sixty cafés with milk from a *crèmerie*, have

---

[3] In a related *factum*, Sax claimed that he was only getting 6000fr per year for patent royalties. *Réponse de Sax à une note de M. Besson* (Paris: n. ed., [Imprimerie centrale de Napoléon Chaix et Cie,] n.d. [1860]), 10.

[4] For example, even if it was true that saxophones brought Sax 100% profit, Besson neglected to include expenses for R&D, production, advertising, etc. It was also true that the Belgian entrepreneur's saxhorns cost 60fr, but only the sopranos (1848 and 1850/51 brochures); the rest—such as the contrabass—could cost up to 250fr.

Table 14.1 Production costs and profit of a low brass aerophone according to Sax

Material, concept, or technique	Cost
Brass (*cuivre*)	15fr
Valve set (*jeu de cylindres*)	12fr
Bell (*Pavillon*)	2fr
Worker action (*façon de l'ouvrier facteur*)	20fr
Polishing (*polissage*)	8fr
Coal (*charbon*), rags (*chiffon*), weldings (*soudures*), accessories (*accessoires*), etc.	15fr
Overheads (taxes?) (*frais généraux*)	12,5fr
Debts or unpaid invoices from consumers (*mauvaises créances*)	2.5fr
Unsuccessful manufacture, lost trials (*fabrication perdue, essais infructueux*)	2.75fr
Subtotal 1	89.75fr
Adaptation to certain buyers (*remise à certains acheteurs entre 60 et 50 fr., soit*)	55fr
Subtotal 2 (*ensemble*)	144.75fr
Selling price (*le prix de vente*)	200fr
Net profit (*bénéfice net de*)	55.25fr

Note: In the original, Sax made a mistake in his subtraction and claimed a clean return of 56.25fr (*Il me restait un bénéfice net de*).

Compiled from *Note pour M. Adolphe Sax contre M. Gautrot: tribunal correctionnel de la Seine: sixième chambre*, 20–1.

lunch twelve times in a restaurant (for example, the Gosselin in the rue Vivienne, 48), or take fifty bus rides in a bus with its interior protected.[5] These 12fr for a mechanism of pistons seem equally costly, especially if they could be ordered from a specialist. However, what is most striking is the 20fr that he paid for labour, which was equivalent to the work of one person for more than four days at a rate of ten or twelve hours a day and is supposed to be entirely dedicated to it. It is also shocking that the polishing or burnishing of a specimen took 8fr, which would be practically equivalent to the full time of a worker for two days. The cost of charcoal, rags, and other auxiliary materials is also high, especially as they could be used until they were used up.

The price of Sax's saxhorns and saxotrombas compared to those of his competitors, namely his licensees, is also illustrative (Table 14.2).[6] However, it must be borne in mind that the Army had set itself certain maximum

---

[5] *Stanford's Paris Guide* (1858), 29, 35, 37, and 50.
[6] To date, no price advertisements for Sax from this period (*c.*1860–5) have come to light. The last known commercial inventory with economic amounts is from 1850/51 and the next one from 1869, which is too far away and the patents in question were already in the public domain. We will therefore use an indirect source (Elwart's *Manuel* of *c.*1862) in which its author specified 'the instrumental composition of the Imperial Guard' on foot and horseback, and the price of each instrument, noting that all these instruments could be purchased (*se trouvent*) in Sax's shop.

Table 14.2 Comparison of the retail prices of Sax's with those of three of his licensees (Millereau, Lecomte, and Gautrot)

Sax 1850/51	(Sax 1862)	Army 1861	Instrument	Millereau 1864	Lecomte 1864	Gautrot 1865
50–75fr	110fr	100–300fr	Piccolo-Flute	70–160fr		4.5–350fr
80–150fr	225fr	250fr	Clarinet	110–250fr		15–400fr
	150fr	250fr	Oboe	125–150fr		80–400fr
			Bassoon	180fr		180–350fr
40–100fr	115fr	115fr	Cornet	55–180fr	32–76fr	32–120fr
75fr	115fr	125fr	Trumpet	135fr	72fr	34–100fr
14fr			Bugle (*clairon*)	17.50fr		16–24fr
55fr	80fr	80fr	Soprano saxhorn	85–90fr	44–54fr	44–60fr
60fr	85fr	85fr	Contralto saxhorn	90fr	54–64fr	52–70fr
		90fr	Alto saxhorn		90fr	80–115fr
85fr	110fr	110fr	Alto saxotromba	110–130fr		
	125fr		Baritone saxotromba			
			Tenor saxhorn		85fr	
95fr	120–125fr	120fr	Baritone saxhorn	150–155fr	100fr	96–128fr
100fr	150fr	160fr	Bass saxhorn	180–190fr	120–140fr	112–150fr
100fr	150–250fr	170–270fr	Contrabass saxhorn	180–190fr 300–310fr	140–200fr	140–190fr
100fr			Ophicleide	120–150fr	72fr	68–120fr
160–250fr	160–250fr	200–250fr	Saxophones			
			Sarrusophones			160–210fr
85–125fr	90fr	115–130fr	Valve trombone	120–160fr	80fr	40–100fr
50fr	90fr		Trombone	60–80fr	40fr	26–40fr
125–150fr			French horn	140–160fr		80–170fr
45–80fr	80fr	75fr	Snare or side drum	28.25–70fr	40–60fr	40–56fr
100–150fr	150fr	160fr	Bass drum	150–180fr	76–100fr	76–140fr
60–100fr	100fr	110fr	Cymbals	120–300fr		16–160fr
			Triangle	9–12fr		5–6fr
			Metronome	20–30fr		20–32fr

Compiled from *Adolphe Sax & C*^{ie}. *Manufacture d'Instruments en cuivre et bois* [1850/51], 1 and 4, Antoine Elwart, *Manuel des aspirants aux grades de sous-chef et de chef de musique de l'armée* (Paris: Gérard, n.d. [1862]), 82, *Journal militaire officiel*, [no exact date, first half of] 1861 [no. 27], 689–90, *Manufacture d'Instruments de Musique. Millereau & C*^{ie}. *Fournisseurs de l'Armée. 6 Passage Chausson, près la caserne du Prince Eugene* (Paris: n. ed., n.d. [1864]), 1, *Almanach des orphéons et des sociétés instrumentales* (Paris: Pagnerre, 1864), n.p [154], and *Catalogue des instruments de musique de la Manufacture Générale de Gautrot aîné*, 1865, 7–76.

amounts—which will be discussed subsequently—and the monopoly was (partially) limited. In any case, it is interesting that, while Sax's saxhorns were concordant to military standards, Millereau's saxhorns became more expensive as they became lower in pitch. This was probably because the assignee had to pay more royalties as the instrument got deeper. Lecomte's cornets, trumpets, and trombones offered greater savings than those of his colleague, although the interest was again in the saxhorns, which were appreciably cheaper than those of Sax. This reduction begs the question, how he would bear the costs of production, such as the wages of 100 workers, the rent of an operation located in the heart of Paris (12, rue Saint-Gilles), and the licence fee (minimum 2000fr per year since 1860). Undoubtedly, this skilful entrepreneur (he never went bankrupt) had to count on certain advantages—that his investors would be satisfied with lower dividends or postpone them over time?, save the rent?, use procedures of dubious honourability, such as the precarization of labour?—or employ a methodology that is not known to us.[7] The prices of Gautrot's saxhorns are slightly better than those of Lecomte, but we do know how he dealt with monopoly. In his case, it is worth noting the very wide range of prices and variety in the other brasswinds—he had twelve qualities of cornets—and, especially, in woodwinds, which confirms the existence of an amateur market (named *Seconde Division*, to avoid the negative connotation of the word *pacotille*) and a professional one.

As previously mentioned, the government renewed (*Décret impérial* of 26 March 1860) the regulations of 1854–5 which detailed the instrumental palette of the military bands. In reality, this new provision concealed the predominant position of the Army, which was implicitly taking part in the parliamentary debate on the extension of Sax's patents. However, the number of soldiers in the infantry was also reduced to forty, that is, by fifteen; and the cavalry also lost ten players, leaving them with twenty-seven.[8] The official explanation was the laxity that these musical activities provoked in recruits, as well as a lack of troops in the fighting ranks (*l'inconvénient de distraire des rangs un trop grand nombre d'hommes*).[9] Although the inclination towards bands (and Sax) remained predominant, there were also other generals and senior officers who considered them useless and a waste of money. The colonel of the 12th Infantry Regiment sent (1859) a report to General Pirion in which he proposed to abolish the bands—including even the drums—and replace them with a small corps of buglers (*clairons*). According to his

---

[7] Arsène-Zoé Lecomte previously worked (1850s) for Gautrot as 'responsible for all the commercial side'. He had a partner, Henry-Joachim Houzé—boilermaker in his youth—who was also employed (1845–8) and later the foreman (*chef d'atelier*) at Gautrot (c.1855). After his independence, Lecomte continued to trade with Gautrot and Besson. Christian Chagot, 'Petite histoire de la marque "A. Lecomte & Cie"', *Larigot* 62 ([October] 2018), 8–15. Houzé had been the de facto patron of the *Association fraternelle d'ouvriers* which was created after the 1848 Revolution and which received a loan of 24,000fr out of the three million that the Republican government of 1848 granted to various workers' associations. Armand Audiganne, *Les populations ouvrières et les industries de la France dans le mouvement social du XIXe siècle*, vol. 2 (Paris: Capelle, 1854), 214–18 and 336–7.

[8] To be precise, what they did was to repeal the figure of pupil-soldier-musicians (*soldats élèves musiciens*) from the previous regulation, which reached the number of fifty-five and thirty-seven persons.

[9] *Journal militaire officiel*, [no exact date, first half of] 1860 [no. 14], 261 or Duvergier, *Collection complète des lois*, tome 60, 1860, 109.

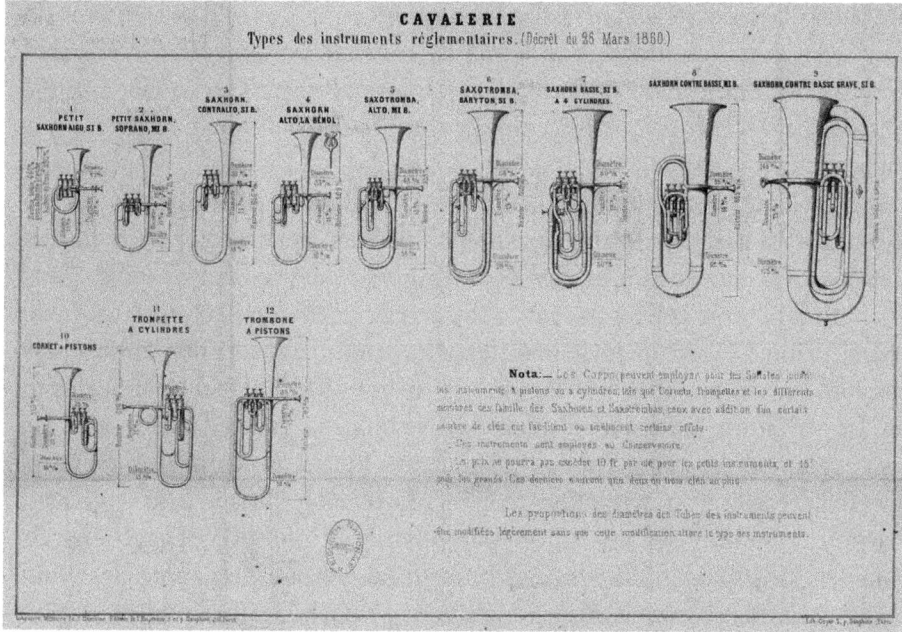

Figure 14.1 Types of regulation instruments for ensembles mounted with the precise shapes of saxhorns, saxotrombas, cornets, trumpets, and trombones
Journal militaire officiel, [no exact date, first half of] 1861 [no. 27], table no. 2 (BnF).

calculations,[10] this would save 4760fr per regiment, with annual savings of 224,000fr in means and more than 6 million francs in personnel; plus, of course, 13,000 additional combatants. France had just been involved in two major armed conflicts (Crimea and Italy) and there were interests in Mexico.

The development of the new instrumental arrangement (*Note ministérielle* of 24 May 1861) contained the precise shapes (actually, closed) and technical specifications of each instrument (the diameters of the pipes, the system of keys, their useful life, the raw materials of their composition, etc.) (Figure 14.1). It also listed the price at which the Army would purchase them—and even the cases—which allows us to know the exact cost per band. And, curiously, it is clear that the cutback was not at all drastic, as the infantry went from spending 8650fr (1854–5 regulations) to 7768fr, while the mounted ones went from 4460fr to 3823fr; that is, a reduction of just over 10% and 16% respectively. We also know that at that time (1862) there were 195 artistic military formations[11]—not counting the fanfares of the Zouaves,

---

[10] 'Archives du duc de Guise, carton G3, enveloppe 1858–1859', cited in Bouzard, *Les usages musicaux dans l'armée française*, 328–9.

[11] Bouzard, *Les usages musicaux dans l'armée française*, 349.

the Sharpshooters (*tirailleurs*), the African Light infantry, and the Hunters on foot[12]—so that the number had remained almost the same (192) compared to the 1858. Thus, there was still (quite) a lot of business to be made in the supply of instruments to French military brass bands, although the trend was slightly downward.

Besson and his incendiary statements had not managed to stop the bill to extend the saxophone and saxotromba patents, but they certainly infuriated his rival. Sax sued him, this time for libel. The pretext was the content of another letter that Besson sent to the Senate on 28 June 1860, which he of course printed in *factum* form in order to have more impact and public repercussion. Besson said that he was being run over by Sax and that he appealed to the Upper House to look after the collective interests granted by the laws. He also explained the simultaneous episode he had shared with Kretzschmann and the atrocious strangulation they were suffering. Besson also suggested pressure from the Executive and reported that one of the Attorney Generals [Mahler?] involved in the previous procedural sets of events came clean and said that he bit his tongue to keep from saying what he really thought (*S'il faut dire mon opinion, je la dirai*). Finally, Besson was imploring justice, as this situation was leading him to ruin and damaging his honour and his work.[13] However, Sax's complaint was successful at the first level (*Tribunal de police correctionnelle*) on 21 February 1861[14] and also at the second level (*Chambre des appels de police correctionnelle*), which finally ruled (10 August) that Gustave-Auguste Besson be punished financially (double fine of 1000fr) and sentenced to two months in prison for the insults.[15]

However, Besson had a contingency plan in place to try to avoid the plausible corrections, or at least minimize them. Although we do not know exactly when (1858–60?), this entrepreneur transferred the business to his wife—who therefore became the first woman in history to run a brasswinds business—and moved to London, we understand, at least until his crimes prescribed. Even before that, however, his visits to the British capital were frequent, as he had established a division of his French parent company there (*c*.1855), which flourished and continued to grow until it became a European fixture and whose brand still survives.[16] Without deviating from the legal axis,

---

[12] Pontécoulant (1861) noted 229 artistic formations in total. Pontécoulant, *Organographie*, vol. 2, 613.
[13] *Pétition adressée au Sénat par M. Besson, facteur d'instruments de musique en cuivre, le 28 juin 1860* (Paris: n. ed., [Impr. de E. Brière,] 1860), 1–14.
[14] *RGMP*, 17 March 1861, 78 and 86. The chamber was presided over by Massé, the representatives were Boudet de Paris and Rouvray, and Bondurand acted as prosecutor.
[15] *RGMP*, 17 November 1861, 366.
[16] See Algernon-S. Rose, *Talks with Bandsmen* (London: Tony Bingham, n.d. ([reprint of 1895]), 69–70, 123–8, 176, 194, 224, and 280; and <www.besson.com/en/our-story/> (accessed 29 May 2023).

Sax did not let himself be intimidated by a woman and inflicted two raids on the now establishment of *Madame* Florentine [Mélanie Ridoux] Besson. The first of these took place on 8 December 1860 and the police seized 'a large number of brass musical instruments' belonging to several army regiments, namely the 2nd Hussar Regiment (*Hussards*); 14th, 86th, and 90th Line; 5th Artillery; 5th and 9th Hunters; 10th Dragoons, and 1st Lancers. In a second raid on 2 March 1861, Sax took eighteen brasswinds (mostly *altos* and *barytons*, but also a *contre-basse* and a French horn, five of them belonging to Muller of Lyon), also belonging to the *Armée* and coming from the 61st and 85th Line Regiments.[17]

After several hearings in the sixth chamber of the Paris Court of First Instance, which the sources do not develop in detail, the president accepted on 11 April 1861 as an extenuating circumstance that Mme Besson was not aware of her husband's criminal affairs in the preceding years; or rather, that this could not be reliably proven (*Qu'il n'est pas établi, par conséquent, qu'elle se soit rendue complice de la contrefaçon*). Another important detail of the order was that the confiscated instruments were sent to her factory to be adapted to conventional tuning (*diapason*),[18] which, on the one hand, exculpated her from illicit manufacture, but on the other hand, made her guilty of possessing corrupted merchandise—concealment, *recel* in French—was aware of it, and prolonged its use by fixing it. According to the judge, those *altos* and *barytons* had not only the shape of the saxotromba, but also its timbre (*voix*). Likewise, the formal modification (*déviation*) that her husband had applied to the bell of those brasswinds (Figure 14.2) in order, according to the president, to disguise the copying (*dissimuler la contrefaçon*) of a protected object, was not admitted as exculpatory. The court therefore found her guilty and fined her—on the basis of articles 40, 42, and 49 of the 1844 law—with 500fr, to which was added 3000fr for damages and the costs of the trial.

Mme Besson appealed and after only three hearings (28 June, 4 and 11 July 1861) presided over by De Guajal and attended by the councillor Portier, the lawyers Senard and Lefèvre-Pontalis, the latter representing Sax, and

---

[17] *Annales de la propriété industrielle*, tome 7, 1861, 230–5.

[18] In early 1859, the French public authorities set up a working group (*Commission du diapason*) to establish a uniform musical tuning, that is, an acoustic reference standard for pitch. The aim was that the same note would have the same cycles (or hertz) in any musical instrument, situation, and space; and that this warning would commit all agents, from makers and musicians, to ensembles and halls. It was established at 870 vibrations par second, or 435Hz for our present-day A4 (following the pitch index of the Scientific Pitch Notation). *Le Ménestrel*, 27 February 1859, 97–9, 6 March 1859, 108–9, and 13 March 1859, 116–17. Of course, the military groups were no strangers to this normalization—the provision of 26 March 1860 stated as much in its article 6—and the press also picked up on it. *Le Ménestrel*, 8 April 1860, 150 and *RGMP*, 8 April 1860, 137.

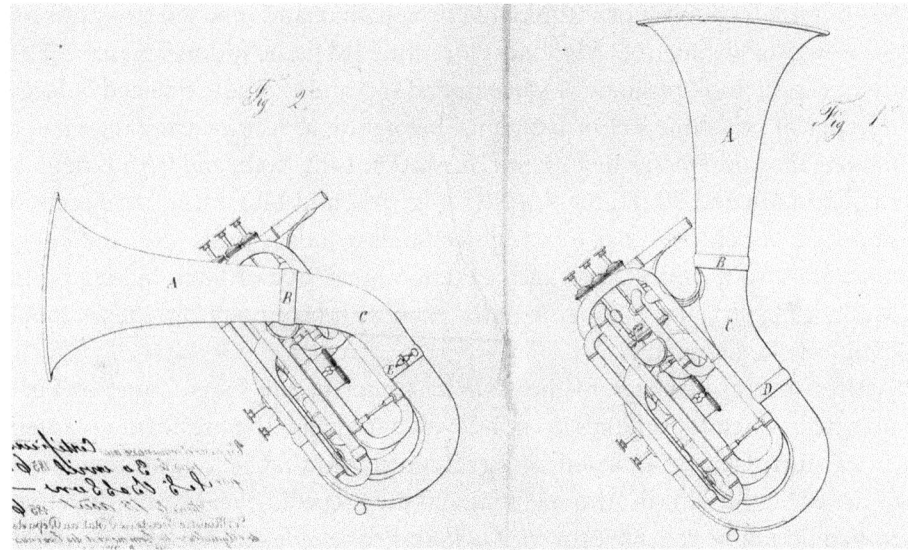

Figure 14.2 Possible variables of the shape of the saxotromba from a patent of Besson
Certificate of addition of Besson of 30 April 1856 on the Patent [no. 22072] of 18 January 1855 [for fifteen years] for 'Improvements to brass instruments of all kinds (*perfectionnements aux instruments de musique de tous genres en cuivre*)', 39 (INPI).

the public prosecutor (Lafaulotte), the Imperial Court ratified that she was guilty. The court did not exonerate her from the crime of concealment, even though the instruments were originally the work of her husband.[19] However, the court considered 'that the damages and interest were fixed at too high a figure' and, amending the previous ruling, reduced the financial compensation to 500fr, which meant a partial victory that sealed (momentarily) the hostilities between her and Sax.

---

[19] Pataille considered Mme Besson's offence *sui generis* [sic] because the court had relied on the 1844 regulations (art. 41 and 43) to harbour relations of concealment or backscratching. According to him, 'articles 59 and 60 of the Penal Code which criminalized this type of offence (*complicité*) were not applicable to piracy'. *Annales de la propriété industrielle*, tome 7, 1861, 233–4.

15
Drouelle or the Valve Big Business

The Challenges of Maintaining a Monopoly

The division of labour of brasswind manufacture was more than usual in the midst of the French Second Empire, as was the subcontracting of part of that production if it saved costs and/or required a certain specialization. The manufacture and assembly of valve sets was one such discipline that could be worth branching out into, and Sax (like many of his colleagues) made use of such auxiliary companies from the outset.[1] Precisely one of them was that of Sébastien Drouelle, who basically supplied these and other components and accessory parts of wind instruments to larger operations, which then assembled them with the rest of the tubes. Drouelle (1818–80) was actually the half-brother of François-Félix-Marie Sassaigne (1802–62), another manufacturer—originally a locksmith in Rennes—who had acted as a prosecution witness against Sax in his confrontation with Rivet. Sassaigne seems to have moved to Paris in the 1830s and began working as a mechanic and key-maker for wind instruments and pistons soon after, a specialization that brought him numerous customers.[2] Near the middle of the nineteenth century, he transferred his business to his relative and named him his successor ('Drouelle, formerly Sassaigne, manufacturer of pistons, keys, and fittings [protectors or accessories] for brass musical instruments').[3] Incidentally, one of Sassaigne's daughters, Marie-Angélique-Françoise (b. 1826) was married to Jacques-Christophe Labbaye, another of the leading figures and makers of the time; and Sébastien Drouelle himself married (1845) Héloïse-Augustine Guichard, a surname with tremendous pedigree in the instrument-making industry.[4]

---

[1] Archives de Paris, D11 U3, box year 1852, dossier 10,509: Faillite d'Adolphe Sax du 5 juillet 1852, *Bilan*, n.p. [1 and 3].

[2] Planque, *Agenda musical ou indicateur des amateurs*, 110 and *Almanach-Bottin du Commerce de Paris, des départements de la France et des principales villes du monde* (Paris: Bureau de l'almanach du Commerce, 1842), 188. According to Sax, Saissagine paid Périnet a licence (*rétribution convenue*) to manufacture his piston model while his patent was in force (1838–43) and had 'Halary, Labaye [sic], Courtois, and others' as his customers. *Note pour messieurs les conseillers [de la troisième Chambre de la Cour d'Appel, 16 février 1850]* (Paris: n. ed., [Impr. Simon Dautreville & Cie,] 1850), 3–4.

[3] *Annuaire général du commerce (Didot-Bottin)*, 1850, 614 and 797.

[4] <http://luthiervents.blogspot.com/search/label/Drouelle> (accessed 24 February 2023).

The conflict between Sax and Drouelle dates back to 24 December 1857.[5] Pataille's chronicles point to 5 February 1858,[6] but this referred the second attack. In the first, the Belgian inventor inflicted a disruptive raid on Drouelle because, according to him, his rival was making pistons and other loose parts for the saxotromba. However, the initiation of the present proceedings had been frozen—*en suspens* said the industrial property specialist—because at that time Sax was fighting with larger companies ('Gautrot, Besson, Halary, and others') and was trying to assert the offensive character of his patent.

Thanks to a *factum* by Drouelle himself, we know exactly how one of these raids took place, an episode that deserves some attention. Louis-Jules-Michel Drion, bailiff of the Court, was in charge of the seizure; he was accompanied by Groufier (police commissioner) and possibly by more agents; Charles-Joseph Sax, Adolphe's father, who acted as incriminating advisor; and finally Benoist-Laisement and Joseph Loutrel, specialists or technicians (*praticiens*). First of all, the ordinance authorizing the committee to proceed against the accused was read out, and a copy of it was left for him. Drouelle initially defended himself by claiming that he did not engage in piracy and that he only made accessories for brass instruments on behalf of other manufacturers; he was therefore not responsible for what his customers did with these components. He also claimed that among his purchasers were licensees of Sax and that he had always acted in good faith. After reading him his rights, the judicial retinue entered the defendant's home-factory and found three work spaces—two workshops (*ateliers latéraux*) on the ground floor and another one on the second floor—where they noted the employment of twenty-five people. Charles-Joseph Sax identified and classified the illegal parts and pieces which were deposited in a box that would be closed and sealed by the chief of police to be kept in the Court's secretariat. Subsequently, Drouelle was asked to produce his book of movements and other registers (*ses livres et papiers*). He offered two notebooks, the first of 504 pages starting on 1 December 1854 and ending on 10 July 1856. The other, beginning on the latter date, had a last entry of 20 December 1857. Among his clients, the names of Michaud, Besson, Darche, Distin [from England], Labbaye, Courtois, Labitte, Jahn, Henry et Martin, Roehn, Halary, Raoux, Rivière, Coeffet, Michon, Peffer, Roth, Key et Cie, Mongin, 'and others whose list would be too long', appeared. Drouelle reiterated that he 'did not know and did not want to know' how his customers used the goods and that, in any event, they should

---

[5] *Affaire Drouelle contre Sax. Renvoi devant la Cour impériale de Rouen après cassation. Cour impériale de Rouen. Troisième chambre. Présidence de M. Le Président Le Tendre De Tourville* (Paris: n. ed., [Impr. Renou et Maulde,] n.d. [1866]), 3–7.

[6] *Annales de la propriété industrielle*, tome 7, 1861, 72–3.

be asked. Lastly, he stressed the financial loss which the raid would cause him and reiterated that he worked for some of Sax's licensees (Labbaye, Courtois, and Henry et Martin). Moreover, he showed a written order from Labbaye for 144 'short pistons' for *aigus* [sopranos?], *si* [?], *altos*, *barytons*, *basses*, and *contrebasses*; and said that he had only verbal orders for the others. He also alleged that the bells seized were for Roth and other licensed builders.[7]

During the trial, *Maîtres* Marie and Dufaure reappeared. The former put forward four defences, some of them with some wit. The first, as was to be expected in order to make sense of his argument, argued that the type of valves Drouelle manufactured (which he called *pistons à amorces tombantes* or 'with dropping slides')[8] were in the public domain and, in any case, pre-dated the Sax's patent. The second, which was interesting because of the particularity of this supplier, opened a new avenue of escape by pointing out that he was indeed working for licensees of Sax. The third and fourth insisted upon Drouelle's innocence on the basis of the neutrality of his merchandise—including the bells—being isolated and separate parts, a detail which would exonerate him from any subsequent assembly which could give rise to a protected instrument.

However, the judge did not give the necessary credence to these arguments because, among other reasons, he linked the accused to Besson, Raoux, and Halary. Moreover, the magistrate made public—on the basis of the documents seized from Drouelle—the accounts linking them. These entries revealed that the accused had manufactured and sold valves for Besson for a value of more than 87,000fr (23,700fr in 1855, 26,000fr in 1856, 22,000fr in 1857, and 15,330fr in 1858; although, according to legal doctrine—articles 637 and 638 of the Code of Criminal Procedure—Sax could only ask for explanations for the three years preceding the raid). As far as Raoux was concerned, the invoices were lower (3580fr in 1855 and 1749fr in 1856); and regarding Halary, no large amounts were reported either (4200fr in 1855 and 2160fr in 1856). Of course, these figures are very significant, especially those of Besson, because with all the money he had invested in valves, we would pay for almost three years the full salary of a senator, seventeen academic years a year for a university professor, or more than 168 monthly payments for a police commissioner. With the 5329fr that Raoux spent on valves during

---

[7] *Affaire Drouelle contre Sax. Renvoi devant la Cour impériale de Rouen après cassation*, 3–7. Incidentally, the cost of the raid amounted to 90.5fr, which someone should make good in the future, depending, we understand, on who won.

[8] In Drouelle's own words, it consisted of a 'rudiment' [sic] of curved tubing that exited directly from the valve describing a curve from top to bottom. A second version had a ring or ferrule welded between the slide and the tube at a right angle curved downwards. *Cour impériale de Rouen. Drouelle contre Sax. Les amorces tombantes* (Paris: n. ed., [Impr. Crété,] 1866), 5–8.

those two years, it would be possible to pay more than fifteen times the fee for evading jury duty, the salary of a school teacher for more than three years; similarly, it would also be possible to pave 410 square metres of streets. On the other hand, the more than 6300fr that Halary spent would be enough to rent a room in Paris for more than sixty months, the maintenance for ten and a half years of an old person in the Asylum of the Providence, or to pay more than 1938 working days to the employees of the Imperial Tobacco Factory; 2520 working days if they were all women. We could also enter 3150 times the Salle Valentino, according to Galignani, the 'most diverting' in Paris, with cancan music assured; or, in another way, ride a donkey for 12,600 hours in the Bois de Boulogne.[9]

Marie also argued that, in any case, no more than a third of those pistons that his client had manufactured could be attached or fit into the tubing of the protected instruments. However, the judge considered it sufficiently proven that Drouelle 'was aware of all the processes that Sax endured' and his manifest link with piracy (*volonté de s'associer à la contrefaçon*). In addition, the magistrate accused him of having been part of the coalition of manufacturers who wanted to overthrow and circumvent the patents of the inventor of the saxophone.[10] The final hearing between these two businessmen took place on 21 March 1861 under the presidency of Massé (sixth chamber of the Paris Court of First Instance). After hearing the conclusions of the prosecutor Bondurand, the judge found Drouelle guilty of forgery and, applying the regulations (articles 40, 41, and 49 of the law of 1844), fined him 500fr, in addition to the costs of the trial and compensation for damages to be determined. However, Massé exempted him from any corrective action in relation to the seized bells and orders from Sax's licensees.

Neither of the parties was satisfied with the judgement and both appealed, hiring the same cadre of representatives. At the Imperial Court, Marie pointed out that his client only manufactured pistons and therefore he was not ultimately responsible for attacking Sax's patent which protected 'the instrument as a whole and not the valves'. On the other hand, he insisted that the manufacture of this type of mechanism was widely known, but that in any case, as far as the twenty-seven seized specimens were concerned,[11] he was backed by thirteen licensees to whom the merchandise was addressed. Finally, Marie said that Drouelle had never sold such a model of conflicting valves to Besson, Raoux, or Halary. But, after hearing the conclusions of Attorney General Barbier, president De Guajal—who had ignored the

---

[9] *Galignani's* (1856), 10, 32, 60, 74, 76, 101, 107, 127, 349–50, 487, and 499.
[10] *Annales de la propriété industrielle*, tome 7, 1861, 74.
[11] *Annales de la propriété industrielle*, tome 8, 1862, 21.

reading of the preliminary report by one of his colleagues—decided on 4 July 1861[12] to open an investigation that could clear up so many uncertainties. Dufaure had also ensured that the bells—previously exonerated—were now included in an enquiry that was entrusted to Surville.

Drouelle filed an appeal in cassation, which was based on two points. The first was grounded in articles 2, 40, and 41 of the 1844 law and basically sought to show that this regulation had been badly applied with regard to valves (thus isolated parts) and that his opponent did not have exclusive rights over them. The second was based on article 7 of the law of 20 April 1810 and argued that the previous ruling was not sufficiently reasoned. However, following the reading of the report by councillor Legagneur, the allegations of *Maître* Mimerel for Drouelle, and the conclusions of the public prosecutor (Savary); president Vaïsse did not admit the protest on 20 January 1862,[13] which, for to all intents and purposes, triggered Surville's audit.

After this setback for Drouelle, and the end of the long and complicated investigation that lasted more than two years (29 April 1862–13 July 1864), the parties met again on 27 January 1865 at the Imperial Court in Paris under the presidency of Haton de la Goupillière. This judge, who heard the pleadings of *Maîtres* Bétolaud and Hébert and the conclusions of the public prosecutor (Merveilleux-Duvignaux), decided to validate Surville's work despite Drouelle's continued protests. However, the defendant had succeeded in proving conclusively that the seized bells were produced for Roth (licensee) and, therefore, 'there was no offence'. The issue of the lawfulness of the valves was more complex; furthermore, that ninety sets had in fact been seized[14] and not twenty-seven as the same source (Pataille) had previously pointed out. (The higher figure probably corresponds to the sum of those caught in the two raids.) Naturally, Drouelle insisted that the mechanism was public knowledge, but the president again rejected this statement on the grounds that, 'according to the report of the expert [Surville], the shape of these pistons was suitable for fitting into the composition of a Sax instrument'. However, Drouelle proved that fifty-four of them were a commission (22 November 1857) from Labbaye—another assignee of Sax—and were exonerated. Drouelle also claimed that he had another verbal commission from [Henry et] Martin and Michaud for the other thirty-six remaining copies, but Haton de la Goupillière considered that, in the absence of written

---

[12] According to Pataille, there were at least two contradictory hearings on 20 and 27 June 1861. *Annales de la propriété industrielle*, tome 15, 1869, 294.
[13] *Annales de la propriété industrielle*, tome 8, 1862, 21–3. Sax's lawyer is not known.
[14] *Annales de la propriété industrielle*, tome 15, 1869, 290–1.

contracts and records from both parties, there was no valid justification and that they were therefore forgeries.

There remained the most uncomfortable and sensitive point: calculating the amount of financial compensation to Sax for the illicit business revealed by Drouelle's account books and movements from 1855 to 1858. According to Surville's information, the defendant manufactured and sold over all those months a total of 3287 sets of pistons of which ninety-three were of the Périnet system and the remaining 3194 'no indication'. Drouelle argued that the latter were generic versions of valves to be fitted to Raoux's, Besson's, and Halary's own particular brass, and were therefore exempt from any problems. However, the judge said that 'at the time when the events took place [1855–8], only instruments in the shape of those patented by Sax were commercially manufactured, and it would have been difficult to place pistons of a different model on the market'.[15] Although Haton de la Goupillière's assertion is unclear—cornets, trumpets, and trombones never gave up their conventional form despite the experimentation of the time that proposed new morphologies, including that of the all-powerful saxotromba—it is clear that Sax had woven a dense web from which it was very difficult to escape. On the one hand, there was the protection granted by the patent, the most powerful tool and one that could be invoked and interpreted in numerous individual and subjective ways. Secondly, the Army's instrument regulations and specifications were blatantly biased in Sax's favour and had to be adhered to in order to do business with this very willing customer. When a builder made similar instruments and tried to circumvent the patent—as in the case of Halary, Besson, or Gautrot himself, Figure 15.1—he risked making the merchandise unavailable. It is also striking how much coverage was still given to him by most of the official, unofficial, and private media.[16]

Drouelle also tried to evade responsibility by defining himself as a subordinate worker (*ouvrier à façon*) who worked for other, more important makers.

---

[15] *Annales de la propriété industrielle*, tome 15, 292.
[16] An example of the latter was the most important handbook for military musicians of the time, which, in addition to spreading praise to Sax, reproduced the model-types of the 1860–1 regulations. Its author included the sympathies he had received from various personalities, but also a circular dated 4 October 1860 from the Minister of War (Randon) in which he urged inspectors and generals that, 'under no circumstances' should there be extra-regulation instruments in the ranks of bands. Elwart, *Manuel des aspirants*, 86. This author, a personal friend of Sax—there are several photos of him in the Sax family album of the Association Internationale Adolphe Sax (AIAS), Dinant, Belgium—was a teacher at the Conservatoire and also offered to prepare the examinations for conductors or assistants: twelve lessons, forty francs (pages vi and 72). As a curiosity, Elwart had also at the time embraced republican values and wrote (1848) a *Hymne à la fraternité* and a *Te Deum républicain*. Bouzard, *Les usages musicaux dans l'armée française*, 271–2. In any case, the change of regime in 1852 was not a problem either and, adapting to the circumstances, he composed a *Marche triomphale* to commemorate the proclamation of the Empire, performed on 2 December by the 6th Light infantry, thus obtaining the approval of Napoleon III himself, who even asked for an encore. *RGMP*, 12 December 1852, 463.

Figure 15.1 Performer with a chromatic bugle or deep brasswind with valves perpendicular to the bell, probably by Gautrot

Photograph attached to André Adolphe-Eugène Disdéri's patent [no. 21502] dated 27 November 1854 [for fifteen years] for 'Improvements relating to the photographic technique (*perfectionnements en photographie, notamment appliqués aux cartes de visites, portraits, monuments, etc.*)', n.p. (INPI).

However, the judge did not believe him and said that he was in fact 'manufacturing on his own account and employing a large number of workers'. Finally, Haton de la Goupillière definitively validated Surville's investigation which uncovered thirty-six unalibied valves and illegal profits for 3009 mechanisms manufactured and sold between 1855 and 1858. The president ruled on 27 January 1865 against the defendant and fined him 500fr—on the basis of article 40 of the 1844 law—made him pay the costs, and estimated the damage due to Sax at 30,000fr. Drouelle lodged an appeal in cassation seeking to prove procedural irregularities in the judgments of the hearings of 4 July 1861 and 27 January 1865, and won. In fact, Drouelle had already gone against the first of these before, but this time he based his protest on the violation of articles 153, 190, and 210 of the Code of Criminal Procedure. Basically,[17] he asserted that the Imperial Court presided over by De Guajal at the hearing on 4 July 1861 had failed to read the preliminary reading of the attestation and had therefore not followed the regulatory procedural steps laid down by law. This failure, which, as the cassation order itself acknowledged, 'was not indispensable', was now interpreted as a sufficiently serious defect because it was part of a summary that led to the ordering of an expert opinion. Thus, the president of the Court of Cassation (Vaïsse), after having heard the report of counsel Legagneur, the plea of Drouelle (*Maître* Mimirel), and the conclusions of the prosecutor Savary, annulled on 28 July 1865 the judgement of 4 July 1861. Vaïsse also and consequently reversed the judgements that subsequently followed and, 'in order to proceed in accordance with the law', referred the appeals from the hearing of 21 March 1861 back to the Imperial Court of Rouen;[18] which, for all practical purposes, reversed by more than four years all that had previously been decided.

After a twelve-month wait, and when the two patents for the saxotromba and the saxophone were in the public domain, the interested parties were once again involved in a new interpretation of the facts at the Rouen Court. The president of the court, Letendre de Tourville, heard the lawyers Lemarcis and Deschamps, the former for Drouelle,[19] the representative of the public prosecutor (Martin) and, of course, and before all of them, the councillor Fouan, who, this time, read the preliminary report. The judge ruled that the patent for the saxotromba protected not only the instrument as a whole, but also its constituent parts, 'especially the valves which represented the character of the invention and were one of its organs, ... although these have not been the subject of a special description'. Sax was therefore acting in accordance with the law in ordering the seizure of those pistons, bells, and account books. Letendre de Tourville also placed Drouelle 'at the head of an important company (*fabrication*), aware of all Sax's inventions, and in league (*mêlé*)' with the other manufacturers who wanted to overthrow those

---

[17] Rogron, *Codes français expliqués*, tome 2 [Code d'instruction criminelle expliqué] (1836), 69–71, 92–4, and 107.
[18] *Annales de la propriété industrielle*, tome 15, 1869, 293–5. Sax's lawyer is not known.
[19] *Cour impériale de Rouen. Drouelle contre Sax. Les amorces tombantes*, 1–20.

patents. The president therefore considered him to be the active protagonist of a counterfeiting offence, against which he could not raise false shields or extenuating circumstances such as 'being a subordinate or secondary agent of other manufacturers'.[20]

The judge also cut back the claims of Sax, who had tried to enforce the terms contracted with his licensees, one of which prohibited them from transferring all or part of the acquired right to a third party. Letendre de Tourville considered this clause to be exorbitant, especially given that it obliged them to manufacture at least fifty valve sets per year and for which he charged a percentage. Thus, the judge ruled as lawful the fifty-four sets ordered by Labbaye, as he was the only one who had written documents on the subject; but not those of the alleged verbal orders of Martin and Michaud, i.e. the remaining thirty-six 'which have inspired nothing but mistrust'. Moreover, Sax should fit that Drouelle would not be prosecuted for the valve mechanisms that his rival manufactured and sold to Besson, Halary, and Raoux.[21] Letendre de Tourville considered that there was insufficient evidence to prove that the merchandise these miscreants had bought from Drouelle was corrupt, 'even on the basis of the report of the expert [Surville]', whose report, the judge noted, had been taken as mere advice. Sax also failed to obtain financial compensation for the bells (thirty-three was the amount, by the way)[22] seized. Finally, the imperial judge concluded on 7 June 1866 that Drouelle should be fined 500fr and reduced the compensation due to half of what the other magistrate had established earlier, i.e. 15,000fr. He also released—after almost eight years and with the saxotromba patent already in the public domain—the material seized, i.e. everything except the thirty-six pistons which had no justification.[23]

However, there was still one last episode at the Court of Cassation following the appeals lodged by the two businessmen, which this time were dismissed on two counts by Vaïsse on 26 January 1867. Previously, the president had heard the report of the adviser Lagagneur and then the conclusions of the public prosecutor Bédarrides.[24] Drouelle and his lawyer (Mimirel) had insisted stubbornly that his opponent had registered the whole instrument

---

[20] Drouelle, who considered himself an honest man, who acted in good faith (*de bonne foi*), and who only wanted to save his honour (*sauver son honneur*), acknowledged having a 'modest' [sic] business that fed his family and twenty-five other people. *Cour impériale de Rouen. Drouelle contre Sax. Pavillons. Pistons saisis. Piston Besson* (Corbeil: n. ed., [Impr. Crété,] 1866), 9.

[21] *Conclusions pour Monsieur Drouelle, intimé et appelant, contre Monsieur Sax, appelant et intimé. Cour Impériale de Rouen. 3ème Chambre. Présidence de M. Letendre de Tourville. Audience du 18 mai 1866* (Paris: n. ed., [Impr. Dubuisson,] 1866), 12–13.

[22] *Annales de la propriété industrielle*, tome 15, 1869, 299.

[23] *Annales de la propriété industrielle*, tome 15, 1869, 295–9.

[24] François Malepeyre, dir., *Le Technologiste ou archives des progrès de l'industrie française et étrangère*, tome 28 (Paris: Roret, 1867), 446.

and not its separate parts. Sax and his advocate (Léon Clément) remained adamant that the licensing contract was exclusive and therefore not transferable. However, in order to better justify his decision, Vaïsse argued that there was a defect of precision in the form of the written agreement which established the impediment to transfer the licence to a third party.[25] After more than nine years of interminable and bitter litigation, Drouelle and Sax ended up out of pocket and, no doubt, dissatisfied. The former had not been able to validate his merchandise and was being severely punished, which would cause his establishment to collapse a few years later. The outlook was not very promising for the latter either, which, despite the financial injection, continued to hide major accounting problems that would be compounded by new difficulties.

---

[25] *Annales de la propriété industrielle*, tome 15, 1869, 299–301.

16
Endgame and Epilogue

Pressing Charges against Ex-Associates and the Confirmation of the Brasswinds Consumer Society

There remains one last episode in this procedural saga, which surprisingly had the saxophone as its protagonist. Sax waited until the exact day before this patent expired (20 March 1866) to cause several simultaneous raids on Gautrot, Halary, Millereau, Leroy et Goumas, Buffet *jeune*, Jules Martin, Mme Besson, Barbu father and son, Massabo, Kroll, the Martin brothers, Couturier from Lyon, and Gaubert and Bohem, both from Lille. At least five of them (Gautrot, Halary, Millereau, Jules Martin, and Couturier) had been his licensees with regard to saxotromba. François Millereau started working for Besson, but set up on his own in 1861 and the following year was already offering brasswinds under licence from Sax.[1] His business prospered and shortly thereafter these confrontations he took over the funds (1878) of Labbaye who in turn had taken over Raoux in 1857. Twenty years later (1881), Millereau employed more than fifty-five workers who worked not only brass- but also woodwinds. From that point on, a slow decline would begin, with ill-advised political family successors who would eventually ruin the company in 1931. Jules Martin (and his former partner E. Henry) were the nephews and successors of Darche, another important mid-century maker who negotiated (1855) a licence with Sax. His, but rather Couturier's, was one of those firms that mass-produced wind musical instruments even when Napoleon III's regime had not yet collapsed. Couturier worked from Lyon, although like many of his colleagues he had a branch in Paris (92, rue Turenne)[2] to finish the merchandise and as a simple office. According to his publicity, he employed 100 people and, significantly, had improved his production technique '[by] employing a new practice which enabled him to differentiate himself from any other manufacturer and [produce] in less time without

---

[1] Pierre, *Les Facteurs d'instruments de musique*, 333–4 and 360–1
[2] *Manuf^{re} d'Instruments de Musique Couturier. 73, Cours Lafayette. Lyon. Rue Turenne, 92. Paris* (Paris: n. ed., n.d. [1869?]), cover. See also Pontécoulant, *Organographie*, vol. 2, 510–11 and Pierre, *Les Facteurs d'instruments de musique*, 346.

the aid of any mandrel, [creating] any type of instrument in the desired key and timbre'. This (dubious) method that gave rise to the *mésophones* was the hook for making the plain version of his merchandise more attractive. Another relevant detail about this entrepreneur is that Bonaparte appointed him 'Manufacturer of the Military Household of His Majesty the Emperor' on 15 February 1867.[3] It seems, therefore, that the exclusivity that Sax and a few others[4] enjoyed was increasingly shared by more and more people, as well as suggesting that the central power was not only looking for new allies with money, but also perhaps cutting old ties that no longer served it so well. Barbu's and Massabo's were modest companies that traded in mouthpieces and reeds, which again shows that it was possible to make a living from segmentation.[5] Massabo even appears among the creditors of Sax's bankruptcy in 1852, as does Gaubert from Lille, a rather convoluted family that focused on clarinet and saxophone key systems.[6]

The prosecution was based on the fact that these businessmen manufactured and sold minor components (mouthpieces, ligatures, reeds, pads, etc.) which were specific to the saxophone and its patent, and therefore prohibited.[7] In addition, Sax also accused several of them of having repaired saxophones, a right that he considered exclusively his own. Likewise, he incriminated Buffet *jeune* for even selling saxophones, another individual privilege.[8] The raid also resulted in the seizure of a sarrusophone, which Sax took advantage of to denounce Gautrot in particular. The Belgian businessman alleged that the instrument 'was nothing more than a disguised copy of the saxophone, obtained by narrowing (*rétrécissant*) the dimensions of the former, and applying to it instead of a single reed mouthpiece, a double reed mouthpiece similar to that of the bassoon'.[9]

Five months after that treacherous raid (23 August 1866), the Paris Court of First Instance, under the presidency of Vivien, considered Sax's incriminations to be capricious and dismissed all charges against the defendants.

---

[3] *Manuf^{re} d'Instruments de Musique en Cuivre et en Bois de Couturier de Lyon. A. Rustant concessionnaire. Paris. Rue de Turbigo, 70 [in addendum]* (Paris: n. ed., n.d. [1868?]), 1.

[4] Montal, Kriegelstein, Alexandre, Debain, Raoux, and Halary. See also 'Archives nationales, 05-747, Acquisition d'instruments, 1851–1870', cited in Haine, *Les facteurs d'instruments*, 319.

[5] Waterhouse, *The New Langwill*, 18.

[6] <http://luthiervents.blogspot.com/search/label/Couturier> and <http://luthiervents.blogspot.com/search/label/Gaubert> (accessed 11 June 2023). Unfortunately, we have not found anything about Kroll or Bohem, but everything suggests that they were small companies dedicated to saxophone and/or clarinet reeds or mouthpieces. We are also unclear who Leroy was, although he may have been a famous clarinettist of the time who occasionally associated with Goumas in order to profit from his experience.

[7] *Annales de la propriété industrielle*, tome 15, 1869, 302–5.

[8] Buffet *jeune* claimed that he only resold them after having 'bought them from the military bands', so we understand that those musical phalanxes were quite autonomous in the purchase and renewal of their material. *Annales de la propriété industrielle*, tome 15, 1869, 304.

[9] *Annales de la propriété industrielle*, tome 15, 1869, 305.

Of course, the seized material would be returned to them and they would be compensated for what the magistrate considered to be minimal damage, with sums of between 100fr and 150fr. However, Vivien retained Gautrot's sarrusophone and requested the advice of a specialist, again Surville, to investigate the affinity of this instrument with the saxophone. This prompted Gautrot to defend himself and to pay for a private report which he commissioned from a civil engineer (Victor Bois) and its subsequent publication as a *factum*. The technician compared a Sax alto saxophone to an alto sarrusophone and concluded that they were different instruments. With basic general observations—for example, that the latter was less conical than the former—and very precise measurements to within half a millimetre, he provided interesting tables of the distances of each hole from the embouchure and between the holes themselves, as well as other dimensions of the diameters of the holes and the taper at that point. Expertly, Bois concluded that these data did not follow any arithmetical or geometrical progression, nor were they made according to an established acoustic rule. Rather, the makers had based their work on general facts (*données générales qui sont prises sur des constatations de faits*) and their own background, study, and experience (*ou plutôt sur l'expérience*); an amalgam that had enabled them to arrive at these instruments by groping (*tâtonnements*) and with much effort (*peine*) and expense (*beaucoup de dépenses*).[10]

All the victims appealed—some makers wanted compensation fifty times higher than what had been ruled—and Sax also registered his own protest. This is where a *factum* that this businessman sent to the editor-in-chief of *La Liberté* would fit in, in which he complained that he had not been allowed to counter a previous publication in that medium where it was claimed that the persecutions he was conducting were unfounded and would prove to be sterile.[11] This document is interesting because Sax spoke in the first person and summarized his position (with the experience of twenty years of litigation). One of his main purposes was to expose his opponents and to show that he did not suffer from a persecution mania (*une sorte de manie*). His basic

---

[10] *Affaire Sax contre Gautrot. Attaque du sarrusophone en contrefaçon du saxophone. Consultation de Monsieur Victor Bois, Ingénieur, sur la différence existant entre ces deux instruments* (Paris: n. ed., [Impr. E. Blot,] 1866), 1–8. Sax complained about the technician's interference, criticizing his work ('he is not based on the patent or a serious, reasoned comparison') and recalled that his report had no legal value. *Note sur le brevet du saxophone. Réponse aux conclusions de Monsieur l'Avocat général. M. Sax contre MM. Gautrot, Leroy et Goumas, Jules Martin, Martin frères, Lecomte et Cie, Millereau, Buffet jeune, Halary, femme Besson, Barbu père, Barbu fils, Massabo, Kroll, Couturier, Bohem et Gaubert. Chambre des appels de Police Correctionnelle. M. Saillard Président. M. le conseiller Falconnet, Rapporteur. M. Ducreux, Avocat général* (Paris: n. ed., [Impr. E. Brière,] n.d. [1867]), 31–5.

[11] *Réponse à la Liberté. Lettre adressée à M. Émile de Girardin par Adolphe Sax* (Paris: n. ed., [Libraire Centrale,] 1867), 3–11.

reasoning was that if the saxophone was brand new and protected, so should be its component parts. He later commented that, of the fifteen years that a patent normally lasted, he spent half of it defending himself against the 'rapacity of counterfeiters'. Although the courts ruled in his favour (Rouen 1854) and there were barely five and six years of exclusivity left on his main patents, his adversaries continued to raid his property ('alone against a redoubtable league that didn't withdraw before anything'). Therefore, being within his rights, he provoked several raids on them. However, his counterfeiters did not stop then and did not stop after the law that extended his concession by five more years. Sax complained that justice itself allowed certain loopholes and that his opponents were fined for three years of misdeeds instead of fourteen. Finally, he claimed that he had only received some 21,000fr in damages, which he felt was insufficient 'after having endured twenty-two years of incessant piracy'.

The Imperial Court received a number of lawyers (Lefèvre-Pontalis, Bétolaud, Berthoud, Calmels, Cléry, Carraby, Colfavru, Dabot, Fauvel, Gambetta, and Philbert) who did not succeed (hearings of 4, 11, and 18 January 1867) in getting the judge (Saillard)—who was assisted by the public prosecutor Ducreux—to correct on 15 February the previous sentence. (Hardly any of these builders succeeded in having these fines increased from 100fr to 200fr.)[12] However, this was not to be the worst news for Sax who, once again, had to accept that the magistrate would turn a deaf ear to his request to consider the seizure of the mouthpieces and other related equipment as legitimate. His desperate argument was the same as the one he had advanced to the director of *La Liberté*.[13] At the same time, the president neutralized the order of the previous chamber which had requested the supervision of an expert (Surville),[14] a 'useless commission', since 'the instrument called

---

[12] *Annales de la propriété industrielle*, tome 15, 1869, 306–8.

[13] *Note sur le brevet du saxophone. Réponse aux conclusions de Monsieur l'Avocat général*, 4–24.

[14] Surville (b. 1790) was a retired (1841) engineer of bridges and roads, but still active as one of the thirty-seven 'engineers' who worked for the Paris Court of First Instance, curiously none of whom had anything to do with music or acoustics. It is also significant that Surville left 111,918fr at his death, a succulent asset that was rejected by his widow—incidentally, the sister (Laure) of the novelist Honoré de Balzac—evidently because the debts must have been much larger. *Annales des ponts et chaussées. Mémoires et documents relatifs à l'art des constructions et au service de l'ingénieur. Lois, décrets et autres actes concernant l'administration des ponts et chaussées* (Paris: Carilian-Goeury, 1841), 175, [J-M.] Quérard, *La France littéraire*, tome 9 (Paris: Firmin Didot, 1838), 297–8, *Almanach Impérial pour 1866*, 1026–9, Pierre Laszlo, 'Deux polytechniciens et la chimie' *Bulletin de la Sabix* 50 (2012), 5–13, and Édith Marois, 'Les relations entre Laure Surville et son frère Honoré . . . de Balzac', in Académie des Sciences, Arts et Belles-Lettres de Touraine, ed., *Mémoires de l'Académie des Sciences, Arts et Belles-Lettres de Touraine*, tome 24 (Touraine: Académie de Touraine, 2011), 80–3.

Earlier, Drouelle also complained about the choice of 'a retired engineer of bridges and roads, whatever his science and merit profession', to assess such specific musical and technical issues. *Cour impériale de Rouen. Drouelle contre Sax. Pavillons*, 20.

sarrusophone, made by Gautrot, is not a forgery of the saxophone'. Gautrot would also receive a compensation of 1000fr for all the trouble Sax had caused him and he would also not have to bear the costs of the trial.

But there was still a fleeting opportunity to overturn this situation in the Court of Cassation, and Sax did not hesitate to exhaust it by basing his appeal on three pillars. The first, drawing on the 1844 law, held that mouthpieces, ligatures, reeds, and pads were inherent elements of the saxophone patent and therefore protected by it. However, Cassation said that they were widely known components of other instruments, for example, the clarinet. The second argument also relied on the aforementioned general rules and insisted tenaciously that the sarrusophone was a saxophone in disguise. Nevertheless, Cassation stated that 'the characteristics of the saxophone are not found in the sarrusophone, that these two instruments differ from each other by the shape, the name and the size of the holes, the number of notes produced, the shape of the reed and the mouthpiece, the way in which the air is emitted, and the results and sounds obtained'. The third, desperate, and final argument attempted to demonstrate procedural flaws—articles 190, 210, 408, and 413 of the Code of Criminal Procedure—by unduly increasing the amount of damages. The president of the court (Vaïsse), who was hearing the inventor of the saxophone for the tenth time in all these years, after having heard the preliminary report of the councillor Legagneur, the positions of the lawyers Clément (Sax) and Morin and Groualle (the rest of those summoned) and the conclusions of the public prosecutor (Bédarrides), dismissed the appeal in its entirety on 22 August 1867.[15] Sax was left without legal arguments and forums to which to lodge a protest; concluding, at last, all[16] (Figure 16.1) the judicial confrontations which had as their object the brasswind production.

Some of the final sentences of this saga of trials overlapped with the French International Exhibition of 1867, an event that also brought together all the contradictions that had accumulated the French brass manufacturing. The

---

[15] *Annales de la propriété industrielle*, tome 15, 1869, 308–10.

[16] Outside of musical instrument making, Sax had other and varied disputes with other people, for example with Marie Sasse (1866), a successful singer who had chosen Marie Sax as her stage name. On the other hand, the Belgian inventor succeeded in having the courts compensate him with 2000fr from Malibran for defamation (1857). In 1866-7 he got into a dispute with Bernard, Couly, and Jonquet because, according to him, they had unlawfully copied his *goudronnières* or hygienic exhalers. Finally, he also had a complaint from the Society of Composers and Music Publishers which took him to court (1876) for having performed several musical works in his concert hall without express authorization. Haine, *Adolphe Sax*, 216–17, *Annales de la propriété industrielle*, tome 12, 1866, 255–9 and tome 13, 1867, 261–6. See also *Affaire des émanateurs et des inhalateurs. Mémoire pour M. Bernard contre M. Sax. Procès en contrefaçon d'appareils inhalateurs de goudron pour les voies respiratoires. Notes explicatives* (Paris: n. ed., [impr. P. Cordier,] n.d. [1867]) and *Affaire des émanateurs hygiéniques. Contrefaçon. Monsieur Adolphe Sax contre Messieurs Bernard, Couly et Jonquet* (Paris: n. ed., [impr. E. Brière,] n.d. [1867]).

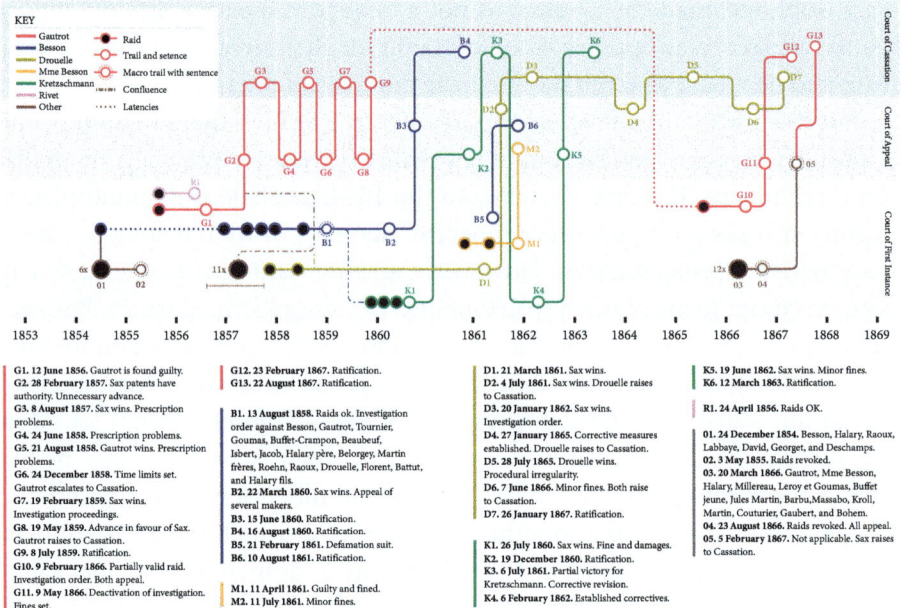

Figure 16.1 Timeline of the attack phase
Compiled by the author.

1867 Fair was the most representative and lavish event of Napoleon III's regime which, in reality, hid numerous deficiencies and structural problems that were to be revealed three years later.[17] This world of appearances, nepotism, and corruption was also reflected in the musical instruments section, particularly in the brass section, where Sax was once again the protagonist. Evidently, the patents for the saxotromba and saxophone had fallen into the public domain and it was open to offer any brass—whatever the name or form—without its author being able to take any legal reprisals. In fact, several French and even foreign firms displayed saxophones in their showcases. Victor-Charles Mahillon from Brussels, for example, exhibited two saxophones and a whole family of saxhorns 'from soprano to contrabass'. However, this builder and the rest of the 486 music-related participants (201 French, 29 winds) were not worthy of the 'Only Grand Prix (*Seul Grand Prix*)', which went unanimously to Adolphe Sax. His closest rivals (Gautrot, Besson, Courtois, Labbaye, Roth, Millereau, J. Martin, Buffet-Crampon, Godfroy) were awarded the silver medal, i.e. two levels below;

---

[17] Édouard Vasseur, 'Pourquoi organiser des Expositions universelles? Le « succès » de l'Exposition universelle de 1867' *Histoire, économie et société* 4 (2005), 573–94.

and others (Couturier, Lecomte, Breton, Martin, Thibouville aîné, Buffet, etc.) even lesser prizes.[18] The president of the international jury was Émile-Henry Mellinet, general, senior commander of the Paris National Guard, and former senator (1863–5).[19] This military veteran (b. 1798) with an impeccable career—he was wounded several times in combat—held (1859) the Grand-Croix (the highest degree of the Legion of Honour) and was also Grand-Master (1865) of Freemasonry.[20] More interestingly, however, he was also Inspector General of Military Music in France. In fact, Mellinet was protecting Sax from the early days of the Empire, as he was the main person responsible for the military instrumental regulations of 1854[21] and probably co-ordinated with him the subsequent instructions of 1860–1.

However, the prize would be of no use if it did not translate into instrument sales, and with patents expiring and competition growing, the situation was very worrying; even for someone who had been the biggest monopolist in the music industry in history. On the eve of the expiry of the saxotromba patent (1864), Joseph D'Ortigue (head of *Le Ménestrel*) was promoting Sax's 'New six-piston instruments with independent tubes' as representing 'the supreme effort' and 'the crowning of his work'.[22] In reality, this idea had been around for a long time (1852),[23] and Sax was going to bet (almost) everything on a proposal that unnecessarily complicated the functioning of the brass and, what was worse, had an impact in the price, more than doubling it.[24] His remaining military friends in the Army at the beginning of the Third Republic tried to help him and included in the regulations of 1873— as will be discussed subsequently—a specific section for *Instruments Sax à 6 pistons* [sic] which affected trombones, trumpets, cornets, and all types of

---

[18] The English reporter Frederic Clay questioned why Sax was given such an award when the products of 'Gautrot, Courtois, Besson, and Distin are all entitled to the highest commendation'. *Reports on the Paris Universal Exhibition, 1867*, vol. 2 (London: George Edward Eyre and William Spottiswoode, 1868), 214–17.

[19] The press was also surprised that a military man should be in charge of music, but evidently defended it by arguing that it was 'an act of justice which would have its positive echo (*sympathique*) in the world of the arts. No one, in fact, is unaware of General Mellinet's wise (*éclairé*) taste in music; for he is one of the most ardent and devoted protagonists'. *Le Ménestrel*, 19 March 1865, 125.

[20] Robert, Bourloton and Cougny, *Dictionnaire des Parlementaires*, tome 4, 334. There are several photos of him and his wife in the Sax family album of the AIAS, which reinforces a deep friendship.

[21] *Journal militaire officiel*, [no exact date, second half of] 1854 [no. 59], 288.

[22] *Le Ménestrel*, 17 July 1864, 261–2.

[23] Sax's 1852 patent [no. 14608] for 'Dispositions to be applied to wind instruments, particularly brass' explored the possibility of two instruments sharing the same bell and the first part of the tube. That experiment was improved (1859) in another patent ('Dispositions to be applied to brass instruments' [no. 39371])—supposedly these duplex instruments were exhibited in London 1862—and led to further advances, complications, and exotic forms in the patent of 1 April 1867 [no. 75861] for 'Various improvements made to brass instruments'.

[24] *Manufacture d'Instruments de Musique en Cuivre et en Bois Adolphe Sax. 50, rue Saint-Georges, Paris* (Paris: n. ed., n.d. [1870–72]), n.p. [2].

saxhorns.[25] That instrumental concept was doomed to failure and he himself recognized this in his business bankruptcies of 1873 and 1877.[26] In any case, he did not let up, understand, or cope with a consumer reality that prioritized the practical, and in his last patent (1881) he continued to fantasize about eleven-valve instruments, keys on the piston cases themselves, whimsical shapes, etc.

The 1867 Fair also uncovered the lights and shadows of the French military bands and, above all, the immense business that always accompanied them. Although they continued to enjoy great popularity—an international competition was organized with representation from France, Austria, Prussia, Russia, Bavaria, Baden, Holland, Belgium, and Spain[27]—their ancillary character made them more vulnerable to a difficult economic and/or political situation. Indeed, Adolphe Niel (Marshal and Minister of War) bore the brunt of the calamitous second French intervention in Mexico (1862-7) and the growing German threat.[28] A general overhaul of the French war apparatus was therefore necessary, and the musical ensembles of the Chasseurs regiments in Africa were the first to suffer on 23 February 1867.[29] This cutback was nothing compared to that of 4 April 1867, which eliminated all mounted musical ensembles,[30] including those of the Guides, which were to cease to exist—even the ground band—after the Exposition of 1867. Niel argued that those groups had enjoyed very advantageous benefits, including the status of the performers and substantial financial endowments. He did not deny the 'inordinate' [sic] artistic level they had reached—and that the size of some instruments made them non-functional—but 'it had to be recognized (*il faut reconnaître*)' that such policies absorbed too many resources (men and horses) and cost the state too much. This bad news—and the well-founded fear that the cuts would spread to the rest of the mainstream artistic

---

[25] *Journal militaire officiel*, [no exact date, second half of] 1873 [no. 67], 544–6. The adoption of trombones and trumpets on this principle would be obligatory for the music of the artillery schools that would be created in the future, and optional (*facultatif*) for the existing corps of this type, as well as for the rest of the infantry and cavalry. The wording of this regulation and its discretionary nature lead one to believe that it was a concession—to a high-ranking officer, a friend of Sax?—who had insisted on the introduction of this new provision.

[26] Archives de Paris, D11 U3, box year 1873, dossier 17,524: Faillite d'Adolphe Sax du 6 août 1873, *Rapport*, n.p. [2–8] and box year 1877, dossier 3731: Faillite d'Adolphe Sax du 14 mai 1877, *Rapport*, n.p. Sax's last advertising leaflet (1886) showed an abundance and profusion of articles that did not correspond to the reality of a much diminished business.

[27] Oscar Comettant, *La musique, les musiciens et les instruments de musique chez les différents peuples du monde* (Paris: Michel Lévy frères, 1869), 92–109, 218–29, and 241, *RGMP*, 21 July 1867, 230, Pontécoulant, *La musique à l'Exposition Universelle de 1867*, 94, *Le Ménestrel*, 21 July 1867, 266 and 28 July 1867, 276, *Le Monde Illustré*, 3 August 1867, 65, and *Le Guide Musical*, 18 and 25 July 1867, [1–2].

[28] Édouard Ebel, dir., *Les ministres de la Guerre, 1792–1870* (Rennes: Presses universitaires de Rennes, 2018), 446–9

[29] *Journal militaire officiel*, [no exact date, first half of] 1867 [no. 3], 39–40.

[30] *Journal militaire officiel*, [no exact date, first half of] 1867 [no. 7], 166–8.

formations—was to permeate the heterogeneous circles of opinion, most of them gravitated from professional and, above all, economic perspectives of influence.[31] When the conflict with Prussia broke out (1870), the State continued to cut back and suspended 'until further notice' [sic] the classes for military students at the Conservatoire which were taught by Sax and several of his friends.[32]

However, despite what one might expect, the French Third Republic was to be a very good time for military formations. It is not known how many formations were created in the last years of the Second Empire, but the 1873 *Armée* counted 190 bands (153 infantry and 38 artillery) and 110 fanfares (three Light infantry from Africa, 30 foot Chasseurs, and 77 cavalry).[33] Moreover, the new government ordered them early (1872-3) with an entirely conservative approach. Apart from continuing with forty troops (including the director and his assistant), the most characteristic feature was that they referred to the *Modèle 1861* and retained the particular appellations of the brass, i.e. the saxhorns and the saxotromba.[34] The instrumental system that had been designed at the end of the July Monarchy and optimized during the Second Empire remained and would remain valid for the rest of the nineteenth century. The last regulation of that time (1898) also called for seven saxophones, one soprano saxhorn (or *petit bugle*) [sic], two alto saxhorns (*bugle*) [sic], three alto saxotrombas [sic], and seven low saxhorns (including baritones, basses, and contrabasses).[35] There is no data on how many French military bands there were at the time, but it is estimated that there were just over 400 before the outbreak of the First World War.[36]

However, the number of military bands and their business was almost negligible compared to civilian and amateur ensembles, which in 1894

---

[31] *Le Ménestrel*, 21 April 1867, 165 and 5 May 1867, 181-2, *RGMP*, 3 November 1867, 534, Comettant, *La musique, les musiciens*, 229-38, and Neukomm, *Histoire de la musique militaire*, 136-7. Sax also launched his own manifesto (*De la nécessité des musiques militaires*) in which he acknowledged an economic saving, but also that nearly 7000 careers would be cut short (*brisées*), France would lose cultural influence, and the instrumental industry would suffer a severe setback.

[32] 'Archives Nationales de France, AJ37 84, dr. 9, Fonds du Conservatoire, Création et suppression des classes pour élèves militaires', cited in Haine, *Adolphe Sax*, 117.

[33] Bouzard, *Les usages musicaux dans l'armée française*, 342.

[34] *Bulletin des lois de la République française. XIIe Série. Premier semestre de 1875. Partie principale*, tome 10 (1875), 605-68 and *Journal militaire officiel*, [no exact date, second half of] 1873 [no. 67], 543-5. See also 'JMO [*Journal militaire officiel*], 1872, 2e semestre, p. 263', cited in Bouzard, *Les usages musicaux dans l'armée française*, 335-9. The musical journals also commented that instruments should be named according to the nomenclature annexed to the decision and follow the proportions as far as possible. *RGMP*, 29 June 1873, 205 and *Le Ménestrel*, 6 July 1873, 256.

[35] *Journal militaire officiel*, [no exact date, second half of] 1898 [no. 110], 219-21.

[36] Thierry Bouzard, *1845. L'armée française met au point le premier orchestre de plein air*. Talk given on 6 July 2018 during the biannual conference 'France: Musiques, Cultures, 1789-1918' organized by the Universities of Cambridge and Southampton, Bibliothèque historique de la ville de Paris.

numbered around 7000 between fanfares (5500) and bands (1500).[37] Pontécoulant (1867) noted this booming market and 'the development and interest that all nations had taken in the taste for music'. At the same time, he noted that 'the demand [for instruments] was constantly increasing' and that 'every day small groups were being created everywhere, both in the cities and in the smaller towns, [which] seemed to ensure the prosperity of this interesting industry'.[38] In reality, this journalist observed a trend that had been present for a while affecting not only France, but also several Western countries that saw the flourishing of numerous civilian groups populated with brass. In Belgium, for example, there were 465 civilian bands in 1851, 531 in 1860, and 1694 between fanfares (1216) and ensembles with woodwinds (478) in 1910.[39] The British Isles enjoyed a similar trend and reached their peak (c.5500) in 1895; and in the USA it could be around 3500—probably more—before the turn of the century.[40] The reality is that it was not only the love of music, but the affordability of these instruments that meant that more people could bear the expense of them. Moreover, those modest brass—cornets, trumpets, bugles, saxhorns, fugelhorns, altos, baritones, helicons, tubas, etc. or whatever they were called—had (and have) a relatively easy and quick learning curve in their amateur side,[41] which offered leisure time and, when played in a group, socialization.

The French brass industry of the Third Republic has not left precise data,[42] but everything seems to point to the maturation and improvement of the productive approach that we have already seen during the central years

---

[37] E. Guilbaut, *Guide pratique des sociétés musicales et des chefs de musique* (Paris: L'Instrumental, 1894), 111–12.

[38] Pontécoulant, *La musique à l'Exposition Universelle de 1867*, 86.

[39] Ernest Closson and Charles Van Den Borren, *La musique en Belgique* (Brussels: La Reinaissance du livre, 1950), 423–4.

[40] Galvin Holman, *How Many Brass Bands?—An analysis of the distribution of bands in Britain and Ireland over the last 200 years* ([March] 2018), article available on the Internet at
<http://www.ibew.org.uk/GH018-howmanybands.pdf> (accessed 14 September 2023). My sincere thanks to Professor Gavin Holman for his advice in this regard.
See also Christine Condaris, *The Band Business in the United States between the Civil War and the Great Depression* (Thesis, Middletown, Wesleyan University, 1987), 6–10
Other authors estimate that there were many more in the UK. Arthur-R. Taylor, *Brass Bands* (London: Hart-Davis MacGibbon, 1979), 62–92 (who takes data from *Amateur Band Teacher's guide and Bandsman's Adviser of 1889*) and Rose, *Talks with Bandsmen*, xi.

[41] The only exception would be the French horn, possibly the most difficult instrument in the brass family; and, obviously, it was not usually the preferred instrument of the workers or labourers.

[42] A comparison of three references reveals three very different numbers of music-related companies (679, 407, and c.510) and of brass in particular (120, 28, and c.50). *Enquête sur les conditions de travail en France pendant l'année 1872. Département de la Seine* (Paris: Chambre de Commerce, 1875), 122–3, Émilie Coyon, *Annuaire musical et orphéonique de France* (Paris: Administration de l'Annuaire musical et orphéonique de France, 1875), 66–71, *Annuaire-Almanach du Commerce (Didot-Bottin)* 1873, 641–2, 1007, 1051–3, 1109, 1186–7, and 1240–2. See also 'Archives nationales, F 12-4726, Travail des enfants, 1872', cited in Haine, *Les facteurs d'instruments*, 109–10. Part of the disparity in the data is due to the fact that specialities were mixed, there are repeated companies and no discrimination between producers and sellers, etc.

of Napoleon III's regime. It is also worth mentioning the existence (and survival) of small and medium-scale firms—some of them distinguished themselves as 'specialists'[43]—which gravitated around dominant firms such as Lecomte, Gautrot, or Jérôme Thibouville-Lamy, which were not only dedicated to brass and exploited the potential of their machinery and workforce in other ways. The catalogues (1873 and 1878) of the latter boasted of feeding 420 families on three operations. The first of these, at Mirecourt, employed 125 workers and made inexpensive bow instruments, barrel organs, and large organ parts; the second, at La Couture, focused mostly on woodwinds, employed 40–5 people; while the one at Grenelle (15th arrondissement of Paris) employed 80 workers in brass and as equal number in silk and gut harmonic strings (*cordes harmoniques en soie et en boyaux*). In addition, the company's headquarters and point of sale (rue Réaumur) operated another workshop which received the instruments to be finished and adjusted.[44] Thibouville-Lamy had achieved such a turnover by absorbing the 'workshops, factories, and plants' formerly run by Husson et Duchêne, Porot, Gaudot *jeune*, Thibouville-Grandin, Henry Savaresse, Husson et Buthod, and Thibouville.[45]

The prices of the main brass instruments of these companies and the references of the army regulations during the Third Republic confirm the development of a municipal and working-class market, the existence of a very wide range of prices for the same instrument (except for saxophones), and the persistence of certain asymmetries (Table 16.1). The company that perfectly encapsulates these three ideas is Couesnon,[46] which offered (1893)

---

[43] Auguste Feuillet, for example, worked as an employee of Sax and received a small award (bronze medal) at the 1867 Exhibition as a collaborator (*coopérateur*). In the same year he became independent and distinguished himself as a saxophone expert. Millereau was second only to Sax in registering a saxophone patent (1866)—excluding the rare case of Soualle—and exhibited his new version of the instrument at the 1867 Fair. According to his publicity, he claimed that he applied 'new mathematical combinations' to his instruments which produced 'satisfactory results, universally accredited by civil and military artists'. *RGMP*, 5 December 1871, 348, Comettant, *La musique, les musiciens*, 720, Waterhouse, *The New Langwill*, 114, and José-Modesto Diago, 'Ali-Ben-Sou-Ale's Turcophone patent (1860): the closest bridge between clarinet and saxophone', *The Galpin Society Journal* 72 (2019), 154–7 and 175–91.

[44] *Manufacture de Cordes Harmoniques et d'Instruments de Musique. Jérôme Thibouville-Lamy. 68 & 70 Rue Réaumur. Paris* (Paris: n. ed., 1873), 2 and *Manufacture d'Instruments de Musique Jérôme Thibouville-Lamy. 68 & 70 Rue Réaumur. Paris* (Paris: n. ed., 1878), 2. As a curiosity, La Couture (1887) had twelve operations employing 250 male and 40 female workers. Marconi, *La Couture-Boussey*, 19.

[45] Of course, all this hoarding of capital and resources by Jérôme Thibouville was perfectly calculated, including his marriage (1857) to *Mademoiselle* Lamy, niece of Charles Husson, once owner of the powerful Husson et Buthod. Julien Turgan, *Les grandes usines, études industrielles en France et à l'étranger*, tome 11 (Paris: Calmann-Lévy, 1878), 1–36 and Grenot, 'La facture instrumentale des cuivres', 37–8.

[46] After Gautrot's death (1882), his then son-in-law (Amédée Couesnon divorced Mathilde Gautrot in 1885) managed the instrument manufacturing company which was to be renamed (1888) 'Couesnon et Cie'. The new company had a capital of 1,800,000fr of which 862,500fr belonged to its owner. Thomas Le Roux, 'Le patrimoine industriel à Paris entre artisanat et industrie: le facteur d'instruments de musique Couesnon dans la Maison des métallos (1881–1936)' *Le Mouvement Social* 199: 2 (2002), 11–36, Waterhouse, 'Gautrot-Aîné, first of the moderns', 130–2, and Grenot, 'La facture instrumentale des cuivres',

Table 16.1 Standard prices of some brasswinds during the early part of the Third Republic (c.1870–98) from various catalogues, Army regulations, and Pierre's book

Instrument	Sax 1870–72	Army 1873	Thibouville-Lamy 1878	David 1883	Association Générale Ouvriers 1884	Couesnon 1893	(Pierre 1893)	Army 1898
Soprano saxophone	160–200fr	175fr	174fr	175fr	165fr	178–200fr	140–150fr	145fr
Alto saxophone	175–225fr	200fr	194fr	200fr	180fr	200–230fr	145–170fr	155fr
Tenor saxophone	185–225fr	200fr	200fr	210fr	195fr	208–240fr	150–170fr	155fr
Baritone saxophone	200–250fr	225fr	220fr	230fr	230fr	230–260fr	180–190fr	180fr
Cornet	50–140fr	100fr	24–89fr	32–135fr	34–190fr	28–110fr	116fr	65fr
Trumpet	60–125fr	125fr	48–100fr	54–90fr	34–100fr	64–140fr	128fr	80fr
Trombone	30–90fr		22–40fr	27–54fr	40–100fr	28–120fr	110fr	70fr
Bugle		85fr	35–44fr	47–90fr	60–74fr	46–110fr	95fr	55fr
Bb Soprano saxhorn								
Eb Alto			50–88fr	67–108fr	72–115fr	64–130fr	75–128fr	
Alto saxhorn	65–120fr	100fr						65fr
Alto saxotromba								
Bb Baritone	65–150fr	110fr	54–103fr	72–126fr	80–130fr	68–140fr	80–150fr	75fr
Baritone saxhorn								
Bb Bass	75–175fr	150fr	67–116fr	108–180fr	100–160fr	85–210fr	120–200fr	115fr
Bass saxhorn								
Eb Contrabass	95–170fr	160fr	100–170fr	126–234fr	140–210fr	120–260fr	125–240fr	120fr
Bb Contrabass								
Contrabass saxhorn	115–325fr	250fr	170–246fr	162–342fr	180–300fr	150–380fr	200–330fr	190fr

Compiled from *Manufacture d'Instruments de Musique en Cuivre et en Bois Adolphe Sax* [1870–2], [2–3], *Journal militaire officiel*, [no exact date, second half of] 1873 [no. 67], 544, *Manufacture d'Instruments de Musique Jérôme Thibouville-Lamy* (1878), 118–25, 130–1, and 134, *Catalogue de la Manufacture d'Instruments de Musique de l'Association Générale des Ouvriers. L. François, Maitre & Cie. 81, rue Saint-Maur, Paris* (Paris: n. ed., 1884) 1–8 and 18, *Catalogue général Illustré des Instruments de Musique fabriqués par la Maison David. 5, boulevard de Sébastopol* (Paris: n. ed., [Imprimerie N-M. Duval, 17, rue de l'Echiquier], 1883), 4–8 and 14–15, *Manufacture d'Instruments de Musique. La plus importante du monde* [sic] *Couesnon & Cie. 94, rue d'Angoulême, Paris* (Paris: n. ed., 1893–4), 5–18, 16–38, and 41–2, Pierre, *Les Facteurs d'instruments*, 390–1, and *Journal militaire officiel*, [no exact date, second half of] 1898 [no. 110], 219–21.

innumerable types of brasswinds (bugles, altos, baritones, trombones, basses, contrabasses, helicons, etc.) with eight versions of ranked by quality (Excelsior, H, BA, MO, GM, AM, CG et GA, and CF). Even the bugles (*clairons*), cavalry trumpets, and hunting horns had four models, while the standard French horns had six, without taking into account the (presumed) improvement of the *nickelage* or *argenture* baths. Couesnon only had only two types of saxophones; most of his fellow entrepreneurs only one. The demand for this instrument was not high compared to that of the other brass; this is also reflected in the lack of investment in innovation—we have barely counted fifteen dedicated French patents during the entire nineteenth century, and three of them were the inventor's own. The reasons are heterogeneous, but we can point to the lack of a grave alter ego—not so the trumpet, trombone, French horn, or other brasswinds for which masterpieces had been written as early as the Baroque—that military and amateur bands did not need a high-performance instrument to tackle a simple and light repertoire, and that perhaps the traditional brass ecosystem and its particular idiosyncrasy in small ensembles (fanfares) did not always feel comfortable accepting a reed instrument in its ranks. Incidentally, although the saxophone had military, municipal, and regional teaching in France—frequently taught by clarinettists, oboists, or bassoonists—the Paris Conservatoire turned its back on it until 1942; as did the 'B♭ saxhorn' (c.1951) and the 'saxhorn tuba' (1956).[47] The asymmetry referred to above is related to the latter, for at the end of the nineteenth century it was still a question of what to call that paradigm of brasswind with predominantly conical tubing that developed in the mid-Industrial Revolution and was supposedly invented by Sax. The Army (1873 and 1898) retained the terms saxhorn and saxotromba—the 1898 provision also offered the word 'bugle' for the high-pitched version of saxhorns—but France's leading manufacturer and musicologist at the time (Couesnon and Constant Pierre) execrated them and advocated generic names related to the register.

In the aftermath of this latest episode, we have witnessed the end of a lucrative irregular corridor made possible by the drive of Sax and the help of influential political and military officials. Rival manufacturers tried to undermine this hallway, but not being as well positioned as he was, they lost the battle. However, those makers—especially Gautrot and Besson; others

---

68–9. Incidentally, Couesnon's father was a banker—Amédée was an only child—and Gautrot married his second and elder daughter (Cécile) to another rich rentier, Léon Durand.

[47] Philippe Lescat, *L'enseignement musical en France de 1529–1927* (Courlay: Fuzeau, 2001), 199–201 and 212–15. It is clear that these instruments were dogged by an uncomfortable military label (see, for example, *Le Ménestrel*, 28 May 1893, 174) which they had difficulty shedding.

followed—became better able to read and understand that the manufacture and marketing of musical instruments demanded a change of model towards standardization and democratization of prices. At the time of his monopoly, Sax sold overpriced products that really had no such standard. His contacts in the Army tried to delay this advantage, but money was obviously a very determining factor and some directors tried to stretch their budget as far as possible and resorted to other suppliers. In any case, those military bands full of multi-coloured brasswinds played a fundamental role, because they radiated admiration and created a following among the people. By imitation, the civilian ensembles that were created in the Second Empire, but especially during the Third French Republic, adopted those amusing brasswinds. But, in reality, and beyond their potential artistic value, there was nothing special about these instruments; they were ordinary consumer items of the Industrial Revolution and, as such, obeyed the rules of the capitalist system. As was the case in other areas of bourgeois society, only that which was capable of adapting to the demands of the market and the demands of consumers could survive over time. And perhaps beneath all this pressure lies something sweet: despite changing fashions and the passing of the years, brasswinds are still very much in demand today, largely due to the popularity they enjoyed in the mid to late nineteenth century.

17
Conclusions

Compared to other related controversies, the judicial process described in this book was the longest and most merciless seen by the arts and music in the nineteenth century. In the wind sector, there were hardly any confrontations that reached the courts, other than Courtois vs Drouelle.[1] An earlier one involving pianos was more substantial, with the classic triangle of conflict over an (insubstantial) gadget. Henri Herz sued (1836) Jean-Baptiste Cluesman for having copied his *dactylion*,[2] that is, a gymnastic apparatus for the fingers. However, before this lawsuit and shortly after the original patent was filed, the author (Herz) was pursued by Meyer d'Alembert, who supposedly owned the idea.[3] Jean-Henri Pape was another piano builder who got into a lot of trouble and fought with other colleagues for using, without his permission, a novel arrangement of felt to cover the hammers that struck the strings.[4] In the music box sector, L'Épée and Bolviller clashed in court over the validity of a raid on products manufactured abroad, but which were allegedly in transit to a third country and were not to be marketed in France.[5] The prosecutions of the powerful harmonium builder Debain were more notorious, and he hunted down the Alexandres (father and son),[6] and Marix et Bruni for questions of authorship and patent infringement.[7]

The conflicts that had one foot in music and the other in a different or derivative art (the publishing of scores, photography,[8] and the plagiarism of melodies, themes, and even entire works) were even more numerous and involved leading figures. For example, Victor Hugo sued Etienne Monnier

---

[1] *Observations pour M. Courtois contre M. Drouelle* (Paris: n. ed., n.d. [1860]), 1–4.
[2] *RGMP*, 19 August 1838, 333.
[3] Catherine Michaud-Pradeilles and Jean Haury, *Touches à touches. Pianos et brevets d'invention au XIXe siècle* (Paris: Édipso, 1997), 21–6, Martha Novack, *Makers of the Piano: 1820–1860* (New York: Oxford University Press, 1999), 85, and *RGMP*, 24 January 1836, 32.
[4] Quesneville, dir., *Revue Scientifique et industrielle*, tome 1 (2nd series), 385–6.
[5] *Annales de la propriété industrielle*, tome 6, 1860, 307–11.
[6] *Annales de la propriété industrielle*, tome 5, 1859, 411–17.
[7] *RGMP*, 3 December 1843, 413, 19 January 1845, 24, and 28 September 1845, 320. See also Patrick-Alain Faure, 'Procès en contrefaçon des harmoniums Debain', *L'harmonium français* 3 (2008), 3–20.
[8] Brandus and Dufour succeeded in having Ben-Tayoux's patent for the reproduction of sheet music by means of instantaneous techniques (*application de la photographie à la reproduction et à la publication de la musique*) annulled, in addition to making him pay a fine of 500fr. *RGMP*, 5 March 1865, 76.

(head of the Théâtre de Metz) for an unauthorized adaptation of a *Lucrezia Borgia* translated into Italian, and then the director of the Théâtre-Italien (Toribio Calzado) for a performance of Verdi's *Rigoletto* which he considered to be an appropriation of his *Le roi s'amuse*.[9] There were also cases of publishers claiming infringement of copyright.[10] The most important battle in this sector took place when a group of firms (Escudier, Brandus et Dufour, Boisselot, Leduc, Colombier, Grus, Strauss, Gambogi brothers, Prilipp, Catelin, Richault, De Choudens, Pâté, Heugel, Schonenberger, and Debain) succeeded in getting the courts to authorize several collective raids against twelve manufacturers and sellers of mechanical instruments (L'Épée, Masnata, Remy et Grosbert, Bolwiller, Guillet, Borel, Marti, Wurtel et Pief-ford, Hoffmann, Paillard, Bissen, and Schwab et Marx); damage estimated at some 32,000fr.[11] The performance and/or printing of music in other countries without having secured the rights,[12] as well as the illicit copying of sheet music—handwriting[13] or taken without permission from a public collection, as occurred in the library of the Paris Conservatoire—were also relatively common.[14]

However, none of these latter trials came anywhere near the virulence, stubbornness, and breadth of the one narrated in this book: ex-ministers acting as lawyers and protecting or trying to overturn those brasswinds, legal files that were continuously appealed and escalated to cassation—even several times in the same case—parliamentary commissions and the plenary sessions of the French National Assembly and Senate debating the legality of those musical upstarts, gigantic economic agreements that exceeded half a million francs, direct and indirect support from the very top of the state to a private company, and so on. Thus, if we evaluate these facts globally, one of the cardinal points of this book and at the same time the great paradoxes of nineteenth-century culture come to the surface. Romanticism made the arts—and especially music—a lofty expression, a sign of the greatness of

---

[9] *RGMP*, 8 August 1841, 374–5, 14 November 1841, 503–4, 18 January 1857, 22, and 1 February 1857, 38–9.

[10] The Troupenas vs Aulagnier and Maurice Schlesinger *affaire* regarding Rossini's *Stabat mater* (*RGMP*, 24 October 1841, 470, 28 November 1841, 534, 12 December 1841, 553–5, 23 January 1842, 29–31, and 12 June 1842, 244–5), and Brandus et Cie, Heugel et Cie, Richault, Schonenberger, and the François-Jules Colombier vs bookstores Pierre Nauvert, Pourny, Marin, and Perdereau case (*RGMP*, 9 February 1851, 45 and 16 March 1851, 87) are two examples.

[11] *RGMP*, 2 June 1861, 172.

[12] Namely, Germany (letter from Schott publishing regarding the arrangements of Gounod's *Roméo et Juliette* by other firms from that country)—*RGMP*, 8 December 1867, 395, Hungary (Choudens, also due to a similar issue)—*RGMP*, 19 July 1868, 229–30, Belgium (Brandus et Dufour, along with other Parisian firms, against Aymard-Dignat)—*RGMP*, 18 April 1869, 132–3, or Spain, with Fernández Caballero and his zarzuela adaptation of Auber's *Le premier jour de bonheur*—*RGMP*, 28 April 1872, 135.

[13] *RGMP*, 24 July 1870, 237.

[14] *RGMP*, 21 May 1876, 165.

the human being; in reality, of the magnitude and importance of the new group in power: the bourgeoisie. The confusion of legal confrontations we have gone through (provoked precisely by entrepreneurs) has shown how the strategic parameters of the Industrial Revolution and, essentially, the system that sustained them (capitalism), permeated everything. Music—in all its dimensions, from the one who makes an instrument to the one who pays a ticket to listen to a concert—had definitively become a business and, as such, demanded without mercy or exceptions the rendering of profits.

As far as the French brasswinds manufacturing and marketing sector specifically was concerned, and bearing in mind that all of this is part of a dialectical process within the continuum of technological progress, the nineteenth century could be divided into three distinct stages. The first, which lasted until 1845, was characterized by the domination of a sort of lobby that shared out profits, largely from the Army; the second, until 1866, was the key phase and the period of greatest friction between obsolete structures in the process of disappearing and the new capitalist model which, paradoxically, allowed a monopoly; and the third, confirms the definitive activation of civilian clientele and the democratization of the market. However, these guidelines are insubstantial if we do not connect them with the arena where other stronger sectors—mainly economic and political—were battling, layers where agreements and exchanges of pledges and favours are not usually aired.

But first we must reflect on the object that provoked this conflict (the patent), one of the parameters of which we spoke earlier and which turned out to be a very strong competitive resource, but, in the end, just another element of the established economic organization. In other words, business success was not directly related to the collection of certificates, nor did the latter guarantee legal victory in case of conflict.[15] The key was that patents had to be harmonized with the implementation of other business strategies and synchronized with the changing market. This crucial—and seemingly obvious—approach did not prove so easy in practice because of the immaturity and clumsiness of some entrepreneurs, but also because of the very situation brasswinds were in. The Industrial Revolution and the capitalist system were forcing a readjustment of this sector which, in the middle of the nineteenth century, had not yet abandoned the corporate structures of the

---

[15] Certain manufacturers such as Debain (harmoniums), the Érards (pianos), or Gautrot himself (winds) were able to reach around forty titles each and had periods of extraordinary performances; but Bord or Herz (pianos), Cavaillé-Coll (organs), or Jean-Baptiste Vuillaume (strings) also succeeded and did not reach five registers—even adding up the addition certificates—and, of course, brought improvements in the design or production of their instruments.

Ancien Régime. Before the judicial confrontation broke out, the 'small' French brass industry—still artisanal or semi-craft in many ways—still retained considerable influence. Its main customers were the artistic military formations and some private individuals (*gagistes* or professional civilian musicians) who were employed not only in the orchestras, but also in the military formations. The (rather expensive) brass aerophones had an outlet due to a supposedly careful and outstanding finish; and the consumer—the regiments themselves, which performed quite autonomously and at the expense of the state coffers—did not complain about the price. However, industrialization (and more specifically the implementation of new technologies related to brass—most significantly, the ones concerning procedures and machines that provided rapidity and precision), the trend towards the standardization of instrumental palettes, the emergence of hegemonic operations, the incipient public demand for cheaper products, etc., made the survival of the old model unfeasible.

One only has to look at the total number of patents relating to music to see that the middle period of the nineteenth century was the peak of innovation and technological fever for brass (Figure 17.1). The patents of brass instruments experienced an extraordinary rise between 1840 and 1860—which coincided with the judicial events narrated in the book—surpassed only by the almighty piano.[16] In any case, it should be borne in mind that these brasswinds were in an adolescent period, that is, excited by that industrialization which seemed exponential and which even let loose numerous fanciful instruments. The sector was going through its own intense contradictions, although it was irremediably moving towards satisfying the demand of a growing number and type of consumers. Recall the English quintet of the Distin, an elitist brass group that emerged in the 1840s in France with precisely those products that only twenty years later could be afforded and enjoyed by the humble employees and workers of a factory or municipality.

Brass instruments had certain intangible properties that were difficult to explain or show; this was a channel—an opportunity—to break into this increasingly competitive segment. It was through one of these cracks that Adolphe Sax (by push and pull) carved a niche for himself in this market. His 1843 patent did not even bear the name of the instrument it was based on, the saxhorn. It is assumed that it was the musicians themselves, the press, or the Distin who gave it to him; but, in reality, it matters little. The word was given substance and legitimacy during the early years of those court

---

[16] The free reed family seems to occupy the second place, but it is only apparent, since the yellow line reckons every instrument sharing the same performance principle even when they have different structures, like the harmonium or accordions.

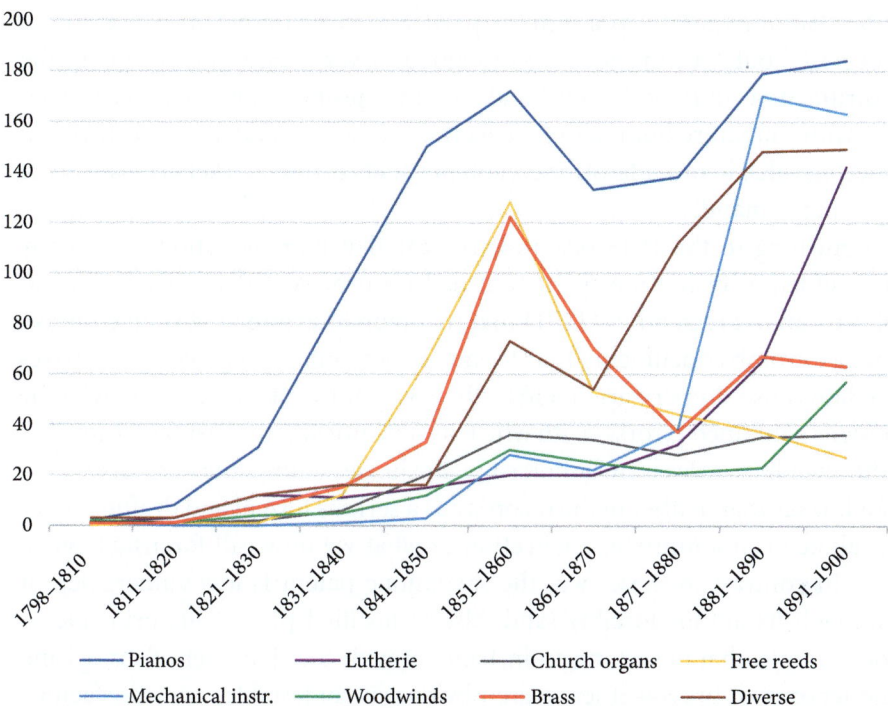

Figure 17.1 (Added) quantity of patents and certificates of addition of the main eight branches of instrumental manufacturing in nineteenth-century France
Compiled from Malou Haine, *Les facteurs d'instruments*, 396.

battles (1847–54) and finally gained it in 1854 when the Court of Rouen closed the civil prosecutions. Perhaps more important than the legality of the instrument itself and its patent were the dissemination and differentiating possibilities that the word *saxhorn* itself had. By using the inventor's own surname and adding a very basic English generic entry (*horn*, the bony extension of the head of some animals and, by extension and anthropological function, wind instrument), the resulting noun worked (sounded) very well; certainly much better than *instruments chromatiques*, as they were christened. Moreover, it was short and had a commercial appeal, a not insignificant detail to differentiate oneself in that capitalist context. (By the way, *tromba* in Italian is trumpet, another choice of noun that was not unmotivated.)

The saxophone was approached in a similar way—another eponym with the root of the author and a suffix of Greek origin meaning sound or voice—but it was promoted with the notion of 'parabolic cone'. This assertion had appeared in the patent itself; it was even repeated in the most important learning manual of the time, and the 1847 *rapport* made express reference to it by claiming that it was a form of 'particular curvature'. This concept does not exist,[17] but it does function as a (feigned) advertising argument, giving the instrument a supposedly novel and attractive profile. In reality, we are dealing with immature but relatively effective marketing strategies, creating and offering value in order to place certain products on the market and satisfy the growing demand.

Returning to the 1843 patent, it is clear that its registration was clearly in a situation of inferiority, since it had been protected for five years and obeyed an old regulation (1791) that was soon to expire (1844). In contrast, the saxotromba document (1845) is much more interesting because its pages contain those slippery arguments—they were rather sophisms and even the designs contained errors—with which its inventor was to defend and attack.[18] Although both titles were endorsed by the judges of the time (1854), we cannot but say that neither of the records has a serious formal and drafting basis, let alone even a minimal application of what we now call forensic linguistics. In contrast to these two, the saxophone patent is less vulnerable, for although its author forcibly (and falsely) justified part of his principles—for example, that of seeking an instrument with the character of strings and the fervour of brass—others were obvious, incontestable, and satisfactory. Hence, even when challenged and judged in a hostile climate (1848), the fourth chamber of the Paris Court of First Instance cleared the instrument of all suspicion as to its originality and lawfulness. The saxophone was a radical invention—unlike the incremental ones;[19] it not only was a truly new and original instrument, but it also gave rise to its own line of commercial activity.

In fact, equally or more important than the patents themselves were the reforms that the government introduced in 1845, one of the keys to the whole matter and which exemplify how political power uses economic power (and vice versa), employing the very system and procedures that are on the edge of, if not outside, legality. These patents and consequently the resulting instruments would be useless if no one bought them, which again shows

---

[17] Gary-Paul Scavone, *An acoustic analysis of single-reed woodwind instruments with an emphasis on design and performance issues and digital waveguide modelling techniques* (Thesis, Stanford, Stanford University, 1997), 68–74.

[18] A patent is, after all, a malleable legal instrument and consisting of claims strategically drafted by the patentee. Christopher Beauchamp, 'Dousing the Fires of Patent Litigation', in Stephen H. Haber and Naomi R. Lamoreaux, eds, *The Battle over Patents: History and Politics of Innovation* (New York: Oxford University Press, 2021), 145–53.

[19] Bruno Kampmann, 'French Makers' Improvements to Brass Instruments in the Mid-19th Century, Compared with Those by Adolphe Sax', in Adrian von Steiger, Daniel Allenbach, and Martin Skamletz, eds, *Das Saxhorn Adolphe Sax' Blechblasinstrumente im Kontext ihrer Zeit. Romantic Brass Symposium 3* (Schliengen: Argus, 2020), 175.

the categorical role of the market. But, if the Administration created a public regulation (as it did) and forced the supply of the same products, i.e. forced the demand, the fate of those saxhorns and saxophones would be completely different. Moreover, this regulation had a wide impact, as it affected several members of these families, divided into treble, middle, and bass; which is also very interesting from an economic point of view.

Before the Champ de Mars contest (1845), a typical regimental band of 45 would contain 1 flute, 2 oboes, 2 bassoons, 1 E♭ clarinet, 12 clarinets, 3 trumpets, 4 cornets, 1 keyed bugle, 4 French horns, 4 trombones, 6 ophicleides, and 5 percussionists.[20] This was the formation to beat and there was certainly a chance to win and, specifically, to 'fanfare' it, i.e. to introduce brass instruments. Not only were there obvious fundamentals—brasswinds are portable and work very well in the open air—but the aesthetic tastes of the prevailing Romanticism were favourable and the development of metallurgy was entering its most vigorous phase yet. This, rather than the substance that might exist in his patents, is perhaps Sax's visionary point, rather immature and impetuous, but ahead of competitors who were too comfortable within the walls of Paris and the times that were unfolding. Obviously, the Belgian businessman's purpose was to tidy up and improve the instruments of these military formations; the question is to know what lay behind this laudable intention—which was none other than to introduce a monopoly—and how to justify (mask) it, as it was supposedly forbidden.

In any case, the manufacturers' faction failed to take advantage of the advent of the Second Republic (1848) when the new public authorities took that side and modified the military regulations governing those instruments (and which de facto liberalized the market). In fact, the structure of these bands remained basically the same as had been decided three years earlier—confirming the overwhelming dominance of brass and its path towards standardization—but now saxhorns would be called chromatic bugles (*clairons chromatiques*), baritones (*barytons*), basses (*basses*), or contrabasses (*contrebasses*). Evidently, this new and generic terminology was a political concession to those instrument makers, which is a clear indication that these people constituted a lobby with their contacts and supporters in that government. In addition, and for practical purposes, this blunt redefinition also served to neutralize and sober Sax by disabling his exclusivity even if the courts ruled in his favour regarding the legality of his patents in the immediate future; but—here was the miscalculation of those businessmen—within a necessarily republican scenario.

[20] Péronnet, 'Saxons et Carafons', 57.

However, winning in court—especially in the initial civil summary proceedings—was an imperative condition for both parties because of the very strong authority that legal arbitration would bring. Although those instrumental ordinances (1845 and 1848) emanating from the Army were mandatory, they also had to overcome de facto other resistance and penetrate into the citizen sphere, i.e. the promising (and real) market. The key to convincing judges and, to a certain extent, public opinion, was therefore to build up credibility, another of the system's fundamental ingredients, which would translate into sales and customer loyalty. As far as the trials were concerned, both sides knew that they were dealing with intangible capitals such as sound and supposed artistic premises. Therefore, the testimonies of witnesses and other authoritative persons would be decisive in sustaining the thesis one way or the other. And here, Sax gained overwhelming support, which he himself did not hesitate to amplify through the press and his *factums*. With regard to this first period (1847–54), it is worth recalling several representative and decisive examples from fields such as the Army and politics (notably Rumigny and Fleury, both aides-de-camp and advisors to their respective heads of state), the nobility (Albert de La Ferronays and Charles Dupin), intellectuals (Fétis, Jobard, Séguier, Boquillon, and Savart), the high civil service (Édouard Monnais), and the arts (Berlioz, Habeneck, and Halevy, among others). Moreover, the Belgian manufacturer's curricular merits at the exhibitions of 1844, 1849, and especially the international one of 1851 supported his proposal. Of course, the judges were not independent of these prizes, so it appeared very unlikely to rule as false those patents that supposedly gave substance to instruments that won prizes at home and abroad. Another thornier question was the extent to which these competitions (and the national system of innovation that underpinned them) were impartial,[21] since the 1849 president was Séguier, and Berlioz—an avowed supporter of Sax from the outset—also took part in the London competition. Likewise, it is also difficult to fit in the fact that some of these allegedly neutral agents—such as Boquillon, co-author of the 1847 legal report—lent money to the Belgian inventor and/or were shareholders in his company.

The weight of the press during all these processes was decisive and has honoured the role of the Fourth Estate so characteristic of bourgeois capitalist society. The three most important specialized magazines of the time (*Le Ménestrel*, *La France musicale* and, especially, the *Revue et Gazette Musicale de Paris*) protected and supported Sax; and we do not even rule out the possibility that there were channels of financing or common economic interests.

---

[21] Kahn, 'History Matters', 332–41.

These newspapers promoted the Belgian entrepreneur—except when it was in their interest to create a small polemic to entertain their readers or, conveniently, when rivals paid for advertising—and also acted as a warning loudspeaker so that his products would not be copied by the other manufacturers. The latter were deluded to think that newspapers would remain neutral in court cases; clearly, these media were businesses and also positioned themselves, so having contacts on the board or in the editorial office was a competitive advantage. In addition, these magazines took a stance when faced with an issue (e.g. political preferences) that might reduce subscribers, or they changed their flag outright; the aim was to survive, make money, and retain influence.

This book's thread has not been oblivious to one of the classic and fundamental elements required by the system, which is none other than good legal advice and representation, especially in these sectors where there is competition for large market positions and shares. Those lawyers had to argue very blurred and uncertain positions and, again, Sax's representatives did so with more solvency. *Maître* Dufaure's reasoning seemed to us to be very solid, but we would like to draw more attention to Chaix-d'Est-Ange who, for the first time and in a decisive and crucial way for the course of events, had to explain (1847) to a court what saxophones were and, especially, the problematic saxhorns and saxotrombas. His performance was excellent, for based on the established principles of brass evolution and valve incorporation, he was able to connect them with the few rays of light emanating from those two conflicting patents (1843 and 1845). Conveniently, he tried to reinforce them with the testimonies of authoritative and knowledgeable people (Spontini), in addition to the reports of the open competitions—for example, the 1844 Exhibition—which had not detected anything irregular. Of course, he washed his hands of the drafting of the documents and did not even provide an interpretation of the murkier technical aspects, such as the measurements of the tubes. Moreover, he was able to conveniently and rightly attack the heart of the other side by calling the French wind instrument makers 'heroes', when in fact he was exposing them and denouncing a stale and guild-like position.

On the other side, and while not doubting Marie's tremendous worth—perhaps more political than prosecutorial—he was overconfident and made important and easily refuted errors. His metaphor of 'chimeras (*chimères*)' was a scathingly offensive concept; and, assiduously combined with the word 'monopoly', the effect was even more lacerating. However, he did not get the ammunition right, perhaps simply because he was ill-advised or because he saw himself as a winner before his time. In any case, the issue was very messy and finding the right thread to pull was very difficult. Even so, he had decisive failures such as attacking the bulk, for example by comparing the saxhorn with the *Bass-tuba*, or the saxophone with the *Batyphone*, losing a lot of credibility in both cases. Etienne Blanc, another of the lawyers in charge, also hit the bull's eye and was able to see what was going on in the other layers of political and economic reality; for example, qualifying as a hoax or parody (*simulacre*) the Champ de Mars competition (1845) where the germ of a kind of legality had been created for patents that were de facto supported by a military regulation. In other words, a 'double privilege' that obliged them to go to the negotiating with or a visit to the shop of the Belgian businessman. This begs the question as to why the government did not expropriate those patents and compensate Sax for it, or try to reach an agreement with him and avoid all these fights and public exposure. In truth, those brasswinds were not profoundly technological—and not just from our perspective today, but from that of the time; metallurgy was sufficiently developed to produce them, and several entrepreneurs in the industry had the means and machinery to work those brass tubes and sheets. What's more, without resorting to the patent and by reverse engineering (i.e. having an example as a model), they could easily replicate it.[22] If Louis-Philippe did not do this, it suggests that his administration had other, more specific intentions.

The experts and their reports (1847 and 1860) were—and still are—a fundamental technical tool for judges. However, it is difficult to give reliability to those analyses, both formally and substantively. From the outset, this book has doubted the impartiality (and ability) of the three authors of the first dossier, since Halevy and Savart had already come out in favour of Sax before the commission; and everything pointed to Boquillon being of the same opinion, an assumption that was confirmed over the years. This report—digressions aside—reads more like an editorial or essay than a forensic memoir. The second report (1860) was better prepared; at least Surville established a (conflicting) measurement procedure common to all instruments. In any case, it is striking that he recognized major flaws in the sketch of the saxotromba patent and still found it to be correct. It is curious how this ambiguous and showy prism was combined with the other side of the right, much more austere, serious, and complex.

The tremendous and heterogeneous support garnered by one of the factions has been another of the striking elements of this whole story; all the

---

[22] To learn about a different case and how a patentee balanced the disclosure of knowledge with continuing to enjoy a competitive advantage, see Patricio Sáiz and Rubén Amengual, 'Do Patents Enable Disclosure? Strategic Innovation Management of the Four-Stroke Engine', *Industrial and Corporate Change* 27: 6 ([December] 2018), 975–97.

more so when the forging of this brilliant professional image did not correspond to the reality and health of a business that was in severe trouble. In this book, influential politicians, military men, journalists, theoreticians, artists, etc., the vast majority of them French, have appeared, who practically and from the very beginning did not stop supporting a foreign businessman in the media. Rival builders must have been deeply envious to see such revered composers as Berlioz and Halevy supporting Sax, and the Paris's press so openly publicizing and praising him. It is also likely that there was a kind of weariness on the part of these celebrities—not only the economic and social system was evolving, but also music as a reflection of it—which they did not dare to openly air, precisely because of the tremendous influence of this lobby. Meyerbeer, Adolphe Adam, Rossini or the two leading examples above did not write a single professional eulogy for those French entrepreneurs in their entire careers. For his part, Sax presented himself as a battering ram to shake up the vitiated atmosphere that supposedly existed in the military formations and, by extension, though with somewhat less impact, in other forums (orchestra and opera). Nor should we think that the support would go beyond a few paragraphs—the Belgian inventor and his impulsiveness were excellent cannon fodder with which to hook new followers—for these music writers did not step down from their pedestal to write band scores,[23] or even to give shelter to his star instrument, the saxophone.[24] It was all part of the prevailing cross-cutting performativity; some sold a profile, others a product.

Another fundamental idea that has been confirmed in the pages of this book is that none of the business, organizational (including artistic military ordinances), and judicial achievements would have gone ahead if the government had not had a parallel plan—the real driving force—to articulate them with its own interests. The key figure at the outset was General Rumigny, who organized and prepared Sax's victory on the Champ de Mars (1845), with the approval of the Minister of War (*maréchal* Soult), of course. We can understand that this high command had a fondness for music, but that he had all those means and took so much trouble to improve the brass of the bands is completely implausible. The real cause was to empower an external agent to reduce the influence and cut off the funding (in 1847 it exceeded 1.5 million

---

[23] There are barely two exceptions, namely Giacomo Meyerbeer and his *Marche aux flambeaux* (*RGMP*, 11 December 1853, 431), and another by Rossini (*La corona d'Italia*). Denise Gallo, 'Rossini's Fanfare for Maximilian of Mexico: A Mysterious Self-Borrowing', Historic Brass Society Journal 23 (2011), 89–102 and Martina Grempler, 'Rossinis politisches Spätwerk: Die Hymne à Napoleon III und La corona d'Italia', in Bernd-Rudiger Kern and Reto Müller, dirs, *Rossini in Paris* (Leipzig: Leipziger Universitätsverlag, 2002), 181–98.

[24] Only Meyerbeer summoned it once—when the theatre did not have bass clarinets, furthermore (*L'Africaine*, 1865)—and earlier (1852), Halévy (*Le Juif Errant*).

francs) of the pressure group of musical instrument makers who did not agree with the Orleanist monarchy.

Napoleon III acted in a similar way to his predecessor in power, but with even greater brazenness, for one need only recall the appointment (April 1854) of Sax as 'Manufacturer of the Military Household of His Majesty the Emperor' just two months before the civil justice system was to pass judgement. This honorary credential put enormous indirect pressure on the judicial court, which had yet to rule on the legitimacy of the instruments of a man who become from then on a *protégé* of the Emperor of France. Moreover, barely a month and a half after the court ruling that validated the patents in question, the government of the Empire sanctioned (August 1854) a new military regulation that re-activated the monopoly. Almost half of the budget of an infantry band and more than two thirds of that of a cavalry band were controlled by a single company. Although in subsequent years the owner granted some licences for the manufacture of saxhorns—on very advantageous terms for himself, of course—and in 1861 the Army stipulated the maximum purchase price for all such brasswinds, it is clear that a velvet carpet had been rolled out for Sax to enjoy an extraordinary commercial advantage. But, assessing the magnitude of favours and protections, what is extraordinary and irrefutably proves the support of the Government was the passing of a law (1860) to allow the extension for five more years of the patents on the saxotromba and the saxophone. Obviously, the granting of such an exceptional privilege required the consortium of all three branches of state, and especially a great deal of involvement on the part of the Executive. No one had ever achieved anything like this before—possibly not even later—and France sanctioned the first extension in its history to exercise a double monopoly in the time following the Revolution. The day would also come when those patents would cease to have effect (1865 and 1866) and a true free market would be introduced. Moreover, the brasswinds sector had been evolving towards a larger and more heterogeneous clientele on which it was necessary to implement new commercial strategies and, equally, to have woven a particular network of contacts.[25] The point is that Sax did not foresee the scenario of making himself useful to Napoleon III[26]—or, in other words, that the cost of his protection would be greater

---

[25] A worker of Millereau threatened his master with disclosing to the press the expensive commercial strategies of his boss, consisting of bribes and extra charges (*dîners d'affaires et des remises de 45–50%*) if the salaries were not raised. Grenot, 'La facture instrumentale des cuivres', 85.

[26] Sax did not manage to rise from the first rung of the Legion of Honour. Fleury (1863) tried to intercede with the Emperor's entourage so that the Belgian businessman, 'one of our longest-standing customers (*un de nos plus vieux clients*)', would be promoted in the order. Mellinet also tried in 1867. In the reports of that year (*Service de l'Exposition*), he was recognized as having many merits (*médaille*

than the benefit that the Belgian businessman and his bands provided to the ruler. In reality, this representative resource had already been squeezed to the limit, and with each passing year there were more and more civilian musical ensembles.

It is paradoxical that an entrepreneur who had enjoyed such a long monopoly would not have understood or been better able to adapt to the change of business model that was already relatively widespread in the second half of Napoleon III's regime. However, it was the French Third Republic that confirmed the change of cycle and the real opportunity to make money with the multiplication of civilian bands and fanfares; or, to put it in socioeconomic terms, a consumer society was conquered with an increasingly wide range of products of various qualities and prices. The target market at the end of the nineteenth century was that of a dilettante musician of a civil/municipal group with limited economic resources, who was primarily looking for collective. This amateur was able to buy a brasswind instrument not only because of the end of that monopoly, but rather because of the technological improvements brought about by the second Industrial Revolution, as well as other productive and competitive factors and strategies, including subcontracting, offshoring, and a continuous crushing of workers' labour that had already gone before.

These simple—also in their apprenticeship aspect—brasswinds multiplied and ended up in the hands of groups of amateurs who used to immortalize themselves proudly with them (Figure 17.2). It is not only photographs that bear witness to this special attunement; also the bulky and generous sales catalogues of the Third Republic attest to this growing popularity and diversity. Moreover, those brochures offered not only instruments and brasswinds, but all the paraphernalia that their new and extremely enthusiastic civilian clientele might need: music stands, mouthpieces, ligatures, reeds, pads, sheet paper, medals for their competitions, music cases, cartridge belts (*gibernes de musique*); caps, badges (fabric or metal); clappers, crowns, and diplomas; dance cards, invitation letters and other handbills; standards and banners; and, of course, good-looking uniforms.

And, in order to provide an outlet for such a large number of articles and products, it was necessary to develop and update a capital component that was increasingly and better exploited, namely advertising. Looking back over the arc of the nineteenth century, the claims of the brasswinds

---

d'or, mérite incontesté, esprit d'invention), but he was also described as a very irritating or annoying person at those appointments (*mais fort gênant dans les Expositions*). Malou Haine, 'Un réseau d'influence: les démarches d'Adolphe Sax pour obtenir la croix d'officier de la Légion d'honneur', *Revue belge de Musicologie* 70 (2016), 9–22.

Figure 17.2 French amateur civilian fanfare (*c*.1895)—including minors—and the usual military look
Author's collection.

shifted from the appraisals of a few dignitaries with seats in wise institutions to the increasingly frequent, explicit, generous, and visual advertisements. The personification of brands with prominent performers also increased—Couesnon signed the entire Republican Guard band for his 1900 catalogue—as did the externalization (and amplification) of medals and positive reports from the Expositions. Precisely in order to seduce and attract potential buyers, and taking advantage of the intangibilities of brasswinds, the entrepreneurs offered specimens and models sheltered from of a new and presumed theory or acoustic principle, or with a certain special characteristic that differentiated them from the competition. This type of manoeuvre was very common throughout the nineteenth century—not only in brasswinds, of course; the point is that there was a need to sell and the brass companies resorted to ambiguous practices or even deceitful.[27]

[27] Referring to the Universal Exhibition in Paris in 1889, Constant Pierre (1890) pointed out the 'deceitful (*charlatanesque*) and ridiculous stratagems [of those businessmen and instrument makers] into which only the naïve fell'. These and other formulas seemed to him 'a reprehensible swindle of an unscrupulous conscience' and he ironized that 'the authors of these improprieties are the most honest people in the

Nor should we completely forget the military customer base during the last third of the nineteenth century, for it remained active and was perfectly regulated. Instead of going back to compiling figures or talking about its hackneyed instrumental palette, we prefer to focus on an element forged during that period and which proved to be a real success for the French government. Despite the cutbacks after the war with Prussia (1871), the central powers maintained the band of the *Garde Républicaine*—former *Garde de Paris*—which, precisely, contained those brasswinds and saxhorns in its ranks. This served to spread the 'French model'[28] throughout the continent and overseas—including twinning with and trips to the United States, Russia, the UK, Italy, Spain, etc.—while the formation acted as a cultural, diplomatic, and also a business tool. France made its military bands an effective tool of 'soft power à la française'[29] and also promoted these products and their exports.[30]

In addition, France's cultural strength in brasswinds provides another interesting derivative that we introduced at the beginning of the book, since the judicial and economic battle had its consequences and is still felt today. In the preceding pages, we have seen that the ecosystem of the brasswinds is very broad, it can be approached in many different ways, it resorts to explanatory ideas that cannot be measured well, and its taxonomy and lexicon are muddled. Nevertheless, many brass instruments are still called 'saxhorns' today, but they are not related to or derived from the 1843 patent (paradoxically, the term saxotromba, which gave them substance and a reason for being together, soon fell into oblivion). The idea is that this composite and pretended name is a trope (catch-all term) that has encompassed a group of certainly heterogeneous brasswinds; and that, in truth, it is nothing more than an ethereal of the constant technological drip on brass and of the resources (differentiating and advertising) of capitalism itself. Another parallel and interesting issue is when this terminology is exploited by certain sectors that want to exert cultural (or commercial) influence, a delicate subject that can raise blisters in the official establishment of musicians, academics, or representatives of institutions—including museums—or other administrations. At the

---

world'. Constant Pierre, *La facture instrumentale à l'Exposition Universelle de 1889* (Paris: Librairie de l'art indépendant, 1890), 7–8.

[28] Péronnet, *Les enfants d'Apollon*, 3–5 and 'Musiques militaires et relations internationales', 49–60.

[29] Bouzard, 1845. *L'armée française met au point le premier orchestre de plein air.*

[30] Japan had asked the French for advice (1884) in the artistic field. Thus, Leroux, director of the band of the 78th Line Regiment, was to travel to the East and take charge of organizing the military music of the Japanese Army, to which the editor reacted by saying 'Goodbye Turkish crescent [a percussion military instrument]! All for the saxophone! (*Adieu le chapeau chinois! Tout pour le saxophone!*)'. *Le Ménestrel*, 20 July 1884, 271. Based on data from the *Statistique des douanes*, Pierre stated that the French brasswinds export (second in volume after pianos) was 2,770,794fr in 1892. Pierre, *Les Facteurs d'instruments*, 419–21.

end of the day, language—the way of expressing oneself and the words we choose—creates our realities and legitimizes them.

The turbulent process that French brasswinds went through in the nineteenth century led to a modern understanding of this type of instruments that not only affected France later on, but was also reflected in other countries. It is also essential to emphasize that these brasswinds are products of the Industrial Revolution, namely the development of metallurgy and new technologies applicable to brass, but under the ubiquitous cover, evolution, and rules of the capitalist system, one of the latter being the codification of these advances and progressions through the patent system. However, it must also be underlined that there was an important social and functional component connected to the economic one, furthermore fuelled by these incessant transformations that made it possible for these items to reach more people. Likewise, we cannot forget that these instruments were able to move forward by aligning themselves with and favouring the new needs that, in the consumption of culture, the bourgeoisie imposed on its rise to power and for the type of society it had designed: a group in which the old stereotypes of the *Ancien Régime* are no longer valid, but neither are the schemes of democratic society. The patterns of bourgeois liberal society are at work, where the pressure groups—linked to the oligarchy and to power—control the springs of all powers. But, returning to culture and music, one of those customs of that time was the taste and enjoyment of music in the open air, for example, listening to a band playing from the bandstands in parks and promenades, or entertaining an evening in the surrounding cafés and restaurants; or, in another way, participating in military protocols, religious ceremonies, sports, or civil festivals, where its sound was effective outdoors. It was at this juncture, in these codes of interaction, that the brasswinds achieved a kind of popularity that still endures today.

APPENDIX I
French Patent Law of 1791

Source: Joseph-Marie Blanc-Saint-Bonnet, *Code des Brevets d'Invention* (Paris: Audin, 1823), 71–94 and *Loi portant règlement sur la propriété des auteurs d'inventions et découvertes en tout genre d'industrie donnée à Paris le 25 mai 1791* (Paris: Imprimerie royale, 1791), 1–12.

Law relating to useful discoveries, and to the means of ensuring the property to those who will be recognized as authors.
7 January 1791.

Whereas any new idea, the manifestation or development of which may be useful to society, belongs originally to the person who conceived it, and it would be an attack on the essence of human rights not to regard *an industrial discovery* as the property of its author; whereas, at the same time, to what extent the non-observance of a positive and authentic declaration of this truth may have contributed hitherto to discourage French industry, and may have caused the emigration of numerous distinguished artists and of a great number of new inventions, from which this kingdom should have taken the first advantages; whereas, finally, that all the principles of justice, of public order, and of national interest, imperiously command that the opinion of the French citizens on this kind of property should henceforth be fixed by a law which enshrines and protects it, we order the following:

Art. I. Any discovery or new invention, in all types of industry, shall be the property of its author; consequently, the law shall guarantee him the full and complete enjoyment thereof, in the manner and for the time hereinafter determined.

II. Any means of adding to any manufacture whatsoever a new kind of perfection shall be considered an invention.

III. Whoever is the first to bring into France a foreign discovery shall enjoy the same advantages as if he were the inventor.

IV. Any person who wishes to preserve or secure industrial property of the kind set forth in the foregoing articles shall be bound:

1. To apply to the secretariat of the Directory of his department [now prefecture],[1] and to declare in writing whether the object he presents is of invention, of perfection, or only of importation;
2. To deposit under seal an exact description of the principles, means, and processes that constitute the discovery, as well as the plans, sections, drawings, and models that may relate to it, so that the said package may be opened at the time the inventor receives his title of ownership.

V. With regard to objects of general utility, and with an execution too simple and imitation too easy to yield any commercial profit, and in case the inventor prefers to

---

[1] Blanc-Saint-Bonnet updated the French administrative and territorial references.

deal directly with the government, he shall be free to contact the administrative assemblies or the Parliament (*corps législatif*), if appropriate, to entrust his discovery, demonstrate its advantages, and request compensation from the Minister of the Interior through the intermediary of the prefects.

VI. When an inventor has preferred to the personal advantages assured by the law the honour of making the nation immediately enjoy the fruits of his discovery or invention, and when he proves by public notoriety, and by legal attestations, that this discovery or invention is of real utility, he may be granted a reward from the funds intended for the encouragement of industry.

VII. In order to ensure to every inventor the ownership and temporary enjoyment of his invention, a *title* or *patent* shall be issued to him in the form indicated in the regulations to be drawn up for the execution of the present law.

VIII. Patents shall be issued for five, ten, or fifteen years, at the option of the inventor; but this last term may never be extended without a special decree of the Parliament.

IX. The exercise of patents granted for a discovery imported from a foreign country may not extend, beyond the term fixed in that country, to the exercise of the first inventor.

X. The patents sent in parchment and sealed with the State seal will be registered in the secretariats of the directorates of all the departments [prefectures] of the kingdom, and it will be sufficient to obtain them by applying to these directorates, which will be responsible for obtaining them from the inventor.

XI. Any citizen shall be free to consult the catalogue of new inventions at the secretariat of his department; any domiciled citizen shall likewise be free to consult the *specifications* of the various patents currently in force at the general depository established for this purpose; however, the descriptions shall not be communicated in cases where the inventor, having judged that political or commercial reasons require the secrecy of his discovery, has presented himself to the *corps législatif* [to the Minister of the Interior] to explain his reasons, and has obtained a specific decree on this subject.

In the event that it is declared that a description shall remain secret, commissioners shall be appointed to ensure the accuracy of the description, according to the view of the means and procedures, without the author thereby ceasing to be subsequently responsible for this accuracy.

XII. The owner of a patent shall enjoy privately the exercise and the fruits of the discoveries, inventions, or improvements for which the said patent has been obtained; consequently, he may, by giving good and sufficient security, request the seizure of the counterfeit objects and bring the counterfeiters before the courts; when the counterfeiters are convicted, they shall be condemned, in addition to confiscation, to pay the inventor damages proportionate to the extent of the counterfeit, and furthermore to pay into the poor box of the district a fine set at a quarter of the amount of the said damages, without however the said fine exceeding the sum of 3000 livres,[2] and double in the event of a repeat offence.

XIII. In the event that the denunciation of infringement on the basis of which the seizure took place is found to be devoid of evidence, the inventor shall be ordered to pay damages to the opposing party proportionate to the disturbance and the prejudice that the latter may have suffered, and in addition to pay into the district poor box

---

[2] The livre is a French coin that was used during the *Ancien Régime*. The value at the time is somewhat similar to the later franc, so the figure for that fine was around 2963 francs. [Patrick] Kelly, *Le cambiste universel*, tome 1 (Paris: Bossange frères, 1823), 141–2.

a fine set at a quarter of the amount of the said damages, without however the said fine exceeding the sum of 3000 livres, and double that amount in the event of a repeat offence.

XIV. Any owner of a patent shall have the right to set up establishments throughout the kingdom, and even to authorize other private individuals to apply and use these means and procedures; and in all cases, he may dispose of his patent as if it were movable property.

XV. At the expiration of each patent, the discovery or invention having to belong to society, the description thereof shall be made public, and the use thereof shall become permitted throughout the kingdom, so that any citizen may freely exercise and enjoy it, unless a law has extended the exercise of the patent, or has ordered its secrecy in the cases provided for in article XI.

XVI. The description of the discovery set forth in a patent shall likewise be made public, and the use of the means and processes relating to such discovery shall also be declared free throughout the kingdom when the owner of the patent is deprived thereof, which shall only take place in the cases hereinafter specified.

1. Any inventor who is found to have concealed his true means of execution in his description shall forfeit his patent.
2. Any inventor who is convicted of having used in his manufacture secret means that were not detailed in his description, or for which he did not give his declaration in order to have them added to those stated in his description, shall forfeit his patent.
3. Any inventor, or inventor claiming to be such, who is convinced that he has obtained a patent for discoveries already recorded and described in printed and published works, shall forfeit his patent.
4. Any inventor who, within a period of two years from the date of his patent, has not put his discovery into practice, and who has not justified the reasons for his inaction, shall forfeit his patent.
5. Any inventor who, after having obtained a patent in France, is found to have taken out a patent for the same object in a foreign country, shall forfeit his patent.
6. Finally, any acquirer of the right to exercise a discovery set forth in a patent shall be subject to the same obligations as the inventor, and, if he contravenes them, the patent shall be revoked, the discovery published, and use thereof shall become free throughout the kingdom.

XVII. The exclusive privileges previously granted for inventions and discoveries shall remain unaffected, when all the legal forms have been observed for these privileges, which shall have their full and entire effect, and shall, in addition, be subject to the provisions of the present law.

Other privileges based on simple rulings of the Council, or on unregistered *lettres-patentes*, shall be converted without charge into patents, but only for the time remaining to them, by proving that the said privileges were obtained for discoveries and inventions of the kind set out in the preceding articles.

The owners of the said former registered privileges, and of those converted into patents, may dispose of them as they wish, in accordance with article XIV.

XVIII. The Committee on Agriculture and Commerce, meeting as a Committee on Taxation, shall present to the National Assembly a draft regulation which will set the fees for inventors' patents according to the duration of their exercise, and which will cover all the details relating to the execution of the various articles contained in this law.

Law regulating the ownership of authors of inventions and discoveries in all types of industry.

Given in Paris on 25 May 1791.

Louis, by the grace of God and by the Constitutional Law of the State, King of the Franks: To all present and future, Hail. The National Assembly has decreed, and we will and order the following:

Regulations for the execution of the law of 7 January 1791, on the property of authors of inventions and discoveries in all types of industry.

Title I.

- Art. I. In accordance with the first three articles of the law of 7 January 1791, relating to new discoveries and inventions in all types of industry, national patents, under the name of patents (*brevets d'invention*) (the model of which is annexed to the present regulation, under no. 2) shall be issued, on simple request to the King, and without prior examination, to all persons who wish to carry out or have carried out in the kingdom objects of industry hitherto unknown.
- II. There shall be established in Paris, in accordance with article XI of the law, under the supervision and authority of the Minister of the Interior, who shall be responsible for granting the said patents, a general depository under the name of Directory of Patents for Invention, to which the said patents shall be sent after prior formalities, and in the manner hereinafter determined.
- III. The Directory of Patents for Invention [Minister of the Interior] shall dispatch the said patents on the basis of applications received from the secretariats of the departments [prefectures]. These applications shall contain the name of the applicant, his proposal and his request to the King; a package shall be attached containing the exact description of all the means proposed to be used, and to this package shall be added the drawings, models, and other documents deemed necessary for the explanation of the statement of the application, all with the signature and under the seal of the applicant.

  On the back of the envelope of this package will be written a declaration (in the form attached to these regulations, under no. 1) signed by the secretary of the department [prefect] and by the applicant, to whom a copy of the said declaration will be issued, in order to record the object of the application, the remittance of the documents, the date of filing, the payment of the fee, or the submission to pay it according to the price and within the time limit which will be fixed in these regulations.
- IV. The directorates of the departments [prefectures], as well as the Directory of Patents for Invention, shall not receive any application which contains more than one principal subject matter together with the detailed subject matter that may relate thereto.
- V. The directorates of the departments shall be required to send the applicant's packets to the Directory of Patents, in the form prescribed above, in the same week in which the application is submitted.
- VI. On arrival of the dispatch from the secretariat of the Department to the Directory of Patents for Invention, the declaration recorded on the back of the package shall be registered, the package shall be opened and the patent shall immediately

be drawn up in accordance with the model annexed to these regulations (under no. 2). This patent shall contain an exact copy of the description, as well as of the drawings and models annexed to the declaration; after which the said patent shall be sealed and sent to the department, under the seal of the Directory of Patents. At the same time, a King's announcement relating to patents shall be sent to all the courts and departments of the Kingdom, in the form attached hereto (no. 3), and these announcements shall be recorded in date order and posted in the said courts and departments.

VII. The descriptions of the objects of which the Parliament, in the cases provided for by article XI of the law of 7 January, shall have ordered secrecy, shall be opened and entered by numbers in the Directory of Inventions, in a special register, in the presence of commissioners appointed for that purpose, in accordance with the said article of the law; these descriptions shall then be sealed again, and a declaration thereof shall be drawn up by the said commissioners. The decree ordering them to be kept secret shall be transcribed on the back of the package; mention thereof shall be made in the King's announcement, and the package shall remain sealed until the end of the term of the patent, unless a decree of the Parliament orders it to be opened.

VIII. Extensions of patents which, in very rare cases and for major reasons, may be granted by the Parliament, only for the duration of the legislature, shall be recorded in a special register in the Directory of Inventions, which shall be required to give notice of this recording to the various departments and courts of the kingdom.

IX. Decisions of the Council, *lettres-patentes*, descriptive memoranda, all documents and papers relating to invention privileges, previously granted for industrial objects, in whatever public repository they may be found, shall be brought together forthwith with the Directory of Patents for Invention.

X. The costs of the establishment shall not be borne by the public treasury; they shall be taken solely from the proceeds of the tax on patents for invention, and the surplus used for the benefit of national industry.

Title II.

Art. I. Any person wishing to obtain a patent for invention shall be required, in accordance with article IV of the law of 7 January, to apply to the secretariat of his department [prefecture], to submit his application to the King, together with a description of his means, as well as his drawings and models relating to the subject matter of his application, in accordance with article III of Title I; he shall attach thereto a duplicate statement signed by him of all the documents contained in the package; one of these duplicates shall be returned to the secretariat of the department by the Director of Patents for Invention, who shall take charge of all the documents by his receipt at the foot of the said statement.

II. The applicant shall have the right, before signing the declaration, to be given a catalogue of all the objects for which patents have been sent, in order to judge whether or not he should continue with his application.

III. The applicant shall be required, in accordance with article III of Title I, to pay the patent fee to the secretariat of the department, in accordance with the tariff annexed to these regulations (under no. 4); however, he shall be free to pay only half of this fee when filing his application, and to submit his tender for payment of the remainder of the sum within a period of six months.

IV. If the patentee's submission is not completed within the prescribed period, the patent granted to him shall be null and void; the exercise of his right shall become unrestricted, and notice thereof shall be given to all departments by the Directory of Patents.

V. Any person in possession of a patent for invention (*brevet d'invention*) shall be required to pay, in addition to the tax for the said patent, the tax for the annual patents (*patentes annuelles*) imposed on all arts and crafts professions by the law of 17 March 1791.

VI. Any owner of a patent who wishes to make changes to the subject matter set forth in his first application shall be obliged to make a statement thereof and to submit the description of his new means to the secretariat of the department [prefecture] in the form and manner prescribed by article 1 of this Title; and in this respect the same formalities shall be observed between the directorates of the departments [prefectures] and that of patents for invention.

VII. If the patentee wishes to enjoy the exercise of these new means privately only during the term of his patent, he shall be sent by the Directory of Patents a certificate in which his new statement shall be mentioned, as well as the delivery of the package containing the description of his new means.

He will also be free to successively take out new patents for the said changes, as and when he wishes to do so, or to have them combined in a single patent when he presents them collectively.

These new patents will be sent in the same way and in the same form as the invention patents, and they will have the same effects.

VIII. If any person announces a means of perfection for an invention already patented, he shall obtain on his application a patent for the private exercise of the said means of perfection, without being permitted, under any pretext, to execute or have executed the main invention; and conversely, without the inventor being able to have executed by himself the new means of perfection.

Changes of shape or proportion, or ornamentation of any kind whatsoever, shall not be included among industrial perfections.

IX. Any licensee of a patent obtained for an object which the courts have judged to be contrary to the laws of the kingdom, to public safety, or to police regulations, shall forfeit his right, without being able to claim compensation, subject to the Public Prosecutor's Office taking such conclusions as it sees fit, depending on the importance of the case.

X. When the owner of a patent is disturbed in the exercise of his private right, he shall appeal, in the manner prescribed for other civil proceedings, to the Justice of the Peace to have the infringer sentenced to the penalties prescribed by law.

XI. The Justice of the Peace shall hear the parties and their witnesses, shall order any verifications that may be necessary, and the judgment that he pronounces shall be provisionally executed, notwithstanding any appeal.

XII. In the event that a legal seizure has failed to uncover any object manufactured or sold in fraud, the informer shall bear the penalties set out in article XIII of the law, unless he legitimizes his denunciation by legal evidence, in which case he shall be exempt from the said penalties, without however being able to claim any damages.

XIII. The same procedure shall be followed in the event of a dispute between two patentees for the same subject matter: if the similarity is declared to be absolute, the patent of earlier date alone shall remain valid; if there is dissimilarity in some parts, the patent of later date may be converted, without payment of a fee, into a patent for perfection, for the means not set forth in the patent of earlier date.

XIV. The owner of a patent may enter into such partnerships as he may see fit for the exercise of his rights, in accordance with commercial practice; but he may not establish his business by means of shares (*actions*), on pain of forfeiture of the exercise of his patent.[3]

XV. When the owner of a patent has transferred his right in whole or in part (which he may do only by a notarial deed), the two contracting parties shall be required, on pain of nullity, to register such transfer (in accordance with model no. 3) with the secretariat of their respective departments, which shall immediately inform the Directory of Patents for Invention, so that the latter may inform the other departments.

XVI. Pursuant to article XVII of the law of 7 January, all holders of exclusive privileges, maintained by the said article, shall be required, within a period of six months after the publication of the present regulation, to register the titles of their privileges at the Directory of Patents for Invention, and to file therein the descriptions of the privileged objects, in accordance with article 1 of the present title, the whole on pain of forfeiture.

Title III.

Art. 1. The National Assembly refers to the Minister of the Interior the measures to be taken for the execution of the regulation on the Law of Patents for Invention and instructs him to present forthwith to the Assembly the provisions he deems necessary to ensure this part of the public service.

No. 1: Model of a patent application.
(...).

No. 2: Model patent.
(...).

No. 3: Model for the registration of transfer of a patent.
(...).

No. 4: Tariff of fees payable to the Directory of Patents (Ministry of the Interior).

Patent fee for five years: 300fr.
Patent fee for ten years: 800fr.
Patent fee for fifteen years: 1500fr.
Patent dispatch fee: 50fr.
Certificate of improvement, change, and addition: 24fr.
Patent extension fee: 600fr.
Registration of patent extension: 12fr.
Registration of an assignment of a patent in whole or in part: 18fr.
For the search and communication of a description: 12fr.

---

[3] According to Blanc-Saint-Bonnet, 'the provision of Article 14 of Title II of the law of 25 May 1701, ..., is abrogated with regard to the defence of the exploitation of patents for invention by shares. Those who wished to exploit their titles in this way were obliged to request authorisation from the Government (decree of 25 November 1806)'.

Tariff of fees payable to the secretariat of the department.
>For the declaration of delivery of a description or of any improvement, change or addition, and of the related documents, all fees included: 12fr.
>For the registration of an assignment of a patent in whole or in part, all fees included: 12fr.
>For communication of the catalogue of inventions and research rights: 3fr.

The National Assembly decrees the following changes to the text of the law of 7 January 1791.

The following new wording has been substituted for article X:

>The inventor shall be required, in order to obtain the said patents, to apply to the directory of his department [prefecture], which shall request a copy thereof. The patent sent to this board will be registered there, and the Minister of the Interior will at the same time notify the boards of the other departments.

The Assembly decreed the deletion of the following words:

>Article XII, by giving good and sufficient security, request the seizure of the counterfeit objects (*en donnant bonne et suffisante caution, requérir la saisie des objets contrefaits*).
>Article XIII, 'of which the seizure took place (*d'après laquelle saisie aura eu lieu*)'.

We mandate and order all the Courts, Administrative Bodies, and Municipalities, that these present provisions be transcribed in their registers, read, published, and posted in their respective jurisdictions and departments, and executed as law of the Kingdom. In witness whereof, we have caused the Seal of the State to be affixed.

In Paris, on the twenty-fifth day of May, in the year of Our Lord one thousand seven hundred and ninety-one, and of Our Reign the eighteenth. Signed, Louis [and below] M. L. F. Du Port [French Minister of Justice]. Sealed with the State Seal.

Certified true.

APPENDIX II
French Patent Law of 1844

Source: *Bulletin des lois du Royaume de France, IXe série. Deuxième semestre de 1844*, tome 29 (Paris: Imprimerie nationale,] 1845), 13–27 or Jean-Baptiste Duvergier, *Collection complète des lois, décrets, ordonnances, règlements et avis du conseil d'état*, tome 44 (Paris: [Duvergier?], 1844), 553–621 to know about the previous debates on the draft law and the final discussions in Parliament.

Law on Patents for Inventions.

Title I.
General Provisions.

Article 1.
Any new discovery or invention in any kind of industry shall confer on its author, under the conditions and for the period hereinafter determined, the exclusive right to exploit the said discovery or invention for his own benefit.

This right shall be evidenced by titles issued by the Government under the name of *patents [for invention]* (*brevets d'invention*).

Article 2.
The following shall be considered as new inventions or discoveries, [i.e.]

the invention of new industrial products, [and]
the invention of new means or the new application of known means for obtaining an industrial result or product.

Article 3.
The following may not be patented:

1. Pharmaceutical compositions or remedies of any kind, the said objects remaining subject to the special laws and regulations on the subject, and in particular to the decree of 18 August 1810 relating to secret remedies;
2. Credit or financial plans and combinations.

Article 4.
The duration of the patents shall be five, ten, or fifteen years.
Each patent shall give rise to the payment of a fee, which shall be fixed as follows, namely:

five hundred francs for a five-year patent;
one thousand francs for a ten-year patent;
fifteen hundred francs for a fifteen-year patent.

This fee shall be paid in annual instalments of one hundred francs, on pain forfeiture, if the patentee allows a term to elapse without paying it.

Title II.
Formalities relating to the grant of patents.

Section I.
Application for Patents.

Article 5.
Any person wishing to obtain a patent shall deposit, in a sealed envelope, at the secretariat of the prefecture in the department in which he is registered, or in another department, designating his domicile,

1. His application to the Minister of Agriculture and Trade;
2. A description of the discovery, invention, or application for which the patent applied for is intended;
3. Such designs or samples as may be necessary for the understanding of the description;
4. A record of the documents submitted.

Article 6.
The application will be limited to a single main object with its constituent detailed objects, and the applications that will have been indicated.

It shall state the duration that the applicants intend to assign to their patent within the limits set by article 4, and shall not contain any restrictions, conditions, or reservations.

It shall include a title containing a brief and precise description of the subject matter of the invention.

The description may not be written in a foreign language. It must not be altered or overwritten. Words crossed out as invalid shall be counted and noted, and the pages and cross-references initialled. It must not contain any denomination of weights or measures other than those shown in the table annexed to the law of 4 July 1837.

Drawings must be in ink and drawn to a metric scale.

A duplicate of the description and drawings must be attached to the application.

All documents must be signed by the applicant or by an authorized representative, whose power of attorney will remain attached to the application.

Article 7.
No filing shall be accepted unless a receipt is produced recording payment of the sum of one hundred francs to be deducted from the patent fee.

A declaration, drawn up free of charge by the Secretary General of the Prefecture, in a register intended for that purpose, and signed by the applicant, shall record each filing, stating the day and time of submission of the documents.

A copy of the said declaration will be given to the applicant, in return for reimbursement of stamp duty.

Article 8.
The term of the patent shall run from the date of filing prescribed in article 5.

Section II.
Issue of patents.

Article 9.
Immediately after registration of the applications, and within five days of the filing date, the prefects shall forward the documents, under the inventor's stamp, to the Minister for Agriculture and Trade, enclosing a certified copy of the filing declaration, the receipt recording payment of the fee and, where appropriate, the power of attorney referred to in article 6.

Article 10.
On arrival of the documents at the Ministry of Agriculture and Trade, the applications will be opened, registered, and the patents dispatched in the order in which they were received.

Article 11.
Patents for which applications have been duly filed shall be granted, without prior examination, at the risk and peril of the applicants, and without any guarantee, either of the reality, novelty, or merit of the invention, or of the truth or accuracy of the description. A decree from the Minister, stating that the application is in order, will be issued to the applicant and will constitute the patent.

The certified duplicate of the description and drawings referred to in article 6 shall be attached to this decree, after their conformity with the original copy has been recognized and established if necessary.

The first copy of the patents shall be issued free of charge. Any subsequent copy requested by the patentee or his successors in title shall give rise to the payment of a fee of twenty-five francs. The drawing costs, if any, shall be borne by the applicant.

Article 12.
Any application in which the formalities prescribed by article 5 (nos 2 and 3), and by article 6, have not been complied with shall be rejected. Half of the amount paid shall be retained by the Treasury, but the applicant shall be entitled to the full amount if he reapplies within a period of three months from the date of notification of the rejection of his application.

Article 13.
Where, in application of article 3, there are no grounds for granting a patent, the fee shall be refunded.

Article 14.
A royal decree, inserted in the *Bulletin des lois*, shall proclaim, every three months, the patents granted.

Article 15.
The duration of patents may only be extended by a law.

Section III.
Certificates of addition.

Article 16.
The patentee or those entitled under the patent shall have the right, throughout the term of the patent, to make changes, improvements, or additions to the invention, by complying, for the filing of the application, with the formalities laid down in articles 5, 6, and 7.

Such changes, improvements, or additions shall be evidenced by certificates issued in the same form as the main patent and shall, from the respective dates of the applications and their dispatch, have the same effect as the said main patent, with which they shall terminate.

Each application for a certificate of addition shall give rise to the payment of a fee of twenty francs.

Certificates of addition taken out by one of the entitled parties shall benefit all the others.

Article 17.
Any patentee who, for a change, improvement, or addition, wishes to take out a main patent for five, ten, or fifteen years, instead of a certificate of addition expiring with the original patent, must complete the formalities prescribed by articles 5, 6, and 7, and pay the fee mentioned in article 4.

Article 18.
No person other than the patentee or his successors in title, acting as aforesaid, may, for a period of one year, validly take out a patent for a change, improvement, or addition to the invention which is the subject of the original patent.

Nevertheless, any person wishing to take out a patent for a change, addition, or improvement to a discovery already patented may, during the said year, make an application which shall be forwarded to, and remain filed under seal with, the Ministry of Agriculture and Trade. Once the year has expired, the seal will be broken and the patent granted. However, the principal patentee will have preference for changes, improvements, and additions for which he himself has applied during the year for a certificate of addition or a patent.

Article 19.
Any person who has taken out a patent for a discovery, invention, or application relating to the subject matter of another patent shall have no right to exploit the invention already patented, and conversely the owner of the original patent may not exploit the invention which is the subject matter of the new patent.

Section IV.
Transfer and Assignment of Patents.

Article 20.
Any patentee may assign all or part of the ownership of his patent.

The total or partial assignment of a patent, either free of charge or for a consideration, may only be made by notarial deed, and after payment in full of the fee determined by article 4.

No assignment will be valid with regard to third parties until it has been registered with the secretariat of the prefecture of the department in which the deed was executed.

The registration of assignments and all other deeds involving transfers will be based on the production and filing of an authenticated extract of the deed of assignment or transfer.

A copy of each registration declaration, together with the extract from the aforementioned deed, will be sent by the prefects to the Minister of Agriculture and Trade within five days of the date of the declaration.

Article 21.
A register shall be kept at the Ministry of Agriculture and Trade, in which shall be recorded the changes made to each patent and, every three months, a royal decree shall proclaim, in the form determined by article 14, the changes recorded during the expired quarter.

Article 22.
Assignees of a patent, and those who have acquired from a patentee or his successors in title the right to exploit the discovery or the invention, shall automatically be entitled to certificates of addition which shall be issued to the patentee or his successors in title. Reciprocally, the patentee or his successors in title shall benefit from certificates of addition subsequently issued to assignees.

All those entitled to benefit from the certificates of addition may collect a copy from the Ministry of Agriculture and Trade, in return for a fee of twenty francs.

Section V.
Communication and publication of patent descriptions and drawings.

Article 23.
The descriptions, drawings, samples, and models of patents granted shall, until the expiry of the patents, remain deposited at the Ministry of Agriculture and Trade, where they shall be communicated free of charge on request.

Any person may obtain, at his own expense, a copy of the said descriptions and drawings, in accordance with the forms to be determined in the regulations issued pursuant to article 50.

Article 24.

After payment of the second annual instalment, the descriptions and drawings shall be published, either verbatim or by extract.

In addition, at the beginning of each year, a catalogue shall be published containing the titles of patents granted during the previous year.

Article 25

The compendium of descriptions and drawings and the catalogue published in accordance with the preceding article shall be deposited at the Ministry of Agriculture and Trade, and at the secretariat of the prefecture of each department, where they may be consulted free of charge.

Article 26

On expiry of the patents, the originals of the descriptions and drawings shall be deposited at the Royal Conservatory of Arts and Crafts.

Title III.

The rights of foreigners.

Article 27.

Foreigners may obtain patents in France.

Article 28.

The formalities and conditions determined by the present law shall apply to patents applied for or granted pursuant to the preceding article.

Article 29

The author of an invention or discovery already patented abroad may obtain a patent in France; but the term of such patent may not exceed that of patents previously taken out abroad.

Title IV.

Nullities and forfeitures, and actions relating thereto.

Section 1.

Nullities and forfeitures.

Article 30.

Patents granted in the following cases shall be null and void, namely:

1. If the discovery, invention, or application is not new;
2. If the discovery, invention, or application is not patentable under the terms of article 3;
3. If the patents relate to theoretical or purely scientific principles, methods, systems, discoveries, and conceptions, the industrial applications of which have not been indicated;
4. If the discovery, invention, or application is found to be contrary to public order or safety, morality or the laws of the kingdom, without prejudice, in this case and in the case of the preceding paragraph, to the penalties that may be incurred for the manufacture or sale of prohibited articles;
5. If the title under which the patent has been applied for fraudulently indicates a subject other than the true subject of the invention;
6. If the description attached to the patent is not sufficient for the execution of the invention or if it does not indicate, in a complete and fair manner, the true means of the inventor;
7. If the patent has been obtained contrary to the provisions of article 18.

Certificates containing changes, improvements, or additions that are not related to the main patent shall also be null and void.

Article 31.
Any discovery, invention, or application which, in France or abroad, and prior to the date of filing of the application, has received sufficient publicity to enable it to be performed shall not be deemed to be new.

Article 32.
All rights shall be forfeited,
1. A patentee who has not paid his annual fees before the beginning of each of the years of the term of his patent;
2. A patentee who does not start working his discovery or invention in France within a period of two years from the date of signature of the patent, or who ceases to work it for two consecutive years, unless, in either case, he can justify the reasons for his inaction;
3. A patentee who introduces into France articles manufactured in a foreign country and similar to those covered by his patent. The provisions of the preceding paragraph do not apply to models of machines which the Minister of Agriculture and Trade may authorize to be introduced in the case provided for in article 29.

Article 33.
Any person who, in signs, advertisements, prospectuses, posters, marks, or stamps, claims to be a patentee without possessing a patent issued in accordance with the laws, or after the expiry of a previous patent; or who, being a patentee, mentions his status as a patentee or his patent without adding these words, without a guarantee from the Government (*sans garantie du Gouvernement*), shall be punished by a fine of fifty francs to one thousand francs. In the event of a repeat offence, the fine may be doubled.

Section II.
Actions for nullity and forfeiture.

Article 34.
Invalidity and forfeiture actions may be brought by any person having an interest therein.

Such actions, as well as any disputes relating to the ownership of patents, shall be brought before the civil courts of first instance.

Article 35
If the action is brought at the same time against the proprietor of the patent and against one or more partial assignees, it shall be brought before the court of the domicile of the proprietor of the patent.

Article 36.
The case shall be heard and judged in the form prescribed for summary proceedings by articles 405 et seq. of the Code of Civil Procedure.[1] It shall be communicated to the prosecutor.

Article 37.
In any proceedings for a declaration of invalidity or forfeiture of a patent, the Public Prosecutor may intervene and make submissions for a declaration of absolute invalidity or forfeiture of the patent.

It may even bring a main action directly to have the invalidity declared, in the cases provided for in nos 2, 4, and 5 of article 30.

---

[1] For those points, see for example, Rogron, *Codes français expliqués*, tome 1 [Code de procédure civil expliqué] [1836], 135 et seq.

Article 38.
In the cases provided for in article 37, all those entitled to the patent whose titles have been registered with the Ministry of Agriculture and Trade, in accordance with article 21, shall be joined as defendants.

Article 39.
When the absolute nullity or forfeiture of a patent has been pronounced by a judgement or ruling which has acquired the force of res judicata, the Minister of Agriculture and Trade shall be notified and the nullity or forfeiture shall be published in the form determined by article 14 for the proclamation of patents.

Title V.
Infringement, prosecution, and penalties.

Article 40.
Any infringement of the rights of the patentee, either by the manufacture of products or by the use of means which are the subject matter of his patent, shall constitute the offence of infringement. This offence shall be punishable by a fine of between one hundred and two thousand francs.

Article 41.
Those who knowingly conceal, sell, or display for sale, or introduce into French territory, one or more counterfeit objects, shall be liable to the same penalties as counterfeiters.

Article 42.
The penalties established by the present law may not be cumulative.

The heaviest penalty alone shall be imposed for all acts prior to the first prosecution.

Article 43.
In the event of a repeat offence, in addition to the fine provided for in articles 40 and 41, a prison sentence of between one and six months shall be imposed.

A repeat offence is deemed to have been committed if the accused person has, within the previous five years, been convicted of one of the offences provided for by this law.

Imprisonment of between one and six months may also be imposed if the infringer is a workman or employee who has worked in the workshops or establishment of the patentee, or if the infringer, having associated with a workman or employee of the patentee, has had knowledge, through the latter, of the processes described in the patent.

In the latter case, the worker or employee may be prosecuted as an accomplice.

Article 44.
Article 463 of the Penal Code[2] may be applied to the offences provided for in the foregoing provisions.

Article 45.
Criminal proceedings for the application of the above penalties may only be brought by the Public Prosecutor's Office on a complaint from the injured party.

Article 46.
When an action for infringement is brought before the Criminal Court, the court shall rule on any objections raised by the accused, either on the grounds of invalidity or forfeiture of the patent, or on questions relating to the ownership of the said patent.

---

[2] To understand the complex and extensive item 463 of this compendium, see, among others, Rogron, *Codes français expliqués*, tome 1 [Code pénal expliqué] [1863], 239–41.

Article 47.
The owners of a patent may, by virtue of an order of the President of the Court of First Instance, have any bailiff make a detailed description, with or without seizure, of the allegedly infringing articles.

The order shall be made on a simple request and on representation of the patent; it shall contain, if necessary, the appointment of an expert to assist the bailiff in his description.

Where seizure is to take place, the said order may require the applicant to provide security, which he shall be required to deposit before proceeding with the seizure.

The security shall always be imposed on the foreign patentee requesting the seizure.

A copy shall be left with the holder of the objects described or seized, both of the order and of the deed recording the deposit of the security, if applicable; all on pain of nullity and damages against the bailiff.

Article 48.
If the petitioner fails to take action, either by civil action or by criminal action, within a period of eight days, plus one day for every three *myriamètres* [ten kilometres] of distance, between the place where the objects seized or described are located and the domicile of the infringer, finder, introducer, or debtor, the seizure or description shall be null and void as of right, without prejudice to any damages that may be claimed, if applicable, in the form prescribed by article 36.

Article 49.
The confiscation of articles found to be counterfeit and, where applicable, that of instruments or utensils specially intended for their manufacture, shall be ordered against the counterfeiter, the dealer, the introducer, or the retailer, even in the event of acquittal.

The confiscated objects shall be returned to the owner of the patent, without prejudice to further damages and the posting of the judgment, if applicable.

Title VI.
Special and transitional provisions.

Article 50.
Royal ordinances, containing public administration regulations, will set out the provisions necessary for the implementation of the present law, which will not take effect until three months after its promulgation.

Article 51.
Orders issued in the same form may regulate the application of the present law in the colonies, with such modifications as may be deemed necessary.

Article 52.
The laws of 7 January and 25 May 1791, that of 20 September 1792, the decree of 17 *Vendémiaire* Year VII, the decree of 5 *Vendémiaire* Year IX, the decrees of 25 November 1806 and 25 January 1807, and all provisions prior to the present law relating to patents for invention, importation, and improvement shall be repealed.

Article 53.
Patents for invention, importation, and improvement currently in force, granted in accordance with laws prior to the present law, or extended by royal decree, shall retain their effect for the entire period assigned to them.

Article 54.
Proceedings commenced prior to the promulgation of the present law shall be terminated in accordance with prior laws.

Any action, either for infringement or for invalidity or forfeiture of a patent, not yet instituted, shall be pursued in accordance with the provisions of the present law, even if it concerns patents granted previously.

The present law, discussed, deliberated, and adopted by the Chambre des Pairs and by the Chamber of Deputies, and sanctioned by us this day, shall be executed as a law of the State.

We instruct our courts and tribunals, prefects, administrative bodies, and all others, that they keep and maintain the present, have them kept, observed, and maintained, and, to make them more notorious to all, they have them published and registered wherever necessary; and, in order that it be a firm and stable thing forever, we have had our seal affixed to it.

Done at the Palais de Neuilly, on the 5 July 1844.
Signed, Louis-Philippe.
For the King,
the Minister Secretary of State for Agriculture and Trade.
Signed, L. Cunin-Gridaine.
Seen and sealed with the Great Seal:
the Keeper of the Seals of France, Minister Secretary of State for the Department of Justice and Religious Affairs.
Signed N. Martin (du Nord).

APPENDIX III

Saxhorn Patent (1843)

Patent for Invention and Improvement [no. 15364] of Adolphe Sax dated 13 June 1843 [for five years] for 'A system of chromatic instruments (*un système d'instruments chromatiques*)' [saxhorns].
Source: Institut National de la Propriété Industrielle (INPI), Département des Systèmes d'Information (DSI), Pôle Archives, Courbevoie (France).

> Note one: We use lower case Roman numerals in the footnotes to provide certain information relating to the document.
> Note two: Adolphe Sax used imprecise and unfortunate terminology, especially for such a technical document. However, in order to facilitate understanding in conflicting places and to remain faithful to the original text, we have completed the underlying information with square brackets and retained the original French word.
> Note three: We have kept the underlining in some words that appear as such in the original text, although in our opinion they are not particularly relevant.
> Note four: The document has a single page where the designs are grouped together, but to better appreciate them, we have distributed them in three figures: III-1, III-2, and III-3.

>> Ministry of Agriculture and Trade.
>> Patent for invention and improvement.
>> Mr Sax
>> Duration five years.
>> No. 15364.

Patents.
The Minister Secretary of State at the Department of Agriculture and Trade,
    Having regard to the laws of 7 January and 25 May 1791;
    Having regard to the report drawn up at the Secretariat of the Prefecture of the Department of the Seine, and noting that Mr Sax deposited, on 13 June 1843, at 3:00 p.m.,

1 An application for a five-year patent for invention and improvement, for a new system of chromatic instruments, which he declares to have invented and perfected,
2 A description of the means and processes that constitute the invention and improvement,
3 A double design.

Having regard to the aforementioned documents noting that all the formalities prescribed by the laws of 7 January and 25 May 1791 have been fulfilled;
    Having regard to the decree of 5 Vendemiaire, Year IX,[i]
    Decides as follows:

---

[i] This regulation, made public on 27 September 1800, dealt with the procedure for granting patents and had only two articles, the first referring to the granting of patents by the Minister of the Interior and their periodical publication in the *Bulletin des Lois*. The second required the model of the application

Appendix III: Saxhorn Patent (1843)   261

Article 1. Note is hereby given to Sieur Sax (Antoine Joseph), known as Adolphe, instrument manufacturer, represented by Mr Perpigna, in Paris, rue Choiseul, no. 2 ter, of his application for a five-year patent for a system of chromatic instruments.

Artticle 2. In support of this certificate shall remain annexed:
1 The description of the means and processes,
2 A copy of the designs.
3 [Empty]

Article 3. A copy of this certificate, followed by the literal copy of the above description and accompanied by a copy of the designs will be sent under seal to the Prefect of the department of the Seine, to be delivered to Mr Sax.

Paris, 17 August 1843.
For the Minister and by delegation,
the person in charge of applications, Director,
[Signed] A. Sénay [?][ii]

Application,
for a five-year Patent for Invention and Improvement in the name of Mr Antoine Joseph, known as Adolphe Sax, manufacturer of musical instruments, residing in Paris, and who has chosen as his domicile for administrative purposes that of Mr Perpigna, rue Choiseul, no. 2 ter,[iii] for a new system of chromatic instruments,

Description,
The improved system which is the subject of the present application makes it possible to make glissando [gliding, sliding, or slipped] sounds (*sons glissés* [sic]),[iv] [and] to modify them at will, without having to change the known fingering. It [this system] also eliminates the angles in the slides added (*tons ajoutés*) to the valves or piston valves (*ajoutés aux cylindres ou pistons*), so as to preserve (*conserver*) the original sonority of the [brass]wind instruments.

When instruments need to change key [i.e. be transported] (*ton*), crooks [or tubing segments] (*pièces*) are generally added to the mouthpiece, but then, as the slides (*tons*) of the valves (*cylindres*) are not extended accordingly, the instrument loses sonority and tuning. To remedy this inconvenience, I fit slides (*coulisses*) [actually, extra tube couplings] to the valve [slides] (*cylindres*) so as to lengthen or shorten them when changing key (*ton*), by the amount necessary to ensure that the instrument, which has changed key (*ton*), retains all the desired tuning.

Other slides (*coulisses*) [actually, slides that do not come out of the valves] brought into play by the finger serve me to make bent [slipped?] (*coulées*) sounds. These slides (*coulisses*) are held open by springs, and the finger makes them re-enter [at] the necessary amount, or they

---

to state in writing that the Government did not examine it beforehand and was not responsible for the priority—whoever had made it effective in the first place—the merit, or its notoriety. Isid. Plaisant, *Pasinomie: collection complète des lois, décrets, arrêtés et réglemens* [sic] *généraux*, tome 2 (Brussels: Tarlier, 1836), 307.

[ii] At the top of the next page, the document is stamped with the words 'MR PERPIGNA, Lawyer. Specialized firm for obtaining patents in France and abroad. Paris, 2 ter, Rue Choiseul (*MR PERPIGNA, Avocat. Cabinet Spécial pour l'obtention de Brevets en France et à l'Étranger. Paris, 2 ter, Rue Choiseul*)'.

[iii] The original has a thin maroon line crossing out this paragraph and adding the words 'dated 17 August 1843 (*en date du 17 août 1843*)' which were certainly added when the document passed through the administrative filter.

[iv] Glissaded or glissandi sounds between two different pitches are achieved by making the frequency (the number of cycles or Hertz) rise or fall in a correlated manner.

are held closed by the springs and then the finger will have to push them out. The pressure to make the slide move is not very considerable.

Therefore, this system comprises the following improvements to the band instruments, which can be used together [referring to the improvements] or separately.

Elimination of angles or curves that are too sharp and which distort the sound.

Adaptation of slides (*coulisses*) [extra tube couplings] to the valve [slides] (*cylindres*) to ensure the tuning (*justesse*) of the instrument when changing key (*ton*).

Slides (*Coulisses*) retracted and extended by means of springs and set in motion by the finger to produce bent (*coulés*) sounds, without changing the known fingering.

The figures in the attached drawings represent various instruments to which my improvements have been adapted.

> **Figure 1.** Bugle; an instrument that does not usually change key (*ton*) and does not need slides (*coulisses*) [actually, extra tube couplings] to the valve [slides] (*cylindres*).
>
> **Figure 2.** Bugle with slides (*coulisses*) [extra tube couplings] on all valve slides (*cylindres*) and that can lower from four to five tones (*tons*).
>
> **Figure 3.** Bugle with slides (*coulisses*) [extra tube couplings] on two valve slides (*cylindres*), which is sufficient when it is not necessary to lower than a tone (*ton*).
>
> **Figure 4.** Tenor trumpet in B-flat [sic], an instrument which, like the bugle, does not change key (*ton*).
>
> **Figure 5.** Three-valve (*cylindres*) contrabass (*contre basse d'harmonie*) in E-flat [sic] that does no change key (*ton*).
>
> **Figure 6.** Six-valve (*cylindres*) contrabass (*contre basse d'harmonie*) in F [sic] that does no change key (*ton*).
>
> **Figure 7.** Chromatic trumpet and spring slides (*coulisses à ressorts*).
>
> **a a.** Slides (*Coulisses*) which must be held (*qu'il faut maintenir*) with the finger placed on the rod (*traverse*) or in the middle of [that rod identified by] two [letters] **b** (*ou l'entre deux b*), and which the spring **c** causes to come out.
>
> **d d.** Slide (*Coulisse*) that the spring **e** keeps retracted and that the finger pressing on the rod (*traverse*) **f** will push out. **g g** valves (*cylindres*).
>
> **h h.** New slides (*tons*) adapted to the valves (*cylindres*); **i i** slides [extra tube couplings] (*coulisses*) adapted to the slides of the valve [slides] (*tons des cylindres*).
>
> **Figures 8 and 9.** Details of the spring slides (*coulisses à ressorts*).
>
> **Figure 10.** Cross-section of the open [line] valve (*cylindre*) when the finger presses on the [push button of the] piston (*piston*).
>
> **Figure 11.** Cross-section of the closed [line] valve (*cylindre*) when the piston (*piston*) is lifted by its spring.
>
> **Figures 12 and 13.** Trumpet crooks (*tons*) to be attached to the mouthpiece of instruments to change key (*ton*).

Descriptive memorandum submitted by Mr Sax in support of a five-year invention and improvement patent registered at the secretariat of the prefecture of the department of the Seine on 13 June 1843.

> Paris, 17 August 1843.
> Paris, 13 June 1843.
> [Signed] Ant^e. [Antoine?] Perpigna.
> For the Minister of Agriculture and Trade, and by delegation.
> The person in charge of applications, the director,
> [Signed] A. Sénay [?].

Appendix III: Saxhorn Patent (1843) **263**

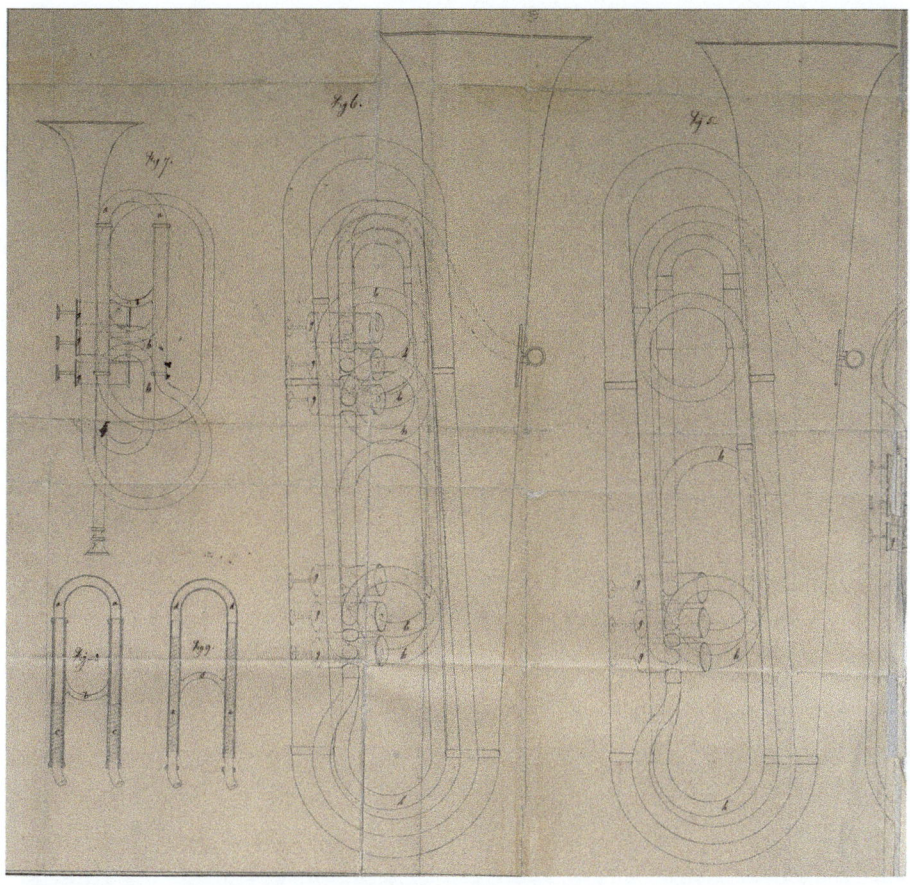

Figure III-1 Main designs of the saxhorn patent (figures 7, 6, 5, 8, and 9)

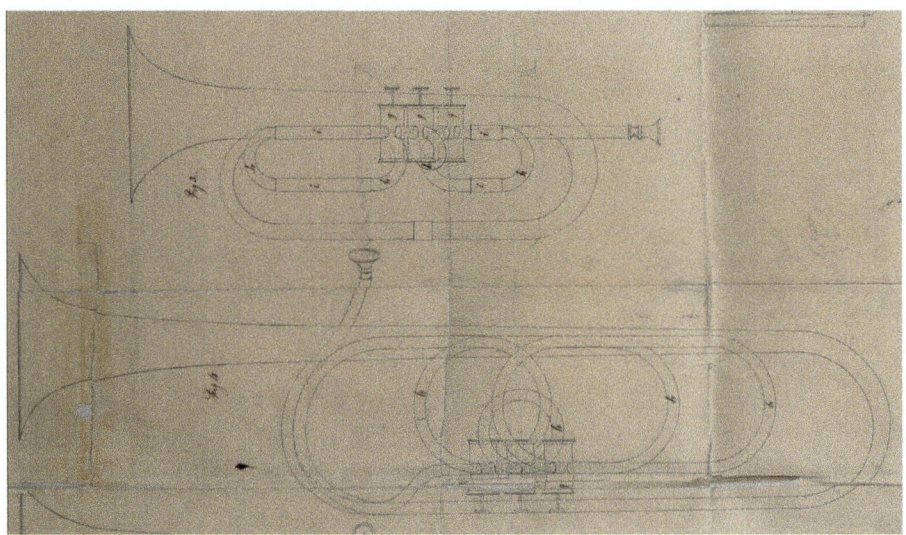

Figure III-2 Main designs of the saxhorn patent (figures 4 and 3)

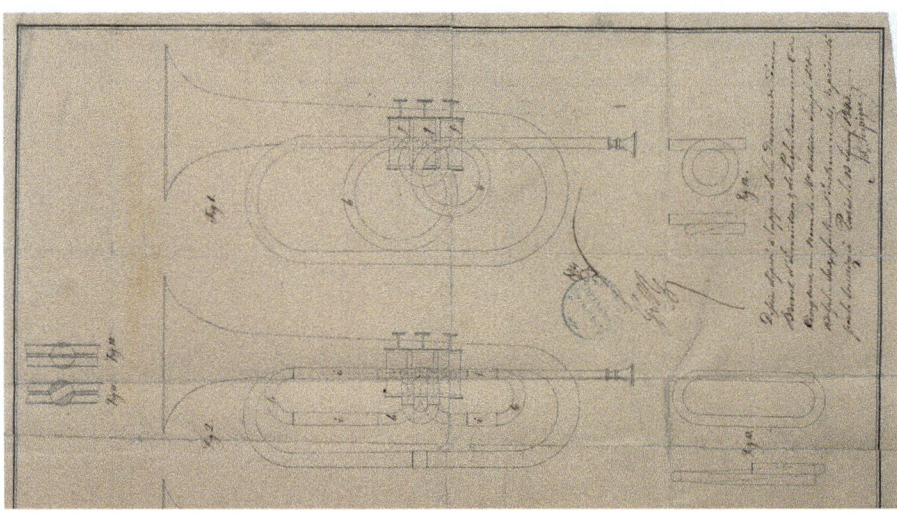

Figure III-3 Main designs of the saxhorn patent (figures 11, 10, 2, 1, 13, and 12)

APPENDIX IV

Saxotromba Patent (1845)

Patent for Invention [no. 2306] of Adolphe Sax dated 13 October 1845 [for fifteen years] for 'A musical instrument called a saxotromba, whose construction, by means of light modifications, can be applied to saxhorns, cornets, trumpets, and trombones (*un instrument de musique, dit saxotromba dont la construction au moyen de légères modifications peut être appliquée aux sax-horns, cornets, trompettes et trombones*)'
Source: Institut National de la Propriété Industrielle (INPI), Département des Systèmes d'Information (DSI), Pôle Archives, Courbevoie (France).

Note one: We use lower case Roman numerals in the footnotes to avoid confusion with the superscripts of the original text and to provide certain information relating to the document.

Note two: Adolphe Sax used imprecise and unfortunate terminology, especially for such a technical document. However, in order to facilitate understanding in conflicting places and to remain faithful to the original text, we have completed the underlying information with square brackets and retained the original French word.

    Ministry of Agriculture and Trade.
    Duration fifteen years.
    No. 2306.
    Patent of invention without Government guarantee.
    The Minister Secretary of State at the Department of Agriculture and Trade,
    Having regard to the law of 5 July 1844;
    Having regard to the report drawn up on 13 October 1845, at 2.30 p.m., at the General Secretariat of the Prefecture of the Department of the Seine, noting the filing by Sieur
    Sax, an application for a fifteen-year patent for musical instrument called a saxotromba, whose construction, by means of light modifications, can be applied to saxhorns, cornets, trumpets, and trombones.
    Whereas the application is in order, hereby decides as follows:

Article 1.

It is issued to Sieur Sax (Antoine Joseph), known as Adolphe, manufacturer of musical instruments; electing domicile that of Mr Perpigna, of Paris, 10, rue neuve St. Augustin, at his own risks and peril, without prior examination, and without guarantee, either of the reality, novelty or merit of the invention, or of the fidelity or accuracy of the description, a patent of invention for fifteen years, which began on 13 October 1845, for a musical instrument called Saxotromba, the construction of which, by means of slight modifications, can be applied to Sax-horns, cornets, trumpets, and trombones.

Article 2.

This decree, which constitutes the Patent of invention, is issued to Mr Sax, to serve as title.

    Attached to this decree shall be a certified duplicate of the description and drawing filed in support of the application, and whose conformity with the original has been duly acknowledged.

Paris, 22 November 1845.
The Minister Secretary of State for Agriculture and Trade.
For the Minister Secretary of State for Agriculture and Trade.
For the Minister and by delegation:
The State Councillor General Secretary.
[Signature]

Descriptive memorandum filed in support of the application for a fifteen-year patent, in the name of Mr Antoine Joseph (known as Adolphe) Sax, manufacturer of wind instruments, residing in Paris at 10, rue neuve St. Georges, and electing domicile for the purpose of the present at Mr Perpigna, lawyer, 10, rue neuve St. Augustin. For a new musical instrument called Saxo-tromba [sic] whose construction, by means of slight modifications, can be applied to Sax-horns, cornets, trumpets, and trombones.

Description

- In deciding on the forms and arrangements of the Saxo-tromba [sic], I have been constantly guided by the conditions that these instruments must fulfil when used in military music, i.e. [to be employed both] on the march as well as at rest, on foot as well as on horseback.
- On horseback, for example, is the position that requires the most care, as the instrument does not rest on the [rider's] hip; it is held between the rider's left arm and flank, so that it is, so to speak (*de manière à faire, pour ainsi dire*), [the instrument is] part of his [rider's] body and accompanies all [his] movements, which considerably facilitates the grasp, embouchure, and fingering.

    The bell, placed in an elevated position and slightly inclined from left to right, directs the sounds over the heads of the performers and does not allow any part of them [the sounds] to be lost in the clothes [or uniforms] (*n'en laisse perdre aucune partie dans les habits*) or [if the sounds were projected] on the ground.
- Therefore, with the instrument at a suitable distance from the horse's head, the rider no longer has to fear that his horse, by raising its head, will strike the instrument and break his teeth or bruise his face, as has happened all too frequently with instruments made to the old model. One of the great advantages of the system I have adopted for the Saxo-tromba is that it can be applied to Sax-horns, trumpets, cornets, and trombones.
- All these instruments have the same fingering and are played in the same way; the sound always emanates from the bell, whereas in keyed instruments it comes out sometimes through the bell, sometimes through the holes closed by the keys, which are pierced at different heights in the tube; this makes the sound sometimes dull, sometimes bright, but certainly very uneven.

    Some of these disadvantages are found in the use of ordinary piston [valves] (*pistons*) because of the angles they present [we understand, in the slides]. As the instruments shown in the attached drawings cover the widest range of the scale, they can be played in all the intermediate keys (*tons*), from the lowest to the highest.
- Crooks (*tons de rechange*) can be adapted to all the instruments in my system; on those in C, crooks (*tons*) can be adapted to B natural or B-flat.
- On those in E-flat contrabass, add the crooks (*tons*) D natural and D-flat.
- These low instruments are fitted with the same valves (*cylindres*) as those instruments] already described in my patent of 17 August 1843 [i.e. saxhorns].[i]

---

[i] This date corresponds to the granting of the patent, although, the document takes practical (legal) effect on the day of deposit, in this case, 13 June 1843.

– Finally, to complete the low octave, I have added a fourth valve (*cylindre*) to those of these instruments that might need it for their range. The third valve (*cylindre*) [that is, the slide of this third valve] may have a length [of tubing] at which the two tones (*tons*) are reached,[ii] which makes it possible to play E-flat with this valve (*cylindre*) alone, and makes it much easier to play certain keys (*tons*) that are particularly suited to military music.

Legend

Fig. 1 Represents a Saxo-tromba in E-flat.
a a. Bell.
b. Semicircle [of tube] leading to the second section [of tube]; part **b** is wider (*développée*) to facilitate the emission of the sound.
c. Second section passing under the valves (*cylindres*) **d d d** and between the slides (*coulisses*) **e e e** of the latter. This has at its end one of the tuning slides (*coulisses d'accord*) **f**.
g. Elbow (*Potence*) rounded [actually, another rounded tube] for the same reason as part **b** and carrying at its end the second tuning slide **f'**.
h. Branch [of tubing] leading to the valves (*cylindres*) **d d d**.
i. Mouthpiece branch which describes a portion of a circle, again to facilitate the emission of sounds.
Fig. 2 Top view of the valves (*cylindres*), shown in elevation in **fig. 1**. The same letters indicate the same parts as in **figure 1**.
e^1 is a ~~potence~~ [sic] double curved tube [actually, the slide] without an angle and gradually widening to receive at their end an elbow (*une potence*)[iii] e^2 wider than that used in the old pistons.
Fig. 2⁺ The same arrangement with the semitone slide uncurved.
Fig. 3 Shows a Saxo-tromba in B-flat.
Fig. 4 Detail of the valves (*cylindres*) adapted to the Saxo-tromba **fig. 3**; they are modified in that the middle valve (*cylindre*) is out of line [is not aligned] with the other two.
Fig. 5. and **5⁺** Sax-horn with four valves (*cylindres*) based on the same system.
d^1. Fourth valve (*cylindre*) which can also be built (*s'adapter*) to the Saxo-tromba.
d^2. Tube and slide of the fourth valve (*cylindre*).
Fig. 6. 8. 9. 10. 11. and **12** Sax-horns based on the Saxo-tromba system with the modifications already indicated.
Fig. 7 Sax-horn in A-flat (form arranged according to my patent of 17 August 1843) to which the arrangements already described have been adapted to allow it to receive crooks (*tons de rechange*) and to tune by the slide (*s'accorder par la coulisse*).
Fig. 13 Arrangement of valves (*cylindres*) which can be adapted to the instruments of **fig. 3. 8. 9.** and **10**.
Fig. 14 Cornet on the Saxo-tromba system **fig.1**.
Fig. 15 Two crooks (*tons de rechange*), for the Sax-horn in A-flat.
Fig. 16 Trumpet with the saxotromba system.
Fig. 17 Tenor trombone on the Saxo-tromba system.

[ii] Although brasswinds were in a period of experimentation (c.1840–60), the use (combination) of three valves (no more and no less) was already defined as a standard because all the pitches of the chromatic scale were achieved quite satisfactorily. (Moreover, it was also said early on in the trials: *Gazette des Tribunaux*, 26 and 27 April 1847, 645). The length of the slides coming out of these valves were proportional to a tone, semitone, and tone and a half; in physical terms, the slide of the first valve lengthens the tube by about 1/8 of its base length, the ratio of the second is 1/15, and the third is 1/5.

[iii] These two words are an addition to the margin and bear the initials 'Ad. S'.

Observations

All instruments which, in the design, have only three valves (*cylindres*) can be fitted with a fourth. Sax-horns have wider proportions than saxotrombas.

Fig. 1 A three-valve E-flat saxotromba.
Fig. 3 Baritone saxotromba in B-flat.
Fig. 5 Four-valve E-flat saxhorn.
Fig. 5⁺ Four-valve saxhorn large width, [and] consequently (*pour seconde partie*), this instrument has a greater volume, larger if I may say so. It lows as deep as the lips [of the performer] allow.
Fig. 6 Sax-horn in A-flat. Crooks (*tons de rechange*) can be fitted to replace the French horn; the slide (*coulisse*) is arranged accordingly.
Fig. 8 Four-valve saxhorn in B-flat
Fig. 10 Contrabass saxhorn in E-flat. It is, as we have already said, stronger and larger than the Saxo-tromba of the same key (*ton*).
Fig. 11 Small saxhorn in E-flat. By adapting a straight crook (*à la coulisse d'accord une rallonge droite*) of one semitone, D is obtained; and by adapting a rounded crook of one tone (*une rallonge d'un ton arrondie*), D-flat is obtained. Acting in the same way with respect to the contralto [saxhorn] in B-flat in **fig. 12**, A or A-flat can be obtained by increasing the tube (*rallonge*) [i.e., by using crooks].

Valve (*cylindres*) system **Fig. 2⁺**. When instruments of a short length have to be fitted with a half-tone tube [i.e. the slide of the second valve], the latter, which cannot be contoured [i.e. bent and placed in the vertical plane] like that of the whole tone or the tone and a half, offers only a very slight contour, a very small curve, thanks to the application of the said system of valves (*cylindres*). In fact, I have found a way of making them less obtrusive (*gênants*) (by arranging them as shown in the drawings), without doing much harm to the sound; I obtain this result by not narrowing the tubes too much, i.e. by taking care that the elbow (*potence*), through a certain arrangement of the curves, is not tightened [or narrow?] (*resserrée*) as is generally the case, and that it [the elbow] offers wider contours.

Summary

–The invention described above comprises not only the individual instruments shown in the attached drawings, but also and above all the different families of which they are members.

> Paris, 1 October 1845.
> [Signed Adolphe Sax]
> Approved [with] one word crossed out [and] void.[iv]
> [Signed Adolphe Sax]
> Seen to be attached to the patent of fifteen years taken on 13 October 1845 by Sieur Sax.
> Paris, 22 November 1845.
> For the Minister and by delegation:
> The Councillor of State. Secretary General.
> [Signature]

[iv] We understand that the word in question is 'potence', which was lined through in the original.

Appendix IV: Saxotromba Patent (1845)

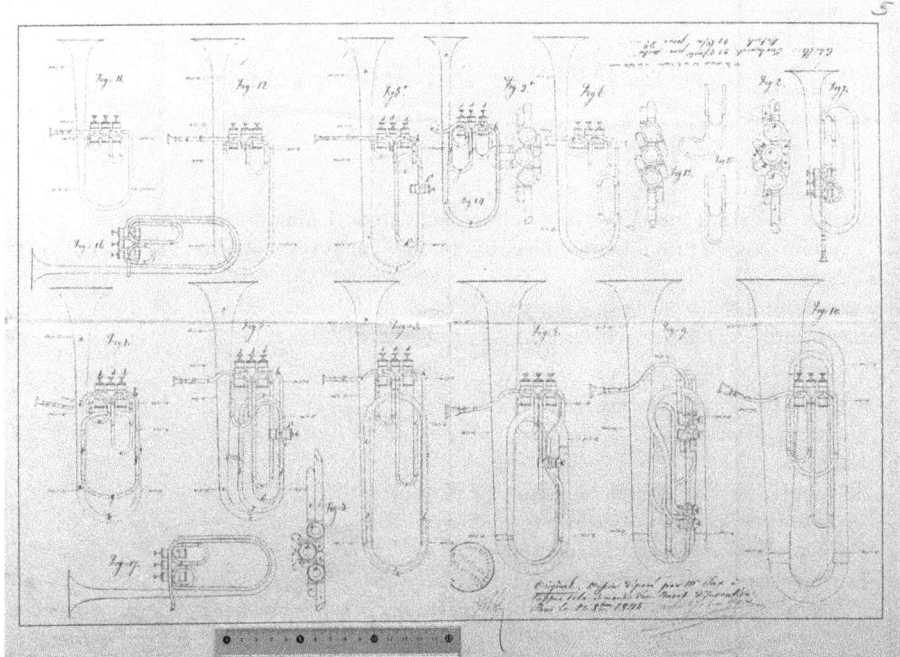

Figure IV General design of the saxotromba patent 1845

Note: The figure has two legends. The first reads 'Original. Drawing submitted by Mr Sax in support of an application for a patent of invention. Paris, 1 October 1845. [Signed] Adolphe Sax (*Original. Dessin déposé par Mr Sax à d'appui de la demande d'un Brevet d'Invention. Paris, le 1er 8bre 1845. [Signée] Adolphe Sax*)' and the second 'N[ote]. The instruments are [reduced] to a quarter of their original size, and the parts to half. Scale: Instruments at 25% per metre. Parts at 50%. (*N. Les instruments sont au ¼ d'exécution et les détails moite. Échelle: Instruments 25% for mètre. Détails 50% pour d°*)'.

APPENDIX V

Saxophone Patent (1846)

Patent for Invention [no. 3226] of Adolphe Sax dated 21 March 1846 [for fifteen years] for 'A system of wind instruments called saxophones (*un système d'instruments à vent, dits Saxophones*)'
Source: Institut National de la Propriété Industrielle (INPI), Département des Systèmes d'Information (DSI), Pôle Archives, Courbevoie (France).

> Ministry of Agriculture and Trade.
> Duration fifteen years.
> No. 3226.
> Patent of invention without Government guarantee.
> The Minister Secretary of State at the Department of Agriculture and Trade,
> Having regard to the law of 5 July 1844;
> Having regard to the report drawn up on 21 March 1846, at 12.20 p.m., at the General Secretariat of the Prefecture of the Department of the Seine, noting the filing by Sieur Sax, an application for a fifteen-year patent for a system of wind instruments called saxophones.

Whereas the application is in order, hereby decides as follows:

Article 1.
It is issued to Sieur Sax, Antoine Joseph, known as Adolphe, manufacturer of musical instruments; rue neuve Saint Georges no. 10, at his own risks and peril, without prior examination, and without guarantee, either of the reality, novelty or merit of the invention, or of the fidelity or accuracy of the description, a patent of invention for fifteen years, which began on 21 Mars 1846, for system of wind instruments called saxophones.

Article 2.
This decree, which constitutes the patent of invention, is issued to Mr Sax, to serve as title.
Attached to this decree shall be a certified duplicate of the description and drawing filed in support of the application, and whose conformity with the original has been duly acknowledged.

> Paris, 22 June 1846.
> The Minister Secretary of State for Agriculture and Trade.
> For the Minister Secretary of State for Agriculture and Trade.
> By delegation:
> The State Councillor General Secretary.
> [Signature]

Descriptive memorandum filed in support of the application for a fifteen-year patent by Mr Antoine-Joseph (known as Adolphe) Sax, manufacturer of musical instruments, residing in Paris at 10, rue neuve St. Georges no. 10, and electing domicile for the purpose of the present at Mr Perpigna, lawyer, 10, rue neuve St. Augustin, for a new system of wind instruments called saxophones.

Statement

Wind instruments are generally known to be either too harsh (*durs*) or too soft in sonority; it is particularly in the basses that one or other of these faults is most noticeable. The ophicleide for example, which reinforces the trombones, produces such an unpleasant sound that it cannot be used indoors because one cannot modify the tone (*timbre*). On the contrary, the bassoon produces such a feeble [or weak] (*faible*) sound that it can only be used for filling in and for accompaniment; or for special orchestral effects in the <u>forte</u> [sic], it is completely useless. It should be noted that this latter instrument is the only one that I combine (*marie*) with the strings.

Only brass wind instruments are satisfactory in the open air; consequently, a band [or group] (*harmonie*) composed of these instruments is the only orchestral combination (*combinaison d'orchestre*) that can be used in such circumstances.

As for stringed instruments, everyone knows that, in the open air, their effect is null because of the weakness of the tone (*timbre*), which makes their use almost impossible in such conditions.

Noticing by these various disadvantages, I sought a way to remedy them by creating an instrument which, in terms of the character of its <u>voice</u> [sic], could be similar (*se rapprocher*) to string instruments, but which possessed more strength and intensity than the latter. This instrument is the <u>saxophone</u> [sic]. Better than any other, the saxophone is capable of modifying its sounds in order to give them the qualities just mentioned and to preserve a perfect smoothness [or homogeneity?] (*égalité parfaite*) over its whole range. I made it of brass and in the shape of a parabolic cone. The saxophone has a simple reed mouthpiece in which the interior is much flared, narrowing to the part which adapts to the body of the instrument.

Description and names of the various individual members of the saxophone family

No. 1. Tenor saxophone in E♭ all closed; B to E♭ sounding <u>D♮</u> to <u>C</u>.

No. 2. Saxophone in <u>C</u> descending to <u>B♭</u> in sound pitch. The same instrument made also in B♭ descends in consequence to <u>A♭</u> which makes B♭ in the same pitch.

No. 3. Contrabass Saxophone in <u>G</u>; which may also be made in A♭.

No. 4. Bourdon saxophone in <u>C</u>, which may also be made in B♭ (a tone lower).

Saxophones numbers 5, 6, 7, and 8 are of the same pitch as the preceding, [but] at an octave above.

Fingerings

No. 1. The fingering of this model has some of the characteristics of the flute and of the clarinet, one may apply to the rest all the possible fingerings and uses.

All closed D♮ to C.
1. Key of C open; 2. C#; 3. D; 4. D#; 5. E; 6. F; 7. F#; 8. G; 9. G#; 10. A; 11. A#; 12. B; 13. C; 14. C#; 15. D; 16. Octave key for the first part of the instrument; 17 D#; 18. E; 19. F; 20. Octave key for the second part of the instrument.

No. 2.
All closed B♭.
1. B♮; 2. C; 3. C#; 4. D; 5. D#; 6. E; 7. F; 8. F#; 9. G; 10. G#; 11. A; 12. A#; 13. B; 14. C; 15. C#; 16. D; 17. D#; 18. Chromatic octave key for the first fifth of the instrument; 19. Octave key for the notes of the next part; 20. Octave key for the rest of the next notes, otherwise for producing the high notes of the instrument.

Description of Mouthpiece
No. 9. Bass saxophone mouthpiece. The other mouthpieces are in the same proportion; they may at all times be made a little smaller or larger (*petites ou plus fortes*) as desired.

Paris, 20 March 1846.
Approved with two words crossed out [and] void.
[signed] Adolphe Sax.
Seen to be attached to the patent for fifteen years taken on 21 March 1846.
Paris, 22 June 1846.
For the Minister and by delegation.
The Councillor of State. Secretary General.
[Signature]

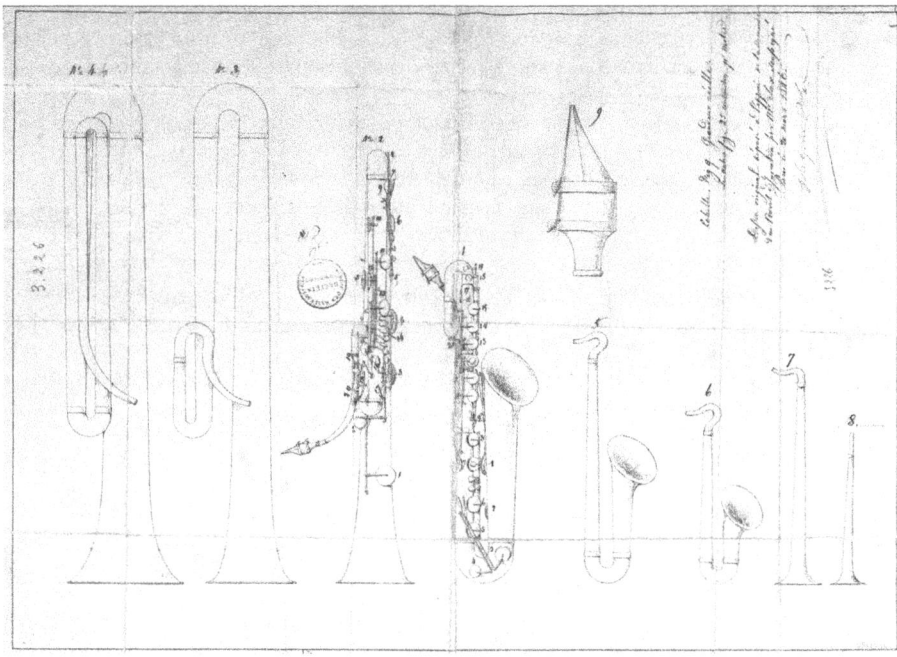

Figure V General design of the saxophone patent 1846

Bibliography

Primary sources

Actes officiels du Gouvernement provisoire dans leur ordre chronologique: arrêtes, décrets, proclamations, etc. Revue des faits les plus remarquables précédés du récit des événements qui se sont accomplis les 22, 23 et 24 février 1848 (Paris: Barba/Garnot, 1848).
Adolphe Sax & Cie. Manufacture d'Instruments en cuivre et en bois. Fondée à Paris en 1843. Rue Saint-Georges no. 50 ([Paris: n. ed., n.d. [1850/51]).
Affaire des émanateurs et des inhalateurs. Mémoire pour M. Bernard contre M. Sax. Procès en contrefaçon d'appareils inhalateurs de goudron pour les voies respiratoires. Notes explicatives (Paris: n. ed., [impr. P. Cordier,] n.d. [1867]).
Affaire des émanateurs hygiéniques. Contrefaçon. Monsieur Adolphe Sax contre Messieurs Bernard, Couly et Jonquet (Paris: n. ed., [impr. E. Brière,] n.d. [1867]).
Affaire Drouelle contre Sax. Renvoi devant la Cour impériale de Rouen après cassation. Cour impériale de Rouen. Troisième chambre. Présidence de M. Le Président Le Tendre De Tourville (Paris: n. ed., [Impr. Renou et Maulde,] n.d. [1866]).
Affaire Kretzschmann contre Adolphe Sax. Cour impériale de Paris (Chambre des appels correctionnels). Présidence de M. De Guajal. Audiences des 8 et 15 mai 1862. Plaidoirie de Me Jules Favre pour M. Kretzschmann. Audience du 7 juin 1862. Extrait des conclusions de M. l'Avocat général Dupré-Lasale. Réplique de Me Jules Favre pour M. Kretzschmann. Arrêt de la Cour du 19 juin 1862 (Strasbourg: n. ed., [Impr. G. Silbermann,] 1862).
Affaire Sax. Arrêt de la cour de cassation. M. Adolphe Sax, d'une part; MM. Raoux, Halary, Gautrot, Buffet Jeune et Gambaro, d'autre part (Paris: n. ed., [Imprimerie H. Simon Dautreville et Cie. Rue Neuve-des-bons-enfants, 3,] 1854).
Affaire Sax: conclusions de M. l'avocat général Oscar de Vallée à l'audience du 26 mai 1860: Adolphe Sax demandeur en condamnation pour contrefaçon contre les sieurs Raoux, Halary, Buffet jeune, Besson, Buffet-Crampon, Tournier et Goumas, Beauboeuf et Victor Jacob, Martin frères et autres. Cour impériale. Chambre des appels correctionnels. Audiences des 11, 12, 18, 19, 25 et 26 mai 1860: plaidoiries (Paris: n. ed., [Imprimerie centrale des Chemins de Fer de Napoléon Chaix et Cie,] 1860).
Affaire Sax contre Gautrot. Attaque du sarrusophone en contrefaçon du saxophone. Consultation de Monsieur Victor Bois, Ingénieur, sur la différence existant entre ces deux instruments (Paris: n. ed., [Impr. E. Blot,] 1866).
Affaire Sax: rapport d'expertise par Messieurs F. Halévy, N. Savart et N. Boquillon, experts nommés par le tribunal civil de la Seine (4e chambre), par jugement en date du 6 avril 1847, dans le procès en déchéance intenté contre les brevets Sax, par MM. Raoux, Halary, Gautrot, Gambaro, Buffet, etc., délégués des facteurs français (Paris: n. ed., [Imprimerie Edouard Proux et Cie,] 1848).
Affaire Sax: réquisitoire: Adolphe Sax demandeur en condamnation pour contrefaçon contre les sieurs Raoux, Halary, Buffet jeune, Besson, Buffet-Crampon, Tournier et Goumas, Beauboeuf et Victor Jacob, Martin frères et autres: tribunal de la Seine. M. Mahler. Audiences des 30 juillet et 13 août 1858, 5 août, 15, 22 et 29 décembre 1859, 5, 12, 19, 26 janvier, 2, 9 et 16 février 1860: enquête, contre-enquête et plaidoiries: audience du 23 février 1860: réquisitoire

de M. Mahler (Paris: n. ed., [Imprimerie centrale des Chemins de Fer de Napoléon Chaix et Cie,] 1860).
Almanach [of France] (Paris: Guyot et Scribe, [several years from 1841 to 1866]).
Almanach de Gotha (Gotha: Perthes, 1846).
Almanach des orphéons et des sociétés instrumentales (Paris: Pagnerre, 1863 and 1864).
Almanach-Bottin du Commerce de Paris, des départements de la France et des principales villes du monde (Paris: Bureau de l'almanach du Commerce, 1842, 1850, and 1873).
Annales de la propriété industrielle, artistique et littéraire, several tomes (Paris: Au Bureau des Annales, 1855–69).
Annales des ponts et chaussées. Mémoires et documents relatifs à l'art des constructions et au service de l'ingénieur. Lois, décrets et autres actes concernant l'administration des ponts et chaussées (Paris: Carilian-Goeury, 1841).
Annuaire général du commerce, de l'industrie, de la magistrature et de l'administration (Paris: Firmin-Didot frères, 1845).
Archive de la Bibliothèque-musée de l'Opéra, 'Dossier d'artiste. Adolphe Sax', *Affaire Sax. Audience du 1 Janvier 1847* and *Audience du 12 Janvier 1847*.
Archives de Paris, D11 U3, box year 1852, dossier 10,509: Faillite d'Adolphe Sax du 5 juillet 1852, *Inventaire, Matériel*, and *Bilan*.
Archives de Paris, D11 U3, box year 1864, dossier 2593: Faillite d'Alphonse Sax du 25 janvier 1864, *Rapport du syndic définitif* and *Concordat*.
Archives de Paris, D11 U3, box year 1873, dossier 17,524: Faillite d'Adolphe Sax du 6 août 1873, *Inventaire* and *Rapport*.
Archives de Paris, D11 U3, box year 1877, dossier 3731: Faillite d'Adolphe Sax du 14 mai 1877, *Rapport*.
Archives de Paris, D1P4 [no. 1032, 1033, 1160, and 1161], [*Cadastres*], 'Saint-Louis, rue (4e), no. 32–112, 1852'; 'Saint-Louis, rue (4e) 1862, 1876, 1900'; 'Turenne, rue de (3e, 4e) 1862'; and 'Turenne, rue de (3e, 4e) 1876, 1900'.
Archives de Paris, D31 U3 [112] [no. 1127], 19 July 1843, no title [*Registration of the formation of the company Sax et Cie.*].
Archives Départementales de Seine-et-Marne, [1] Y 178 [Maison Centrale de Force et de Correction de Melun. Travaux industriels des Condamnés. Instruments de musique. Documents concernant M. Sax], n.d. [10 January 1846], *Cahier des charges pour l'exploitation du travail des détenus dans la Maison Centrale de Force et de Correction de Melun*.
Archives Départementales de Seine-et-Marne, [1] Y 178, n.d. [10 September 1849], *Doit Monsieur Sax*.
Archives Départementales de Seine-et-Marne, [1] Y 178, n.d., no title ['Letter from the Director of the Maison Centrale de Melun, addressed to the Citizen Minister of the Interior [sic] concerning a new deadline of 4 months for the Citizen Adolphe Sax [sic] to pay the debt of 3,317.31fr in accordance with the terms of the act of 29 October 1847'] and ['Letter dated 10 September 1849 from the director of the Maison Centrale de Melun asking Sax to repay the debt of 3,317.31fr'].
Audiganne, Armand, *Les populations ouvrières et les industries de la France dans le mouvement social du XIXe siècle*, vol. 2 (Paris: Capelle, 1854).
Belhomme, [Lieutenant-Colonel], *Histoire de l'Infanterie en France*, tome 5 (Paris: Henri Charles-Lavauzelle, n.d. [1893–1902]).
Berlioz, Hector, *Rapport sur les instruments de musique fait à la commission française du jury international de l'exposition universelle de Londres* (Paris: Imprimerie Impériale, 1854).
Blanc, [M.?], *Mémoires de l'Académie Impériale de Metz* (Metz: Académie de Metz, 1855).
Blanc-Saint-Bonnet, Joseph-Marie, *Code des Brevets d'Invention* (Paris: Audin, 1823).

Blanqui, Jérôme-Adolphe, *Histoire de l'exposition des produits de l'industrie française en 1827* (Paris: Renard, 1827).
Bourquelot, Félix and Maury, Alfred, *La littérature française contemporaine 1827-1849*, tome 5 (Paris: Delaroque, 1854).
Brevets Sax. Motifs à l'appui du rejet du projet de loi (Paris: n. ed., [Impr. E. Brière,] 1860).
Briavoinne, Natalis, *De l'industrie en Belgique: causes de décadence et de prospérité. Sa situation actuelle*, vol. 1 (Brussels: Dubois, 1839).
Brisse, L[éon], *Album de l'Exposition Universelle*, tome 3 (Paris: Bureaux de l'Abeille impériale, 1856).
Bulletin de la société d'encouragement pour l'industrie nationale (Paris: Madame Huzard, 1831).
Bulletin des lois, several tomes (Paris: Imprimerie [de France], [several years from 1814 to 1875).
Bulletin financier [of Paris], 29 July 1853, p. 4.
Catalogue de la Manufacture d'Instruments de Musique de l'Association Générale des Ouvriers. L. François, Maitre & Cie. 81, rue Saint-Maur, Paris (Paris: n. ed., 1884).
Catalogue des instruments de musique de la Manufacture Générale de Gautrot aîné. À Paris, rue Saint-Louis (Marais, 60) et À Château-Thierry (Aisne). ['80 rue Turenne', handwritten] (Paris: n. ed., [Imprimerie Édouard Blot,] 1865).
Catalogue des instruments de musique de la Manufacture Générale de Gautrot aîné & Cie. À Paris, Rue Turenne, 80 (Ancienne Rue Saint-Louis) Au Marais et à Château-Thierry (Aisne) (Rennes: n. ed., [Typographie Ch. Oberthur & Fils,] n.d. [1867]).
Catalogue des instruments de musique de la manufacture générale de Gautrot Aîné, Durand et Cie, Paris, rue de Turenne, 80 et à Château-Thierry (Rennes: n. ed., [Typographie Oberthur & Fils,] 1878).
Catalogue général Illustré des Instruments de Musique fabriqués par la Maison David. 5, boulevard de Sébastopol (Paris: n. ed., [Imprimerie N-M. Duval, 17, rue de l'Echiquier,] 1883).
Certificates of addition of Gustave-Auguste Besson of 30 April 1856 and 12 July 1856 on the Patent [no. 22072] of 18 January 1855 [for fifteen years] for 'Improvements to all types of brass musical instruments (*perfectionnements aux instruments de musique de tous genres en cuivre*)' (INPI).
Chevalier, Émile, *Les salaires au XIXe siècle* (Paris: Rousseau, 1887).
Coghlan, Francis, *The miniature guide to Paris and its environs* (London: Onwhyn, 1853).
Coghlan, Francis, *The Coghlan new guide to Paris* (London: Onwhyn, 1854).
Comettant, Oscar, *Histoire d'un inventeur au dix-neuvième siècle. Adolphe Sax, ses ouvrages et ses luttes* (Paris: Pagnerre, 1860).
Comettant, Oscar, *La musique, les musiciens et les instruments de musique chez les différents peuples du monde* (Paris: Michel Lévy frères, 1869).
Comettant, Oscar, *La Musique de la Garde républicaine en Amérique, histoire complète et authentique* (Paris: Bouallay, 1894).
Conclusions motivées pour Adolphe Sax, professeur au Conservatoire impérial de musique, demandeur en condamnation pour contrefaçon et défendeur en nullité et déchéance de son brevet du 13 octobre 1845, contre les Sieurs Besson, Raoux, Halary, Buffet jeune, Buffet-Crampon, Tournier, Goumas, Martin frères, Beauboeuf et Victor Jacob, inculpés de contrefaçon, défendeurs. Tribunal de la Seine, 6me chambre correctionnelle. M. Gislain de Bontin, Président. M. Mahler, juge suppléant, faisant fonctions d'Avocat impérial (Paris: n. ed., [Impr. N. Chaix,] n.d. [March 1860]).

Conclusions pour Monsieur Drouelle, intimé et appelant, contre Monsieur Sax, appelant et intimé. Cour Impériale de Rouen. 3ème Chambre. Présidence de M. Letendre de Tourville. Audience du 18 mai 1866 (Paris: n. ed., [Impr. Dubuisson,] 1866).

Conclusions pour Monsieur Raoux, appelant, contre Monsieur Sax, intimé. Cour impériale de Paris. Chambre des appels de police correctionnelle. Audiences des vendredi et samedi. M. Partarrieu-Lafosse, Président. M. De Vallée, Avocat général (Paris: n. ed., [Impr. S. Raçon,] n.d. [1860]).

Cour impériale. Chambre des appels correctionnels. Note sur Victor Jacob prévenu de contrefaçon sur la poursuite de M. Sax. Audience du Vendredi 18 mai 1860. M. Parta[r]rieu-Lafosse, Président. M. Oscar de Vallée, Avocat-Général (Paris: n. ed., [Impr. E. Allard,] n.d. [1860]).

Cour impériale de Rouen. Drouelle contre Sax. Les amorces tombantes (Paris: n. ed., [Impr. Crété,] 1866).

Cour impériale de Rouen. Drouelle contre Sax. Pavillons. Pistons saisis. Piston Besson (Corbeil: n. ed., [Impr. Crété,] 1866).

Cour Impériale de Rouen. Faits et documents relatifs au procès entre M. Sax et M. Gautrot. Réponse par M. Sax aux notes fournies par M. Gautrot (Paris: n. ed., [Imprimerie Centrale de Napoléon Chaix et Cie,] 1858).

Cour impériale de Rouen. Note pour M. [Adolphe] Sax, Appelant, Contre MM. Raoux et Consorts, Intimés. Note pour Messieurs les Conseillers (Paris: n. ed., [H. Simon Dautreville et Cie,] n.d. [1854]).

Coyon, Émilie, *Annuaire musical et orphéonique de France* (Paris: Administration de l'Annuaire musical et orphéonique de France, 1875).

Cuënot, Stéph.; Gelle, Th.; and Fabre, A., *Journal du palais: recueil le plus ancien et le plus complet de la jurisprudence*, tome 1 (Paris: Bureaux de l'Administration, 1855).

Dalloz aîné, [Désiré], *Jurisprudence générale. Recueil périodique et critique de Jurisprudence, de législation et de doctrine* (Paris: au bureau de la Jurisprudence générale, 1853 and 1860).

De la Fage, Adrien, *Quinze visites musicales à l'Exposition Universelle de 1855* (Paris: Tardif, 1856).

De Saint-Allais, Nicolas-Viton, *Annuaire Historique, généalogique et héraldique de l'ancienne noblesse de France* (Paris: chez l'auteur, 1836).

Défense de M. Besson contre M. Sax: enquête, contre-enquête et jugement avant faire droit rendu par le tribunal le 13 août 1858: tribunal correctionnel de la Seine (6e Chambre): présidence de M. Berthelin (Paris: n. ed., [Imprimerie de H.S. Dondey-Dupré,] 1858).

Dernières observations pour M. Gautrot contre M. Sax. Cour de Cassation. Chambre Criminelle. M. Legagneur, Conseiller Rapporteur. M. Guyho, Avocat général (Paris: n. ed., [Impr. Madame Veuve Dondey-Dupré,] n.d. [1860]).

Desplaces, Ernest, *Le canal de Suez, épisode de l'histoire du XIXe siècle* (Paris: Hachette, 1858).

Dispositif du jugement rendu le 19 août 1848, par la 4e Chambre du Tribunal de première instance de la Seine, entre MM. Raoux, Halary, Gantrot [sic], Buffet et Gambaro, tous facteurs d'instruments de musique, agissant en leurs noms personnels, et encore comme délégués de tous les facteurs d'instruments de musique en cuivre de Paris et de la France, demandeurs, et M. Adolphe Sax, facteur d'instruments de musique en cuivre, défendeur (Paris: n. ed., [Impr. Appert fils et Vavasseur,] n.d. [1850]).

Dubarle, Eugène, *Histoire de l'Université de Paris* (Paris: Firmin Didot frères, 1844).

Duvergier, Jean-Baptiste, *Collection complète des lois, décrets, ordonnances, règlements et avis du conseil d'état*, tomes 38, 44, 56, and 60 (Paris: [Duvergier?] [several years, from 1839 to 1860]).

Bibliography   277

Elwart, Antoine, *Histoire des concerts populaires de musique classique contenant les programmes annotés de tous les concerts donnés au cirque Napoléon depuis leur fondation jusqu'à ce jour* (Paris: Castel, 1864).

Elwart, Antoine, *Manuel des aspirants aux grades de sous-chef et de chef de musique de l'armée* (Paris: Gérard, 1862).

Enquête sur les conditions de travail en France pendant l'année 1872. Département de la Seine (Paris: Chambre de Commerce, 1875).

Exhibition of the Works of Industry of All Nations 1851: Reports by the Juries on the Subjects in the Thirty Classes into which the Exhibition was Divided, vol. 2 (London: Spicer Brothers, 1851), 724.

Explication des perfectionnements faisant le véritable objet du brevet pris par Monsieur Sax, le 13 octobre 1845 (Paris: n. ed., [Impr. Madame Veuve Dondey-Dupré,] n.d. [1858]).

Exposition 1855. Rapports du jury mixte international (Paris: Imprimerie Impériale, 1856).

Exposition des produits de l'industrie française en 1839. Rapport du jury central, tome 2 (Paris: Bouchard-Huzard, 1839).

Exposition des produits de l'industrie française en 1844. Rapport du Jury Central, tomes 1 and 2 (Paris: Fain et Thunot, 1844).

Exposition Universelle de 1862 à Londres. Section Française Catalogue officiel publié par ordre de la commission impériale (Paris: Imprimerie Impériale, 1862).

Extrait des jugements du Tribunal civil de 1re instance de la ville de Paris du 19 août 1848 et de la Cour d'appel du 16 février 1850 (Paris: n. ed., [Impr. Veuve Dondey-Dupré,] n.d. [1855]).

Fétis, François-Joseph, *Biographie universelle des musiciens*, tome 7 (Paris: Firmin Didot Frères, 1866).

[Fétis, François-Joseph], 'Rapport de M. F. Fétis sur les travaux de M. Sax père', in *Bulletin de l'Académie Royale des Sciences, des Lettres et des Beaux-Arts de Belgique*, tome 18, first part (Brussels: Hayez, 1851), pp. 562–71.

Fleury, Émile-Félix, *Souvenirs du général Cte Fleury*, tome 1 (Paris: Plon, 1897).

Galignani's new Paris guide (Paris: Galignani, [several years, from 1830 to 1868]).

Galopin, Auguste, *Des voituriers par terre, par eau et par chemin de fer ou Traité théorique et pratique des transports* (Paris: Henri Plon, 1866).

Garnier, Joseph, *Le droit au travail à l'Assemblée nationale: recueil complet de tous les discours prononcés dans cette mémorable discussion* (Paris: Guillaumin, 1848).

Gazette des Tribunaux, 26 and 27 April 1847, pp. 645–6; 16 February 1853, [p. 1]; 20 April 1856, p. 394; 30 December 1858, pp. 1280–2; and 31 December 1858, pp. 1286–7.

Gil Blas, 2 April 1887, p. 1.

Grande Diminution Provisoire de Prix. Manufacture d'instruments en cuivre et en bois fondée en 1843. Adolphe Sax et Cie, rue Neuve-Saint-Georges, no. 10 ([Paris: n. ed., n.d. [1848]]).

Great Exhibition of the Works of industry of all nations, 1851. Official descriptive and illustrated catalogue. In three volumes. Vol. I. Index and Introductory (London: Spicer Brothers, 1851) and *Vol. III. Foreign states.*

Guilbaut, E., *Guide pratique des sociétés musicales et des chefs de musique* (Paris: L'instrumental, 1894).

Hoefer, Jean-Chrétien-Ferdinand, *Nouvelle biographie générale*, tomes 15 and 33 (Paris: Firmin-Didot, 1856 and 1860).

International Exhibition 1862. Medals and Honourable Mentions awarded by the In International Juries (London: George Edward Eyre and William Spottiswoode, 1862).

Jacobs, Édouard, *Nomenclature des Sociétés musicales de la Belgique* (Antwerp: Van Merlen, 1853).

Journal des Débats, 8 October 1843, p. 1; 1 April 1845, pp. 1–3; 14 February 1847, pp. 1–2; 12 October 1847, p. 2; 21 August 1849, p. 2; and 17 April 1887, [p. 2].

278 Bibliography

Journal militaire officiel, [no exact date, second half of] 1845, pp. 197–8; [no exact date, first half of] 1848, pp. 155–6 and 291; [no exact date, first half of] 1852 [no. 10], p. 193; [no exact date, second half of] 1852 [no. 47], pp. 212–15; [no exact date, second half of] 1854 [no. 59], pp. 282–92; [no exact date, first half of] 1855 [no. 11], pp. 158–9; [no exact date, first half of] 1856 [no. 13], pp. 394–7; [no exact date, first half of] 1856 [no. 15], p. 430; [no exact date, first half of] 1860 [no. 14], pp. 261–3; [no exact date, first half of] 1861 [no. 27], pp. 689–90 and table no. 2; [no exact date, first half of] 1867 [no. 3], pp. 39–40; [no exact date, first half of] 1867 [no. 7], pp. 166–8; [no exact date, second half of] 1873 [no. 67], pp. 543–6; [no exact date, second half of] 1898 [no. 110], pp. 219–21.

Kastner, Georges, *Traité général d'instrumentation, comprenant les propriétés et l'usage de chaque instrument, précédé d'un résumé sur les voix, à l'usage des jeunes compositeurs* (Paris: Prilipp, [1836]).

Kastner, Georges, *Manuel général de musique militaire à l'usage des armées françaises* (Paris: Firmin Didot Frères, 1848).

Kastner, Georges, *Méthode complète et raisonnée de Saxophone [dédiée à Monsieur Ad. Sax]* (Paris: Brandus et Cie., Successeurs de Maurice Schlesinger et E. Troupenas et Cie,] s.d. [c.1845–50]).

L'Illustration, 5 February 1848, p. 357 and 21 July 1855, pp. 43–5.

L'indépendant, 21 January 1844, pp. 1–2.

La France musicale, 24 September 1843, p. 316; 2 June 1844, pp. 173–4; 11 August 1844, p. 248; 12 March 1848, p. 79; 29 July 1849, p. 236; 5 August 1849, pp. 240–1; 14 October 1849, p. 322; 18 May 1851, p. 156; 4 February 1855, pp. 33–4; 15 April 1855, p. 119; 22 April 1855, p. 123; 6 May 1855, p. 140; and 19 August 1860, p. 343.

La Justice, 26 March 1887, [pp. 1–2] and 20 January 1888, [p. 3].

La musique des familles, 21 April 1887, pp. 215–16 and 28 April 1887, pp. 22–4.

La presse musicale, 23 November 1854, [pp. 2–4].

Laboulaye, Ch., dir., *Annales du Conservatoire Impérial des Arts et Métiers*, tome 3 (Paris: Eugène Lacroix, 1862).

Le Droit. Journal des Tribunaux, 18 March 1847, pp. 268–9; and 27 September 1854, pp. 927–31.

Le Figaro, 1 July 1874, p. 3 and 4 August 1874, p. 1.

Le Guide Musical, 18 and 25 July 1867, [pp. 1–2].

Le Ménestrel, 23 November 1845, p. 3; 26 April 1846, p. 3; 13 June 1847, pp. 3–4; 12 March 1848, p. 3; 1 July 1849, p. 3; 26 August 1849, pp. 1–2; 18 November 1849, p. 2; 19 May 1850, pp. 2–3; 15 June 1851, pp. 1–2; 10 August 1851, p. 4; 25 April 1852, pp. 1–2; 2 January 1853, p. 4; 20 March 1853, p. 3; 15 May 1853, p. 4; 26 June 1853, p. 3; 15 May 1853, p. 4; 22 May 1853, p. 4; 11 December 1853, pp. 1–2; 25 December 1853, pp. 1–2; 16 March 1854, p. 4; 30 April 1854, p. 4; 9 July 1854, p. 1; 1 October 1854, p. 3; 22 October 1854, pp. 3–4; 5 November 1854, p. 4; 26 August 1855, p. 3; 18 November 1855, p. 2; 30 December 1855, p. 3; 1 February 1857, p. 3; 15 February 1857, p. 3; 14 June 1857, p. 3; 13 September 1857, p. 4; 27 February 1859, pp. 97–9; 6 March 1859, pp. 108–9; 13 March 1859, pp. 116–17; 8 April 1860, p. 150; 26 August 1860, p. 311; 23 September 1860, p. 343; 3 May 1863, p. 175; 24 May 1863, p. 200; 17 July 1864, pp. 261–2; 24 July 1864, p. 272; 7 August 1864, pp. 285–6; 21 August 1864, p. 303; 19 March 1865, p. 125; 21 April 1867, p. 165; 5 May 1867, pp. 181–2; 21 July 1867, p. 266; 28 July 1867, p. 276; 29 December 1867, pp. 36–7; 6 July 1873, p. 256; 20 July 1884, p. 271; 3 April 1887, pp. 142–3; and 28 May 1893, p. 174.

Le Monde Illustré, 3 January 1863, pp. 13–14; 2 September 1865, p. 160; 3 August 1867, p. 65; and 29 August 1868, p. 133.

Le Moniteur de l'Armée, 10 September 1845, p. 2; 20 April 1848, p. 4; and 10 June 1848, p. 5; and 16 September 1854, pp. 2–3.

Le Moniteur Universel, Journal officiel de la République française, 12 November 1849, p. 3630.
Le Moniteur universel, 27 June 1860, p. 1; 1 July 1860, p. 2; 2 July 1860, p. 2; 3 July 1860, p. 2; 4 July 1860, p. 2; 5 July 1860, p. 1; 15 July 1860, p. 4; 21 July 1860, p. 2; and 22 July 1860, pp. 2–4.
Le Petit Parisien, 28 March 1887, [p. 2].
Leroy-Beaulieu, Paul, *Le collectivisme: examen critique du nouveau socialisme* (Paris: Guillaumin, 1885).
Lettre adressée à M. le Président de la 4e chambre du tribunal de 1re instance de la Seine par M. Spontini. [Cour d'appel. 3me Chambre. Présidence de M. Poultier. Rôle du vendredi. M. Berville, avocat-général] (Paris: n. ed., [Imp. de Appert,] 1850).
Loi portant règlement sur la propriété des auteurs d'inventions et découvertes en tout genre d'industrie donnée à Paris le 25 mai 1791 (Paris: Imprimerie royale, 1791).
M. Rivet contre M. Sax: tribunal de police correctionnelle: 6e chambre: audience du 27 mars 1856: présidence de M. Dubarle (Paris: n. ed., [Imprimerie de Mme V[euv]e Dondey-Dupré,] 1856).
Malepeyre, François, dir., *Le Technologiste ou archives des progrès de l'industrie française et étrangère*, tome 28 (Paris: Roret, 1867).
Manufacture d'instruments de musique. Adolphe Sax et Cie. Rue Neuve-Saint-Georges, no. 10 (Paris: n. ed., n.d. [c.1845/7]).
Manufacture d'Instruments de Musique en Cuivre et en Bois Adolphe Sax. 50, rue Saint-Georges, Paris (Paris: n. ed., n.d. [1870–2]).
Manufacture d'Instruments de Musique Jérôme Thibouville-Lamy. 68 & 70 Rue Réaumur. Paris (Paris: n. ed., 1878).
Manufacture d'Instruments de Musique. La plus importante du monde [sic] Couesnon & Cie. 94, rue d'Angoulême, Paris (Paris: n. ed., 1893–4).
Manufacture d'Instruments de Musique. Millereau & Cie. Fournisseurs de l'Armée. 6 Passage Chausson, près la caserne du Prince Eugene (Paris: n. ed., n.d. [1864]).
Manufacture de Cordes Harmoniques et d'Instruments de Musique. Jérôme Thibouville-Lamy. 68 & 70 Rue Réaumur. Paris (Paris: n. ed., 1873).
Manuf^{re} d'Instruments de Musique. Rue St Louis 64 au Marais. An^{ne} Maison Guichard. Gautrot aîné et Cie. Album & Catalogue 1850 (Paris: n. ed., [Impr. Plista,] 1850).
Manuf^{re} d'Instruments de Musique Couturier. 73, Cours Lafayette. Lyon. Rue Turenne, 92 Paris. (Paris: n. ed., n.d. [1869?]).
Manuf^{re} d'Instruments de Musique en Cuivre et en Bois de Couturier de Lyon. A. Rustant concessionnaire. Paris. Rue de Turbigo, 70 [in addendum] (Paris: n. ed., n.d. [1868?]).
Meifred, Joseph, *Quelques mots sur les changements proposés pour la composition des musiques d'infanterie* (Paris: Bureau de la France musicale, 1853).
Mémoire ampliatif pour M. Ch. A. Kretzschmann contre M. A. Sax. M. Waisse, président. M. Caussin de Perceval, conseiller rapporteur. Me Michaux-Bellaire, avocat (Strasbourg: n. ed., [Impr. G. Silbermann,] 1863).
Mémoire ampliatif pour M. Kretzschmann, fabricant d'instruments de musique, demeurant rue Sainte-Hélène, à Strasbourg (Bas-Rhin) contre M. A. Sax, fabricant d'instruments de musique, demeurant rue Saint-Georges, 50, à Paris. Cour de cassation. Chambre criminelle. M. Vaïsse, Président. M. Nouguier, Conseiller rapporteur (Strasbourg: n. ed., [Impr. G. Silbermann,] n.d. [1861]).
Mémoire pour M. Gautrot aîné contre M. Sax: cour de cassation: chambre criminelle (Paris: n. ed., [Imprimerie de J. Claye,] 1857).
Mémoire pour M. Gautrot, demandeur en cassation de l'arrêt du 24 juin 1858, rendu par la Cour impériale de Rouen, au profit de M. Sax. Cour de Cassation, Chambre criminelle (Paris: n. ed., [Impr. Le Normant,] n.d. [1858]).

Mémoire pour M. Gautrot, demandeur en Cassation de l'arrêt rendu le 24 décembre 1858, par la Cour impériale d'Amiens, au profit de M. Sax. Cour de Cassation, Chambre criminelle (Paris: n. ed., [Impr. Le Normant,] n.d. [1858 or 1859]).

Mémoire pour M. Rivet contre M. Sax: contrefaçon: instruments en cuivre. Pavillon en l'air—pistons parallèles au pavillon: tribunal civil de première instance. 6e chambre: présidence de M. le président Dubarle: jugement à prononcer le jeudi 17 avril 1856 (Paris: n. ed., [Typographie et Lithographie Maulde et Renou,] 1856).

Neukomm, Edmond, *Histoire de la musique militaire* (Paris: Baudoin, 1889).

Note pour M. Adolphe Sax contre M. Gautrot: tribunal correctionnel de la Seine: sixième chambre (Paris: n. ed., [Imprimerie Charles de Mourgues Frères,] 1856).

Note pour M. Gautrot contre M. Adolphe Sax. Tribunal correctionnel de la Seine. 6me Chambre. Audience du jeudi. Présidence de M. Dubarle (Paris: n. ed., [Imprimerie de Mme Veuve Dondey-Dupré,] n.d. [1856]).

Note pour M. Kretzschmann, fabricant d'instruments de musique, demeurant rue Sainte-Hélène, à Strasbourg (Bas-Rhin) contre M. A. Sax, fabricant d'instruments de musique, demeurant rue Saint-Georges, 50, à Paris (Strasbourg: n. ed., [Impr. G. Silbermann,] n.d. [1861]).

Note pour M. Sax, appelant, contre MM. Raoux et consorts, intimés. Cour impériale de Rouen. Audience solennelle: 1re et 2e chambres réunies (Paris: n. ed., [Impr. H. Simon Dautreville,] 1854).

Note pour M. Sax contre MM. Besson et Kretzschmann: tribunal correctionnel de la Seine: audience du jeudi; jugement par défaut du 26 juillet 1860 auquel Kretzschmann a formé opposition, et dont M. Sax demande au contraire le maintien; Besson prétendant, sans le justifier légalement, qu'il y a aussi formé (Paris: n. ed., [Imprimerie française et anglaise de E. Brière,] n.d. [1860]).

Note pour M. Sax en réponse à la nouvelle note de M. Raoux (Paris: n. ed., [Imprimerie de E. Brière,] n.d. [1860]).

Note pour messieurs les conseillers [de la troisième Chambre de la Cour d'Appel, 16 février 1850] (Paris: n. ed., [Impr. Simon Dautreville & Cie,] 1850).

Note pour MM. Raoux, Halary et consorts contre M. Sax. Cour d'appel. 3me Chambre. Présidence de M. Poultier. Rôle du vendredi. M. Berville, Avocat Général (Paris, n. ed., [Imp. de Schneider,] n.d. [1850]).

Note pour Monsieur Adolphe Sax contre Monsieur Gautrot: tribunal correctionnel de la Seine: sixième chambre (Paris: n. ed., [Imprimerie Charles de Mourgues Frères,] 1856).

Note sur le brevet du saxophone. Réponse aux conclusions de Monsieur l'Avocat général. M. Sax contre MM. Gautrot, Leroy et Goumas, Jules Martin, Martin frères, Lecomte et Cie, Millereau, Buffet jeune, Halary, femme Besson, Barbu père, Barbu fils, Massabo, Kroll, Couturier, Bohem et Gaubert. Chambre des appels de Police Correctionnelle. M. Saillard Président. M. le conseiller Falconnet, Rapporteur. M. Ducreux, Avocat général (Paris: n. ed., [Impr. E. Brière,] n.d. [1867]).

Notice Historique sur la Manufacture d'Instruments de Musique de J. A. Halary (Paris: n. ed., n.d. [c.1864]).

Nouveau prospectus d'Adolphe Sax et Cie. Manufacture d'instruments de musique. Rue Neuve-Saint-Georges, no. 10 (Paris: n. ed., n.d. [1847]).

Nullité de brevet. Instruments et brevets Sax. Tribunal Correctionnel de la Seine, 6me Chambre. Affaire Rivet contre Sax. Documents (Paris: n. ed., [Imprimerie de Mme Dondey-Dupré,] 1855).

Observation pour MM. Raoux, Halary et consorts, appelants incidemment, contre M. Sax, appelant principal (Paris: n. ed., [Impr. Appert fils et Vavasseur,] n.d. [1850]).

Observations pour M. Courtois contre M. Drouelle (Paris: n. ed., n.d. [1860]).

Observations pour M. Sax contre MM. Goudot et Chantepie et M. Vidal, liquidateur de la Société dite Maison Adolphe Sax, Goudot et Chantepie (Paris: n. ed., [Impr. E. Brière,] n.d. [1866]).
Observations soumises aux membres du Corps législatif contre la prolongation des brevets demandés par M. Sax (Paris: n. ed., [Impr. de E. Brière,] 1860).
Palianti, Louis, *Petites Archives des théâtres de Paris. Souvenirs de dix ans, du 1er janvier 1855 au 31 décembre 1864, et des six premiers mois de 1865* (Paris: Gosselin, 1865).
Patent [no. 14608] of Adolphe Sax of 1 October 1852 [for fifteen years] for 'Provisions applicable to musical wind instruments, particularly brass (*dispositions applicables aux instruments de musique à vent, notamment en cuivre*)' (INPI).
Patent [no. 15364] of Adolphe Sax of 13 June 1843 [for five years] for 'A system of chromatic instruments (*un système d'instruments chromatiques*)' [saxhorns] (INPI).
Patent [no. 21502] of Adolphe-Eugène Disdéri of 27 November 1854 [for fifteen years] for 'Improvements relating to the photographic technique (*perfectionnements en photographie, notamment appliqués aux cartes de visites, portraits, monuments, etc.*)' (INPI).
Patent [no. 2306] of Adolphe Sax of 13 October 1845 [for fifteen years] for 'A musical instrument called a saxotromba, whose construction, by means of light modifications, can be applied to saxhorns, cornets, trumpets, and trombones (*un instrument de musique, dit saxotromba dont la construction au moyen de légères modifications peut être appliquée aux sax-horns, cornets, trompettes et trombones*)' (INPI).
Patent [no. 24419] of Jules-Léon Halary of 9 August 1855 and [for fifteen years] for 'Parabolic cut bells applicable to musical instruments (*pavillons à coupe parabolique applicables aux instruments de musique*)' (INPI).
Patent [no. 28034] of Pierre-Louis Gautrot of 9 June 1856 [for fifteen years] for 'A musical instrument called Sarrusophone (*un instrument de musique dit: Sarrusophone*)' (INPI).
Patent [no. 3226] of Adolphe Sax of 21 March 1846 [for fifteen years] for 'A system of wind instruments called saxophones (*un système d'instruments à vent, dits Saxophones*)' (INPI).
Patent [no. 39371] of Adolphe Sax of 3 January 1859 [for fifteen years] 'Dispositions to be applied to brass instruments (*dispositions applicables aux instruments de musique, en cuivre*)' (INPI).
Patent [no. 67433] of Pierre-Louis Gautrot of 20 May 1865 [for fifteen years] for 'Improvements to the sarrusophone family (*perfectionnements apportés à la famille des sarrusophones*)' (INPI).
Patent [no. 6851] of Jean-Auguste Guichard of 29 December 1835 [for five years] for 'Ophicleides with valves (*des ophicléides [ophicleydes] à pistons*)' (INPI).
Patent [no. 75861] of Adolphe Sax of 1 April 1867 [for fifteen years] 'Various improvements made to brass instruments (*divers perfectionnements apportés aux instruments de musique en cuivre*)' (INPI).
Perrin, Albert, *Réorganisation des musiques régimentaires en France* (Mézières: Lelaurin-Martinet, 1851).
Pétition adressée au Sénat par M. Besson, facteur d'instruments de musique en cuivre, le 28 juin 1860 (Paris: n. ed., [Impr. de E. Brière,] 1860).
Pierre, Constant, *Les facteurs d'instruments de musique: les luthiers et le facture instrumentale: précis historique* (Paris: Sagot, 1893).
Pierre, Constant, *La facture instrumentale à l'Exposition Universelle de 1889* (Paris: Librairie de l'art indépendant, 1890).
Pierre, Constant, *Le Conservatoire national de musique et de déclamation. Documents historiques et administratifs* (Paris: Imprimerie nationale, 1900).
Plaisant, Isid., *Pasinomie: collection complète des lois, décrets, arrêtés et réglemens* [sic] *généraux*, tome 2 (Brussels: Tarlier, 1836).

Planque, [No name], *Agenda musical ou indicateur des amateurs, artistes et commerçants en musique de Paris, de la province et de l'étranger* (Paris: E. Duverger, 1837).
Planta, Edward, *A new picture of Paris* (London: Samuel Leigh, 1827).
Pontécoulant, Adolphe de, *Douze jours à Londres. Voyage d'un mélomane à travers l'exposition universelle* (Paris: Henry, 1862).
Pontécoulant, Adolphe de, *Organographie. Essai sur la facture instrumentale*, vol. 2 (Paris: Castel, 1861).
Pontécoulant, Adolphe de, *La musique à l'Exposition Universelle de 1867* (Paris: L'art musical, 1868).
Pour M. Besson. Réponse à la Note publiée par M. Sax sur la saisie faite au greffe des quatre instruments intitulés Antériorités. [Tribunal de première instance de la Seine. 6ᵉ Chambre. Présidence de M. Salmon. Audience du jeudi] (Paris: n. ed., [Impr. Renou et Maulde,] 1862).
Précis analytique des travaux de l'Académie des Sciences, Belles-lettres et Arts de Rouen pendant l'année 1853–54 (Rouen: Alfred Péron, 1854).
Prolongation des brevets Sax. Observations sur le rapport fait au nom de la commission (Paris: n. ed., [Impr. L. Guérin,] 1860).
PROTESTATION [sic] *de tous les Facteurs d'Instruments de musique militaire de France, adressée à Monsieur le Ministre de la Guerre, sur la Commission nommée pour l'examen des nouveaux instruments* (Paris: n. ed., [Typographie et Lithographie de A. Appert,] n.d. [1845]).
Quérard, [J-M.], *La France littéraire*, tome 9 (Paris: Firmin Didot, 1838).
Quérard, [J-M.], *Le Quérard: archives d'histoire littéraire, de biographie et de bibliographie françaises: complément périodique de la France littéraire* (Paris: Le Quérard, 1855).
Quesneville, [Gustave-Augustin], dir., *Revue Scientifique et industrielle*, tome 1 (2nd series) (Paris: Louis Colas, 1844).
Quinze ans de procès!: M. Sax contre MM. Besson, Raoux et consorts: 1846-1860 (Paris: n. ed., [Imprimerie centrale de Napoléon Chaix et Cie,] 1860).
Rapport de M. l'expert Surville, ingénieur, déposé le 18 février 1859 et dire de M. Sax. (Paris: n. ed., [Imprimerie centrale des Chemins de Fer de Napoléon Chaix et Cie,] 1860).
Rapport du délégué des ouvriers en instruments de musique (cuivre) de la ville de Lyon à l'Exposition universelle de Paris en 1889 (Lyon: Association typographique, 1890).
Rapport du Jury Central sur les produits de l'Agriculture et de l'Industrie exposés en 1849, tomes 1 and 2 (Paris: Imprimerie nationale, 1850).
Rapport du jury central sur les produits de l'industrie française en 1834, tome 3 (Paris: Huzard, 1836).
Rapports des délégués des ouvriers parisiens à l'Exposition de Londres en 1862 (Paris: Chabaud 1862–4 [sic]).
Reports on the Paris Universal Exhibition, 1867, vol. 2 (London: George Edward Eyre and William Spottiswoode, 1868).
Réponse à La Liberté. Lettre adressée à M. Émile de Girardin par Adolphe Sax (Paris: n. ed., [Libraire Centrale,] 1867).
Réponse aux observations soumises par Monsieur Besson aux membres du Corps législatif contre la prolongation de brevets demandée par Monsieur Adolphe Sax (Paris: n. ed., [Impr. N. Chaix,] n.d. [1860]).
Réponse de Monsieur Raoux aux conclusions motivées de Monsieur Sax (Paris: n. ed., [Impr. S. Raçon,] n.d. [1860]).
Réponse de Sax à une note de M. Besson (Paris: n. ed., [Imprimerie centrale de Napoléon Chaix et Cie,] n.d. [1860]).

Revue encyclopédique ou analyse raisonnée des productions les plus remarquables dans les sciences, les arts industriels, la littérature et les beaux-arts, tome 45 (Paris: Baudouin frères, 1830).
Revue et Gazette des Théâtres, 3 December 1843, pp. 2–3.
Revue et Gazette Musicale de Paris [*RGMP*], 24 January 1836, p. 32; 19 August 1838, p. 333; 8 August 1841, pp. 374–5; 24 October 1841, p. 470; 14 November 1841, pp. 503–4; 28 November 1841, p. 534; 12 December 1841, pp. 553–5; 23 January 1842, pp. 29–31; 12 June 1842, pp. 244–5; 3 December 1843, p. 413; 31 December 1843, p. 445; 7 April 1844, p. 128; 2 June 1844, p. 195; 19 January 1845, p. 24; 2 March 1845, p. 70; 27 April 1845, pp. 134–5; 9 June 1845, p. 191; 28 September 1845, pp. 316–20; 22 March 1846, p. 95; 19 April 1846, p. 125; 23 May 1847, pp. 172–3; 27 February 1848, p. 65; 23 April 1848, p. 126; 22 October 1848, pp. 327–8; 29 October 1848, p. 334; 12 August 1849, pp. 253–5; 30 December 1849, p. 416; 19 May 1850, p. 171; 25 August 1850, p. 285; 9 February 1851, p. 45; 16 March 1851, p. 87; 10 August 1851, p. 263; 30 November 1851, pp. 385–8; 16 May 1852, pp. 153–4; 12 December 1852, p. 463; 16 January 1853, pp. 21–2; 13 February 1853, p. 55; 20 March 1853, p. 99; 1 May 1853, p. 164; 22 May 1853, p. 187; 12 June 1853, pp. 210–11; 26 June 1853, pp. 22–8; 24 July 1853, pp. 261–2; 11 December 1853, pp. 430–1; 18 December 1853, p. 440; 25 December 1853, p. 447; 9 January 1854, p. 8; 15 January 1854, p. 22; 22 January 1854, p. 32; 12 March 1854, p. 89; 7 May 1854, p. 154; 2 July 1854, p. 218; 1 April 1855, p. 103; 28 October 1855, p. 339; 4 November 1855, pp. 341–3; 11 November 1855, p. 355; 22 June 1856, pp. 200 and 202; 3 August 1856, p. 251; 10 August 1856, p. 257; 17 August 1856, p. 265; 24 August 1856, pp. 272–3; 14 September 1856, p. 298; 26 October 1856, p. 346; 18 January 1857, p. 22; 1 February 1857, pp. 38–9; 8 March 1857, p. 78; 15 March 1857, p. 84; 22 March 1857, p. 94; 5 April 1857, pp. 115–18; 12 April 1857, p. 125; 3 May 1857, p. 150; 9 July 1857, p. 263; 6 September 1857, p. 295; 11 October 1857, p. 335; 25 October 1857, p. 351; 1 November 1857, pp. 353–5 and 359; 19 September 1858, p. 314; 19 December 1858, p. 422; 2 January 1859, p. 6; 9 January 1859, p. 14; 20 February 1859, pp. 61–2; 27 February 1859, p. 75; 29 January 1860, p. 38; 8 April 1860, p. 137; 15 July 1860, p. 262; 8 July 1860, p. 246; 17 March 1861, pp. 78 and 86; 2 June 1861, p. 172; 11 August 1861, pp. 249–50; 17 November 1861, p. 366; 27 March 1864, p. 104; 5 March 1865, p. 76; 21 July 1867, p. 230; 3 November 1867, p. 534; 8 December 1867, p. 395; 19 July 1868, pp. 229–30; 18 April 1869, pp. 132–3; 24 July 1870, p. 237; 5 December 1871, p. 348; 28 April 1872, p. 135; 29 June 1873, p. 205; and 21 May 1876, p. 165.
Revue musicale, 16 November 1833, p. 331.
Robert, Adolphe; Bourloton, Edgar; and Cougny, Gaston, dirs, *Dictionnaire des parlementaires français depuis le 1er mai 1789 jusqu'au 1er mai 1889*, tomes 1–5 (Paris: Bourloton, 1890–1).
Robin, Charles-Joseph-Nicolas, *Histoire illustrée de l'exposition universelle* (Paris: Furne, 1855).
Rogron, Joseph-Adrien, *Codes français expliqués*, tome 1 (Paris: Videcoq/Alex-Gobelet, 1836).
Rogron, Joseph-Adrien, *Codes français expliqués*, tome 2 (Paris: Henri Plon, 1863).
Rose, Algernon-S., *Talks with Bandsmen* (London: Tony Bingham, n.d. ([reprint of 1895]).
Sarrut, Germain and Bourg, Edme-Théodore, *Biographie des Hommes du Jour*, vol. 2 (Paris: Henri Krabbe, 1836).
Soullier, Charles, *Nouveau Dictionnaire de musique, illustré, élémentaire, théorique, historique, professionnel et complet à l'usage des jeunes amateurs, des professeurs de musique, des institutions et des familles* (Paris: Bazault, 1855).
Stanford's Paris Guide (London: Standford, 1858 and 1862).

Statistique de l'industrie à Paris résultant de l'enquête faite par la Chambre de commerce pour les années 1847–1848 (Paris: Guillaumin, 1851).
Statistique de l'industrie à Paris résultant de l'enquête faite par la Chambre de Commerce pour l'Année 1860 (Paris: Chambre de Commerce, 1864).
Statistique de la France. Industrie. Résultats généraux de l'enquête effectuée dans les années 1861–1865 (Nancy: Berger-Levrault, 1873).
Tarbé, Adolphe-Pierre, *Cour de Cassation. Lois et réglements* [sic] *à l'usage de la Cour de Cassation* (Paris: Roret, 1840).
Teyssèdrec, [No name], *Conducteur général de l'étranger dans Paris* (Paris: Garnier Frères, 1842).
The great London Exhibition 1851: awards (Paris: Brière, n.d. [1851]).
The New York Times, 7 August 1881, p. 10.
Tribunal de commerce de Paris. Audience du 8 novembre 1862. Concurrence déloyale. Sax contre Gautrot (Paris: n. ed., [Imp. de N. Chaix,] 1862).
Tribunal de la Seine: 6e chambre correctionnelle: jugement rendu à la suite des audiences des 30 juillet et 13 août 1858, 5 août, 15, 22 et 29 décembre 1859, 5, 12, 19, 26 janvier, 2, 9, 16 et 23 février 1860. M. Gislain de Bontin et M. Mahler (Paris: n. ed., [Imprimerie de E. Brière,] 1860).
Trois publicistes [sic], *Profils critiques et biographiques des 750 représentants du peuple a l'Assemblée législative* (Paris: Garnier frères, 1849).
Turgan, Julien, *Les grandes usines, études industrielles en France et à l'étranger*, tome 11 (Paris: Calmann-Lévy, 1878).
Valette, [Auguste], *Explication Sommaire du Livre Premier du Code Napoléon et des lois accessoires* (Paris: Marescq, 1859).
Waterstone, William, *A Cyclopaedia of Commerce, Mercantile Law, Finance, Commercial Geography, and Navigation* (London: Henry G. Bohn, 1844).

Secondary sources

Ahrens, Christian, 'Technological Innovations in Nineteenth-Century Instrument Making and Their Consequences', *The Musical Quarterly* 82: 2 (1996), pp. 332–40.
Baines, Anthony-C., *The Oxford Companion to Musical Instruments* (New York: Oxford University Press, 1992).
Beauchamp, Christopher, 'Dousing the Fires of Patent Litigation', in Stephen H. Haber and Naomi R. Lamoreaux, eds, *The Battle over Patents: History and Politics of Innovation* (New York: Oxford University Press, 2021), pp. 136–70.
Beltran, Alain, Chauveau, Sophie, and Galvez-Behar, Gabriel, *Des brevets et des marques: une histoire de la propriété industrielle* (Paris: Fayard, 2001).
Bevan, Clifford, *The Tuba family* (Winchester: Piccolo Press, 2000).
Biagioli, Mario, 'Patent Specification and Political Representation: How Patents Became Rights', in Mario Biagioli, Peter Jaszi, and Martha Woodmansee, eds, *Making and Unmaking Intellectual Property: Creative Production in Legal and Cultural Perspective* (Chicago/London: University of Chicago Press, 2011), pp. 25–40.
Bouzard, Thierry, *Les usages musicaux dans l'armée française de 1815 à 1918* (Thesis, Amiens, Université de Picardie Jules Verne, 2016).
Bouzard, Thierry, *1845. L'armée française met au point le premier orchestre de plein air*. Talk given on 6 July 2018 during the biannual conference 'France: Musiques, Cultures, 1789–1918' organised by the Universities of Cambridge and Southampton, Bibliothèque historique de la ville de Paris.

Bouzard, Thierry and De la Tour, Dominique, 'Gagistes et tambours majors. Le statut du musicien militaire au XIXe siècle', *Revue historique des armées* 279 (2015), pp. 61–8.

Bowles, Edmund-A., 'The Impact of Technology on Musical Instruments', The Cosmos Club, *Cosmos Journal* (1999), article available on the Internet at <http://www.cosmosclub.org/journals/1999/bowles.html> (accessed 4 February 2022).

Brenet, Michel, *Les musiciens célèbres: La musique militaire* (Paris: H. Laurens, 1917).

Bruinders, Sylvia, 'Soldiers of God: the Spectacular Musical Ministry of the Christmas Bands in the Western Cape, South Africa', in Suzel-Ana Reily and Katherine Brucher, eds, *Brass Bands of the World: Militarism, Colonial Legacies, and Local Music Making* (London & New York: Routledge, 2016), pp. 139–54.

Campbell, Murray, Greated, Clive, and Myers, Arnold, *Musical Instruments. History, Technology, and Performance of Instruments of Western Music* (New York: Oxford University Press, 2006).

Chagot, Christian, 'Petite histoire de la marque "A. Lecomte & Cie"', *Larigot* 62 ([October] 2018), pp. 8–15.

Chagot, Maxime and Chagot, Christian, 'Cornets modèle Halary et premiers pistons Périnet', *Larigot* 63 ([April] 2019), pp. 6–25.

Chagot, Maxime and Chagot, Christian, 'Courtois, la dynastie enfin retrouvée!', *Larigot* 54 [December] 2014), pp. 24–39.

Chanut, Jean-Marie et al., *L'industrie française au milieu du 19e siècle. Les enquêtes de la statistique générale de la France* (Paris: Ehess, 2000), database included in the CD-ROM.

Citron, Pierre, dir., *Correspondance générale [de Hector Berlioz]*, tome 5 (Paris: Flammarion, 1989).

Čížek, Bohuslav, *Instruments de Musique* (Paris: Gründ, 2003).

Closson, Ernest and Van Den Borren, Charles, *La musique en Belgique* (Brussels: La Renaissance du livre, 1950).

Condaris, Christine, *The Band Business in the United States between the Civil War and the Great Depression* (Thesis, Middletown, Wesleyan University, 1987).

Dahlquist, Reine, 'Some Notes on the Early Valve', *The Galpin Society Journal* 33 (1980), pp. 111–24.

Dalisson, Rémi, *Hippolyte Carnot 1801–1888: La liberté, l'école et la République.* (Paris: CNRS, 2011).

De Keyser, Ignace, 'Adolphe Sax and the Paris Opéra', *Brass Scholarship in Review: Proceedings of the Historic Brass Society Conference, Cité de la Musique, Paris, 1999 (Bucina: The Historic Brass Society series)* 6 (2006), pp. 133–69.

De Keyser, Ignace, 'The Keyed Ophicleide as a Paradigm in the Development of New Wind Instruments in the 1830s and 1840s', in *Vom Serpent zur Tuba (Entwicklung und Einsatz dertiefen Polsterzungeninstrumente mit Grifflöchern und Ventilen), [Proceedings of] XLI. Wissenschaftliche Arbeitstagung und 33. Musikinstrumentenbau-Symposium Michaelstein, 7. bis 9. November 2014.* (Augsburg and Michaelstein: Wißner and Kloster, 2019), pp. 69–88.

Depambour-Tarride, Laurence, 'La création de l'Académie royale de Musique. Théorie et pratique de l'absolutisme français', in Huegues Dufourt and Joël-Marie Fauquet, dirs, *La musique et le pouvoir* (Paris: Aux Amateurs des Livres, 1987), pp. 33–51.

Deschamps, Henry-Thierry, *La Belgique devant la France de juillet: l'opinion et l'attitude françaises de 1839 à 1848* (Paris: Les Belles Lettres, 1956).

Diago, José-Modesto, 'Ali-Ben-Sou-Ale's Turcophone Patent (1860): The Closest Bridge between Clarinet and Saxophone', *The Galpin Society Journal* 72 (2019), pp. 154–7 and 175–91.

Diago, José-Modesto, 'Gautrot and His Sarrusophone Revisited: A Multidisciplinary Approach', *Journal of the American Musical Instrument Society* 48 (2022), pp. 162–90.

Dudgeon, Ralph-Thomas, *The Keyed Bugle* (Oxford: Scarecrow Press, 2004).
Dullat, Günter, *Metallblasinstrumentenbau: Entwicklungsstufen und Technologie* (Frankfurt: Bochinsky, 1898).
Dullat, Günter, *Fast vergessene Blasinstrumente aus zwei Jahrhunderten* (Nauheim: Dullat, 1997).
Dumoulin, Géry, 'The Cornet and Other Brass Instruments in French Patents of the First Half of the Nineteenth Century', *The Galpin Society Journal* 59 (2006), pp. 77–100.
Dutton, Harold-Irvin, *The Patent System and Inventive Activity during the Industrial Revolution, 1750–1852*. (Manchester: Manchester University Press, 1984).
Ebel, Édouard, dir., *Les ministres de la Guerre, 1792–1870* (Rennes: Presses universitaires de Rennes, 2018).
Ericson, John-Q., 'Heinrich Stölzel and Early Valved Horn Technique', *Historic Brass Society Journal* 9 (1997), pp. 63–82.
Farr, Ray, *The Distin Legacy: The Rise of the Brass Band in 19th-Century Britain* (Newcastle: Cambridge Scholars, 2013).
Faure, Patrick-Alain, 'Procès en contrefaçon des harmoniums Debain', *L'harmonium français* 3 (2008), pp. 3–20.
Fougère, Henry, *Les délégations ouvrières aux expositions universelles sous le Second Empire* (Montluçon: Herbin, 1905).
Gallo, Denise, 'Rossini's Fanfare for Maximilian of Mexico: A Mysterious Self-Borrowing', *Historic Brass Society Journal* 23 (2011), pp. 89–102.
Galvez-Behar, Gabriel, *La République des inventeurs. Propriété et organisation de l'innovation en France (1791–1922)* (Rennes: Presses Universitaires de Rennes, 2008).
Gans, Joshua S. and Murray, Fiona, 'Funding Scientific Knowledge: Selection, Disclosure and the Public-Private Portfolio', in Josh Lerner and Scott Stern, eds, *The Rate and Direction of Inventive Activity Revisited* (Chicago/London: University of Chicago Press, 2012), pp. 51–106.
Gerbod, Paul, 'L'institution orphéonique en France du XIXe au XXe siècle', *Ethnologie Française* 10: 1 (1980), pp. 27–44.
Gétreau, Florence, 'Entre l'oral et l'écrit: pratique, transmission et théorie du métier de facteur d'instruments de musique', *Ethnologie Française* 26: 3 (1996), pp. 504–18.
Giannini, Tula, *Great Flute Makers of France: The Lot and Godfroy Families, 1650–1900* (London: Tony Bingham, 1993).
Gould, Roger-V., 'Urban transformations, 1852–70', in *Insurgent Identities: Class, Community, and Protest in Paris from 1848 to the Commune* (Chicago: University of Chicago Press, 1995), pp. 65–95.
Granger, Catherine, *L'empereur et les arts: la liste civile de Napoléon III* (Paris: École des Chartes, 2005).
Grempler, Martina, 'Rossinis politisches Spätwerk: Die Hymne à Napoleon III und La corona d'Italia', in Bernd-Rudiger Kern and Reto Müller, dirs, *Rossini in Paris* (Leipzig: Leipziger Universitätsverlag, 2002), pp. 181–98.
Grenot, Cyrille, 'La facture instrumentale des cuivres dans la seconde moitié du XIXe siècle en France', in Daniel Allenbach, Adrian von Steiger, and Martin Skamletz, eds, *Romantic Brass. Französische Hornpraxis und historisch informierter Blechblasinstrumentenbau. Symposium 2* (Schliengen: Argus, 2016), pp. 11–102.
Haine, Malou, *Adolphe Sax: sa vie, son œuvre, ses instruments de musique* (Brussels: Éditions de l'Université de Bruxelles, 1980).
Haine, Malou, 'Les licences de fabrication accordées par Adolphe Sax à ses concurrents. 26 juin 1854–13 octobre 1865', *Revue belge de Musicologie* 34–35 (1980–81), pp. 198–203.

Haine, Malou, *Les facteurs d'instruments de musique à Paris au 19e siècle* (Brussels: Université de Bruxelles, 1984).
Haine, Malou, 'Un réseau d'influence: les démarches d'Adolphe Sax pour obtenir la croix d'officier de la Légion d'honneur', *Revue belge de Musicologie* 70 (2016), pp. 9–22.
Hazen, Margaret-Hindle and Hazen, Robert-M., *The Music Men* (Washington/London: Smithsonian Institution Press, 1987).
Herbert, Trevor, *The British Brass Band: A Musical and Social History* (New York: Oxford University Press, 2000).
Herbert, Trevor and Barlow, Helen, *Music and the British Military in the Long Nineteenth Century* (New York, Oxford University Press, 2013).
Hervé, Roland, 'La Céleustique. La transmission des ordres par signaux sonores dans les armées françaises', *Revue historique des armées* 279 (2015), pp. 5–12.
Holman, Galvin, 'How Many Brass Bands?—An Analysis of the Distribution of Bands in Britain and Ireland over the Last 200 Years' ([March] 2018), article available on the Internet at <http://www.ibew.org.uk/GH018-howmanybands.pdf> (accessed 14 September 2023).
Hue, Sylvie, *150 ans de Musique à la Garde Républicaine. Mémoires d'un Orchestre* (Paris: Nouvelle Arche de Noé, 1998).
Jenkins, David, *Woodwind Instruments in France 1690-1750. Their Makers, Theoreticians and Music*, vol. 1 (Thesis, Edinburgh, University of Edinburgh, 1973).
Kahn, B. Zorina, 'History Matters', in Stephen H. Haber and Naomi R. Lamoreaux, eds, *The Battle over Patents: History and Politics of Innovation* (New York: Oxford University Press, 2021), pp. 319–64.
Kampmann, Bruno, 'Alphonse Sax vu dans *L'Illustration*', *Larigot* 37 ([May] 2006), pp. 27–31.
Kampmann, Bruno, 'French Makers' Improvements to Brass Instruments in the mid-19th Century, Compared with Those by Adolphe Sax', in Adrian von Steiger, Daniel Allenbach, and Martin Skamletz, eds, *Das Saxhorn Adolphe Sax' Blechblasinstrumente im Kontext ihrer Zeit. Romantic Brass Symposium 3* (Schliengen: Argus, 2020), pp. 168–75.
Kampmann, Bruno, 'Licences accordées par Adolphe Sax à ses concurrents pour la fabrication des cuivres', *Larigot* 42 ([September] 2008), pp. 9–17.
Kampmann, Bruno and McBride, William, 'Martin frères and the Martin Family: Four Generations of Woodwind Instrument Makers', *Larigot* 22 spécial (1995), pp. iv–viii.
Laszlo, Pierre, 'Deux polytechniciens et la chimie', *Bulletin de la Sabix* 50 (2012), pp. 5–13.
Le Roux, Thomas, 'Le patrimoine industriel à Paris entre artisanat et industrie: le facteur d'instruments de musique Couesnon dans la Maison des métallos (1881–1936)', *Le Mouvement Social* 199: 2 (2002), pp. 11–36.
Lerner, Josh, '150 Years of Patent Protection', NBER [National Bureau of Economic Research] Working Paper no. 7478 ([January] 2000), article available on the Internet at <https://www.nber.org/system/files/working_papers/w7478/w7478.pdf> (accessed 5 November 2022).
Lescat, Philippe, *L'enseignement musical en France de 1529–1927* (Courlay: Fuzeau, 2001).
Lesure, François, 'La facture instrumentale à Paris au seizième siècle', *The Galpin Society Journal* 7 (1954), pp. 11–52.
Leterrier, Sophie-Anne, 'Musique populaire et musique savante au XIXe siècle. Du *peuple* au *public*', *Revue d'histoire du XIXe siècle* 19 (1999), article available on the Internet at <https://journals.openedition.org/rh19/157> (accessed 10 March 2023).
Loubet de Sceaury, Paul, *Musiciens et facteurs d'instruments de musique sous l'Ancien Régime. Statuts corporatifs* (Paris: A. Pedone, 1949).
Mactaggart, Peter and Mactaggart, Ann, *Musical Instruments in the 1851 Exhibition* (Welwyn: Mac & Me, 1986).
Maniguet, Thierry, 'La dynastie des Raoux, facteurs de « cors de chasse » du XVIIe au XIXe siècle', *Musique-Images-Instruments* 15 (2015), pp. 226–47.

Marconi, Emanuele, dir., *La Couture-Boussey. Regards sur la facture instrumentale* (La Couture-Boussey: Éditions du Musée des instruments à vent, 2022).
Marois, Édith, 'Les relations entre Laure Surville et son frère Honoré... de Balzac', in Académie des Sciences, Arts et Belles-Lettres de Touraine, ed., *Mémoires de l'Académie des Sciences, Arts et Belles-Lettres de Touraine*, tome 24 (Touraine: Académie de Touraine, 2011), pp. 67–83.
Mauduit, Xabier, *Le ministère du faste. La maison de l'empereur Napoléon III* (Paris: Fayard [Kobo version], 2016).
Mendelssohn Bartholdy, Paul, Mendelssohn Bartholdy, Karl, and Jacobs, Rémi (eds), *Felix Mendelssohn. Voyage de jeunesse, Lettres européennes (1830–1832)* (Paris: Stock, 1980).
Meucci, Renato, 'The *Cimbasso* and Related Instruments in 19th-Century Italy', *The Galpin Society Journal* 49 (1996), pp. 143–79.
Meucci, Renato, 'Brass Bands and the Brass Instrument Industry in 19th Century Milan', in Tiroler Landesmuseen-Betriebsges, ed., *Wissenschaftliches Jahrbuch der Tiroler Landesmuseen* ([Innsbruck?]: Tiroler Landesmuseen-Betriebsges, 2010), pp. 109–13.
Michaud-Pradeilles, Catherine and Haury, Jean, *Touches à touches. Pianos et brevets d'invention au XIXe siècle* (Paris: Édipso, 1997).
Mitroulia, Eugenia, *Adolphe Sax's brasswind production with a focus on saxhorns and related instruments* (Thesis, Edinburgh, University of Edinburgh, 2011).
Mitroulia, Eugenia and Myers, Arnold, 'The Distin Family as Instrument Makers and Dealers 1845–1874', *Scottish Music Review* 2: 1 (2011), pp. 1–20.
Montagu, Jeremy, *The World of Romantic & Modern Musical Instruments* (London: David & Charles, 1981).
Montagu, Jeremy, *The Industrial Revolution and Music* (Oxford: Hataf Segol Publications, 2018).
Moore, Barrington, *Social Origins of Dictatorship and Democracy. Lord and Peasant in the Making of the Modern World* (Boston: Beacon Press, 1966).
Mürner, Martin, 'Meifred und die Einführung des Ventilhorns in Frankreich', in Daniel Allenbach, Adrian von Steiger, and Martin Skamletz, eds, *Romantic Brass. Französische Hornpraxis und historisch informierter Blechblasinstrumentenbau. Symposium 2* (Schliengen: Argus, 2016), pp. 223–33.
Myers, Arnold, *Characterization and Taxonomy of Historic Brass Musical Instruments from an Acoustical Standpoint* (Thesis, Edinburgh, University of Edinburgh, 1998).
Myers, Arnold and Eldredge, Niles, 'Brasswind Production of Marthe Besson's London Factory', *The Galpin Society Journal* 49 (2006), pp. 43–76.
Myers, Arnold and Parks, Raymond, 'How to Measure a Horn', *The Galpin Society Journal* 48 (1995), pp. 193–9.
Novack, Martha, *Makers of the Piano: 1820–1860* (New York: Oxford University Press, 1999).
Patents for Inventions. Abridgments of Specifications Relating to Music and Musical Instruments. A.D. 1694–1866 [1984 reprint from the facsimile of the second edition of 1871 originally published by the Office of the Commissioners of Patents for Inventions] (London: Tony Bingham, 1984).
Péronnet, Patrick, *Les enfants d'Apollon. Les ensembles d'instruments à vent en France 1700 à 1914: Pratiques sociales, insertions politiques et création musicale [Volume 2. Le Triomphe d'Apollon 1815–1870]* (Thesis, Paris, Université de Paris-Sorbonne (Paris 4), 2012).
Péronnet, Patrick, 'Musiques militaires et relations internationales de 1850 à 1914: le cas français', *Relations internationales* 155: 3 (2013), pp. 47–60.
Péronnet, Patrick, 'Saxons et Carafons: Adolphe Sax et le Gymnase musical militaire, un conflit d'esthétique', *Revue belge de Musicologie* 70 (2016), pp. 45–63.

Pierre, René, 'La saga des anges trompettistes ou les Facteurs d'instruments de musique à Strasbourg 1720-1920', *Larigot* 45 ([April] 2010), pp. 20-4.
Pierre, René, 'Charles Kretzschmann (1777-1842), de Markneukirchen à Strasbourg', *Larigot* 48 ([September] 2011), pp. 20-6.
Pierre, René, 'Jean Chrétien Roth, (1816-81). Facteur de tous les instruments à vent à Strasbourg. Successeur de Dobner & Co et de Bühner et Keller', *Larigot* 49 ([February] 2012), pp. 19-23.
Piñeiro, Joaquín, 'La música como fuente para el análisis histórico: la historia actual', *Historia Actual On-Line* 5 (2004), pp. 155-69.
Piñeiro, Joaquín, 'La música como elemento de análisis histórico: el barroco y el clasicismo en la crisis del Antiguo Régimen', *Aula-Historia Social* 17 (2006), pp. 57-64.
Piñeiro, Joaquín, 'Nuevos caminos de investigación en la historia del tiempo presente: la música como instrumento de análisis histórico', *Tiempo Presente. Revista de Historia* 2 (2014), 67-77.
Poinsot, Edmond-Antoine, *Dictionnaire des pseudonymes* (Genève: Slatkine Reprints, 1971).
Powell, Ardal, *The Flute* (New Haven/London: Yale University Press, 2002).
Quéniart, Jean, 'Les formes de sociabilité musicale en France et en Allemagne, 1750-1850', in É. François, ed., *Sociabilité et société bourgeoise en France, en Allemagne et en Suisse (1750-1850)* (Paris: n. ed., 1987), pp. 135-47.
Rauline, Jean-Yves, '19th Century Amateur Music Societies in France and the Changes of Instrument Construction: Their Evolution Caught between Passivity and Progress', *The Galpin Society Journal* 57 (2004), pp. 218 and 236-45.
Reily, Suzel-Ana 'From Processions to *Encontros*: The Performance Niches of the Community Bands of Minas Gerais, Brazil', in Suzel-Ana Reily and Katherine Brucher, eds, *Brass Bands of the World: Militarism, Colonial Legacies, and Local Music Making* (London & New York: Routledge, 2016), pp. 99-122.
Rice, Albert, 'The Early History of the Nineteenth Century Boehm-System Clarinet' *Musique-Images-Instruments* 13 (2012), pp. 130-45.
Risch, Michael 'The Layered Patent System', *Iowa Law Review* 101: 4 (2016), pp. 1535-82.
Rorive, Jean-Pierre, *Adolphe Sax (1814-1894) Inventeur de génie* (Paris: Racine, 2004).
Rostang, Christophe, 'François Georges Auguste Dauverné et les trompettistes de l'orchestre de l'Opéra de Paris au XIXe siècle', *Larigot* 26 Spécial ([June] 2014), pp. 19-74.
Sáiz, Patricio and Amengual, Rubén, 'Do patents enable disclosure? Strategic innovation management of the four-stroke engine', *Industrial and Corporate Change* 27: 6 ([December] 2018), pp. 975-97.
Scavone, Gary-Paul, *An Acoustic Analysis of Single-Reed Woodwind Instruments with an Emphasis on Design and Performance Issues and Digital Waveguide Modeling Techniques* (Thesis, Stanford, Stanford University, 1997).
Schnapper, Laure, 'Entre le théâtre et salon: les premières salles de concert parisiennes au XIXe siècle', in Laure Gauthier and Mélanie Traversier, dirs, *Mélodies urbaines, la musique dans les villes d'Europe (XVIe-XIXe siècles)* (Paris: Presses Universitaires de la Sorbonne, 2008), pp. 201-20.
Scott, Jack-L., *The Evolution of the Brass Band and its Repertoire in Northern England* (Thesis, Sheffield, University of Sheffield, 1970).
Simonett, Helena, 'From Village to World Stage: The Malleability of Sinaloan Popular Brass Brands', in Suzel-Ana Reily and Katherine Brucher, eds, *Brass Bands of the World: Militarism, Colonial Legacies, and Local Music Making* (London & New York: Routledge, 2016), pp. 199-215.
Stanley, Albert-A., *Catalogue of the Stearns Collection of Musical Instruments* (Ann Arbor: University of Michigan, 1921).

Taylor, Arthur-R., *Brass Bands* (London: Hart-Davis MacGibbon, 1979).
Terrier, Agnès, *L'orchestre de l'Opéra de Paris: de 1669 à nos jours* (Paris: Éditions de la Martinière, 2003).
Valynseele, Joseph *Les maréchaux de Napoléon III: leur famille et leur descendance* (Paris: chez l'auteur, 1980).
Vasseur, Édouard, 'Pourquoi organiser des Expositions universelles? Le "succès" de l'Exposition universelle de 1867', *Histoire, économie et société*, 4 (2005), pp. 573–94.
Vigoureux, Claude, 'Napoléon III et Abd-el-Kader', *Napoleonica* 1: 4 (2009), pp. 111–43.
Watel, Denis, 'Luthiers et musiciens à Lyon en 1808–1809 d'après les recensements de population', *Larigot* 49 ([February] 2012), pp. 24–7.
Watel, Denis, 'Facteurs d'instruments et luthiers à Lyon en 1840', *Larigot* 52 ([July] 2013), pp. 17–21.
Waterhouse, William, *The New Langwill Index* (London: Tony Bingham, 1993).
Waterhouse, William, 'Gautrot-Aîné, first of the moderns', *Brass Scholarship in Review: Proceedings of the Historic Brass Society Conference, Cité de la Musique, Paris, 1999. (Bucina: The Historic Brass Society series)* 6 (2006), pp. 121–32.
Wiss, Jérôme, 'Essai sur la datation des ophicléides', *Larigot* 61 ([April] 2018), pp. 8–15.
Wiss, Jérôme and Kampmann, Bruno, 'La Basse d'Harmonie de Sautermeister', *Larigot* 55 ([May] 2015), pp. 3–11.
Zeldin, Theodore, *Histoire des passions françaises (1848–1945)*, tome 3 *(Goût et corruption)* (Paris: Seuil, 1981).

Website resources

Basic explanation of the structure and functioning of the current French judicial system by the Ministry of Justice: 2023 <https://www.justice.gouv.fr/justice-france/cours-tribunaux> (accessed 4 August 2023).
Genealogy of the Thibouville (family of instrument makers) by luthiers Roland Terrier and Yves-Antoine Gachet: 2022 <https://www.luthiers-mirecourt.com/thibouville_genealogie.htm> (accessed 10 December 2022).
Inventory of documents relating to the orchestra in the nineteenth century drawn up by the Archives de l'Opéra de Paris held at the Archives nationales and compiled by Brigitte Labat-Poussin detailing the appointment of Adolphe Sax as head of the fanfare and external musicians of the Opera [8 and 33]: 2020 <https://www.nakala.fr/nakala/data/11280/01026c93> (accessed 4 August 2020).
Professional data of Augustin-Charles Renouard—judge (*conseiller*) of the Court of Cassation—provided by the Institut Français de l'Éducation: 2023 <http://www.inrp.fr/edition-electronique/lodel/dictionnaire-ferdinand-buisson/document.php?id=3519> (accessed 1 December 2022).
Professional data of Besson (manufacturer of wind instruments) provided by its own website: 2023 <www.besson.com/en/our-story/> (accessed 29 May 2023).
Professional data of Buffet-Crampon (manufacturer of wind instruments) provided by its own website: 2023 <http://www.buffet-crampon.com/en/our-story> (accessed 20 August 2023).
Professional data of Couturier (manufacturer of wind instruments) compiled by a specialized blog (Luthiervents): 2023 <http://luthiervents.blogspot.com/search/label/Couturier> (accessed 11 June 2023).
Professional data of Drouelle (manufacturer of accessory parts) compiled by a specialized blog (Luthiervents): 2023 <http://luthiervents.blogspot.com/search/label/Drouelle> (accessed 24 February 2023).

Professional data of Gaubert (manufacturer of wind instruments) compiled by a specialized blog (Luthiervents): 2023 <http://luthiervents.blogspot.com/search/label/Gaubert> (accessed 11 June 2023).

Professional data of the prosecutor Gustave Rouland, Minister of Public Instruction and Religious Affairs under Napoleon III, provided by the Association Artistique de la Banque de France: 2022 <http://www.genea-bdf.org/BasesDonnees/genealogies/rouland.htm> (accessed 3 December 2022).

Serial number, date of manufacture, instrument name, pitch, and other details of Adolphe Sax's instruments compiled by various organologists: 2023 <http://www.euchmi.ed.ac.uk/am/gdsl.html> (accessed 4 August 2023).

Index

For the benefit of digital users, indexed terms that span two pages (e.g., 52–53) may, on occasion, appear on only one of those pages.

Adam, Adolphe 34, 48, 99–100n41, 102–103, 118–119, 236–237
Arban, Jean-Baptiste 103–104, 126
army bands. *see* military bands
Auber, Daniel-François-Esprit 42, 48, 83–85
Aymé de la Herlière, Jacques-Gabriel 152–153n9, 154–155n13, 155–156

Barbu factory 28, 213–214, 214–215n10
Baroche, Pierre-Jules 151–152, 154–155, 158
Bass-tuba 31–32, 235–236
Batyphone 32, 55–56, 91–93, 235–236
Battut factory 26, 177–178
Beaubeuf, Jules-Oscar 26, 31, 178–179, 185–186
Beaubeuf, Lazare-Auguste 26, 31, 123, 177–179, 185–186
Belmont, Marie-Louis-Gabriel-Alfred-Stanislas Briançon-Vachon, Marquis de 103–104
Belmontet, Louis 156–157
Belorgey factory 26, 97–98, 177–178
Bérenger, Alphonse-Marie 101–102, 105–106
Berlioz, Hector 7–8, 34, 47–48, 54–55, 59n40, 63–64, 81–82, 86–87, 95–96, 103–104, 118–119, 234, 236–237
Besson, Florentine 27–28, 31, 200–202
Besson, Gustave-Auguste 25–27, 156–157, 166–167, 170–173, 177–181, 184–192, 194–195, 200–201, 217–219, 225–226
Biot, Jean-Baptiste 53–54n13
Blanc, Etienne 44–45, 235–236
Blanc, Louis 59
Blanchard, Henry 82–83
Boehm, Theobald 93, 127–129
bombardon 131–134

Bontin, Gislain de 123, 184–185
Boquillon, Nicolas 51–55, 97–98, 143, 146, 234, 236
Boucherie, Jean-Auguste 150–151, 155–156
Bourloton, Edgar 32n8, 99–100n39
Boursault, Léonie-Amable-Albertine 47–48
Brandus, Louis 82
Bréton factory 37–38
Briançon-Vachon, Marie-Louis-Gabriel-Alfred-Stanislas *see* Belmont, Marie-Louis-Gabriel-Alfred-Stanislas Briançon-Vachon, Marquis de
Buffet, Jean-Louis (also known as Buffet-Crampon) 26, 28, 31–32, 162–163, 177–179, 217–219
Buffet, Louis-Auguste 126, 177–178, 214n8
Buteux, Claude-François 33–34

Carafa, Michele (Michele-Enrico) 33–34, 48, 63–64
Castil-Blaze (François-Henri-Joseph Blaze) 34
Cavaignac, Louis-Eugène 59–60
Cavaillé-Coll factory 78–79, 127–129, 229–230n15
Chaix-d'Est-Ange, Gustave-Louis 33–35, 39, 40–43, 48, 49, 61–62, 76, 106, 108, 235
Cherubini, Luigi 39, 83–84
Citron, Pierre 47–48
clavicor 32, 38, 42, 76–77, 130–131, 143–144, 181–183
Clinton, Bill 17–18
Cluesman, Jean-Baptiste 227
commerce. *see* economy, industry, and commerce
Couesnon factory 192–193, 223–225, 239–240

Cougny, Gaston 32n8, 83–84n27, 99–100n39, 101–102n45, 106n74
Cour d'appel (Court of Appeal) proceedings (1848-50)
  commencement 76
  factums 76–77
  judgment 83–84, 88
  outline of 21–22
cornet 17, 36–37, 41n42, 51–53n6, 163, 196–198
Court of Cassation proceedings (1850-53)
  commencement 88–89
  composition of Court 88
  judgment (1853) 101–102, 107
  outline of 22–23
Court of First Instance proceedings (1847-48)
  commencement (Mar-Nov 1846) 31
  complainants' case 31–32, 44–49
  defendant's case 33–43, 49
  initial hearings (Jan 1847) 31–32
  July Monarchy (1830-48) and 57–59
  outline of 20–21
  prosecutor's report (Nov 1847) 12, 21, 51–53
  Rapport d'expertise (Nov 1847) 51–57
  saxophone patent discussion 44
  saxotromba patent discussion 42–44
  Second Republic (1848-52) and 59–62
Courtois, Antoine 27, 217–219, 227
Couturier factory 28, 178n9, 213–214
Creuzet, André 139, 152–155
Criminal Court (*correctionnelle*) of Paris proceedings
  confiscation order (1854-55) proceedings, award of order to Sax 123–125
  confiscation order (1854-55) proceedings, Sax/Rivet dispute 124–127

d'Alembert, Jean le Rond 4–5
d'Alembert, Meyer 227
d'Allarde, Pierre 10n14
Darche factory 27, 97–98
David, Jérôme 154–155
De Brisse, Léon 127–129
De Guajal 51–53, 188, 190, 201–202, 206–210
De la Fage, Adrien 127–129, 163, 170–173
De Morny, Count 155
Debain, Alexandre-François 229–230n15

Diderot, Denis 4–5
Distin quintet 27, 57–58, 230–231
Donizetti, Gaetano 79–80, 82
D'Ortigue, Joseph 219–220
Drouelle, Sébastien 26–27, 97–98, 177–178, 203–212, 216–217, 227
Du Miral, Francisque-Rudel 152–155
Dubarle, Eugène 136–138
Dubois, Count E. 151–152, 155
Dubois et Cie 39
Ducroquet factory 91–93
Dufaure, Jules-Armand 107–112, 131–132, 135–138, 205, 206–207, 235
Dujariez, Emmanuel-Jean-Marie 170
Dupin, Charles 78n7, 83–84, 90–91, 102, 234
Duponchel, Henri 56–57n28

economy, industry, and commerce
  Cobden-Chevalier Treaty (1860) (*coup d'État douanier*) 7
  Colbertism 5–6
  customs policy 7
  Exhibition of French National Industry (National Exhibition) (1844) 34, 38, 42, 53–54, 57–58, 65, 78
  free trade policy 7
  industrial development 7
  National Exhibition of French Industry (1849) 21–22, 77–83, 90–91
  Paris-centricity 7–8
  prisoner labour in factories 98–99
  this book's focus on economic themes 2–3
el-Kader, Emir Abd 81–82
Érard, Céleste 33–34
Érard, Pierre 78, 78–79n15
Érard, Sébastien 33–34
Érard factory 93, 229–230n15
Escudier, Léon 82
Escudier, Marie 91–93
Europe, French cultural and political influence 1–2

Fabre, Paul 141–142, 144–147, 186
Ferronays, Albert de la 33–34, 234
Fétis, François-Joseph 53–54, 54–55n22, 91–93, 234
Feuillet, Auguste 222–223n43
Fink, Charles 63–64

Fleury, Émile-Félix 99–100, 104n68, 234, 238–239n25
Florent factory 26, 177–178
Fox, Charles 91
France. *see also* economy, industry, and commerce; law and courts; military bands; music and musical instruments
  capitalism, advent of 1, 6–7
  cultural and political influence in Europe, UK, and USA 1–2, 241
  First Empire (Napoleon I) (1803-15) 7
  July Monarchy (Louis-Philippe) (1830-48) 3, 7, 9–10, 14, 21, 37, 57–59, 82, 83–84, 89
  liberal bourgeois revolutionary period 1
  military bands, saxophone removed from (1848) 62
  Revolution (1789) 6–7
  Second Empire (Napoleon III) (1852-70) 9, 77–78
  Second Republic (1848-52) 62
  socio-economic and political background 1
  this book's focus on economic themes 2–3
  this book's purpose 1–3
Frederick William IV, King of Prussia 51–53
Froment, Gustave 78

Gallay, Jacques-François 42
Gambaro, Jean-Baptiste (Giovanni Battista) 17, 31–32
Gambey, Henri Prudence 42
Gaubert factory 28, 213–214, 214–215n10
Gautrot, Pierre-Louis 24–26, 28, 31–32, 65–68, 70–75, 77–79, 130–150, 153–154, 156–158, 160–169, 173–174, 177–178, 181, 184–185, 188–189, 194–198, 213–219, 222–223, 223–225n46, 225–226, 229–230n15
Godfroy, Clair 36–38, 217–219
Goudot factory 167–168
Goumas, Pierre 26, 31, 177–179
Guichard, Jean-Auguste 32, 38–39, 53, 130–134
Guizot, François 56–57

Habeneck, François-Antoine 42, 56–57n28, 234

Halary, Jean Hilaire Asté 177–178
Halary, Jean-Louis-Antoine (Halari) 17, 23–24, 26, 27–28, 31–32, 72, 77–78, 105–106, 170–171, 177–178, 184–185, 213–214
Halary, Jules-Léon-Antoine 26, 177–178
Halévy, Fromental 33–34, 48, 51–55, 63–64, 82, 97–98, 118–119, 234, 236–237
Haton de la Goupillière 207–210
Henry et Martin 27, 167–168
Henry IV, King of France and Navarre 5
Hérouard factory 37–38
Herz, Henri 227
Heugel, Jacques-Léopold 82
Husson & Buthod factory 162–163

Imperial Court of Rouen proceedings (1854)
  defendants' case 109–110, 112
  defendants' decision not to appeal 115
  disputants' legal representatives 107–108
  prosecutor's judgment and reasoning 112–114, 123
  referral of case to 107
  Sax's case 108–112
  Sax's resulting commercial advantage 115–119
industrial property. *see* law and courts
industry. *see* economy, industry, and commerce
Isbert factory 26, 177–178

Jacob, Victor 26, 31, 177–179
Jahn factory 27, 204–205
Jenkins, David 4–5n4
Jobard, Marcellin 33–34, 143, 234
Jolibois, Eugène 107, 112–114, 144
Josseau, Jean-Baptiste 152–155

Kastner, Georges 34–36, 47–48, 57–58, 63–65, 84–85, 110, 132–134, 142–143
Key et Cie 27
Klosé, Hyacinthe-Eléonore 126
Kretzschmann, Charles-Auguste 26, 184–192, 200
Kreutzer, Léon 103
Kroll factory 28, 213–214, 214–215n10

Labbaye brothers 27, 32, 72, 77–78, 97–98, 207–208, 211, 217–219
Labitte factory 27
Lamartine, Alphonse de 59

law and courts
  Civil Code 11–12
  Colbertism 5–6
  courts, availability of appeal (double instance) 12–13
  courts, types of 12
  courts of appeal (*cours d'appel*), number of 76
  Criminal Code 11–12
  factums, purpose and content of 15–16
  French justice system in nineteenth century 11–14
  industrial property, France/UK comparison of aerophone patents 94
  industrial property, French IP laws in nineteenth century 9–11
  legal actors 11–12
  litigation routes 12
  Ministry of Justice 12
  Patent Law of 1791 9–11, App I, 17
  Patent Law of 1844 9–11, 17, 24–25, 31, 88–89, App II
  patents, Baroque era 5–6
  patents, earliest musical instrument-related edicts 5
  patents, economic power 2
  patents, five-year extension of Sax's patents (1860) 150–159
  patents, purpose and content of 14–15
  patents, Renaissance era 5
  Procedure Code 11–12
  saxhorn patent (1843) 76–77, App III
  saxophone patent (1846) 17, 31, 44, App V
  saxotromba patent (1845) 17, 31, 42–44, 76–77, 83, App IV
  Second Republic (1848-52) 7, 14, 21, 59–62
Le Play, F. 151–152, 155, 156
Lecomte, Arsène-Zoé 153–154n12, 158n23, 167–168, 196–198, 222–223
Ledru-Rollin (lawyer) 59–60
Leroy et Goumas 28
Letendre de Tourville 210–211
Liouville, Félix 61–62, 123, 124–125n9
Liverani, Domenico 33–34, 63–64
Louis XIV, King of France 5–6
Louis-Philippe, King of the French 3, 5, 9–10, 12, 32, 48n55, 48–49, 56–57n28, 57–59, 62, 72, 101–102n46, 107–108, 118–119, 138–139, 177–178, 235–236
Lully, Jean-Baptiste 5–6

Marie [de Saint Georges], Alexandre-Pierre-Thomas-Amable 21, 24, 31–32, 35–36, 41, 47–48, 59–60, 107, 109–113, 131–132, 135–139, 145–146, 205, 206–207, 210–211, 235–236
Marloye, Albert 78, 80
Martin, Félix 26, 28, 162–163, 177–179
Martin, Jean-Baptiste 26, 28, 162–163, 177–179
Martin, Jules 28, 213–214, 217–219
Martin factory 37–38
Massabo factory 28, 97–98, 213–214
Mathieu, Claude-Louis 42, 78
Maudslay, Henry 18–19
Meifred, Joseph 32, 179–180
Mellinet, Émile-Henry 85–86, 217–219, 238–239n26
Mendelssohn, Felix 78–79n15
Meyerbeer, Giacomo 7–8, 34, 63–64, 79, 82–84, 102–104, 118–119, 156–157, 236–237
Michaud, Noel-Firmin 27, 77–78
Michon factory 27, 204–205
military bands
  Champ de Mars bands competition (1845) 35–36, 39–40, 44–45, 47–49, 55
  Garde de Paris 179–180, 241
  Garde Républicaine 241
  Guides band 86–87, 99–100, 103–104, 115, 126–129, 171, 179–180, 220–221
  July Monarchy and 37
  membership of 35–36, 50
  Paris *Gymnase Musical Militaire* buys Sax instruments 40
  Paris National Guard 37
  Sax instruments usage 40, 50, 62
  saxophone removed from (1848) 21
  Second Republic reforms (1848) 62
Millereau, François 28, 196–198, 213–214, 217–219, 222–223n43, 238–239n25
Mohr, Nicolas 103–104
Mongin factory 27, 204–205
Monnais, Édouard 56–57n28, 234
Moritz, Johann-Gottfried 31–32
Muller factory 39

Mürner, Martin 32
music and musical instruments
  Bass-tuba 31–32, 235–236
  Batyphone 32, 55–56, 91–93, 235–236
  bombardon 131–134
  brass/brasswind/woodwind instruments, catalogues 66–75
  brass/brasswind/woodwind instruments, characteristics and aesthetic/emotional associations 16–17
  brass/brasswind/woodwind instruments, classification and naming 16
  brass/brasswind/woodwind instruments, development and success of 9
  brass/brasswind/woodwind instruments, inferior quality instruments 37–38
  brass/brasswind/woodwind instruments, patent awards growth (1840-60) 50–51
  brass/brasswind/woodwind instruments, prices 36–37, 63–75
  brass/brasswind/woodwind instruments, prices of Sax instruments 44–48
  brass/brasswind/woodwind instruments, profitability of 39
  chromatic instruments (*Système d'instruments chromatiques*) patent (1843) 17, 31, 41
  clavicor 32, 38, 42, 76–77, 130–131, 143–144, 181–183
  cornet 17, 36–37, 41n42, 51–53n6, 163, 196–198
  customs protection from UK imports 7–8
  Encyclopédie entry (1756) 4–5
  historical background to French trade of musical instrument trade 4–9
  Industrial Revolution 7–9
  musical and political patronage 77–87
  néo-alto 131–132, 181–183
  ophicleide 35–37, 66–68, 72, 90–91, 132–134, 178, 181–185, 187, 233
  patents disputes *see* saxhorn, saxotromba, and saxophone patents disputes; saxophone patent infringement dispute
  sarrusophone 139–141, 146–149, 214–217
  saxhorn, description of 17–20
  saxhorn, exhibition awards 78–79, 83
  saxhorn patent (1843) 76–77, App III
  saxophone, jazz music association with 17–18
  saxophone, Lisa Simpson (The Simpsons) association 17–18
  saxophone, USA associations with 17–18
  saxophone invention 17
  saxophone patent (1846) 17, 31, 44, App V
  saxotromba, description of 17–20
  saxotromba patent (1845) 17, 31, 42–44, 76–77, 83, App IV
  this book's approach to music-related themes 16
  trombone 17
  trumpet 17
  valve era 7–8

Napoleon I (Bonaparte), Emperor of the French 33–34, 59–60, 150–151n2
Napoleon III (Bonaparte), Emperor of the French 3, 7, 22–25, 35–36, 77–79, 81–82, 83n27, 83–87, 89, 96, 99–100n41, 100, 101–102n45,n47, 103–108, 115n21, 118–119, 126–127, 154–155, 174, 238–239
néo-alto 131–132, 181–183
Neudin factory 178n9, 192–193
Niedermeyer, Louis 63–64

Onslow, Georges 48, 80
ophicleide 35–37, 66–68, 72, 90–91, 132–134, 178, 181–185, 187, 233

patent law and enforcement. *see* law and courts
Paxton, Charles 91
Périnet, Étienne-François 51–53, 109
Perrin, Pierre 5–6
Picard, Louis-Joseph-Ernest 155–158
Pierre, Constant 239–240n27
Pleyel piano company 163–164n15
Pontécoulant, Adolphe de 80, 82–83, 139, 163–164n15, 164–165n19, 165–166, 199–200n12, 221–222
Pouillet, Claude 42, 78
prisoner labour in factories 98–99

Raoux, Marcel-Auguste 17, 23–24, 26, 27, 31–32, 53, 76–79, 105–107, 118–119, 177–178, 186, 205–206
Renouard, Augustin-Charles 101–102n46

Ricci, Federico 34, 63–64
Riedl, Wenzel 132–134
Rivet, Michel 124–127, 130–132, 136–139, 188–189
Rivet factory 39
Robert, Adolphe 32n8, 83–84n27, 99–100n39, 101–102n45, 106n74
Robespierre, Maximilien 48n55
Roehn factory 26–27, 177–179
Roguet, Christophe-Michel 103–104
Rossini, Gioachino 7–8, 33–34, 39, 63–64, 86–87, 236–237
Roth, Jean-Chrétien 27, 170–171, 217–219
Rouher, Eugène 152–153
Rouland, Gustave 101–102n47
Rumigny, Marie-Hippolyte de 48–49
Rumigny, Marie-Théodore de 32, 34–35, 39, 44–45, 47–49, 57–58, 138–139, 234, 237–238

Saint-Laurens [Saint-Laurent], Jules-Henri Nogent 152–155, 157–158
Saint-Yon, Alexandre-Pierre Moline de 82
Sámal, Vaclav 41
sarrusophone 139–141, 146–149, 214–217
Sassaigne, François-Félix-Marie 203
Sasse, Marie 217n16
Savart, Félix 53–54
Savart, Nicolas 42, 48, 51–55, 97–98, 234
Sax, Adolphe
  aesthetic and creative vision 233, 236–237
  amateur/civilian band instruments supplier 239
  appeal case complainant (1848) 20–28, 76–77
  appeal case complainant (1852) 88–94, 96, 99–102
  appeal case complainant (1853) 107–119
  bankruptcy (1852) 96–99
  catalogues 66–75
  Champ de Mars military bands competition winner (1845) 40, 45, 55
  commission of experts' (*lumières*) support for 51–57
  criminal case complainant against rivals (1854-55) 123–129
  criminal case complainant against rivals (1858-60) 177–186
  five-year extension of patents (1860) 150–159, 194–202
  French residency grant (1855) 124, 126–127
  industrial and commercial rivalry with Charles-Auguste Kretzchmann 187–193
  industrial and commercial rivalry with Gustave-Auguste Besson 170–176, 194–202
  industrial and commercial rivalry with Pierre-Louis Gautrot 160–168
  industrial and commercial rivalry with Sébastien Drouelle 203–212
  July Monarchy supporter 89
  legal dispute leader 3–4
  legal representatives, effectiveness of 106, 235–236
  Louis-Philippe's support for 56–59
  military band instruments supplier 40, 50, 62, 99–100, 233, 236–239, 241
  monopolistic ambition 233
  Napoleon III's support for 103–106
  National Exhibition award winner (1844) 42, 53–54, 97
  National Exhibition award winner (1849) 77–80
  National Exhibition of French Industry (1849), and 78–83
  patent enforcement dispute with Gautrot (1865-67) 168–169
  patent enforcement dispute with *Madame* Besson (1861) 201–202
  patent enforcement dispute with Michel Rivet 124–127
  patent enforcement raid against Besson (1854, 1857, 1858) 25–26, 170
  patent enforcement raid against Gautrot 25
  patent enforcement raid against Gautrot (1855) 130–149
  patent enforcement raid against Gautrot (1865) 168
  patent enforcement raid against *Madame* Besson (1860, 1861) 200–201
  patent enforcement raid against rivals (1866) 213–214
  patent enforcement raids against rivals (1854-55) 123–125
  patent enforcement raids by 26–28

Sax, Adolphe (*Continued*)
  patent lawsuit defendant 17, 20–23, 31
  patent owner 17, 21
  price reductions (1848) 63–68
  profitability comparison with rivals (1860) 174–176
  revival of business 99–100
  saxophone inventor 3–4, 231–232
  saxotromba inventor 17, 230–231
  Second Republic, and 89
  Société de la Grande Harmonie concerts (1852-53) 99–103
  support from musicians and politicians 77–87, 234–237
  UK Great Exhibition prize winner (1851) 91–97
Sax, Alphonse 167–168
Sax, Charles-Joseph 33–34, 53–54, 103–104, 204–205
Sax bankruptcy case (Commercial Court of Paris, 1852) 96–99
saxhorn *see* music and musical instruments
saxhorn, saxotromba, and saxophone patents disputes
  background to 1–4
  civil proceedings period (defence phase) (1847–54), 1st appeal case (1850) 21–22
  civil proceedings period (defence phase) (1847–53), 2nd Appeal Court case (Imperial Court of Rouen) case (1853-54) 23
  civil proceedings period (defence phase) (1847–53), 2nd appeal (Court of Cassation) case (1851-53) 22–23
  civil proceedings period (defence phase) (1847–53), 1848 Revolution/July Monarchy interruption and resumption 21
  civil proceedings period (defence phase) (1847–53), beginning of (1846) 17
  civil proceedings period (defence phase) (1847–53), chapter outlines 20–23
  civil proceedings period (defence phase) (1847–53), Court of First Instance proceedings (1847-50) 21
  civil proceedings period (defence phase) (1847–53), outline of 3–4
  criminal proceedings period (offensive phase) (185467), 1866 raid and Court of Cassation case (1866-67) 28
  criminal proceedings period (offensive phase) (1853–67), Besson raids (1854-58) 25–26
  criminal proceedings period (offensive phase) (1853–67), chapter summaries 20–21, 23–28
  criminal proceedings period (offensive phase) (1853–67), Drouelle valves dispute 27
  criminal proceedings period (offensive phase) (1853–67), Kretzschmann raid (1854-58) 25–26
  criminal proceedings period (offensive phase) (1853–67), law on 5-year extension of patents (1860) 24–25
  criminal proceedings period (offensive phase) (1853–67), *Madame* Besson raid (1860) 27
  criminal proceedings period (offensive phase) (1853–67), outline of 3–4
  criminal proceedings period (offensive phase) (1853–67), Sax/Gautrot licence agreement (1859) 25
  criminal proceedings period (offensive phase) (1853–67), Sax's enforcement raids on rivals' premises (1854-66) 23–28
  legal historical significance of 28
  public prosecutor's office's role in 21
  this book's chapter summaries 20–28
  this book's chapters outline 20–28
  this book's focus on legal themes 16–20
  this book's legal sources 14–16
Sax/Drouelle dispute (1857-67)
  background 203–205
  Court of Cassation appeal proceedings (1862-64) 207–208
  Court of Cassation appeal proceedings (1867) 211–212
  Court of First Instance proceedings (1861) 205–206
  Imperial Court appeal proceedings (1861) 206–207
  Imperial Court appeal proceedings (1865) 207–211

Sax/Gautrot dispute
  Appeal Court judgment (1857) 137–141
  background to 130–131
  commencement of proceedings
    (1855) 131–132
  Court of Cassation appeal proceedings
    (1867) 168–169
  Court of Cassation proceedings
    (1857-59) 141–142, 144–145
  disputants' legal representatives 131–132, 137–138
  Gautrot's appeal to Imperial Court in Amiens (1858) 145–146
  Gautrot's appeal to Imperial Court in Paris (1856-57) 137–138
  Gautrot's appeal to Imperial Court in Paris (1857-58) 142–144
  Gautrot's case 131–138
  Gautrot's case at Appeal 137–138
  Gautrot's initial complaint to Paris Court of First Instance 131–132
  Gautrot's Pre-Appeal Hearing success (1856) 137–138
  judgment (1856) 136–138
  Paris Court of First Instance judgment (1866) 168
  Sax/Gautrot business agreement (1859) 147–149, 160, 168
  Sax's case 135–136
Sax/Kretzschmann dispute (1858)
  Court of Cassation proceedings (1863) 190–192
  Paris Criminal Court of First Instance proceedings (1858) 187
  Paris Criminal Court of First Instance proceedings (1862) 188–189
  Paris Imperial Court proceedings (1860) 188
  Paris Imperial Court proceedings (1862) 190
Sax's collective court action (1858)
  background 177–178
  disputants 177–179
  Halary case 178
  Raoux case 177–178
Sax's collective court action (1858-59)
  Appeal Court judgment (1860) 186
  commencement of (1858) 177–181
  defendants' appeals (1860) 185–186

  judgment (1860) 184–185
  resumption of (1859) 181–184
saxophone *see* music and musical instruments
saxophone patent infringement dispute (1866)
  background 213–214
  Court of Cassation appeal proceedings (1867) 217
  Imperial Court appeal proceedings (1867) 215–217
  Paris Criminal Court of First Instance proceedings (1866) 214–215
  Sax's case 214
Schollmieyer, G. 63–64
Séguier, Armand 48, 78, 234
Singelée, Jean-Baptiste 97–98
Sivori, Camillo 33–34
Soult, Jean-de-Dieu 39, 62, 82, 107–108
Spontini, Gaspare 7–8, 33–34, 48, 51–53, 55n23, 63–65, 155–156
Stradivarius, Antonio 37–38
Sudre, François 178, 192–193
Surville, Eugène 168, 180–185, 188–189, 206–207, 211, 216–217, 236

Thibouville-Lamy, Jérôme 222–223
Thibouville, Roussel 97–98
Thomas, Ambroise 34, 63–64
Tournier, François 26, 31, 177–179
Triébert, Frédéric 40
Tulou factory 5

United Kingdom (UK)
  Cobden-Chevalier Treaty (1860) 7
  free trade policy 7
  French cultural and political influence 1–2
  French customs protection against UK exports 7–8
  industrial development 1–2
  Napoleon I's blockade (1806) 7
United States (USA), French cultural and political influence 1–2

Vaillant, Jean-Baptiste-Philbert 85–87, 104n68, 115, 173
Valette, Auguste 124n4
Verdi, Guiseppe 7–8, 82, 83–84

Véron, Louis-Desiré 152–157
Villeneuve, Ernest-Louis Geoffroy de 152–155
Vuillaume Jean-Baptiste 37–38, 91–93, 127–129, 229–230n15

Wagner, Richard 7–8
Ward, Cornelius 94n23, 94–95
Weber, J. 126
Wieprecht, Wilhelm-Friedrich 31–32, 91–93